Encountering China

Evangelical Missiological Society Monograph Series

Anthony Casey, Allen Yeh, Mark Kreitzer, and Edward L. Smither
SERIES EDITORS

_____

A Project of the Evangelical Missiological Society
www.emsweb.org

Encountering China

The Evolution of Timothy Richard's
Missionary Thought (1870–1891)

Andrew T. Kaiser

☙PICKWICK *Publications* • Eugene, Oregon

ENCOUNTERING CHINA
The Evolution of Timothy Richard's Missionary Thought (1870–1891)

Evangelical Missiological Society Monograph Series 1

Copyright © 2019 Andrew T. Kaiser. All rights reserved. Except for brief quotations in critical publications or reviews, no part of this book may be reproduced in any manner without prior written permission from the publisher. Write: Permissions, Wipf and Stock Publishers, 199 W. 8th Ave., Suite 3, Eugene, OR 97401.

Pickwick Publications
An Imprint of Wipf and Stock Publishers
199 W. 8th Ave., Suite 3
Eugene, OR 97401

www.wipfandstock.com

PAPERBACK ISBN: 978-1-5326-6413-7
HARDCOVER ISBN: 978-1-5326-6414-4
EBOOK ISBN: 978-1-5326-6415-1

Cataloguing-in-Publication data:

Names: Kaiser, Andrew T., author.

Title: Encountering China : the evolution of Timothy Richard's missionary thought (1870–1891) / Andrew T. Kaiser.

Description: Eugene, OR: Pickwick Publications, 2019 | Series: Evangelical Missiological Society Monograph Series 1 | Includes bibliographical references and index.

Identifiers: ISBN 978-1-5326-6413-7 (paperback) | ISBN 978-1-5326-6414-4 (hardcover) | ISBN 978-1-5326-6415-1 (ebook)

Subjects: LCSH: Richard, Timothy, 1845–1919. | Missionaries—China | Missions—Educational work—China.

Classification: BV3427 K15 2019 (print) | BV3427 (ebook)

Cover photo credit: Timothy Richard, *Forty-Five Years in China: Reminiscences* (London: T. Fisher Unwin, 1916), 193.

Manufactured in the U.S.A.   03/26/19

To Heather
sine qua non

Abstract

IN PURSUIT OF THE conversion of others, cross-cultural missionaries often experience their own "conversions." This thesis explores the ways in which one particular missionary, the Welshman Timothy Richard (1845–1919), was transformed by his encounter with China. Focusing specifically on the evolution of his understanding and practice of Christian mission during the first half of his career with the Baptist Missionary Society, the study is structured chronologically in order to capture the important ways in which Richard's experiences shaped his adaptations in mission. Each of Richard's adaptations is examined within its appropriate historical and cultural context through analysis of his published and unpublished writings—all while paying careful attention to Richard's identity as a Welsh Baptist missionary. This approach reveals that rather than softening his commitment to conversion in response to his encounters with China, Richard was driven by his persistent evangelical convictions to adapt his missionary methods in pursuit of greater results. When his experiences in Shandong and Shanxi provinces convinced him that Christianity fulfilled China's own religious past and that God's Kingdom promised blessings for souls in this life as well as in the next, Richard widened his theological horizons to incorporate these ideas without abandoning his essential understanding of the Christian gospel. As Richard adjusted to the realities of mission in the Chinese context, his growing empathy for Chinese people and their culture increasingly shaped his adaptations, ultimately leading him to advocate methods and emphases on the moral evidences for Christianity that were unacceptable to some of his missionary colleagues and to leaders in other missions, notably James Hudson Taylor.

As the first critical work of length to focus on the early half of Richard's missionary career, this thesis fills a gap in current scholarship on Victorian Protestant missions in China, offering a challenge to the simplistic conservative/liberal dichotomies often used to categorize missionaries. The revised picture of Richard that emerges reveals his original understanding of "the worthy" in Matt 10, his indebtedness to Chinese sectarian religion, his early application of indigenous principles, his integration of evangelism and famine relief work, his relative unimportance in the China Inland Mission "Shanxi spirit" controversies of the 1880s, and—most significantly—his instrumental rather than evangelistic interest in the scholar-officials of China. By highlighting the priority of the Chinese (religious) context for Richard's transformation, this thesis also contributes to the growing volume of historiography on Christianity in modern China that emphasizes the multi-directional influences present in the encounters between Christianity and Chinese culture and religion. Finally, connections between Richard's evolution and changes taking place within the larger missionary community are also explored, situating Richard within wider discussions of accommodationism in mission, the rise of social Christianity, and evangelistic precursors to fulfillment theology.

[M]issionary history is hardly worth the telling, unless it leads the reader to bring the experience of the past to bear upon the missionary problems of to-day, and enables him to solve the problems of to-day by the insight and the instinct as it were, that reward the patient investigator into the deeds and the purposes of those who have gone before. A knowledge of the history of all the societies is of little service unless the conscience of the reader is enlightened, his love for those for whom Christ died deepened, and his zeal for the furtherance of the great missionary cause strengthened.

—Richard Lovett, *The History of the London Missionary Society, 1795–1895* (London: H. Frowde, 1899), vii–viii.

Contents

Acknowledgments | xv
Abbreviations | xviii

1. Introduction: Researching Timothy Richard | 1
    1.1 Historiography of Richard   7
    1.2 Academic Contributions   11
    1.3 Methodological Considerations   14

Part One: Richard Encountering China
Innovation and Adaptation of His Missionary Thought

2. Beginnings: Preparation in Ministry and Disappointment in China | 25
    2.1 Growing Up Baptist in Wales, 1845–1869   25
    2.2 Protestant Missions in Shandong, ca. 1870   35
    2.3 Disappointment and Adaptation   42

3. "Seeking the Worthy" | 48
    3.1 Reading the Bible   50
    3.2 Edward Irving's *Missionaries after the Apostolical School*   58

4. Indigenous Impulses in Practice: Chinese and Western Influences | 68
    4.1 Learning about the Three Teachings   69
    4.2 Learning from Chinese Sectarians   72
    4.3 Learning from Western Missionaries   80
    4.4 Richard's Qingzhou Adaptations   83

Part Two: Richard Encountering Famine
Application and Justification of His Missionary Thought

5. **Practice Shaping Theory: Moral Evidences in the North China Famine | 97**
   5.1 Missionary Identification and the Famine   99
   5.2 Famine Relief Work   102
   5.3 Evangelism During the Famine   108
   5.4 Famine Relief Work and Early Ministry in Shanxi   117

6. **Richard after the Famine: Accommodationism, the Kingdom of God, and the Broadening of Christian Mission | 126**
   6.1 Fulfillment Theology and Accommodating Mission   127
   6.2 The Social Implications of the Kingdom of God   136
   6.3 Seeking Officials for Strategic Rather than "Worthy" Reasons   148
   6.4 The Coming "National Conversion"   153

Part Three: Richard Encountering Conflict
Confirmation and Conviction of His Missionary Thought

7. **Richard and the China Inland Mission | 159**
   7.1 Mutual Cooperation   160
   7.2 Separating from Richard: The Question of Orthodoxy   163
   7.3 Richard and Attrition within the CIM   171
   7.4 Revisiting the "Shanxi Spirit"   178

8. **Substituting Another Gospel? Timothy Richard and His Critics in the Baptist Missionary Society | 183**
   8.1 The First Furlough: Disappointment with the BMS   183
   8.2 The Contours of the Conflict   188
   8.3 Conclusion of the Conflict: Release for Expanded Ministry   216

9. **Conclusion | 223**
   9.1 Transformation and Continuity   223
   9.2 Implications   226

Appendix 1: Selected List of Chinese Terms | 231

*Appendix 2: Full Chronological List of Publications
    by Timothy Richard to 1891* | 234

Bibliography | 237
   Archival Collections   237
   Periodicals   238
   Published Works Cited   239

Index | 257

Acknowledgments

I AM GRATEFUL TO God for bringing me to New College in the University of Edinburgh, and allowing me the privilege of intensive study.

At precisely the moment when I had made peace with the idea of not pursuing a doctoral degree, three different mentors all independently approached me encouraging me to do so. First of all, Dr. Thomas Askew, my champion and persistent supporter for the last twenty years of my career in China pushed me to pursue further study, offering invaluable time and encouragement at a time when his own health was less than robust. Tom and his wife Jean have been dear friends and passionate encouragers of our entire family throughout all the vicissitudes of life overseas. Professors Richard Lints and Garth Rosell, my advisors while I studied the American missionary to China Samuel Wells Williams for my master's thesis at Gordon Conwell Theological Seminary, added their wise counsel and encouragement, agreeing with Tom's suggestion that Edinburgh was the place for me.

Following their advice, I contacted Professor Brian Stanley, Director of the Centre for the Study of World Christianity at New College within the University of Edinburgh. His quick reply and warm interest in my proposed topic were a foretaste of the dedicated assistance and sage guidance that characterized all my interactions with him. I cannot imagine completing this project with anyone else: his high standard of scholarship, pastoral concern for his students, and sincere empathy for the evangelical missionary project made the task enjoyable. His detailed and insightful critiques of my work as it developed have made it far better than it otherwise would have been. I am indebted.

I am also grateful for the camaraderie and encouragement I enjoyed with my fellow students at New College. Conversations in Rainy Hall over lunch, the stimulation of the World Christianity seminars, and especially the collegial atmosphere of the Semples study room made my time more productive and stretched me in many positive ways. Fellow student Marina Wang reminded me that the history of Christianity in

China was important, and that I had a small contribution to make. David Kirkpatrick was a constant source of encouragement and assistance as we struggled in parallel to produce theses that would satisfy the demands of our wise and gifted supervisor. Alexander Chow, then Chancellor's Fellow in World Christianity, arrived at New College just in time to provide welcome China-specific guidance for my work, and to become a friend and companion in my life-long study of China. Mark McLeister, employed as a Senior Teaching Fellow in Chinese Studies, also came to Edinburgh at just the right time, ensuring that I would not forget the contemporary Chinese church during my time in Scotland.

Over the years, many scholars from around the world have generously shared their knowledge and resources to help expand my understanding of Chinese history. Professor Roy Grow and his wife Mary Lewis are perhaps most responsible for my having ended up in China in the first place. From the very beginning I had the tremendous benefit of being taught to view China with wonder and anticipation, rather than fear; for this I will always be grateful. The late Drs. Edvard Torjesen and Norman Cliff were always happy to pass along photocopied bits from their decades of study, making possible my earliest attempts to understand Shanxi. Once I began my formal work on Richard, Margaret Wyatt's provision of food and housing made possible my extended time exploring the Baptist Missionary Society Archives at Regents Park College, Oxford. Archivists Emily Burgoyne and Emma Walsh were my sure guides, making what might have been arduous a pleasurable and productive experience.

I am especially grateful to Professors Kathryn Edgerton-Tarpley and Henrietta Harrison, two gifted scholars of Chinese history with abiding interests in Shanxi. Their kindness and graciousness toward me—a far less rigorous historian—and their willingness to include me in their conversations about Shanxi are an example of the open-mindedness and generosity toward which all scholarship aspires. The footprints of their ideas, no doubt distorted by the waves of my muddled prose, can be seen throughout this work.

My colleagues in China have had to take on an extra share of the work there during our years in Edinburgh; they encouraged me in spirit, and through their labors freed me to undertake this study. We are family, and without their support this thesis would not have existed. I look forward to repaying them in kind over the next few decades. I am also grateful to the many individuals and churches that have continued to support our family during this detour through Edinburgh. In the coming years we will endeavor to remain faithful stewards of their investment.

My parents have always been my strongest advocates, even when my life has gone in paths different from theirs. Their prayers, their emotional and material support, and especially their willingness to send their only son to the other side of the world, are a constant demonstration of their faith in an eternal glory that truly outweighs all earthly rewards or troubles. Their sacrifices have made my life of service possible. I regret that I can only hope to be faithful, never worthy.

Finally, my family has always been with me. The life we have chosen makes it possible for us to spend so much of our time together, and I am grateful for the joy they have brought by accompanying me on this Scottish adventure. My children Sophia and Rebekah gamely entered a schooling situation so different from their experiences in China, and negotiated new social and academic minefields with tremendous grace. I know how much it cost them to give up these last few years in China, and I will always be grateful for their sacrifices. My wife Heather is my partner in all things, and so I dedicate this thesis to her. She worked far harder than I during our time in Scotland, making it possible for me to finish this degree. This thesis is as much hers as mine, except for the clunky language and wandering ideas: she is far too bright to have written such follies. As always, each new phase of life has been a joy with her at my side. I look forward to what will come next.

Andrew T. Kaiser
Edinburgh
July 2014

Abbreviations

ABCFM	American Board of Commissioners for Foreign Missions
ABCFMA	Microfilms of the American Board of Commissioners for Foreign Missions Archives, Billy Graham Center, Wheaton College, Wheaton, IL
APM	American Presbyterian Mission
BFBS	British and Foreign Bible Society
BMS	Baptist Missionary Society
BMSA	Baptist Missionary Society Archives, Regents Park College, Oxford
CES	Chinese Evangelization Society
CIM	China Inland Mission
CLS	Christian Literature Society for China
CM	*China's Millions*
CR	*The Chinese Recorder and Missionary Journal* or *The Chinese Recorder*
CSWCA	Archives, Centre for the Study of World Christianity, School of Divinity, University of Edinburgh
GCPMC	General Conference of Protestant Missionaries in China
HTCOC	*Hudson Taylor and China's Open Century*
IBMR	*International Bulletin of Missionary Research*
KJV	*The Holy Bible*, King James Version
LMS	London Missionary Society
MH	*The Missionary Herald*

NCH	*The North China Herald*
NLS	National Library of Scotland, Edinburgh
SDCK	Society for the Diffusion of Christian and General Knowledge Among the Chinese
SOAS	School of Oriental and African Studies Library, London
WGGB	*Wan'guo gongbao* [*Globe Magazine*, also known as *Review of the Times*]
WMMS	Wesleyan Methodist Missionary Society

1

Introduction
Researching Timothy Richard

IN HER EARLY WORK on the Christian colleges in China, Jessie Lutz drew attention to the challenges to effective cross-cultural communication inherent in the missionary encounter with "the other-ness of Chinese culture and people."[1] For most nineteenth-century missionaries to China, their ties to Western cultural norms led them initially to view this other-ness in negative or even hostile terms.[2] The hoped-for conversion of the other required that the missionaries learn to communicate effectively across this gulf of cultural other-ness. Ironically, crossing these cultural boundaries—"translating the message"—involved the missionary in a multi-directional adaptive process whose goal of changing others necessitated at least some degree of change on the part of the missionary as well.[3] This process of mutual transformation that results when groups of individuals from different cultures come into continuous first-hand contact is known as acculturation.[4] Beginning with their initial struggles to learn a new language, missionaries to China were forced to divest themselves of the culture they wore so comfortably. While the degree of resistance or acquiescence in this process of acculturation varied greatly, effective cross-cultural communication ultimately demanded at least some degree of accommodation—linguistic, social, and in some ways even religious—from every missionary. Ostensibly focused on

---

1. Lutz, *China and the Christian Colleges*, 4–10.

2. On hostility to local religion, see Reinders, *Borrowed Gods*, iii, and throughout. On hostility to the local language, see Glover and Lyall, *Thousand Miles*, 265.

3. Walls, "Translation Principle," 28–29.

4. This is the classic definition from Redfield, Linton, and Herskovits, "Memorandum for the Study of Acculturation," 149. Different from the Catholic use of acculturation to contrast with the more empathetic missional methods of inculturation, acculturation is employed in this thesis in its sociological sense, as it is typically used to analyze how migrant communities change and are changed by their new contexts. Sam and Berry, *Cambridge Handbook*, 1–42; Liu, "Chinese Converts in the Chinese Rites Controversy," 315–21.

the transformation of the Chinese people they had come to evangelize, the missionaries themselves were being transformed.

While nearly all China missionaries shared this experience of change and adjustment, they did not have the modern language of cross-cultural communication to describe their transformation. Prior to the twentieth-century development of a functional anthropological understanding of plural cultures, culture was merely a gloss for civilization.[5] And yet, despite the absence of the terminology, the phenomenon itself was readily evident as different missionaries to China negotiated their cultural accommodation in different ways. Some, such as Martha Foster Crawford of the American Southern Baptist mission, developed such a marked degree of empathy for the Chinese context that they experienced a "cultural conversion."[6] Having devoted several decades of her life to the civilizing mission project and its attempt to introduce Western and specifically American Southern cultural norms as a precursor or companion to the gospel, Crawford in 1883 abandoned all such efforts and, under the influence of fellow Shandong missionary Alfred G. Jones of the English Baptist Missionary Society (BMS), committed herself to a deeply indigenous "three-self" model of mission that focused on serving and respecting the Chinese Christian community.[7] For others, such as Eva Jane Price with the American Board of Commissioners for Foreign Missions (ABCFM) in Shanxi, the increased empathy that emerged from her growing awareness of the hardness of Chinese life resulted in a still stronger push for the civilizing aspects of mission that she believed would be the natural by-product of evangelical conversion.[8]

In his 1997 book *The Conversion of Missionaries*, Lian Xi brought a new level of sophistication to discussions of missionary adaptations in the face of Chinese cultural distinctness. This study of the interactions between Republican China, the American Protestant missionary community in China, and American sending churches in the first half of the twentieth century focused on "the unraveling of nineteenth-century missionary mentality" and its relation to the rise of American theological liberalism.[9] Throughout the book, Lian Xi highlighted the ways in which cultural differences were negotiated by various subjects, drawing attention to two kinds of ironic missionary conversion. The first referred to the intentional and unintentional "reflux influence" or "reverse missionary

---

5. Stanley, "From 'The Poor Heathen,'" 3–10.
6. Vaughn Cross, "Missionary Returns," 244.
7. Vaughn Cross, "Missionary Returns," 251–55.
8. Price, *China Journal*, 192–93.
9. Lian, *Conversion of Missionaries*, 10.

impulse" of the missionaries on their home constituents, and the ways in which missionaries converted their own communities by problematizing certain theological assumptions and bringing a new complexity to long-cherished perceptions of the world.[10] The second kind of conversion referred to the ways in which sympathizing missionaries themselves were converted from their exclusivist conceptions of Christian salvation to embrace more theologically liberal motivations for mission.

For Edward Hume, Frank Rawlinson, and Pearl Buck, the three subjects of Lian Xi's study, the transformation was particularly acute. In sympathy with Chinese nationalist movements, and out of respect for China's religious and cultural traditions, these three abandoned their earlier commitments to Christian conversion by rejecting the traditional salvific justification of evangelical mission and preserving only "the moral and social message of Christianity."[11] As Lian Xi makes clear, the comparatively extreme nature of their transformations in the face of Chinese other-ness was made possible by a number of significant contextual factors that did not pertain to the earlier nineteenth-century experience of Crawford, Price, or their peers. Confronted with the rapid institutionalization of China mission during the "golden period" of the first two decades of the twentieth century, the growing influence of theological liberalism within the American home bases, and the powerful rise of Chinese nationalism, Lian Xi's subjects "began to cast doubts on their Christian missions."[12]

Andrew Walls's article, "The Multiple Conversions of Timothy Richard," offers a similar exploration of acculturation—this time focusing on how the Welsh missionary Timothy Richard (1845–1919) responded to his encounter with China.[13] Having served in China with the BMS from 1870 to 1915, Richard is best known for his political, educational, and literary contributions near the end of the nineteenth century. In Richard, Walls identifies yet another kind of missionary conversion or, in his terms, "multiple conversions"—referring both to Richard's desire to see the rapid conversion of many Chinese people to Christianity, as well as to the series of reactive adaptations that transformed Richard's own understanding and practice of mission during his years in China.

Like so many of the Protestant missionaries in China, Richard's acculturation and its resultant effects on his idea of mission evolved over time. Raised, baptized, and educated within Welsh nonconformity, Richard's

---

10. Lian, *Conversion of Missionaries*, 207–28.
11. Lian, *Conversion of Missionaries*, 10–13.
12. Lian, *Conversion of Missionaries*, 10–11.
13. Walls, "Multiple Conversions," 236–58.

intense experiences in China—his isolation in the interior, frequent interaction with Chinese religious leaders, and intimate involvement in the North China Famine (1876–1878)—produced in him a deep sense of identification with the local people. Beyond conventional missionary acculturation, this paradigmatic shift in sympathies combined with his evangelical interest in conversion to produce a series of adaptations to his missionary methods that made Richard, at the halfway mark in his career in China, the subject of strong criticisms from his closest colleagues in the BMS.

Richard is a particularly fruitful subject for exploring the nature of missionary adaptation in response to cross-cultural encounter. Unlike some China missionaries, much of Richard's early years were spent in what was at the time considered China's remote "interior"—in places such as Taiyuan, Shanxi and Qingzhou, Shandong, far from the culturally reinforcing foreign enclaves of the coastal treaty ports. As he pioneered these two fields, Richard spent years living with little or no foreign contact in communities noted for their extensive and active communities of religious sectarians. Additionally, the pioneering nature of much of his early work in China gave him an unusual degree of freedom to experiment with his adaptations and put them into practice. Following the North China Famine, Richard and his ideas received national attention, influencing several generations of China workers. Finally, having spent nearly all his adult life in China as a missionary, Richard was more deeply and personally invested in the questions of acculturation than those of his peers—such as London Missionary Society (LMS) missionary and Oxford Professor James Legge—who spent much of their careers as academics in the West.

With very few book-length treatments of Richard in print and a preponderance of studies focused on Richard's later years, there are a number of unfounded assumptions about Richard's development as a missionary that require revision. Scholars have tended to view Richard, with his cultural accommodation and interest in Chinese elites, as a modern Jesuit; and yet, while there are certain superficial parallels with Matteo Ricci, one of the most intriguing aspects of Richard's response to his encounter with China is precisely the way in which he *differed* from the earlier Jesuits: as this thesis will demonstrate, during the period under study Richard's interest in Chinese scholar-officials was not primarily evangelistic. Likewise, despite a pervasive sense on the part of modern researchers that Richard was progressive for his days, close analysis of Richard's supposed conflicts with his fellow missionaries in the 1880s reveals the degree to which many of his practical adaptations were welcomed on the ground—particularly among his evangelical peers. Accordingly, an in-depth study of Richard's early transformations not only illuminates the ways in which he adapted theologically in response to his experiences in China, but also provides invaluable insights into the theological changes taking place within the Protestant missionary movement in China on the doorstep of the twentieth century.

More fundamentally still, unlike our current understandings of Crawford, Price, or the subjects of Lian Xi's study, the precise nature of Richard's "multiple conversions" is still unclear, confused by the apparently contradictory nature of his theological development. On the one hand, numerous instances of Richard's positive influence on the deeply evangelical adaptations of others—such as those of his colleague Alfred Jones and, through him, Martha Foster Crawford—suggest that while his methods were becoming increasingly accommodating toward the local context, his commitment to evangelical conversion persisted. Similarly, like Eva Jane Price, Richard continued to expect that personal Christian conversion would produce material benefits that would reduce Chinese suffering. On the other hand, so much in Richard's narrative echoes the experiences of Hume, Rawlinson, and Buck that—despite differences in context—it is difficult to avoid seeing him as an early example of a similar move toward theological liberalism. Richard's later positive writings on Buddhism, his extensive involvement in turn-of-the-century Chinese political reform, as well as his close association with the institutions of education and publishing in late imperial China all seem to presage developments within the liberal wings of twentieth-century British and American Protestant mission in China. In particular, Richard's early interest in humanitarian service as an essential part of Christian mission appears at least superficially similar to the Social Gospel movement of the late nineteenth and early twentieth century that so influenced Lian Xi's subjects. Given these similarities, it seems equally plausible to suggest that Richard abandoned his initial evangelical convictions to espouse a more liberal and less conversionist form of Christianity.

Andrew Walls points toward a possible resolution of these competing interpretations by suggesting that the apparent connections between Richard and later liberal missionaries may be misleading. Walls views Richard's theological transformation as more complex, and something quite different from the loss of evangelical justification for mission experienced by the twentieth-century Americans surveyed in Lian Xi's book.

> It is a distortion, I think, to treat [Richard's] career as that of a simple evangelical who moved progressively in a liberal direction; still more distorting to see him as a missionary who departed from the original missionary vocation by transforming it into something else.[14]

14. Walls, "Multiple Conversions," 240.

These distortions have been compounded by the relative ascendancy of James Hudson Taylor and his China Inland Mission (CIM) within the hagiography of post-war evangelicalism. The successful international expansion of the CIM (today known as the Overseas Missionary Fellowship), the continued publication and persistent popularity of Taylor-related materials, and the uninterrupted participation of Taylor's descendants in the ministry has overshadowed Richard and his now somewhat reduced BMS, resulting in a reading of both men that obscures their evangelical similarities while overemphasizing Richard's apparent similarities to early twentieth-century theological liberalism. Lauren Pfister explains the problem:

> In English language media these two missionaries have since the 1950s had their strategies placed in relative opposition, generally portraying Taylor as the "conservative" and Richard as the "liberal." Despite occasional qualifications, the general effect has been to portray them as representing nearly diametrically opposed positions within Chinese missionary circles. *This picture requires significant revision* for both its theological suggestions and its general understanding of both late nineteenth-century Chinese missions and the nature of the Qing dynasty.[15]

This study is an attempt to repair the distortion mentioned by Walls—to provide the kind of revision to our understanding of Richard that Pfister recommends.

At its most basic level, then, this thesis is an exploration of acculturation—of the ways in which Western missionaries were changed by their encounters with China. Specifically, it will use Timothy Richard as its subject, and analyze the ways in which his understanding and practice of mission evolved during his formative early years in China. While a longitudinal study covering Richard's theological development over the course of his entire career would be ideal, Richard's complexity, the scope of his activity, and the vast amount of material he produced during his lifetime makes such a work impractical within the constraints of a doctoral thesis. But there are thematic reasons for limiting the historical time frame as well. The study begins with the year 1870, simply because this was when Richard arrived in China; and while his background prior to commencing his work in China is by no means irrelevant and will be discussed, this project is primarily concerned with the development of his understanding and practice of mission in response to his encounter with China. The study ends in 1891 when Richard moved to Shanghai to superintend the literary and educational work of the Society for the Diffusion of Christian and General Knowledge

15. Pfister, "Rethinking Mission in China," 186 (emphasis added).

Among the Chinese (SDCK), marking his transition from more traditional mission station work to the kinds of institutional mission work that would become so prevalent after the turn of the century.[16]

1.1 Historiography of Richard

During the first half of the twentieth century many different English-language biographies of Richard were produced—several for the 1945 centenary of his birth.[17] All were positive and essentially uncritical, providing no scholarly references and drawing the vast quantity of their material from Richard's own autobiography. While Evans provided the most readable of the biographies, MacGillivray's work was the most original, including many quotations and recollections from people who knew Richard personally. Despite its age, Soothill's biography still holds primacy of place as being most detailed and most widely referenced, with later scholars relying heavily on its portrayal of Richard. Unfortunately, many of these biographers have shaped their accounts to reflect either the exigencies of their own historical moment or their own personal preferences.

Ding Zeliang's biography of Richard, written immediately after the 1949 Chinese liberation, is a clear example of a demonizing portrait.[18] Not surprisingly, Richard emerges from Ding's Leninist critique as a slave of Western imperialist forces bent on the subjugation of China. Much like the proverbial frog in the bottom of the well who imagined his limited view of the sky above encompassed the sum total of the heavens (*jing-di-zhi-wa*), Ding was either unable to see or unable to publish a picture of Richard that departed from the controlling narrative of demonization of the West.

William Soothill's biography of Richard is likewise burdened with bias, although it produces a very different picture of Richard. Unlike Ding, Soothill stood at the top of the well, and as he looked down into its deep waters he all too often saw his own face staring back at him from the midst of Richard's narrative. Arriving as pioneer of the United Methodist Free Church's mission in Wenzhou in 1882, Soothill served in China until the 1911 revolution, after which he supported a number of mission initiatives

---

16. The SDCK (*tong wen shuhui*) changed its name in 1906 to the Christian Literature Society for China (*guang xue hui*). Johnson, "Timothy Richard's Theory," 57 n. 1.

17. Reeve, *Timothy Richard*; MacGillivray, *Timothy Richard of China*; Soothill, *Timothy Richard of China*; Evans, *Timothy Richard, a Narrative*; Garnier, *Maker of Modern China*; Holloway, *Timothy Richard of China*; Warr, *Far Into China*.

18. Ding, *Li Timotai*. A similar later work suggested that Richard used famine relief work in Shanxi as a cover for collecting secret statistics on Shanxi for the British Empire: Guo, "Li Timotai zai Shanxi," 11–15.

before accepting a post as Professor of Chinese at Oxford in 1920. In his 1926 biography of Timothy Richard, Soothill's love for his subject is apparent, most likely shaped by his brief acquaintance with Richard during his years as principal of the Imperial University of Shanxi, as well as his professional affinity for Richard's later writings on Buddhism.[19] Whether including unattributed quotations that claimed Richard "did not think human nature altogether bad, and that he believed Darwin knew more of science than Moses," explaining away Richard's faith in prayer and its ability to elicit divine intervention in the natural world, or crediting Richard with bringing a "new Ideal" to China that began by asking "whether already [China] had not a better [religion] than our own," Soothill at times colored his narrative according to his own preferences rather than the demands of the material.[20] With Soothill's biography still in use, less careful readers may mistakenly confuse Soothill's theological views with those of Richard.

The first modern critical reading of Richard was undertaken by Rita Johnson in her unpublished 1966 doctoral dissertation.[21] Johnson made use of archival sources to reconstruct the outlines of Richard's narrative, presenting him with sensitivity as a theologically sincere and admirable figure. Little attention, however, was given to Richard's relationship with Victorian evangelicalism or the complex nature of cross-cultural encounters. Paul Bohr's 1972 monograph on Richard's role in the North China Famine was the next monograph on Richard, and remains the only scholarly book-length treatment of Richard to be published after 1945.[22] Owing to its thorough use of archival material—both in English and Chinese—as well as its informed reading of the late Qing famine context, it remains a valuable source of Richard-related insights. Bohr was careful to respect Richard's theological convictions, but his focus on Richard's role in famine relief means that relatively less was said about his missionary work before or after the disaster. Lastly, building on Rita Johnson's earlier research, Eunice Johnson's 2001 doctoral dissertation examined Richard's contributions to the development of education in China. Johnson's overwhelming concern with Richard as educator, however, led her to focus primarily on

---

19. Following the death of Moir Duncan, Soothill served as Principal of the Western Studies Department of Richard's university from 1906–1910. On their life in Taiyuan, see chapter 33 in Soothill, *Passport to China*.

20. Soothill, *Timothy Richard of China*, 37, 86–87, and 151.

21. Johnson, "Timothy Richard's Theory."

22. Bohr, *Famine in China*. There is also a recent and very basic reworking of the other Richard biographies by one of Richard's descendants: Chambers, *Tim China*.

his later years in China, and to ask questions that are different from those being considered in this thesis.[23]

Apart from these three longer treatments of Richard, a handful of scholars have published articles analyzing Richard and his practice and understanding of mission. Probably the earliest published critical essay to discuss Richard, Paul Cohen's 1957 comparison of Richard and James Hudson Taylor is still referenced by scholars today.[24] Perhaps not surprisingly, the pessimism that surrounded the Christian missionary project in China at the time colors Cohen's analysis. Already mentioned above, Andrew Walls's article on "The Multiple Conversions of Timothy Richard" is especially insightful, not only acknowledging more of the similarities between Richard and Taylor, but also allowing Richard to be seen as a missionary operating within the evangelical world of his day.[25] Also mentioned above, Lauren Pfister's 2003 comparison of Richard and Taylor brings additional nuance and complexity to this emerging picture of Richard.[26] Pfister goes even further in highlighting the similarities between the two missionaries, suggesting that the differences that did emerge between them were the result of their divergent approaches to different problems in Chinese mission and society. Most recently, Gregory Adam Scott has written helpfully about Richard's relationship with the emerging field of comparative religion and the ways in which his interactions with Chinese religions problematize scholarly applications of Edward Said's notion of orientalism to the nineteenth-century Protestant mission project.[27] While Scott's inclusion of a survey of Richard's early years is admirable, his article is concerned primarily with Richard's views of Buddhism as reflected in his twentieth-century publications rather than his earlier theological development. Finally, two Hong Kong scholars have published article-length English-language treatments of Richard: Timothy Wong's 1999 article uses Richard's Chinese-language periodical contributions to analyze his advocacy of reform, while Peter Ng's 2012 essay attempts to trace in less detail some of the same theological developments discussed in this thesis.[28]

While these articles each have their valuable insights, their contributions are necessarily constrained by length. Walls's insight into the organic

---

23. Johnson, "Educational Reform in China." Johnson's work makes use of her extensive collection of Richard's English-language writings, but would have benefited from interaction with Chinese-language primary and secondary sources.

24. Cohen, "Missionary Approaches," 29–62.

25. Walls, "Multiple Conversions," 236–58.

26. Pfister, "Rethinking Mission in China," 183–212.

27. Scott, "Timothy Richard," 53–75.

28. Wong, "Timothy Richard," 47–59; Ng, "Timothy Richard," 111–32.

and evolutionary nature of Richard's missional development sets the stage for this thesis, yet its lack of detailed engagement with the relevant primary source material leaves its argument unproven. The comparative nature of Cohen and Pfister's essays presents Richard in chiaroscuro with his qualities only observable when viewed against those of Taylor, resulting in a picture—particularly in Cohen's essay—that highlights the differences between Richard and Taylor while deemphasizing their areas of similarity. Peter Ng's essay, largely building upon the work of the other three articles, is ultimately prevented from advancing the conversation by its spatial constraints and limited access to Richard's letters. More problematic still, studies of Richard as a reformer, relief administrator, scholar of Buddhism, or educator examine aspects of Richard that are all derivative of his fundamental yet inadequately understood role as a missionary. Hence this study: a detailed, long-form analysis of the relevant primary source materials that seeks to reveal Richard the missionary on his own terms.

Toward the end of the twentieth century Mainland Chinese scholarship on Richard began to move away from the Leninist-imperialist critiques of the post-liberation years. While Gu Changsheng's reading continues to influence many scholars, a growing number of Chinese academics are now offering tentative reevaluations of Timothy Richard's contributions to China.[29] Richard's participation in famine relief work in China has received particular attention, with many scholars drawing on Chinese gazetteers and local source materials to add welcome context to analyses of missionary roles during the disaster.[30] A number of Chinese and especially Hong Kong scholars have published sophisticated explorations of Richard's later interest in Chinese Buddhism.[31] More recently, encouraged by the Chinese state's current interest in soft-power projection, younger Chinese scholars have tentatively begun to view Timothy Richard as a successful model of cultural transmission.[32] Unfortunately, limited use of English-language primary

---

29. Gu, *Cong Malixun dao Situ Leideng*, 315–56. For more sympathetic readings, see Ma, "Lun Li Timotai"; and Zhang, "Xifang xinjiao chuanjiaoshi," 21–28.

30. For example, Xu, "Lun 'Dingwu qihuang,'" 102–5.

31. Lai, "Li Timotai dui da sheng fojiao de huiying," 30–39; Lee and So, "Hua-di-wei-you," 105–29; Li, "Li Timotai yu fojiao," 13–15.

32. See the discussion of "cultural transmission," or *wenhua chuanbo*, in Wang, "Shixi Li Timotai de chuanjiao celue," 91–96; and Zhao, "Li Timotai de chuanjiao huodong." A consensus is building that views admirably Richard's integration of evangelism and secular work, using the following four categories for analysis: relief and medical work, the introduction of Western knowledge, the establishment of Shanxi University, and reform advocacy with Chinese officials. The two works listed here use nearly identical language for these categories, though this admittedly may be due to plagiarism. For a recent example of the more traditional suspicious reading of Richard's

source materials and a lack of theological sophistication limit the quality of most Chinese-language works when dealing directly with Richard, at times resulting in misreadings.³³

The single Chinese-language academic work that comes closest to the interests of this thesis is Lee Chi-Ho's 2007 doctoral dissertation on Christian-Buddhist dialogue and translation in the lives and work of Timothy Richard, William Soothill, and Karl Ludvig Reichelt.³⁴ Lee devotes one chapter to exploring Richard's early years in China in the hopes of uncovering a theological grounding for Richard's subsequent fascination with Buddhism. While Lee's explicitly theological interest in Richard's early China experience is echoed in this thesis, his preoccupation with Buddhism leads to a different understanding of Richard. His heavy reliance on Richard's 1916 autobiography compounds this emphasis, exposing Lee to the danger of reading later Buddhist preoccupations into Richard's earlier life.³⁵

1.2 Academic Contributions

By engaging directly with Richard's evolving theology of mission, this thesis will provide the interpretive tools necessary for advancing views of Richard that move beyond the simplistic conservative/liberal dichotomy that Pfister so rightly deplores. A detailed analysis of primary source materials shows that from 1870 to 1891 Richard's commitment to evangelistic mission persisted alongside what P. Richard Bohr, following Kenneth Scott Latourette, has called Richard's "widening vision of the task of the Christian missionary."³⁶ Throughout this process of widening, three characteristics were consistently present shaping Richard's evolution: the evangelical, the pragmatic, and the empathetic. Put simply, it was Richard's evangelical convictions that motivated him to adapt his understanding and practice of mission. The process by which these changes came about was reactive rather than reflective—pragmatic rather than theoretical—with each adaptation

---

cultural sympathies, see the final chapter in Wang and Hu, *Wenhua zhan lue*, 338–61.

33. See, for example, Li's ill-informed assertion that Richard's "hegemonic attitude" toward "inferior" Chinese religions and cultures set him apart from most other missionaries of his time. Li, "Shixi Li Timotai de jiduxinjiao sixiang," 49.

34. Lee, "Qing mo ming chu jiduxinjiao."

35. Though Lee's use of Chinese sources such as the writings of Yang Wenhui and Richard's contributions to the *Wan'guo gongbao* is noteworthy, his work suffers from insufficient reliance on Richard's English-language archival materials. See Lee, "Qing mo ming chu jiduxinjiao," 36, 57–58.

36. Bohr, "Legacy of Timothy Richard," 78; quoting Latourette, *History of Christian Missions in China*, 378.

developing organically from his experiences in China. The result was a series of missional adjustments that demonstrated an increasing empathy toward and even identification with the Chinese other.

In the process of building this argument, this thesis will also reveal a number of new discoveries that alter current understandings of Richard and his career as a missionary in China. One of the more surprising findings relates to Richard's appropriation of Edward Irving's reading of "seeking the worthy" in Matt 10 and how this shaped his extensive interactions with Chinese scholar-officials. Rather than pursuing the kind of elite-focused "top down" evangelistic strategy often associated with the earlier Jesuit mission in China, Richard pursued devout followers of China's religions—the worthy seekers of the truth of Matt 10—because he was convinced that they were predisposed to accept the gospel. Accordingly, when Richard did turn his attention to Chinese political and intellectual elites following the North China Famine, he did not seek them because they were "worthy."[37] Rather, his new focus represented a strategic shift: Richard's interest in using Christian publishing and the accouterments of Western civilization to engage Chinese scholar-officials was primarily related to his post-famine drive to reduce Chinese suffering and to transform negative opinions of Christianity among Chinese elites. Evangelism, while never eschewed, was a secondary goal, in so much as his efforts among the socially and politically powerful were designed to improve conditions for Christian evangelists throughout China.

Though little recognized by scholars, Richard's relationship with the sectarian religious groups located in Shandong and Shanxi made him one of the earliest Westerners to draw attention to these groups. The extensive interaction with Chinese religionists that resulted naturally from Richard's unique application of seeking the worthy led him to adopt methods for propagation, support, and governance from the sectarians—a surprising demonstration of his Chinese empathy.[38] Impressed by their piety and their perseverance in the face of government persecution, Richard saw much to admire in these sectarian "brethren in nonconformity."[39]

Analyzing Richard's evolution within the proper historical and cultural contexts will also shed new light on a number of theological and missiological trends affecting the nineteenth-century Protestant mission

---

37. This will be introduced in chapter 3, and discussed again in chapters 6 and 8.

38. Richard's interest in sectarianism will be discussed in chapters 3 and 4.

39. Richard, *Wanted: Good Samaritans for China*, 13–15. This pamphlet was reproduced later in Richard, *Conversion by the Million*, 2:28–59.

to China.[40] First of all, Richard's integration of humanitarian aid and evangelism did not mark a departure from his identity or work as a missionary. Like his evangelical counterparts in late Victorian Britain with their burgeoning interest in social Christianity, Richard simply reacted compassionately to his context; only afterwards did he "discover" the implications of the Kingdom of Heaven for this earth. Secondly, Richard's interest in Christianity's ability to fulfill what was good within China's own religious and cultural traditions also arose out of the combination of his evangelical convictions with his compassionate identification with Chinese people. Standing somewhere between James Legge's "supplemental" form of accommodationism and the more radical fulfillment theology of John N. Farquhar, Richard's accommodationism was not so much theological as it was instinctive and practical; ultimately, it was inseparable from his efforts to indigenize both evangelism and local church practice.[41] Thus, Richard's widening of the mission task—both his willingness to engage in activities that were less directly evangelistic and his insistence on doing things in ways that resonated with Chinese people —was a practical response to the realities of the mission field in Shandong and Shanxi; theological justification of these adaptations was an afterthought.

Finally, the overall picture of Richard that emerges from this thesis also brings a new level of complexity to current understandings of the interplay between missionaries, culture, and religion in nineteenth-century China. Theological development and cultural accommodation within the missionary movement cannot be properly assessed without proper attention to multiple contexts. Viewed in this way, Richard's adaptations demonstrate the surprising creativity and sensitivity with which some adjusted their missionary methods to meet Chinese needs and desires. Richard's insistence on the effectiveness of indigenous Christian ministers, his emphasis on Christianity as fulfilling rather than destroying Chinese culture, and especially his willingness to borrow from Chinese sectarians all draw welcome attention to the diverse and empathetic ways in which Christianity could interact with late imperial Chinese society.

---

40. The themes from this paragraph will be discussed in chapter 6.

41. On Farquhar's fulfillment theology, see Sharpe, *Not to Destroy but to Fulfil*. For Legge's idea of Christianity as essential supplement to the good in China's religions—especially Confucianism—see, for example, Legge, *Confucianism*, 7; as well as the discussion throughout Girardot, *Victorian Translation of China*, especially 218–34.

1.3 Methodological Considerations

As a study of the ways in which a British missionary responded to his encounter with China, this thesis will pay close attention to the interplay between the religious idealism of a Victorian evangelical Protestant and the political, cultural, and social realities of late Qing China. The current academic climate has brought a welcome emphasis on doing history from the bottom up and on the essential significance of what has been termed hyphenated Christianity (or Christianities)—meaning that Christianity takes its shape from the cultural environment in which it takes root. While this awareness has illuminated heretofore under-appreciated dimensions of the missionary project, care must still be taken to maintain balance. As the Hong Kong scholar Philip Leung has rightly observed, whatever distinctions may exist between mission history (the story of the foreign) and church history (the story of the local), both accounts—and more—are needed to do justice to the rich diversity of Christianity in its manifold global embodiments.[42]

Biography has begun to resurface in scholarship, finding a welcome position in missionary studies informed by the new themes and correctives provided by the current emphasis on the global nature of Christianity.[43] Sensitivity to the common dignity and multiplicity of characters present in historical narratives sets biographies free from the predilections of demonization or hagiography, and encourages the asking of questions of a wider academic significance. Two recent studies of the Jesuit Matteo Ricci by leading historians of early modern Europe model this new approach. R. Po-chia Hsia's narrative highlights the significant ways in which the Italian and Portuguese contexts shaped Ricci's life and work in China, while Mary Laven's record reveals the heretofore unnoticed preponderance of non-elite converts within the early Jesuit Chinese community.[44] Even if it be granted that Richard is not of the same stature or significance as Ricci, the positive reception of Hsia and Laven's studies of a European missionary in seventeenth-century China suggests that a similarly biographical work on a European in nineteenth-century China—and one that deals with similar issues—might reasonably expect to make valuable contributions to scholarly discourse.[45]

Due to the diachronic nature of the questions being asked, as well as the reactive nature of so many of Richard's adaptations, biographical narrative plays a significant role in this thesis. The primary tools for reconstructing

---

42. Leung, "Mission History versus Church," 177–213; 200–205, especially.
43. Manktelow, *Missionary Families*, 10–11.
44. Hsia, *Jesuit in the Forbidden City*; Laven, *Mission to China*.
45. Criveller, "Review," 768–73.

Richard's narrative within his historical and cultural context are the volumes of correspondence and reports preserved within the Timothy Richard Papers, part of the Baptist Missionary Society Archives held at Regent's Park College, Oxford. A number of more personal letters in Welsh between Richard and his parents are also held in the National Library of Wales; however, these documents were translated into English and copies deposited in the Richard Papers at Regent's Park by Thomas Evans in the 1960s. A second smaller collection of primary and mostly secondary source materials relating to Richard has recently been deposited in the archives of the Yale Divinity School Library, preserving a decade worth of travels and research carried out by Richard scholar Eunice Johnson. In addition to these letters and official papers, Richard also produced a number of articles for publication in the BMS periodical, the *Missionary Herald*, and the main periodical of the Protestant mission community in China, the *Chinese Recorder and Missionary Journal*. During this period, a number of Chinese-language publications were also developed by Richard for use in the China mission—a few of which survive, including his 1878 *Xuedao cixu* [*The Order of Learning Doctrine*] and his 1881-82 *Jinshi yaowu* [*Present Needs*].[46] Additionally, he produced several articles for the influential Chinese-language periodical *Wan'guo gongbao* [*Globe Magazine*] or *WGGB*. When read alongside Richard's three major autobiographical accounts—his 1885 address to the BMS Committee "Fifteen Years' Missionary Work in China," his 1906 "Autobiography of the Author," and his 1916 *Forty-five Years in China*—these materials make it possible to reconstruct the significant experiences of his early years in China, and to make some preliminary statements regarding his understanding and practice of mission.[47]

Previous works on Richard have tended to rely heavily on his 1916 autobiography *Forty-Five Years in China*. References to his diaries made by Richard within the text, as well as verifications from other source materials suggest that this account is reasonably accurate and trustworthy when recounting Richard's experiences.[48] This autobiography is less helpful, however, for tracing the development of his feelings and ideas, since it is

---

46. Bibliographic entries for Richard's published works are given in the chronological list at the end of this thesis.

47. Richard, "Autobiography of the Author" in *Conversion by the Million*, 1:79–109; Richard, *Fifteen Years' Missionary Work*; Richard, *Forty-Five Years in China*.

48. A number of Richard's diaries are preserved in the Baptist Missionary Society Archives. Unfortunately, Richard's records were spartan giving only scheduling details, and the collection is incomplete with the earliest diary dating from August 1888. Timothy Richard Diaries, August 1888 to September 1889; 1890–1892; 1898; and 1899–1903, BMSA CH/4B.

unrealistic to expect Richard to recollect with perfect accuracy impressions and patterns of thought from forty-five years in the past: like Soothill, Richard may also be guilty of refashioning the younger Timothy Richard in the image of his later self. Accordingly, this thesis will whenever possible rely on documents written by Richard at the time being discussed, using *Forty-Five Years* only with reference to narrative events. As Richard's writing output increases over time, particularly following the North China Famine, this becomes more practicable.

Particular effort has been made to situate Richard in relation to his fellow China missionaries. Accordingly, biographies and autobiographies of many other China missionaries from the time have been examined, along with relevant archival materials for some of the more prominent individuals. The American Presbyterian missionary John Nevius's writings from this period have been utilized, along with the David Hill Papers held in the (Wesleyan) Methodist Missionary Society Archives at the School of Oriental and African Studies Library (SOAS) in London. SOAS also holds the archives of the China Inland Mission, including the papers of James Hudson Taylor, two important sources for information about Richard and those who worked alongside him in Shanxi. The CIM periodical *China's Millions* has been especially helpful, providing an unexpected wealth of information about Richard and his missionary world. Reading all these materials alongside the more specific Richard sources adds depth and contrast to the emerging picture of Richard, making Richard's departures from and similarities with the rest of the China missionary community much more clear.

For this study to progress properly, however, narrative alone is inadequate. To borrow the language of Clifford Geertz, a "thick description" is needed—a self-conscious attempt to provide sufficient information regarding Richard's context to allow the reader to see Richard on his own terms.[49] The cross-cultural aspect of Richard's life as a missionary necessitates a sensitivity to the interplay of both the Chinese and the British contexts throughout the narrative, while recognizing that Richard may in fact be representative of neither context, but rather of some new hybrid third culture unique to himself. Nor is this awareness alone sufficient, for the too-broad categories of "Chinese" and "British" say very little regarding the specific associations and affinities that shaped his life. Accordingly, the relevant secondary literature will be employed to help situate Richard, his faith, and his theological evolution not only within the world of late Victorian Welsh nonconformity, but also within late imperial Chinese sectarianism, the broader China mission community, and the lived reality of the North China

---

49. Geertz, *Interpretation of Cultures*, 5–6, 9–10.

Famine in Shandong and Shanxi. To try and understand Richard without detailed reference to these multi-dimensional identities and influences is to risk misrepresenting him.[50]

Admittedly, referencing these contexts responsibly requires sensitivity. While there have been recent suggestions from theologians that the term "evangelical" has outlived its usefulness, it is surely a helpful one when thinking historically about the Western Protestant Christian community during the eighteenth and nineteenth centuries.[51] When viewing from the outside the historical phenomena commonly referred to as evangelicalism, W. R. Ward's suggestion that eighteenth-century Christians who "felt spiritually bound to create Orphan Houses" could be considered evangelicals is quite helpful.[52] Richard's participation in humanitarian activities while in pursuit of evangelistic goals certainly lends him the outward appearance of a stalwart evangelical. Reading the inner life is much more problematic, and here David Bebbington's well-known quadrilateral (of conversionism, activism, biblicism, and crucicentrism) is still the most useful tool for identifying evangelicalism in its nineteenth-century forms.[53] For Richard, the ways in which he reacted to his experiences in China cannot be understood without reference to his abiding interest in conversionism. His activism was uncontested, as seen in his innovative integration of humanitarian service and evangelism.[54] While perhaps falling short of the bibliolatry of many of his fellow Victorians, Richard's biblicism was evident in his insistence upon the biblical rootedness of his adaptations.[55] And his commitment to the importance of Jesus's substitutionary death on the cross as the only means of personal salvation—while less significant for Richard than the other three sides of the quadrilateral—nevertheless remained a constant throughout the period of this study, from his revivalist conversion and subsequent call, through to the confirmation of his theological views by the BMS Committee at the conclusion of the 1880s BMS conflicts.[56] To refer in this thesis to Richard or his ideas as "evangelical" is to do so with Bebbington's framework in mind.

50. Li and Guo, "Rethinking the Relationship," 45–60.

51. Wells, *Courage to Be Protestant*, 18–20.

52. Ward, "Evangelical Identity," 12–13.

53. Bebbington, *Evangelicalism in Modern Britain*, 2–3. Ward, however, has questioned the suitability of Bebbington's categories, particularly with reference to the role of mysticism among eighteenth-century continental Protestants. Ward, "Evangelical Identity," 11–30.

54. For the evolving nature of evangelical activism in the second half of the nineteenth century, see Bebbington, *Nonconformist Conscience*, 37–60.

55. Larsen, *People of One Book*.

56. Richard's conversion and call are discussed in chapter 2; the confirmation of his

Similar care must be taken to guard against an over-essentialized view of China's religions. When this thesis speaks of "China's religions," it does so acknowledging the diversity of religious practice and belief within China that persists despite the "eclectic" sharing of many themes.[57] While there are limitations to the generic signifier "Chinese," grounding the analysis in specific local contexts can help minimize problems, as a number of recent scholarly works have demonstrated.[58] "Religion," either as an English term or in its Chinese form, *zongjiao*, is likewise problematic:[59] here, too, attention to the specifics of context—in this case, to the actual practices and beliefs of specific communities—can help bound and root the term.[60] Keeping in mind Richard's situatedness in rural Shandong and post-famine Shanxi thus guards against reifying either "the Chinese" or their "religions."

Beyond narrative and contextual concerns, close attention must also be paid to Richard's character. As the working son of a Welsh blacksmith farmer, Richard acquired a practical bent from his earliest days—a character trait that predisposed him toward action and experimentation rather than systematic reflection. By disposition, Richard was not a systematic theologian, and so he left many theological issues unaddressed in his writings. He showed little concern for building a cohesive philosophical or theological system, and much more interest in developing and applying methods that worked in the real (Chinese) world. Richard was also reactive, as was the case with many missionaries, changing and adjusting his missionary practice in response to events and the challenges of his particular context. Finally, Richard was an intellectual magpie, collecting new ideas and incorporating them into his existing practice and understanding, rather than rejecting the old and replacing it with the new.[61]

Given Richard's character, it is thus important to avoid the temptation to over-theologize or impose any unwarranted order upon his thoughts or

---

understanding of the gospel by the BMS Committee is discussed in chapter 8.

57. Gentz, "Rational Choice," 538–39. Many scholars favor a more unified view of religion in China: Feuchtwang, "Chinese Religion Exists," 139–61; Goossaert and Palmer, *Religious Question*, 20–21.

58. See, for example, Chau, *Miraculous Response*; and Johnson, *Spectacle and Sacrifice*.

59. Clart, "Concept of 'Popular Religion,'"166–203; Fitzgerald, *Ideology of Religious Studies*, 3–32. Shandong historian Lu Yao argues that *zongjiao* was also being used by Daoist and folk religious groups to differentiate discrete sets of teachings by the middle of the tenth century. Lu, "Zhongguo chuantong shehui minjian xinyang zhi kaocha," 86. The more generally accepted reading of *zongjiao* is outlined in Goossaert, "1898: The Beginning of the End for Chinese Religion?," 320–21.

60. See, for example, Dunch, *Fuzhou Protestants*.

61. Walls, "Multiple Conversions," 258.

his theological development. Allowing the narrative to dictate when various issues are addressed—and readdressed—within the thesis is one tool for avoiding such pitfalls. And if this muddies the various strands of his theological development, so be it: this is not a study of a particular theological trajectory, after all, but rather a study of how China can change people. Specifically, it is a study of how one particular man—a Victorian Baptist missionary from Wales—was transformed by his encounter with China. When confronted with the other-ness of China, Richard reacted practically in ways that preserved his evangelical distinctives while at the same time accommodating the other, resulting in a way of doing mission that was both conversionist and culturally empathetic.

1.3.1 Note on Languages

Limited agreement existed within the nineteenth-century Protestant mission community in China regarding how best to transliterate Chinese characters into the Roman alphabet. Dialectical variations within China heightened the confusion. For the sake of clarity, this thesis renders all Chinese terms into the standard *hanyu pinyin* romanization, with the exception of the older place name of Chefoo, which has been retained owing to its prevalence within the relevant missionary correspondence.[62] For specialists, a list of characters for Chinese terms referred to in the text is supplied in the back matter, and Chinese characters are included in the concluding bibliography. When available, the English translations of Chinese-language titles are printed as supplied by the original author or publisher, preserving original wording and spelling. An asterisk (*) is used to denote instances where English translations were not provided, and the translated title is my own.

Nineteenth-century Welsh spellings also lack consistency. Place name spellings have been rendered in this thesis in accordance with the accepted authorities whenever possible.[63] Finally, curious spellings for Chinese, Welsh, or English terms within quotations have been preserved as they originally appeared. This should cause little difficulty for most readers, and has the added advantage of bringing modern readers one step closer to the world of Richard and his contemporaries. Emphases in quotations, unless otherwise noted, are taken directly from the original material.

---

62. The history of the name "Chefoo" is discussed in chapter 2.
63. Davies, *Gazetteer of Welsh Place Names*; Dugdale et al., *Topographical Dictionary*.

1.3.2 Structure of the Thesis

Reflecting Richard's pragmatic, reactive development as a missionary, this thesis takes its structure from Richard's narrative.

The first part of the thesis establishes Richard's evangelicalism and analyzes his initial adjustments to his practice of mission. Chapter 2 demonstrates the evangelical nature of Richard's experience of revival and subsequent conversion, call, and theological training before probing his initial disillusionment on the field. Chapter 3 analyzes Richard's first adaptation in response to the ineffectiveness of contemporary mission practice in China. Richard's appropriation of the Matt 10 idea of seeking the worthy—as encountered in the writings of Edward Irving—is shown to reflect both Richard's evangelical drive for Christian conversion as well as his pragmatic interest in methods that work. Chapter 4 explores Richard's interactions with China's religions, particularly in their sectarian forms. As Richard acted in accordance with his newfound method of seeking the devout worthy, his desire to find methods that produced evangelical conversions led him not only to promote the use of "moral evidences" in evangelism but also to borrow techniques for his mission from Chinese sectarian groups. Combined with his own previous theological proclivities and the practical constraints of limited field resources, Richard's interactions with Chinese religionists encouraged his remarkable implementation of indigenous ministry principles within the BMS mission in Shandong.

Part two of the thesis analyzes how Richard applied and further developed these ideas in the context of the North China Famine. In chapter 5 the reactive and sympathetic nature of Richard's initial participation in famine relief work is demonstrated, along with the continuing interest in evangelism that naturally accompanied his humanitarian efforts. The traumatic and isolated nature of Richard's famine experiences contributed to his strong identification with the local people that found expression, as explored in chapter 6, in his post-famine reform advocacy and his efforts to ensure that no similar disaster would strike North China again. Already convinced of the practical effectiveness of combining evangelism with humanitarian action, Richard grounded his new methods in his "discovery" of the social implications of the Kingdom of God. A similar conviction regarding the gospel's ability to fulfill rather than destroy what was positive in China's religions and cultures also emerged from his heightened post-famine identification, further strengthening Richard's support for indigenous ministry and the development of evangelistic materials that were more empathetic to Chinese cultural priorities. Chapter 6 also demonstrates that Richard's post-famine shift toward Chinese officials and scholars was the result of his desire to prevent human suffering and reduce the persecution of Christians, rather than an expression of a trickle-down theory of evangelization.

Part three uses the two major conflicts of Richard's post-famine years in Shanxi to demonstrate both the strength of Richard's commitment to his adaptations as well as the areas where his fellow missionaries accepted or rejected his new ideas and techniques. Chapter 7 begins by outlining the cordial relations that existed between the various missionaries present in Shanxi immediately after the famine, and their respect for Richard as an evangelical missionary. The so-called Shanxi Spirit controversy is then revealed to be fundamentally an internal conflict that swept through the CIM China field, rather than a direct attack on Richard or his theology. Chapter 8 outlines the explicitly personal and theological nature of the criticisms leveled against Richard by some of his BMS colleagues in the second half of the 1880s. Analyzing these criticisms alongside Richard's responses and the final decision of the BMS Committee reveals Richard's persistent evangelical convictions and his insistence on a more empathetic approach to China's religions and cultures. Ultimately, his 1891 decision to undertake the work of the SDCK is shown to have been not a rejection of evangelical goals nor of the missionary task itself, but rather a strategic decision to eschew more direct forms of evangelistic work in order to bring about the conditions in China necessary for "conversion by the million."[64]

---

64. This phrase comes from the opening of Richard's 1907 anthology: Richard, *Conversion by the Million*, 1:16–17.

Part One

Richard Encountering China

Innovation and Adaptation of His Missionary Thought

2

Beginnings

Preparation in Ministry and Disappointment in China

TIMOTHY RICHARD'S YOUTH IN Wales—his home life, religious experience, education and training for ministry—was fundamentally evangelical. After his arrival in China, it was this same evangelicalism that led to his disappointment with the mission methods of his day. Further influenced by both the faithfulness of the fledgling Chinese Baptist community and the absence of expatriate Baptist colleagues, Richard responded to his dissatisfaction with the slow rate of conversion in the mission by pursuing an increasingly empathetic trajectory of acculturation to his Chinese context. Combined with his desire for practical results, these two impulses—his evangelicalism and his empathy for the needs and priorities of China and her people—comprise the primary tools for understanding the ways in which this Welsh missionary to China adapted his practice and understanding of mission during his first twenty years of ministry.

2.1 Growing Up Baptist in Wales, 1845–1869

The nonconformist spirit in Wales traces its roots back to the late sixteenth-century Welsh Puritans who were impatient with what they perceived to be a true lack of reform as well as outright immorality among the laity and in particular among the religious leaders.[1] The availability of a Bible and Book of Common Prayer in the Welsh language from the year 1567 materially aided the cause of these early Protestants.[2] From the 1593 martyrdom of the Welsh evangelist John Penry—the "pioneer" of Welsh nonconformity—to the establishment of the first Baptist congregation in Wales by John Myles in 1649 and the effective church planting work of "the Whitfield of Wales,"

---

1. Williams, *Recovery, Reorientation, and Reformation*, 306–16.

2. 1567 saw the first printing of a Welsh New Testament, translated by William Salesbury (with help from Davies and Huet); the complete Bible in Welsh was not available until Morgan's enduring 1588 translation. Ballinger, *Bible in Wales*, 16–22.

Vavasor Powell, in the latter half of the seventeenth century, vital Protestantism quickly grew in influence and popularity among the Welsh laity, thriving especially outside of the established Anglican church.[3] By Richard's lifetime, Dissenting Protestantism was the predominant form of religious expression in Wales.[4] On the Sunday of the 1851 census, nonconformists made up 486,242 of the total attendances in Wales versus 138,438 Church of England attendances, with Independents, Calvinistic Methodists, and Baptists representing the largest groups of Dissenters.[5] By the end of the nineteenth century, Baptists alone would claim over one hundred thousand adherents, or more than one out of every twenty Welsh people.[6]

Timothy Richard was born in October 1845, the youngest of nine children in a blacksmith's household recently settled at Tanyresgair farm on the outskirts of Ffald-y-brenin on the road to Ffarmers in Cynwyl Caio, Wales.[7] This was a Baptist home. In addition to his responsibilities as farmer, Richard's father also served as secretary and deacon of the Baptist churches of Bethel and Salem in Caio, earning for himself a reputation as a peacemaker.[8] One of Richard's uncles had been the means of conversion of Griffith John's first wife, while one of his father's nephews, Joshua Lewis, was a well-known nonconformist preacher in Pembrokeshire. Richard's maternal grandfather was deacon in a prominent Baptist chapel in Aberduar, Llanybedder, the same

---

3. Rees, *History of Protestant Nonconformity*, 19–30; Williams, *Recovery, Reorientation, and Reformation*, 321–22, 325–26. On Myles and the earliest Baptists in Wales, see Vedder, *Short History of the Baptists*, 269–72; Morgan, *Wales and the Word*, 5–15.

4. In his 1883 historical survey, Thomas Rees claimed confidently that on the basis of his statistical analysis "the Welsh are now emphatically a nation of nonconformists." Rees, *History of Protestant Nonconformity*, 485. In 1904 Lewis cites figures from Howard Evans listing the total number of Welsh nonconformists as 462,017, with Baptists coming in third behind Congregationalists (Independents) and Calvinistic Methodists with a respectable 113,597 communicants. Lewis, *Nonconformity in Wales*, 104–7.

5. Attendances for Roman Catholic or other religious bodies in Wales were negligible. Mann, *Census of Great Britain*, 142. For the relative size of the groups—at least as reflected in the discrete number of "sittings" on the census day—see Mann, *Census of Great Britain*, 136–37.

6. The total number of 106,566 Baptists in 1900 Wales is taken from Vedder, *Short History of the Baptists*, 271. For the total Welsh population see *Census of England and Wales: Summary Tables*, 6.

7. The October date comes from Price, *History of Caio*, 58. The geographical details are from a 16 July 2012 email sent to the author by Rev. Peter Thomas, General Secretary of the Baptist Union of Wales and great-great-nephew of Timothy Richard.

8. While it need not necessarily be doubted, the claim that the elder Timothy Richard was a peacemaker among the various local religious parties came from the younger Richard. Richard, *Forty-Five Years*, 20.

chapel the celebrated Christmas Evans had first joined in 1788.[9] Shaped by the warm evangelicalism of her own upbringing, Richard's mother Eleanor was known throughout the area for her graciousness and piety.[10]

The first Baptist chapel in Caio was built in 1741 on the site of the current Bethel Chapel, most likely as an outgrowth of the remote Bwlch-y-rhiw Baptist Chapel.[11] Located closer to human settlements, the young Bethel Chapel grew much faster than Bwlch-y-rhiw and was rebuilt in 1836, having been served by one pastor shared with Bwlch-y-rhiw since 1817. In 1829 Salem Baptist Chapel—also in Cynwyl Caio—was built on the road toward Pumsaint as an extension of Bethel, leaving the Richard family farm outside of Ffarmers roughly equidistant between the Bethel and Salem chapels. Sometime after the establishment of the Salem Baptist Chapel, Bethlehem and Salem agreed to share one pastor between them.[12] Hence, Richard's father's role as secretary and deacon of both chapels was not unreasonable.

Welsh laymen were known during Richard's life for their interest in theological issues, displaying willingness in their leisure time to discuss religious controversies "with such acumen and intelligence as would delight professors."[13] Richard's parents seem to be no exception, with his father enjoying visits from noted Broad Churchman Rowland Williams during Williams' tenure as vice-principal and Hebrew instructor at nearby St. David's College in Lampeter.[14]

In the course of the nineteenth century, Wales experienced a number of revivals large and small.[15] By the middle of the century Welsh nonconfor-

9. Evans, *Timothy Richard*, 11. For Christmas Evans's conversion to the Baptist cause and his influence on Welsh nonconformity, see Morgan, "Christmas Evans," 116–24.

10. Richard himself gives his mother's maiden name as "Eleanor Llethercoch," almost certainly derived from her childhood farm's proximity to the village of Llethercoch, an unknown location perhaps in the vicinity of Pencarreg. Richard, *Forty-Five Years*, 20. On the rise of evangelicalism in Wales and within Welsh nonconformity in particular, see Morgan, *Wales and the Word*, 88–105.

11. Price, *History of Caio*, 36. The Bwlch-y-rhiw Baptist Chapel was built shortly after the passing of the Five Mile Act in 1665, hence its remote location. Price, *History of Caio*, 31.

12. By 1866—just one year prior to Rev. J. D. Evans's appointment as their pastor—the combined membership of the two congregations numbered 326. Price, *History of Caio*, 38.

13. Rees, *History of Protestant Nonconformity*, 463.

14. Richard, *Forty-Five Years*, 19–20. Though it is tempting to make inferences, there is no indication of Richard's father's attitude toward Williams's views. On Williams and "Lampeter Theology" see Morgan, *Wales and the Word*, 37–54.

15. One typical example: in 1849, shortly after Richard's birth, a cholera outbreak swept across South Wales. In its wake followed a "Divine blessing" with many thousands repenting and coming to church. Rees, *History of Protestant Nonconformity*, 461.

mity, while remaining predominantly orthodox in its theology, was having little positive influence on society. Accusing their fellow Welsh Christians of being "lukewarm" or "asleep," a growing number of believers longed for a renewed sense of spiritual urgency.[16] News of the dynamic revivals sweeping the United States in 1857 soon spread to Wales, and helped inspire a movement of prayer for revival which took hold in many congregations. In the summer of 1858 Humphrey Jones returned to his native Cardiganshire, promoting the revivalism that many had been seeking and to which he himself had become converted during his previous few years in the United States.[17] Though skeptical of things American and Arminian—for Jones was a Wesleyan—the Calvinistic Methodist minister David Morgan attended one of Jones' addresses, and was promptly struck by the same sense of spiritual deepening. By the end of 1858, one out of every five adults in Morgan's own Cardiganshire hometown were newly converted.[18]

In 1859 the revival expanded to include nearly all parts of Wales, with the itinerant Morgan in particular employing a direct and intimate style of preaching often decried as "Finneyism."[19] In addition to numerical growth (out of one hundred ten thousand added to the rolls of Welsh churches at the time fourteen thousand joined Baptist congregations), the 1858–1860 Revival influenced the church and society in a number of long-lasting ways.[20] Regular times of family worship became common in Wales, while support for temperance and unity among churches increased dramatically.[21] Preaching was transformed, with formality and reserve giving way to a sermon style both personal and direct. It was prayer, however, that emerged as

---

16. Evans, *When He Is Come*, 23–27. Evans's record of the mid-century revival in Wales is the most thorough.

17. Though inspired by the American revivals of the same time, the revival in Wales developed along its own course with little additional input from the United States and remained independent of similar events taking place in Ireland and Scotland. Evans, *When He Is Come*, 107–8.

18. The standard account of the mid-century revivals is Orr, *Second Evangelical Awakening*. For events in Wales, see pp. 78–94. The most detailed record of the roles played by both Jones and Morgan in the 1858–1860 Revival in Wales is Evans, *Two Welsh Revivalists*.

19. Recognizing the real danger of insincere conversions, Morgan adjusted his techniques, adding meetings designed to impart basic Christian knowledge to new converts. Evans, *When He Is Come*, 111–12. Jones, on the other hand, seemed to be more self-consciously adopting Finney's techniques. His reliance on technique is evident in his use of "the anxious seat" in the front row of the chapels to better impress his call upon his listeners. Evans, *Two Welsh Revivalists*, 9–10, 14–18.

20. Evans, *When He Is Come*, 97, 99.

21. Evans, *When He Is Come*, 100–101.

the hallmark of the revival. As recorded in one contemporary revival report from the market town of Llangefni,

> The great fruit of this revival is prayer. It was preceded by prayer, and it issues in prayer, which remains its chief agent. In previous awakenings, the ministry of the Word was the chief means . . . but the particular means of this present movement is "the prayer";—everyone is coming to believe in the efficacy of prayer.[22]

The revival also left its mark on Timothy Richard. In March of 1859 David Morgan traveled to Carmarthenshire where, according to one correspondent,

> [t]he week-day and Sabbath-day services at churches and chapels were crowded. Hundreds are coming over to the Lord's side . . . a deep and genuine work of grace is coming on. . . . There is no excitement; but a deep, silent and awfully solemn impression prevails everywhere.[23]

On one Sunday early in the month, Richard was in attendance as Morgan preached at the Bethel Baptist Church in Caio on "Ephraim's grey hairs" from Hos 7:9. Though Morgan himself found it to have been "a very hard service," the local minister rejoiced to see forty penitents converted on the following Sunday, and an additional thirty-nine converted during his next service at Salem Baptist Chapel.[24] Like many children at the time, young Richard was caught up in the revival and was among those in Caio who made decisions that March.[25] On 10 April 1859 Timothy Richard and fifty-one others were baptized in the River Twrch by John Davies, pastor of the Salem Baptist Chapel.[26] Such a large number of additions to the Caio Chris-

22. This unreferenced quotation is taken from Evans, *When He is Come*, 109.

23. From the March 1859 issue of *The Nonconformist* as quoted in Evans, *When He Is Come*, 82.

24. Evans, *When He Is Come*, 81–82. The quoted "local minister" is almost certainly John Davies. The Ddolwen Brook mentioned by the minister most likely refers to the local name of the stem of the River Twrch wherein Richard and the others were baptized.

25. On the prominent role and high degree of participation of young people in the 1858–1860 Revival in Wales, see Evans, *When He Is Come*, 103–6. In a number of instances, the revival first took hold of communities through children's prayer meetings.

26. For the exact date see Evans, *Timothy Richard*, 15. Richard's own recollection of his baptism date is less precise, claiming at first to have been twelve years of age, and then giving no date other than "during the great revival." Richard also claimed that Davies chose to baptize him first as he was the lightest and easiest to manage in the water: the Twrch was in flood and the pastor wished to make a test before committing the rest

tian community must have been quite striking, given that church membership in the 1830s was 112, which by 1866 after the revival had grown to 326: moreover, these new converts "formed the strength of the church in ten years."[27] Richard recalls hearing a sermon not long afterwards on 1 Sam 15:22, "Obedience is better than sacrifice." Walking back from Salem Chapel later that day, he remarked to his brother Joshua how throughout the pastor's message he had felt as if God was commanding him to "go abroad as a missionary"—this despite the fact that, as his brother wondered, the sermon was "not particularly missionary in character."[28]

After leaving the local primary school at the age of fourteen, Richard began to pursue education more seriously, both as a profession and as an end in itself. This was very much in line with his evangelical upbringing: prior to 1870 education in Wales was intimately connected to religion, typically of a nonconformist bent.[29] Alternating work on the farm with studies in institutions throughout Carmathenshire, Richard soon became an educator in his own right, eventually supporting himself in a string of teaching positions at various schools in the region, finding particular success as master at the endowed school in Cynwyl Elfed. The convictions of his baptism remained evident during this period, and at the age of eighteen Richard held a very popular evening Bible class on the life of Paul for the senior form at the Cynwyl Elfed school. Richard was pleased to note that every child from the class had joined the chapel within a year of his leaving the school.[30]

As an educator, Richard would have been aware of the growing English challenge to Welsh-language instruction in Wales. The criticisms of both the Welsh people and especially their language contained within the 1847 government-commissioned report on education in Wales—the Welsh-speaker was described as using "a language of old-fashioned agriculture, of theology, and of simple rustic life, while all the world about him is

---

to the river. Richard, "Autobiography of the Author" in *Conversion by the Million*, 1:79; Richard, *Forty-Five Years*, 22.

27. Price, *History of Caio*, 38. This same source notes that Davies was pastor of Salem Baptist Chapel perhaps up until 1866, but the exact date at which Bethel was separated from Blwch-y-rhiw and twinned with Salem is uncertain. The quotation (most likely Davies again) is from Evans, *When He Is Come*, 82.

28. Richard, *Forty-Five Years*, 22. Richard's interest in vocational ministry was part of a trend: in the wake of the 1858–1860 Revival, the Welsh Baptist chapels contributed disproportionately to the number of Baptists going into ministry in Britain: between 1860 and 1890 the 23.5 percent of British Baptists located in Wales supplied 29 percent of the denomination's new ministers. Brown, "Baptist Ministry," 111. For some of the reasons behind this trend, see Jones, "Culture," 157–83.

29. James, *Older Mother Tongues*, 14.

30. Richard, *Forty-Five Years*, 22–25.

English"—inaugurated a period of increasing emphasis on English instruction in Welsh schools, culminating in the 1870 Education Act's provisions for educational uniformity across the United Kingdom.[31] Increasing urbanization of the Welsh population also contributed to the gradual decline in the Welsh language during this period: while 70 percent of the population spoke Welsh in 1850, less than half did so at the end of the nineteenth century.[32] Although Richard was not of the generation who as children experienced "Welsh Not" boards and other forms of corporal punishment to enforce English-only learning in Welsh schools, his strong connections with the educational community in Wales would have kept him well informed of these growing conflicts, and sensitized him to the importance of language for shaping and preserving cultural identity.

In 1865 Richard enrolled as a student at the Baptist College in Haverfordwest. Though the decision was likely inspired by Richard's youthful sense of missionary vocation, the career path from school to chapel ministry was one of the most promising available to those outside the Welsh gentry.[33] Although the ministry offered an escape from the more common agricultural and industrial labors, Richard's classmates were unlikely to have entered ministry out of a desire for prestige or financial gain: mid-Victorian Welsh Baptist pastors were poorly compensated, and being economically disadvantaged and barred from the accepted educational institutions they were necessarily socially handicapped as well.[34] Under these conditions, the comparatively small percentage of nonconformists who pursued formal theological training did so out of a genuine interest in Christian service.[35]

Matriculating fifteen years after Richard, Thomas Lewis, the noted alumnus and missionary to the Congo, was happy to find at Haverfordwest not only a proper interest in promoting Richard's legacy as an example for the students, but also a general and "decided Christian character" among the men.[36] Richard had similarly found his new environment to be an effective preparation for ministry in the evangelical mode, as well as an

---

31. Commissioners of Inquiry, *Reports of the Commissioners*, 4.

32. Edwards and Newcombe, "When School Is Not Enough," 301.

33. Griffith, "'Preaching Second to No Other,'" 64.

34. Few Welsh Baptist ministers earned more than £100 a year, with one survey showing an average salary in 1862 of less than £25. Brown, "Baptist Ministry," 105–20, especially 115.

35. Richard's reasons for studying formally at Haverfordwest are not entirely clear, and may in fact reflect his own personal love for education: as late as 1871 only 58 percent of English and Welsh Baptist ministers received formal theological training. Brown, "Baptist Ministry," 110.

36. Lewis, *These Seventy Years*, 11–13.

academically challenging one, since Richard's education up to this point had been more slapdash than many of his classmates.[37] Richard soon made up the deficiency, in time covering a demanding range of theological subjects, including: "the being and attributes of God, the Trinity, the Divinity and Humanity of Christ, the Personality and work of the Holy Spirit, and the Divine Purposes" as well as "Imputed Righteousness, election, Original Sin, Conversion and Restoration of the Jews, Pre-millennial advent, Prophecy, Imprecatory Psalms, Salvability of the Heathen, Authenticity of the Pentateuch, and of Daniel, Various theories of Infant Baptism."[38] Among the texts encountered by Richard at Haverfordwest, Bishop Butler's *Analogy of Religion* and, to a lesser degree, his *Fifteen Sermons* seem to have left an outsized impression.[39] Butler, whose works remained popular among nonconformists throughout the nineteenth century, was mentioned several times by Richard during his years in China, and his influence can be seen behind many of Richard's later adaptations.[40] In particular, Butler's insistence that the truthfulness of Christianity can be demonstrated from "the moral experience of the individual man" and "the facts of the experience of society" informed Richard's later convictions regarding the efficacy of what he termed "moral evidences" in evangelism.[41]

In addition to the expected formal studies focusing on biblical languages and the various standard theological texts of the day the students were set to preaching right from their first year.[42] Writing to his parents in January of his first year, Richard mentioned having "preached at Sill Park last Thursday Evening" as well as having heard two other preachers speaking at college that same week.[43] The twenty or so students enrolled at the college during Richard's days were the main source of pulpit supply for many

37. Richard was conscious that he had not read as much theology and philosophy as many of his classmates prior to his enrollment at Haverfordwest. Richard to his parents, 13 January 1866, translated from the Welsh by Thomas Evans, 1 January 1965, BMSA Box CH/4A.

38. These two lists represent only a selection of the theological material Richard covered during his years in college. *Report of the Baptist College, 1867*, 9; *Report of the Baptist College, 1869*, 12.

39. Butler, *Fifteen Sermons*; Butler, *Analogy of Religion* (1736).

40. On the continuing influence of Butler and his moral theology, see Bebbington, *Dominance of Evangelicalism*, 115–16.

41. From Ronald Bayne's introduction to Butler, *Analogy of Religion* (1906), xviii. On Richard's use of moral evidences, see chapters 4 and especially 5 below.

42. *Report of the Baptist College, 1867*, 10.

43. Richard to his parents, 13 January 1866, translated by Thomas Evans, 1 January 1965, BMSA CH/4A. One source claims his first public sermon was preached even earlier, in May of 1864. Price, *History of Caio*, 58.

of the chapels in the surrounding countryside: during his senior year he and his classmates roamed across Pembrokeshire preaching over one thousand sermons.[44] While most of this preaching would have been in Welsh, at least a portion was conducted in English; one of the sermons for the annual meeting of the college board as well as large portions of the general instructions of the college were presented in English. Richard must have had some success as a preacher, for while at college he agreed to provide regular monthly services for one church before eventually receiving pastoral calls from Welsh congregations in Pembrokeshire and Glamorganshire.[45]

It is significant that the Welshman Richard was able to preach in English as well. As Andrew May has argued, it may have been the case that bilingualism gave Welsh missionaries an advantage when approaching a third language, such as Chinese.[46] Building upon his early association with education in Wales and its growing nationalistic implications, Richard's developing role as a Baptist preacher both in Welsh and in English placed him near the center of the mid-century conflict over Welsh identity. The "Welsh style" of nonconformist Welsh-language preaching, with its intimacy, homely extempore images, and poetic forms, served as a primary vehicle for the preservation of Welsh national identity at the exact time of Richard's upbringing.[47] It is not unreasonable to suggest that his nonconformist and Welsh-medium education during a period of relative English linguistic and cultural aggression may have predisposed him to empathize with Chinese habits and values when they were threatened by Western imperialism.

During these years, Richard's own evangelical piety—particularly his high view of the Bible and his commitment to evangelism in Asia—was evident to his classmates. One student, John Gomer Lewis, who later became a well-known Welsh Baptist minister, recalled Richard's devoted attention to the deep study of the Bible, and his strong belief in

> the Gospel to be the secret of the world's redemption. There would be no other, there could be no other; to him it was absolute and all-sufficient. He was convinced that art, literature, science,

---

44. *Report of the Baptist College, 1869*, 11.

45. Richard's first sermon at the college was so well received that he was erroneously accused by the faculty of having plagiarized his text from Horace Bushnell. Richard, *Forty-Five Years*, 26–28.

46. May, "Mountain Views," 244–45.

47. Griffith, "'Preaching Second to No Other,'" 61–83, especially 65–68. Well into the middle of the twentieth century, chapel going continued to function as one of the key means for preserving the Welsh language's place in Welsh society. James, *Older Mother Tongues*, 12.

wealth, and learning—all the forces of civilisation combined—could not save the world. By Grace the world is saved.[48]

Within their small community of evangelicals preparing for the ministry Richard's commitment to the gospel stood out.

Lewis also noticed that Richard's "strong inclination to do pioneer work in the Celestial Empire" filled him with a "thirst for the knowledge necessary to qualify him for service in the foreign field." Richard's desire to learn and willingness to work hard for his education had been obvious throughout his youth, as he juggled a busy rotation of farming, teaching and studying.[49] This eagerness was then bolstered by his conviction that China, "being the most civilized of non-Christian nations," not only was well suited to accept the gospel, but also would be able in time to carry the gospel to the other "less advanced nations."[50] Richard recognized that effective ministry in that nation required special preparation. Demonstrating his ongoing passion for learning, as well as his practical approach to missionary training, Richard joined a student drive at Haverfordwest to reform the curriculum to include modern languages, the history of places outside of Europe, and recent scientific advances—subjects beyond the traditional limits of ministerial training.[51] While theology remained the "main subject" and students were still set to preaching during their first year, the college administration agreed to the students' demands for reform for at least part of Richard's time at the college.[52] Grafted onto his formal theological training, Richard's life-long and wide-ranging love of knowledge proved instrumental for some of his later missionary adaptations, encouraging his use of scientific demonstrations in evangelistic contexts as well as his commitment to the dissemination of knowledge through literature.[53]

---

48. This and the following, as quoted in Reeve, *Timothy Richard*, 25–27.

49. Evans, *Timothy Richard*, 12–15.

50. Richard, *Forty-Five Years*, 29. On the national implications of Welsh nonconformist participation in British imperial missions, see Evans, "Nonconformity and Nation," 235.

51. On the additional courses taught, see *Report of the Baptist College, 1869*, 12. Science and ancient history were not taught until after 1867, possibly beginning in 1868. *Report of the Baptist College, 1867*, 9–11.

52. Richard to his parents, 13 January 1866, translated by Thomas Evans, 1 January 1965, BMSA CH/4A. According to Richard, the old curriculum was back in place when he next visited his college fifteen years later. Soothill, *Timothy Richard of China*, 26.

53. Richard's founding of Shanxi University best exemplifies these interests. The prominence of local officials and educators in its establishment, as well as Richard's desire to make the institution explicitly Christian are elucidated in Li, "Competition and Compromise."

Growing up in a pious Christian home with parents who were theologically inclined and actively serving in their local churches, and finding his faith confirmed in the midst of revival, Richard had religious foundations that were firmly evangelical. His experiences moving between rural villages in pursuit of or endeavoring to deliver education gave him a familiarity with itineration and the passing on of knowledge to the most reluctant audiences—skills that prepared him well for ministry in the interior of China. Finally, after his four years of study at Haverfordwest, he was not only familiar with a wide range of intellectual, scientific and theological questions and issues, but was a well-experienced preacher in two languages.

In 1868 Richard applied to join the CIM, having been deeply impressed with the attitude of heroic missionary sacrifice presented in a lecture from Fanny Guinness, the wife of CIM missionary trainer Henry Grattan Guinness.[54] In light of his studies at the Baptist College and association with that denomination, the CIM advised him instead to seek service with the BMS.[55] Richard duly applied to the BMS and was accepted in April 1869.[56] Following his ordination at the Salem Chapel in Caio in November 1869, Richard sailed for China from Liverpool on the seventeenth day of that same month.[57]

2.2 Protestant Missions in Shandong, ca. 1870

With the conclusion of hostilities following the Second Opium War, British Baptists, like many other Christians, saw the hand of God at work in the provisions of the June 1858 Treaty of Tianjin.[58] Inspired and challenged by the well-known Congregational minister John Angell James's popular pamphlet *God's Voice from China to the British Churches*,[59] the BMS Committee

54. Richard, *Forty-Five Years*, 29.

55. Contrary to his own citations from Broomhall and Soothill, Alvyn Austin mistakenly claims that Richard applied with the CIM in 1865 during the organization of the *Lammermuir* party, and was rejected due to his unwillingness to submit to authority. Austin, "Pilgrims and Strangers," 63–64, 180.

56. Richard, *Forty-Five Years*, 29.

57. The date and location of Richard's ordination is taken from a memorial plaque mounted on the walls of Salem Baptist Chapel, as photographed by Richard's great-grandson Bjorn Hansen. From the unpublished personal account of Bjorn Hansen, "An Historic Trip to Wales and Golders Green Crematorium," November–December 2011.

58. On the treaty guarantees and early BMS difficulties securing their "rights," see Latourette, *History of Christian Missions*, 273–81; Morse, *International Relations*, 2:226; and Richard, *Forty-Five Years*, 52–54.

59. James, best known for his *Anxious Inquirer*, produced *God's Voice* during the last year of his life. James, *God's Voice from China*. For one example of James's influence see Edward Steane, "Plea for the Proposed Mission to China," *Baptist Magazine* (1859)

announced immediately following the publication of the Society's Annual Report their commitment to begin missionary work in China:

> This committee, having had their attention drawn to the great providential fact, that China has now for many months past been open to the introduction of the gospel, and that this fact constitutes an urgent call upon the churches of Christ to send missionaries to that great country, desires to feel impressively that this duty devolves in part upon the Society they represent; and they resolve, in humble dependence upon the grace of God, to address themselves solemnly to its fulfilment.[60]

These intentions took concrete shape on 13 July 1859 with the formal appointments of Hendrik Z. Kloekers, Charles James Hall, and their wives to minister in China on the Society's behalf.[61]

Initially selecting Shanghai for their base, Kloekers and Hall made exploratory visits to nearby cities, including Nanjing, in 1860 and 1861.[62] Both men soon became involved in the Taiping cause, supporting independent American Baptist Issachar Roberts and spending extended periods of time meeting with, and in Kloekers's case setting up and operating a chapel for, the Taiping in their Nanjing capital. Despite Kloekers's initial excitement—Hall was more reticent—disillusionment with the supposedly Christian character of the Taiping movement soon set in, and both men began to look elsewhere for effective ministry opportunities. Hall headed for Chefoo, as the coastal city of Yantai was known at the time, and by the end of 1861 had established there the first residential station of the BMS in China.[63] British authorities denied Kloekers his request to reside in Beijing, and so, after a cholera epidemic claimed the life of Hall and one of his children in the spring of 1862, Kloekers and his wife settled in Chefoo as the only remaining BMS workers in China.

333–39.

60. "Proposed New Mission to China," *Baptist Magazine* (1859) 320.

61. Williamson, *British Baptists in China*, 22. The British General Baptists had been moved by similar concerns in the wake of the First Opium War to undertake mission work in Ningbo through T. H. Hudson and W. Jarrom from 1845 to 1860. Williamson, *British Baptists in China*, 18–19.

62. The financial troubles of the CES led Kloekers and Hall—with their linguistic skills and cultural experience—to offer to transfer to the BMS. On this and their Taiping experiences, see Stanley, *History of the BMS*, 178–79.

63. Presumably derived from an attempted romanization of the name of nearby Zhifu Island (located just off the coast of Shandong), the name Chefoo was a popular nineteenth-century expatriate misnomer for the port city of Yantai.

1863 saw the arrival of Richard Frederick Laughton and his wife, with the McMehan and Kingdon families joining them over the following two years.[64] The McMehans resigned after barely a year of service due to ill health, with Kloekers leaving shortly after.[65] In 1867 the Kingdons departed as well in an effort to avoid having "a breakdown." Only Laughton and his wife remained, with Laughton struggling to maintain the work of the mission despite his own poor health. The setbacks and losses during these early years, combined with waning interest in China from the home churches, led the BMS to consider withdrawing from China; in January 1868 the Committee voted to maintain the mission but only with the lowest possible expenditure and investment.[66] On 21 June 1870, after seven years of effective ministry devoted to building a "native church [that was] self-governing, self-supporting and free from every kind of foreign influence which tends to hinder its free native natural development and extension," Laughton succumbed to typhus. Having only recently arrived on 27 February 1870, Timothy Richard found himself the sole foreign representative of the society in China, left to care for the fledgling thirty-five member Chefoo Baptist church alongside its leader Pastor Zheng Yuren, the first BMS-trained native pastor.[67] Pastor Zheng served the church in Shandong faithfully for some fifty years.[68]

64. James Hudson Taylor very nearly became the third addition to the BMS China field. While Taylor was involved in speaking and deputation work for the BMS in the early 1860s, efforts to recruit him for the BMS China field ultimately collapsed owing to Taylor's comparatively ecumenical approach to baptism and his dissatisfaction with the BMS Committee's inability to send extra workers to China due to shrinking financial resources. Broomhall, *HTCOC*, 3:251–52.

65. Kloekers's wife E. E. L. Kloekers née Winterbottom passed away in Shanghai in December 1860, and her nineteen-month-old daughter Emily P. perished in June 1862. See Elliston, *Shantung Road Cemetery*, 21; and Williamson, *British Baptists in China*, 22.

66. Stanley, *History of the BMS*, 179.

67. Williamson, *British Baptists in China*, 25–32. The Laughton quotation is from an unreferenced 1869 letter "home" as recorded in Williamson, *British Baptists in China*, 31. Forsyth mistakenly lists Laughton, "MacMahon," and Kingdon's arrival date as "1888." Forsyth, *Shantung*, 263–64.

68. For the Chinese pastor's full name see Lai, *Negotiating Religious Gaps*, 113. Williamson's "first Chinese pastor Ch'ing" who was the "Chinese Pastor-elect of the Chefoo church," and Forsyth's reference to "the mission's first pastor" as being Chung Yu-jen most likely refer to this same individual. Forsyth, *Shantung*, 263. According to Williamson, Laughton was responsible for the training of Pastor Zheng, who not surprisingly shared Laughton's commitment to indigenous agency. Williamson, *British Baptists in China*, 31. For an indication of the close cooperation that may have existed between Laughton and Zheng, see F. J. Laughton, "The China Mission," *MH* 62, no. 11 (1866) 184–85.

The British Baptists were not alone in Shandong, nor were they the first Western missionaries to work there. Catholic Western missionaries had been active in the province since the seventeenth century, and several Protestant sending agencies had responded more rapidly than the BMS to the opportunities provided by the mid-century treaties. Following a brief exploratory visit from LMS missionaries Joseph Edkins and Griffith John in 1858, the American Southern Baptists were the quickest to mobilize workers for Shandong. James and Sally Holmes were sent straight from Virginia to Shandong, but owing to the Arrow War were unable to settle in Chefoo until the end of 1860 when they were joined by fellow Baptist compatriots from Shanghai Jesse and Elizabeth Hartwell.[69] The Hartwells headed to the port city of Dengzhou (modern day Penglai) some fifty miles to the northwest of Chefoo,[70] where they were joined by other Shanghai colleagues, Tarleton and Martha Crawford, in 1863.[71] Alexander Williamson arrived in Chefoo with his wife Isabelle in 1860, returning to China as a representative of the National Bible Society of Scotland after having been invalided out of the LMS following a brief attempt at mission service in Shanghai. Using Chefoo as a base for excursions throughout North China, Williamson would eventually leave his mark as Secretary of the SDCK in China. The American Presbyterian Mission (APM) also made an early and aggressive commitment to Shandong: the Gayleys of Shanghai and the Danforths of Ningbo were the first to move to Dengzhou, followed by John and Helen Nevius—most recently from Ningbo—in 1861, with the addition of the Mills family in the following year.[72] In 1864 Calvin

---

69. For the chronology of the early mission settlements in Shandong, see Cliff, "A History of the Protestant Movement in Shandong," 35–43.

70. According to Article XI of the 1858 Treaty of Tianjin, the port city of "Tengchou [Dengzhou]" in Shandong (not to be confused with Dengzhou, Henan) was to be opened to foreign ships and merchants. Dengzhou's harbor, however, was "totally inadequate in size and depth for steamers," and so "for Tengchow was substituted the harbour of Chefoo, forty miles to the east, as offering a better anchorage, the port being at Yentai, on the opposite shore." Morse, *International Relations*, 1:562–63; Ning and Pruitt, *Daughter of Han*, 7.

71. The Crawfords fled to Shandong to escape (with almost immediate success) ill health, though financial pressures owing to the American Civil War and the effect of the vicissitudes of the Taiping Rebellion on their Shanghai real estate investments also played a role in their decision. Foster, *Fifty Years in China*, 135–37. See also Vaughn Cross, "'Living in the Lives of Men,'" 102–28.

72. Following an extended stay in Japan to explore opening a new mission station there, the Neviuses returned to find the Taiping occupation of Hangzhou and the surrounding countryside to be of such a decided nature that they were forced to consider new locations. Nevius, *The Life of John Livingston Nevius*, 195, 207–10. Nevius also mentioned that at the time of their arrival Dengzhou was a large prefectural port city, while Chefoo was only a small fishing village.

and Julia Mateer and Hunter and Lizzie Corbett arrived, with the Corbetts soon moving down to Chefoo.[73]

By the time of Richard's arrival in 1870, Protestant mission work in Chefoo was substantial and the city had become a thriving center of trade. Responding to the growing expatriate population, Laughton had helped establish an English-language Union Church under the shared pastorate of the gathered missionary community.[74] Laughton's death only four months after Richard's arrival encouraged Richard's interactions with the other foreigners in Chefoo, many of whom were businessmen. During the winter months when the ice on the harbor meant a temporary stoppage of trade, the expatriate community maintained a wide range of social and educational gatherings. Richard participated in the various societies, on one memorable occasion reading a paper of his own on "Demoniacal Possession in China."[75] The paper revealed Richard's already impressive knowledge of the various forms of spirit possession commonly found within Chinese society, as well as his informed confidence in the relative efficacy of the Christian faith in combatting these forces. With an evident respect for the people involved, Richard accepted the supernatural nature of these phenomena noting that "in considering this subject, one feels himself transported back to the days of the Apostles; and is compelled to believe that the dominion of Satan is by no means broken yet."[76]

Within this expatriate community Richard was the sole native Welsh speaker, perhaps reminding him of his earlier years in Wales where English was increasingly pressed as the language of public life. Of all the expatriates he came to know in Chefoo, Richard later remembered Alexander Williamson, John Nevius, Hunter Corbett, and J. B. Hartwell as all being "splendid missionaries" through whom he had received "excellent training in comparative religion." Through lectures delivered by various missionaries on Chinese religions as well as weekly studies on the methods used by the apostles to meet "the need of their times in their preaching," Richard claimed to have received during these early years on the field a missionary education that

---

73. On the APM work in Shandong prior to 1870, see Corbett, *Record of APM Work*, 1–13.

74. Williamson, *British Baptists in China*, 31.

75. Evans, *Timothy Richard*, 33–34. While the full text of Richard's paper does not seem to have survived, a lengthy excerpt can be found in Nevius, *Demon Possession*, 62–72. Richard mentioned some of the discussion following his paper, including supporting comments from Williamson and Corbett, in Richard, *Forty-Five Years*, 67–68.

76. Nevius, *Demon Possession*, 71.

"was superior to any theological training given at home and [that] enabled me to find a clue whereby to win converts in the future."[77]

Protestant missions in China at the time of Richard's arrival revolved around two major activities: street preaching from a central chapel in a population center, and wide-ranging itinerant preaching.[78] In both of these activities, literature distribution could feature more or less prominently, though its role in itineration was particularly stressed. Pioneer Protestant missionary Hunter Corbett had begun itinerant evangelism in 1865, covering "more miles itinerating than any man in the North" while maintaining a steady regimen of preaching in the Chefoo chapel he established in 1867.[79] Calvin Mateer also engaged in itinerant preaching and literature distribution throughout Shandong, often meeting with resistance and on at least one occasion brandishing a revolver to secure his "right" to sell Christian books in a local market.[80] In Mateer's estimation, "This method of work is very excellent, and at the same time very laborious. It reaches obscure places, and a class of people—those who stay at home—not otherwise reached."[81]

When the delegates to the 1877 Shanghai General Conference of the Protestant Missionaries of China (GCPMC) turned their attention to discussing the means to be employed in the evangelization of China, the first two topics considered were preaching and itineration. Following LMS missionary William Muirhead's paper on "Preaching to the Heathen," D. N. Lyon (APM) of Hangzhou expressed the community's shared convictions on the matter with his comment that out "of a hundred ordained missionaries, ninety-eight should devote their whole strength to the direct preaching of the Gospel to the heathen. Of the remaining two, one might be a philologist, and the other a school teacher."[82]

77. These reflections on Richard's early mentors are taken from Richard, "Autobiography of the Author" in *Conversion by the Million*, 1:81. As Richard wrote these comments in 1906, it is difficult to know exactly what these 1870s "comparative religion" studies involved. For more on this subject, see the discussion in chapters 4 and 6 below. In his lengthier and later autobiography, Richard adds Calvin Mateer to his list of early influences in Shandong. Richard, *Forty-Five Years*, 32–35.

78. For a helpful introduction to the differing missionary methods that evolved within nineteenth-century China missions, see Tiedemann, "Social Gospel and Fundamentalism," 83–105.

79. Corbett, *Record of APM Work*, 21–23. One of Corbett's biographers claims that each of his biannual itinerations across Shandong covered 1000–1200 miles. Craighead, *Hunter Corbett*, 84–87.

80. Fisher, *Calvin Wilson Mateer*, chapter 7, especially pp. 122–24.

81. Mateer writing in the mid-1870s as quoted in Fisher, *Calvin Wilson Mateer*, 127.

82. Yates, *Records of the GCPMC: Shanghai, 1877*, 76–83, 85.

The next two essays, "Itineration Far and Near" by Benjamin Helm of the American Southern Presbyterian Mission in Hangzhou and "Itineration Far and Near as an Evangelizing Agency" by James Hudson Taylor of the CIM, both argued for the necessity and efficacy of wide-ranging itinerant preaching with—to a lesser extent—scripture distribution.[83] The lone voice of dissent came from the American Southern Baptist missionary M. T. Yates, who directly challenged the wisdom of rapid, wide-ranging itineration. Questioning the actual effectiveness of missionary street preaching, and giving eyewitness testimony to the ignominious fate of so much of the literature so painstakingly distributed by the missionaries, Yates made a case for concentrated ministry among a particular group of people in a particular location.[84] But for the overwhelming majority of the Protestant mission community in China, the missionary's task was to cover as much territory as possible, preaching in the streets—and perhaps passing out some literature—along the way.

While language acquisition naturally consumed the majority of Richard's time and energy upon arrival in China, he nevertheless found ample opportunity to engage in the expected rounds of itineration and preaching. Richard's 1877 report described the work of the English Baptists prior to 1875: "As to method, —distant and rapid itinerating, like traveling, was once the practice."[85] Indeed, Laughton's death so shortly after Richard's arrival forced these tasks upon him. At the end of 1870, most likely just prior to the arrival of his new (albeit short-lasting) BMS colleague and medical missionary Dr. William Brown of Edinburgh, Richard joined Robert Lilley of the National Bible Society of Scotland on a 150-mile tour to distribute scripture portions in the major towns throughout eastern Shandong. This was followed by five trips in 1871 including a pioneering excursion into Korea. Between journeys, the other responsibilities of the mission remained, including regular preaching in the BMS street chapel in Chefoo—a task Richard performed on a daily basis throughout 1872.[86] Unfortunately, no records of these early Chinese sermons survive.

---

83. Yates, *Records of the GCPMC: Shanghai, 1877*, 93–101 and 101–7, respectively. Taylor's essay was notably practical, advocating the employment of single females in the interior and reliance on local Chinese banks.

84. Yates, *Records of the GCPMC: Shanghai, 1877*, 111–12.

85. Richard, "Sketch of the English Baptist Mission," 381.

86. Richard, *Forty-Five Years*, 48.

2.3 Disappointment and Adaptation

Much like American Southern Methodist missionary Young J. Allen a decade before, Richard soon became disheartened by mission work.[87] By late 1872 or early 1873 he was reporting the practice of street preaching to be "not very productive of good results" and yielding "no success worth mentioning." Moreover, it seemed that the merchant guilds in Chefoo had collectively enjoined their charges by oath to eschew all foreign preaching: Richard observed that apart from occasional travelers and visitors from the surrounding countryside, the only attendees at street preaching in Chefoo were those who "out of curiosity" decided to come and "see the foreigner and his barbarous costume."[88] Richard also suspected that ten years of missionary effort and three separate chapels among the twenty thousand inhabitants of Chefoo meant that the curiosity of the local people had for the most part been satisfied. There were days when the people in the surrounding countryside were busy—such as harvest time—and unable to travel to the city, leaving Richard sitting all day in the chapel with no visitors and no one to talk to.[89] Surely, this was not the most effective way to evangelize China.

At the same time, Richard had been warned by a more experienced fellow missionary of the limitations of wide itineration. Recalling this advice over ten years later, Richard wrote, "Before we can establish churches there must be an opportunity for intimate heart and soul intercourse. Rapid traveling over wide areas does not afford this."[90] Returning from one itineration in the less evangelized regions east of Chefoo, Richard showed his growing sympathy for this perspective by taking a step indicative of his evolving approach to mission in China. On 26 February 1871 at the annual meeting of the Baptist church in Chefoo, Richard asked the Chinese believers to consider sending out "a preacher of their own choice . . . who would be supported by the native brethren in money, sympathy and prayers." To Richard's satisfaction, the congregation eagerly took up the challenge. He wrote,

> A good brother was chosen to be supported by the Native Church. He is since that day the home missionary of the native brethren. Thus, at last, an initiatory step has been taken, which

---

87. Given Richard's eventual contributions to literary work, the parallels between Allen and Richard's experiences of disillusionment are striking. Bennett and Liu, "Christianity in the Chinese Idiom," 163–69.

88. The quotations are from Richard, *Forty-Five Years*, 48.

89. Richard, "Reception of the Gospel in China," 749–50.

90. Richard does not name the American Baptist missionary from Southern China who provided this advice while staying with the English Baptists in Chefoo to recover his health. Richard, *Fifteen Years*, 5–6.

I trust God will abundantly bless. Not wishing that our dear brother should labour alone amongst strangers, I sent Sun Hwei Teh, another good brother who has been a student under Ching S.S., for two years along with him. They started full of love for their work March 27th, to that part of the promontory which I visited last December.[91]

Certainly, Richard was focusing his mission's itinerant ministries; but more importantly, he was learning that indigenous mission was not just preferable but practicable.

One early experience seems to have been particularly formative for the young missionary. As he sought for more effective ways to evangelize China, Richard decided to see how successful he could be at preaching to large gatherings of Chinese people; and so he arranged to accompany a native evangelist to attend a temple fair outside the market town of Songcun roughly eighty kilometers south of Chefoo. The fact that Richard devoted so much space to discussing this one event in his otherwise laconic 1885 address to the BMS Committee suggests the depth of the impact this experience made on his missionary thinking.[92]

What Richard referred to as the "Fair at Hwui Lung San" most likely took place at the temple at Huilong Shan ("Returning Dragon Mountain") near what is now Songcun Zhen in Wendeng, Shandong. The details Richard provided in his account of the festival—the processions to the temple, the fireworks, the throngs of people in attendance, and especially the attention-grabbing theatrical performance—are all typical of temple fairs in late imperial China.[93] Along with the New Year's festival, temple fairs and in particular the theatricals associated with the fairs were some of the more significant events in rural China, marking both the cycle of the seasons and the local village's place within and relationship to the larger world.[94] The fairs also provided collective gatherings that were vital to rural trade and commerce:

---

91. This and the preceding quotation are from an unspecified letter from Richard reprinted in his "Progress in China," 750–51.

92. Richard's account of the festival is found in two places: Richard, *Fifteen Years*, 6–8; Richard, *Forty-Five Years*, 49–52. The event is absent from both Evans's biography of Richard, and Richard's own 1907 "Autobiography of the Author."

93. The best scholarly analysis of North China temple festivals (albeit from Shanxi) and their significance in village life is found in Johnson, *Spectacle and Sacrifice*, 177–319.

94. The role of theatricals—primarily experienced at various temple fairs and festivals—in shaping (though not creating) the popular rural Boxer Uprising at the end of the nineteenth century has been recognized for some time. Cohen, *History in Three Keys*, 106–7; Esherick, *Origins of the Boxer Uprising*, 62–65, 231–34, 328–31; Doar, "Boxers and Chinese Drama," 106–7.

the economic value of the festivals was quite significant.⁹⁵ Recent scholarship has also highlighted the surprising degree to which these fairs and their attendant rituals tended to reflect the concepts and desires of the villagers themselves more than the priorities of local or national elites, with religious professionals being employed only in so far as they complied with the villagers' own intentions and values.⁹⁶ Though Richard may not have been aware of the fact at the time, the sectarian groups that would soon receive his attention mirrored this emphasis on local autonomy. While in this instance Richard's intention was merely to seek out and address a large gathering of Chinese people, his participation in the fair exposed him to a profoundly local event that both shaped and reflected the worldviews of many villagers: it was the people gathered around the local temple through its ritual events that comprised the village community in its essential form.⁹⁷

Since at least 1714, temple fairs have been held at Huilong Shan on the second day of the third lunar month to commemorate the birthday of the mother of the "black dragon without a tail" who eventually settled in Heilongjiang province, from whence that province derives its name.⁹⁸ In the spring of 1872, accompanied by a Chinese evangelist and a few boxes of Christian literature, Richard arrived in the town of Songcun two weeks prior to the anticipated fair. The villagers were alarmed by the presence of a foreigner, and none of the inns would offer him a room. He waited patiently with his horse in the middle of the street, feeling confident that "if I had been called to work there God would somehow open up a way."⁹⁹ Richard made small talk with the rapidly growing crowd—discussing local celebrities, crop conditions, and the local market until the villagers felt sufficiently at ease for the "chief man" of the village to send for Richard and offer him a room. For the next few weeks Richard spoke with the man's son and nephew (both scholars) and received visits from educated individuals throughout the surrounding countryside. He was more than happy for the "long talks on foreign civilization and religion, I on my part getting as much information

95. Ren, "Rural Market in Late Imperial China," 42–49.

96. Johnson, *Spectacle and Sacrifice*, 13–16; Overmyer, *Local Religion*, 1.

97. Litzinger, "Rural Religion," 41–52. With their tremendous local variations, the festival rituals and practices were a primary means for shaping and expressing shared village values. See Johnson, *Spectacle and Sacrifice*, 321–37. For a modern example of a revitalized temple fair in Shandong, see Overmyer, *Local Religion*, 119–20.

98. Kown today as the Dragon Li Culture (*li long wenhua*) festival, as many one hundred eighty thousand people attend the annual weeklong celebrations in Songcun. "Li long wenhua shanhui," China News Service; "Li long shanhui sheng kuang," Xinlang Shipin. For a summary of the "dragon without a tail" or *tu weiba laoli* story that is at the center of Dragon Li Culture, see Zhao, "'Place Where the Sage Wouldn't Go,'" 124–25.

99. Richard, *Fifteen Years*, 6.

BEGINNINGS

as I could as to their religion and civilization. When not besieged by visitors I studied Chinese literature."[100]

As the time for the weeklong temple festival approached, Richard tentatively enquired as to whether he might be allowed to address the crowd from the bell tower of the mountain temple where the fair was to be held. To his surprise, his request was granted and a ladder was provided by the resident Buddhist priests to facilitate his climb. On the day of the festival, Richard was literally carried off his feet by the surging of the crowd, as some thirty villages passed through in procession to make their obeisance in the temple courtyard. Beneath the cacophony of the gongs, cymbals, drums and fireworks, the masses on the hillside were engaged in every kind of business or trade imaginable. Once the last village had completed its rituals at the temple, Richard—from his position above the crowd with one of the sons of the village chief at his side—seized upon a lull in the noise to preach the gospel "for a long time as well as I could to the people in both courtyards, who manifested great patience in listening to the foreigner addressing them in imperfect Chinese."[101] Exhausted, and unable to speak any more, Richard's voice dropped. "After my silence, the throng outside the courts, which hitherto were listening to me, now turned their faces to the south, where a historical play—half-political, half-moral or immoral—was being acted out."[102] As the day grew to a close, Richard reflected on this his "most memorable attempt at preaching to a vast crowd."[103] "I wrestled in my soul with God to hasten the time when these thousands would meet together with their hearts centred in Him and in His Christ."[104]

Richard's time at Huilong Shan was the nexus for a number of significant adaptations in his thinking. In some ways the culmination of earlier experiences, in other ways the beginning of a series of fresh realizations, from this time onwards Richard increasingly saw Christian mission in China as a task that must be carried out on Chinese terms. From the hospitality he experienced from the village head and the scholars in the community, to the warm acceptance of his request to preach, Richard was learning that the relationship between foreign missionaries and local people need not be adversarial. With time, patience, and the right cultural sensitivities, Richard had found even a large mass of people to be willing to listen to his gospel message.

100. Richard, *Forty-Five Years*, 50–51.
101. Richard, *Forty-Five Years*, 51.
102. Richard, *Fifteen Years*, 8.
103. Richard, *Forty-Five Years*, 52.
104. Richard, *Fifteen Years*, 8.

The poor results he had observed from both preaching in the street chapel in Chefoo and Christian literature distribution throughout the countryside had already led Richard to question "why it was that the Gospel did not attract more people."[105] After his experience at Huilong Shan, the answer became clear.

> I had had my desire of preaching at the fair fully gratified, and a short residence in their midst had removed prejudices and inspired some confidence. I then asked myself how many Chinese difficulties did I meet? I gave the best replies I could to questions which might arise in European minds. Were Asiatic minds stored with the same difficulties? Are *our ideas* of their difficulties real ones or imaginary? Was I yet qualified to teach the *leaders* as one of the secretaries advised me to do? I came to the conclusion, remembering the questions which the schoolmasters in this place had put to me, that I was not.[106]

Richard now recognized the degree to which his understanding of evangelism and conversion was shaped by his European perspective, and thus was ill suited to the Chinese context. Showing the strength of his convictions, and his determination to give his all to advance the gospel in China, Richard packed up his books in Chefoo and removed to Jinan, the capital of Shandong province, some four hundred miles inland. There he set himself "to continue my study of the Chinese classics, and to read up the current Chinese religious books and tracts of the day, so as to be able to give answers to *Chinese* difficulties and such answers as would satisfy *them* and compel genuine inquirers to become Christians."[107] After a few months of study, as well as significant interaction with the scholars and soldiers who were present for the official examinations, Richard baptized a young lieutenant from Henan—a sign which he saw as confirmation that he was ready to return to Chefoo.[108]

Richard was beginning to take seriously the cultural and religious milieu of the Chinese people he wished to bring to faith—a bold step that would in time move Richard away from the thinking and practice of many of his fellow missionaries. In other words, the process of acculturation for

---

105. Richard, "Autobiography of the Author" in *Conversion by the Million*, 1:80–81.
106. Richard, *Fifteen Years*, 8.
107. Richard, *Fifteen Years*, 8.
108. The 1874 annual report of the BMS claims Richard spent "several weeks" visiting Jinan in the autumn, but that he also spent "two months" providing daily instruction to the army officer prior to his conversion. "Eighty-Second Report," *MH* 70, no. 5 (1874) 318.

Richard was avowedly empathetic, as he was drawn toward accepting rather than rejecting many of the values and priorities he had encountered in the Chinese "other." Richard later described his mindset at the time as one of having come "to the conclusion that what God would have was the *adaptation* of Christian truth to the wants of China, not mere imitation of Christian institutions transplanted from the West."[109]

With the trajectory of his acculturation set, and compelled by his evangelical desire to see more Chinese converted to Christianity, Richard over the next few years developed two of his earliest and most significant innovations in mission. First of all, inspired by his study of scripture and the writings of a Church of Scotland minister from fifty years beforehand, Richard identified the kinds of people who were most likely to respond favorably to the gospel message—the "genuine inquirers" that he hoped to convert. Second, informed by his recent study of Chinese literature and other religions present in China at the time, Richard adjusted the way he presented the gospel to appeal more effectively to Chinese minds—by addressing "*Chinese* difficulties" and by providing "such answers as would satisfy *them*." The following two chapters discuss each of these innovations in turn.

---

109. Richard, *Fifteen Years*, 9.

3

"Seeking the Worthy"

TIMOTHY RICHARD'S PERSONAL EXPERIENCES preaching in a variety of Chinese contexts led to his rapid disappointment with 1870s mission praxis. Far from revealing disillusionment with the mission task in general, Richard's frustration arose precisely because of his passion for Christian mission. For Richard, the common practices simply were not sufficiently effective. Reflecting both his evangelical desire for conversions and the increasingly sympathetic trajectory of his acculturation, Richard's strategic decision to seek the worthy—to take his message to the spiritually devout seekers after the truth, and not, as some modern scholars mistake, to seek the conversion of the political, social or religious elites—was one of his earliest attempts to increase the effectiveness of his evangelistic efforts.

Though he did not appreciate it at the time, the idea was first suggested to Richard in embryonic form before he left Britain. According to his earliest autobiographical record, Richard received advice from two figures immediately prior to his departure for China. The first advisor listed by Richard, Dr. Frederick Trestrail, served in cooperation with the second, Dr. Edward Bean Underhill, as joint Secretary for the BMS from 1849 to 1870—after which Underhill served independently for an additional six years. In Richard's own words, "On leaving for China in the autumn of 1869, the two venerable secretaries, Drs. Trestrail and Underhill, gave me very sound advice."[1]

In his text, Richard went on to explain how "one" of these two secretaries advised him to refrain from commenting on matters in China during his early years, keeping his opinions to himself until he had had sufficient time to study things thoroughly. Such a simple habit was urged by this advisor as an important means for securing peace within any mission community overseas. As will be discussed in chapter 8, Richard would personally suffer from colleagues in the 1880s who failed to heed this advice.

---

1. Richard, *Fifteen Years*, 4.

Next, Richard recorded how "the other" advisor passed on to him a series of suggestions all loosely related to the general recommendation that Richard pay great attention through prayer and study to what he refers to as Jesus's "high instructions and commands" in the tenth chapter of the Gospel of Matthew. Specifically, Richard remembered being told to "strive to get hold of the schoolmasters—the teachers of the land—for, by converting these, we might look for the nation turning to God."[2] Finally, this second advisor also admonished Richard to pursue work in the interior along with the development of self-supporting churches.

The order in which their names were listed seems to suggest that the Home Secretary, Trestrail, was the advocate of restraint when giving opinions, while the focus on Matt 10 came from the Foreign Secretary, Underhill. But this may not be the case. Richard's own grammatical construction, while suggesting such a reading, does not necessarily require such an association. Moreover, the recollection and recording of impressions fifteen years after the fact often lacks precision—and it may be just this ambiguity that prevented Richard from clearly linking one or the other secretary to each piece of advice.

Underhill's influence upon the BMS was more extensive than Trestrail's, with his slightly longer tenure (1849–1876) and particular spheres of interest (including finance) aligning more closely with the expansion of BMS work around the world. Underhill was a staunch proponent of indigenous participation in mission, as will be discussed in chapter 4. He also produced a number of important books on missions and the BMS in particular during his lifetime, and has attracted some attention from modern historians in a way that Trestrail has not.[3] More practically, Trestrail's retirement from the office of Secretary in 1870 meant that Underhill exercised the role on his own during Richard's first few years on the field and thus may have left a more lasting impression on the missionary.

Trestrail, however, was also an outspoken advocate of the application of indigenous principles in foreign mission. His paper "On Native Churches" delivered before the 1860 Conference on Missions held at Liverpool is a striking call for a more robust dependence on indigenous workers throughout the mission endeavor.[4] Whether calling for literature and training in native tongues, the exclusion of missionaries from local pastorates, or more concerted intercessory prayer on the behalf of native

---

2. Richard, *Fifteen Years*, 4.

3. Underhill authored a number of well-received missionary biographies, as well as *Christian Missions in the East and West*, and his influential *The Principles and Methods of Missionary Labour*. See also chapter 4 in Hall, *Civilising Subjects*.

4. *Conference on Missions Held in 1860 at Liverpool*, 279–83.

churches, Trestrail's passionate advocacy of the centrality of indigenous Christians in the mission task was strikingly clear. Richard made no mention of this particular address; however, one of Richard's later biographers claims that at his valedictory service Trestrail exhorted Richard to study closely Jesus's instructions to his disciples as recorded in the Gospels.[5] Thus, although the evidence is not conclusive, it is not unreasonable to credit Trestrail as contributing to Richard's second set of recommendations—particularly with respect to Matt 10.

Despite this early advice—remembered, admittedly, with suspicious clarity fifteen years later—some time elapsed before Richard began to implement any of these suggestions. Only after he had witnessed for himself the disappointing results of his own preaching experiences did he begin to cast about for a superior method by which to convert larger numbers of Chinese people to Christianity. In his searching, Richard—perhaps as early as 1872, and certainly by 1873—became convinced that the Bible taught "not only Christian doctrine but also methods of Christian evangelism."[6] Finally recalling the advice he had received before leaving Britain, Richard turned his attention to the tenth chapter of Matthew. In the eleventh verse, Jesus exhorted his disciples that "into whatsoever city or town ye shall enter, enquire who in it is worthy; and there abide till ye go thence (KJV)." It was the word "worthy" in this passage that became the focal point of one of Richard's key innovations in mission. Richard claimed that his understanding of the importance of the worthy came from two sources: first, his own personal study of this passage; and secondly his reading of what he termed "Edward Irving's matchless exposition of it."[7]

3.1 Reading the Bible

Assessing Richard's claim to have discovered his new missionary method of "seeking the worthy" through reading the Bible is not an easy task. Timothy Richard was not a systematic theologian, nor was he interested in theology as an abstract discipline. Despite his sustained exposure to serious theology at Haverfordwest, as well as his many years spent producing religious literature within the SDCK in China, Richard never produced a theological work in his own words. Although Richard himself preached many times throughout his life in English, Welsh, and Chinese—especially during his time at Haverfordwest and his early years in Chefoo—there are also no

---

5. Evans, *Timothy Richard*, 25.
6. The early date and the quotation are both from Evans, *Timothy Richard*, 25.
7. Richard, *Fifteen Years*, 9.

records of his sermons. Since he did not approach the world as a systematic theologian, he left behind no academic statements of his views on the Bible, or almost any other theological topic.[8]

It is true that two of the earliest titles chosen by Richard for translation were of a theological nature, but Richard's interest in them was always practical. For his first substantial translation work, Richard selected Jeremy Taylor's classic text in Christian spirituality *Holy Living* (1839) for its value as a guide to devotional life for new Christians, rather than as a theological catechism.[9] He particularly hoped it would encourage local believers to trust in God rather than in foreign missionaries.[10] While Richard's Mandarin version of *Holy Living* appears to be his own work, his subsequent 1875–1876 translation of James Walker's *Philosophy of the Plan for Salvation* (1851) into literary Chinese required the assistance of Pastor Zheng of the Chefoo Baptist Church, since Richard's significant linguistic ability did not extend to the writing of *wenyan*.[11] It seems likely that Richard had first encountered Walker's work, which was initially published anonymously and then reprinted several times in Britain, while he was at Haverfordwest. *Philosophy of the Plan for Salvation* relied on logical arguments from scripture and especially Western history to establish the truthfulness and vital necessity of the Christian faith, and it was this apologetic method and potential—rather than any particular theological viewpoint—that attracted Richard to Walker's book.[12] For his interpretive principle, Richard chose

---

8. Though no copies exist today, Richard supposedly produced his own Chinese-language catechism based on existing English-language catechisms, as discussed in chapter 4 below.

9. Jeremy Taylor, *Holy Living and Dying*. Titled *Tiandao gongke*, "the first part," including chapter 1 with its practical instructions in the spiritual disciplines and in chaste Christian living, was translated by Richard into Mandarin (*guanhua*) sometime in the early 1870s, and republished in 1904 by the SDCK. MacGillivray, *Descriptive and Classified*, 77; Lai, *Negotiating Religious Gaps*, 138–39.

10. Richard, *Forty-Five Years*, 105–6.

11. Lai, *Negotiating Religious Gaps*, 113. What Richard called his *wenli* version (or, in today's terms, his *wenyan* or literary version) of Walker's text was published in serial form as *Jiushi dangran zhi li* in *WGGB* in 1874–75. Richard claims to have also produced a Mandarin version at a later date. On missionary understandings of differing styles of written Chinese see Lai, *Negotiating Religious Gaps*, 41–47.

12. For an example of Richard's editorial hand on this work, see the title for Walker's chapter 9 "Concerning the Transition from the Material System, by which religious ideas were conveyed through the senses, to the spiritual system, in which abstract ideas were conveyed by words and parables," which Richard and his colleague translated as "lun shangdi shi ren qingshi guiju zhongkan dao [Concerning God instructing men to pay less attention to superficial rules and emphasize right living*]." Richard and Zheng, *Jiushi dangran zhi li* in *WGGB* (15 October 1874) 134a. See also Walker, *Philosophy of the Plan of Salvation*, 114.

to preserve Walker's argument while adapting the actual text—in particular the illustrations and the introduction—to the Chinese context.[13] This choice, along with his decision to publish his version of Walker's text in Young J. Allen's increasingly popular Chinese-language periodical *WGGB*, demonstrated Richard's practical interest in appealing to Chinese readers rather than upholding theological rigidity. Richard was first and foremost interested in missionary activities that worked.

Though not overly concerned with theological systems, Richard was still very much an evangelical missionary and as such shared in the biblicism that was so central to Victorian evangelicalism and the Protestant missionary project.[14] As Brian Stanley has explained, the missionaries themselves

> were unambiguously people of the Book, men and women whose consciousness was soaked in the Bible and whose experience confirmed the scriptural testimony to the natural depravity of humanity and the sovereignty of divine grace.[15]

During the nineteenth century, the ways in which British evangelicals read the Bible changed dramatically. Romanticism and eventually higher criticism exerted their influences upon the British evangelical community, the latter leading many to question the historic and scientific accuracy of the Bible.[16] Among nonconformists, lingering belief in the verbal inspiration of scripture encouraged styles of exposition based upon single words that—when combined with a preference for inner "spiritual" meanings that many inherited from Romanticism—often resulted in an allegorical approach to scripture that was a less rigorous cousin of the typological interpretations that had been so common in the mid century.[17] In his writings Richard showed no interest in the finer points of biblical criticism, and he never discussed his view of scripture in the abstract. And while, as in his developing understanding of the worthy, Richard at times dabbled in the allegorical, seizing upon individual words and sentences and investing them with larger if not different meanings than their context originally

---

13. Richard, "An Appeal from China," 233.

14. On the pervasive religious and cultural influence of the Bible throughout Victorian England, see Larsen, *People of One Book*.

15. Stanley, "Christian Missions and the Enlightenment," 9. Some have suggested that respect for the Bible was less defining than a commitment to put it into the hands of others. See Ward, "Evangelical Identity," 12.

16. By 1885 nonconformist colleges had reconfigured their teaching to accord with higher criticism—well after Richard had graduated. See Bebbington, *Dominance of Evangelicalism*, 162–65. On changing views of the Bible, see also Wigram, *Bible and Mission*, chapter 3; and Glover, *Evangelical Nonconformists*.

17. Landow, *Victorian Types*, 51–57.

warranted, his interpretive practices were merely the reactive result of his evangelical desire to increase conversions rather than the expression of any well-considered theological stance.

There is little evidence regarding Richard's use of scripture prior to his missionary career in China. Analysis of his written material after his arrival on the field, however, reveals that when reading the Bible Richard tended to prioritize interpretations that fitted his immediate concerns for evangelical action. While neither setting the Bible aside nor rejecting its authority, Richard typically began with his circumstances and then moved to scripture, adapting his missionary methods in accordance with his own experiences before bringing scripture in at the end as an after-the-fact justification. Richard claimed to have acquired this approach from his Haverfordwest education: "in all my after [graduation] missionary life I endeavoured to seek the methods most productive of results, rather than adhere to old ones not adjusted to the changing needs of the times."[18] Though Richard claimed that the Bible itself inspired several of his innovations including his idea of seeking the worthy, this activist pursuit of practical results was often the real driving force, shaping the way in which he used scripture.

A significant and typical example arose from his famine relief work, as discussed in chapter 5 below. While battling against the North China Famine in Shandong in 1876, Richard struggled to prevent injury or even loss of life due to the press of crowds that naturally accompanied aid distribution. Richard claimed to have found in Mark 6 what he felt to be the perfect solution:

> I, after trying various plans with ill success, read how our Lord had compassion on the multitude, and bade them sit down by fifties. The difficulty was solved. I ordered the people to be seated in rows every morning on a threshing-floor that was close by. When my little all came to an end the last day I distributed relief, they were as quiet as if they had been in the house of God.[19]

Within Mark's record of Jesus's feeding of the multitude, Jesus's bidding of the crowd to be seated is ancillary to the narrative's purpose of demonstrating both Jesus's compassion and his divine power and authority. Richard, however, was led by his need to solve the practical difficulties presented by

---

18. Richard, *Forty-Five Years*, 26.

19. Richard, *Fifteen Years*, 13. The same story is told with slightly different details in Richard, *Forty-Five Years*, 102–3. The only biblical passage to mention both Jesus's compassion and the sitting of the crowd in groups of fifty is Mark 6:30–44. Richard may have conflated several miracle accounts in his mind, but Mark's narrative of the feeding of the five thousand accords best with Richard's recollections.

the famine to seize on this one aspect of the narrative. His desire to demonstrate the love of Christ through providing effective famine relief was driving his reading of the Bible, rather than vice-versa.

This reactive, practical hermeneutic was employed by Richard throughout his first two decades in China. In several cases, it was only after methods had proven effective that he turned to the pages of the Bible to find their justification. Richard claimed that his use of "moral evidences" in evangelism was built upon his reading of Matt 25 and the Sermon on the Mount; in fact, as chapter 4 below explains, Richard was first impressed with the openness of Chinese responses to his demonstrations of Christian ethics. Likewise, chapter 6 will show how several of Richard's later innovations—both his "discovery" of the implications of the Kingdom of God for life on earth prior to death, and his insistence that the gospel "fulfills" rather than destroys truths contained within other religious or ethical traditions—evinced this same pattern: Richard first developed effective pragmatic responses to the missional challenges around him, and then found justification for those practices within the Bible.

This willingness to begin with the current crisis and read the text accordingly was not unique to Richard. To take a particularly well-known evangelical contemporary of Richard as an example, James Hudson Taylor allowed similar priorities to shape his Bible reading, as evident in the two different sermons he delivered on the miraculous feeding narratives. During his first visit to Shanxi province in the summer of 1886, Taylor arranged a series of meetings for the CIM workers spread throughout the region. Some BMS missionaries stationed in and around the city of Taiyuan—Richard was on furlough in Britain at the time—were also present on the evening of Tuesday 6 July, when Taylor spoke on Jesus's feeding of the multitude as recorded in John 6.[20] Taylor's reading of John's narrative differed from Richard's, with even the most practical details given tremendous spiritual import:

> Now our Lord does not explain His plans to His disciples; but He says, "make the people sit down." I believe that before He gives us a full blessing, and takes us up and uses us, He says, "Be at rest in My presence; do not be asking for My *plans*." *Jesus is the great plan*; and in the presence of Jesus Christ, no matter how large the need is, *lie down and rest*. "He maketh me to lie down." He does this before, "He leadeth me." Everything in its own order.[21]

---

20. Beauchamp, *Days of Blessing*, 21–29.
21. Beauchamp, *Days of Blessing*, 22.

Eclipsing both the original context and the communicative intent of this miracle narrative, Taylor revealed his Romantic tendencies as he expounded a hidden spiritual—almost gnostic—meaning that seems far removed from Richard's reading of the text.

This maudlin emotionalism so prevalent in Taylor and his organization's literature was strikingly different in tone from most of Richard's writings, which tended to focus on questions of method and strategy.[22] However, Richard's seeming reluctance to engage with the spiritual or the mystical should not be taken as an indication that his personal life was lacking in spiritual experience. On one occasion when writing to his pious evangelical mother, Richard explained his reasons for not returning to Britain in language that would have been familiar to Taylor: "I do not consider that so far the call is from God. When I shall believe that God wants me to go then the way will be clear."[23] On another occasion he joyfully informed his mother of the orphans who were abandoning idols under the evangelistic influence of his wife.[24] This belief in prayer and the reality of the spiritual life extended beyond his understandably pious correspondence with his mother, as seen in his confident request for prayer from Baptist readers in Britain on behalf of Chinese believers who must "bear their cross when they leave the faith of their fathers."[25] As Richard explained during his first furlough back in Britain, his experiences in China with miraculous healings, exorcisms, and conversions had only strengthened his belief that "the age of miracles is not past."[26] Though typically eschewing the mystic, emotional language of some

---

22. On rare occasions Richard was capable of writing with melodrama: compare the focus on prayer and martyrdom of the CIM appeal for workers and funds in "Appeal for Prayer on Behalf of More than One Hundred and Fifty Millions of Chinese," *The Baptist Magazine*, (February 1875) 95–96; with Richard's plea for more workers in his "An Appeal from China," 233–34. More typical of Richard's style is the cool yet demanding catalogue of needs and opportunities he presented to the BMS in his 1885 pamphlet *Wanted: Good Samaritans for China*.

23. Richard to his mother, 13 October 1880, translated by Thomas Evans, 25 January 1965, BMSA CH/4A.

24. Richard to his mother, 17 January 1880, translated by Thomas Evans, 25 January 1965, BMSA CH/4A. On Richard's wife, see chapter 5 below.

25. Richard, "Missionary Labour in China," 160. Curiously, this article was removed by the editor from the edition of the 1874 *Missionary Herald* that was bound together with the *Baptist Magazine*, most likely in deference to the different interests of the subscribers to the two different bound editions (broad versus specialist readers). The absence can be noted on page 516 in the 1874 combined *Baptist Magazine/Missionary Herald*. At least one other article by Timothy Richard was similarly excised: Richard, "An Inquirer's Thoughts on the Gospel," 193–94 [bound out of sequence at 191–92] is absent from the combined 1875 *Baptist Magazine/Missionary Herald*, 638–39.

26. Richard, *Fifteen Years*, 21.

of his peers, Richard was not estranged from the rich spiritual experiences of Taylor and his fellow evangelicals.

When Taylor spoke on the miraculous feeding narratives at the 1890 GCPMC, his sermon was different in its main emphases and strikingly free from the personal spiritual language of his 1886 message.[27] A brief glance at the different contexts for the two sermons—Taylor's desire for submission on the field in Shanxi, and his appeal for better organization among the attending mission agencies in Shanghai—reveals that in both cases Taylor evinced the same approach to scripture demonstrated by Richard, allowing his prior experiences and interests to function as controlling interpretive principles.[28] At a time when so many evangelicals felt comfortable reading themselves into the biblical text, Richard—compelled by his commitment to conversion—was following a popular trajectory, allowing his activist drive to demonstrate the truth of the gospel to take priority over his commitment to submit to the authority of the Bible.[29]

The same was true in Richard's appropriation of the idea of seeking the worthy in Matt 10. Impressed by the sincere desire for truth that had characterized so many of his interactions with local Chinese religious leaders, Richard found in Jesus's instructions to the disciples a biblical warrant for his already effective policy. By no means a unique perspective within evangelicalism of the time, this hermeneutic helps explain how Richard elevated this one concept to such prominence within his understanding and practice of mission: doing so would lead to conversions.

This is not to say that Richard was completely blind to other, broader implications of the Matt 10 passage. Although Richard's appropriation of the worthy was clearly his main inheritance from this passage, as seen in the relative priority it received in his writings, he also recognized that Jesus's words in this text did have implications for other aspects of life and ministry. When summarizing his discoveries in Matt 10 for his 1885 autobiographical address to the BMS Committee, Richard wrote:

> In that chapter it was evident that Christ would not have his disciples *begin* their work in the public streets. They were to seek the worthy. To these they were to go without purse or scrip. They were also to heal the sick as well as preach the Gospel. These

---

27. Barber, Hykes, and Lewis, *Records of the GCPMC: Shanghai, 1890*, 1–10.

28. Broomhall, *HTCOC*, 6:375, 405; Austin, *China's Millions*, 283–85. On Taylor's preaching, see Wigram, *Bible and Mission*, 119–21.

29. See, for example, Catherine Booth's insertion of herself and others into scriptural narratives, as well as her tendency to equate what is "truthful" with what is "biblical." Larsen, *People of One Book*, 107–8.

ideas, however far from attained, I ever endeavoured to make my ideal of missionary work.[30]

While there is no record of Richard following Jesus's other instructions in the passage by limiting the number of cloaks he carried, casting out demons, or refusing to purchase rooms in local inns when such were available, the above quotation suggests that Richard was convicted by Jesus's instructions regarding finances and medicine—two practical teachings, besides the idea of seeking the worthy, that colored Richard's distinctive missionary method throughout his days.[31]

With respect to the first instruction that Richard singled out, Rita Johnson has demonstrated that Richard, while not entirely "without scrip," nevertheless "lived frugally" and made a habit of giving from his salary back to the mission work.[32] Writing home to his mother in 1880, Richard explained:

> The Society is giving me sufficient salary and I do not wish to ask for more than my costs. . . . I am only dressing and eating just as I was at home. The money is used in books and instruments to teach the Chinese. . . . My rule is since so many poor people contribute towards the Society, after paying my expenses I do not keep one half penny. *All* my money goes every year towards the Society.[33]

Growing up on a small farm, working to earn his education, as well as his subsequent experiences working and living in rural China all would have encouraged thrift in Timothy Richard—a habit which his religious upbringing and nonconformist theological training would only have strengthened. Moreover, Richard differed from many of his missionary colleagues in that he does not seem to have complained about or bickered over money.[34] Likewise, he did not seek after or pursue possibly lucrative

---

30. Richard, *Fifteen Years*, 9–10.

31. These are some of the ideas mentioned in Jesus's instructions to his disciples in Matt 10. While exorcism does not seem to have been a significant aspect of his own ministry, Richard acknowledged the prevalence of demon possession in China as well as his confidence in the efficacy of Christian exorcism in his presentation on "Demoniacal Possession in China." Richard, *Forty-Five Years*, 66–68; Nevius, *Demon Possession*, 62–72.

32. Johnson, "Timothy Richard's Theory," 145, 218.

33. Richard to his mother, 13 October 1880, translated by Thomas Evans, 25 January 1965, BMSA CH/4A.

34. As will be discussed in chapter 7 below, many of the early CIM Shanxi transfers, as well as many of the squabbles between the ABCFM workers in Shanxi were over questions about money. For one example, see Brandt, *Massacre in Shansi*, 98–102.

employment outside the mission—even when offered—but instead devoted himself and his finances to the work of mission trusting God to provide in a way not entirely different from Taylor.[35]

In regard to the second instruction from Matt 10 noted by Richard, throughout his first term of service in China he was quick to participate in medical projects whenever called upon to do so. Medical mission was already recognized by most China missionaries as a key component of effective ministry in the Chinese context.[36] Richard's experiences with BMS colleague Dr. William Brown during his early years in Shandong gave him a confirmed opinion of the effectiveness of medical missionary work that continued throughout his years of service.[37]

It is, of course, unlikely that the rural Welshman Richard owed either his frugality or his willingness to engage in medical work entirely to the influence of Jesus's words in Matt 10. As with his concept of seeking the worthy, previous experience suggested that these traits would further evangelism and—just like with the worthy—these ideas were understood by him to have scriptural warrant. Rather than discovering ideas in the Bible and then trying them out in his ministry, Richard's activist concerns took precedence, leading him to adapt and experiment in pursuit of conversions before seeking biblical justification for whatever effective methods he discovered. As an evangelical, it was important to Richard that his missionary methods be grounded in scripture; but his idea of seeking the worthy was not shaped exclusively by his reading of the Bible, as the next section will demonstrate.

3.2 Edward Irving's *Missionaries after the Apostolical School*

In addition to his own personal reading of Matt 10, Timothy Richard pointed to Edward Irving's *Missionaries after the Apostolical School* as being the second source for his emphasis on "seeking the worthy" in evangelism.

Raised in Scottish Presbyterianism, Edward Irving trained in divinity at Edinburgh for the Church of Scotland before earning a name for himself working among the poor of Glasgow as Thomas Chalmers's asssistant.[38]

35. Johnson, "Timothy Richard's Theory," 216.

36. The 1877 GCPMC delegates heartily endorsed medical mission in general—James Hudson Taylor's support was notable—though some stressed the inadvisability of missionary doctors taking up practice among the expatriate communities. Yates, *Records of the GCPMC: Shanghai, 1877*, 126–32.

37. Richard was distributing smallpox vaccines as early as 1874, quite possibly prior to his reading of Irving. Richard, *Forty-Five Years*, 62–66.

38. The most thorough and most recent critical biography of Irving is Grass, *Edward Irving*.

Accepting a call to London in 1821, Irving achieved popularity in the pulpit of the Church of Scotland Caledonian Church, where he became associated with influential figures of his day, including the Romantic poet Samuel Taylor Coleridge.[39] Irving's publications on eschatological historicism and his subsequent participation in Henry Drummond's influential Albury Park conferences also made him a figurehead for the resurgence of premillennialism.[40] His support for a short-lived charismatic revival in Scotland alienated many of his supporters before he was formally deposed in 1833 by the General Assembly of the Church of Scotland for his alleged support of Sabellianism.[41] Having already removed to Newman Street the year previously to form the Holy Catholic Apostolic Church, Irving continued to teach those who shared his radical ideas until his untimely death from consumption in 1834.[42]

Were it not for one event from early in his ministry, Irving and his ideas would have had no bearing on Timothy Richard's life or mission. In 1824, at the height of his popularity in London, Edward Irving was invited by the LMS to give the key address at their annual anniversary convocation during the May meetings. Having "searched the Scriptures in secret . . . [with] much prayer to God and self-devotion," Irving commenced his remarks an hour earlier than scheduled, owing to the tremendous press of attendees already overcrowding Whitefield's Tabernacle on Tottenham Court Road.[43] Recognized as one of the great missionary appeals of the nineteenth century, Irving's address lasted for three and a half hours, interrupted only twice to allow for a hymn and presumably for the orator to catch his breath.[44] In the first five paragraphs Irving appealed to historical precedent, arguing that he need not on this occasion discuss either the LMS or any of its works

---

39. Oliphant, *Life of Edward Irving*, 51–70.

40. Gilley, "Edward Irving," 106. On Irving's interest in eschatological historicism see Flegg, *"Gathered Under Apostles,"* 304–42, especially 326–27.

41. Brown, *Providence and Empire*, 71–73. While Irving's interest in charismatic gifts was profound and relatively early, later Pentecostalism does not owe its emergence to his influence or his ideas in any significant ways. Gilley, "Edward Irving," 103.

42. On the Holy Catholic Apostolic Church see chapter 1 in Flegg, *"Gathered Under Apostles,"* 33–96.

43. The most detailed account of the day is in Oliphant, *Life of Edward Irving*, 94–99. The quotation is Irving's own words from the preface to his address in Irving and Carlyle, *Collected Writings*, 1:429. Richard's primary interaction with Irving was through the first volume of his *Collected Works*, quite possibly this 1866 edition. This text will be used throughout the present study, apart from a few indicated references to unique matter in Richard's 1877 republished edition Irving, *Missionaries After the Apostolical School*.

44. See A. T. Pierson's description in Merricks, *Edward Irving*, 56–58.

from the past or present. The lengthy remainder of Irving's message was an extended scriptural exposition of the "Messiah's instructions to the first missionaries" as recorded in Matt 10. Decrying the lack of faith evident in what he criticized as the expediency and prudence of missionary endeavors during his days, Irving proclaimed in elevated and at times bewildering style the need for a radical and essentially literal conformity to Jesus's instructions to the first disciples. Irving had discovered that "wisdom to address the worthiest people, entire dependence upon God, exemplification of the doctrine, and constant debate with the spirits of men, are surely four of the great principles in the propagation of the gospel."[45]

Irving's speech was not well received: his passionate plea for the individual servant of the Lord to be set free from any organizational supports or constraints was hardly what the LMS leaders had been expecting when they asked him to speak at an event whose intent was to raise further subscriptions for their society.[46] In response to his critics, Irving returned to the scriptures, reading and re-reading the words of Jesus and the apostles. Finding his convictions only strengthened, he decided to publish the address on his own initiative. Confounding his detractors still further, Irving chose to dedicate the work, entitled *Missionaries after the Apostolical School,* to none other than Samuel Taylor Coleridge, whom he credits as having been "more profitable to my faith in orthodox doctrine, to my spiritual understanding of the Word of God, and to my right conception of the Christian Church, than any or all the men with whom I have entertained friendship and conversation."[47] The only completed volume of a proposed four-volume treatise on the subject, Irving's *Missionaries after the Apostolical School* was not popular during his lifetime, and this near universal opprobrium makes Richard's enthusiasm for Irving's text fifty years later all the more striking. As the Canadian Presbyterian missionary, Donald MacGillivray, observed, "What a contrast [was Richard's positive response] to the effect of the original oration . . . ! Did Richard know of the wrath it aroused in the L.M.S.? And if he did, would he care?"[48]

How or when Richard came across Irving's work is not clear, but possibly as early as 1873—and almost certainly by the time of his move to Qingzhou in 1875—Richard had made a study of Irving's address.[49] Certainly,

45. Irving and Carlyle, *Collected Writings,* 1:462.

46. Grass, *Edward Irving,* 98.

47. Irving and Carlyle, *Collected Writings,* 1:427. Richard, in his 1887 republication of Irving's address, does not include the original dedication to Coleridge.

48. Soothill, *Timothy Richard of China,* 79 n. 1.

49. While his 1885 and 1906 autobiographies agree in placing his reading of Irving prior to his move to Qingzhou, Richard's 1916 account places it just after his move for

Irving's address seems to have figured prominently in Richard's early discussions with his Baptist colleague Alfred Jones following his arrival in 1876.[50] As observed by a number of Richard's early biographers, Richard's interest in the address can be seen in his well-worn copy of Irving's *Collected Writings*. Apparently passed on to his wife as a gift in 1883, the volume "bears the marks of frequent reading, with many underlinings and some marginal notes."[51] Richard's successor as Secretary of the Christian Literature Society for China (CLS, formerly SDCK), Donald MacGillivray, had occasion to examine Richard's copy while it was still held in the CLS library in Shanghai, noting that in many places the text had been mended with strips of paper. More tantalizing still, MacGillivray claimed that Richard "had also written out in his own hand a full analysis of the discourses."[52] While this analysis appears to have been lost, it is indicative of the high regard with which Richard viewed Irving's address.

Curiously, at least one other fellow missionary shared Richard's fondness for *Missionaries after the Apostolical School*. Although he does not credit Irving with having contributed to his own ideas about mission, in 1885 James Hudson Taylor opened the October installment of the CIM periodical *China's Millions* with a three-page excerpt from Irving's address, concluding just prior to his comments on Matt 10:11.[53] The simplification of the mission task to a pure "apostolic" model, combined with Irving's strong

---

apparently editorial purposes, employing his reading of Irving to introduce his subsequent interactions with Qingzhou's sectarian leaders. Richard, *Forty-Five Years*, 86; Richard, "Autobiography of the Author" in *Conversion by the Million*, 1:87; Richard, *Fifteen Years*, 9–10. Rita Johnson implies that Richard read Irving's address in 1869, "forty-five years" after Irving spoke to the LMS. It is unlikely that this reflects any conviction on the part of Johnson as she gives only a single page of her dissertation—despite its title—to discussing Irving. Her reference follows a paragraph outlining the advice Richard received from Trestrail/Underhill, an editorial decision that is likely driven by thematic convenience rather than conviction about the precise order of historical events. Johnson, "Timothy Richard's Theory," 133.

50. Richard, *Forty-Five Years*, 121.

51. Evans, *Timothy Richard*, 26. Evans and Soothill appear to have taken their information on Richard's (now lost) copy of Irving's *Collected Writings* from MacGillivray, *Timothy Richard of China*.

52. He also noted that Richard's pen showed little interest in any of the other selections in the first volume of Irving's *Collected Writings*. MacGillivray's excerpts from Richard's notes are quoted verbatim in Soothill, *Timothy Richard of China*, 77–79.

53. Taylor ended with the paragraph quoted at length in the next paragraph of this thesis. "Missionaries after the Apostolical School," *CM* (October 1885) 119–22. Taylor's excerpt is taken verbatim from Irving and Carlyle, *Collected Writings*, 1:449–56. While Benjamin Broomhall was involved in editing and distributing *China's Millions*, Taylor continued to exercise a high degree of control over the content and message of each issue. See Broomhall, *HTCOC*, 6:45–48, 162–65.

preference for the spiritual over the practical was very much in sympathy with much of Taylor's understanding of faith and mission.

The actual text of *Missionaries after the Apostolical School*, lengthy and awkward in its prose, bears the mark of its author quite clearly: Irving's mysticism and dualistic preference for the spiritual over the material are apparent throughout. Immediately prior to his treatment of Matt 10:11 and the worthy, Irving summarizes his understanding of the kind of missionary God was seeking for his gospel work in a passage that is typical of his voice and style.

> It was a spiritual work they had to do, therefore He disembodied (if I may so speak) and spiritualised the men who were to do it. It was faith they had to plant, therefore He made His missionaries men of faith, that they might plant faith, and faith alone.[54]

This dialectical preference for the "disembodied" runs throughout the essay, as Irving argues at great length for the practice of mission by heroic individuals unencumbered by sending agencies or their resources.

When he begins his exposition of Matt 10:11 and the worthy, Irving continues to emphasize the same "unearthly and spiritual strain."[55] The vast majority of Irving's exposition of the verse is taken up with expounding the importance and significance of the missionary relying on others for hospitality. Irving's actual description of those whom he considers worthy is less than a paragraph:

> Inquire, said he, the most worthy. There was to be no stealthy progress, nor keeping in the shade, but open dealing with the most open-hearted and even-minded of the people. There was to be no preference of ranks shewn by these men of no rank, who counted kindred with Messiah, the Missionary of heaven, and were God's adopted children and honoured ambassadors to the earth. They were not, like the Jesuits, to lay their artful toils around the high and noble and princely of the nations; nor like the Mendicant Friars, to go about preaching a crusade of poverty or meanness; nor were they to take their distinction by the grade of intellect or of taste, which compose, even at the best, but a fractionary part of human nature, and may exist in strength surrounded with the most dwarfish and pestilent forms of the moral, social and spiritual man: but like messengers and missionaries from heaven, they were to take their distinction by the grade of worth, or practical goodness; to inquire, whom

---

54. Irving and Carlyle, *Collected Writings*, 1:455–56.
55. Irving and Carlyle, *Collected Writings*, 1:456.

the judgment of their fellow-citizens had pronounced worthy, judicious, well-disposed men; those who, like Cornelius, were devout towards God, and full of alms towards the poor; or who, like Dorcas, employed their leisure and their labour to promote good and charitable works.[56]

Decrying any reliance upon artifice or technique, Irving advocates seeking after those, who like Cornelius, are "devout towards God," regardless of their social or intellectual stature.

This idea resonated with Richard, and by at least the late 1870s it had become a key component of his understanding of effective mission. Writing in 1878 to his BMS colleague and sympathetic friend Alfred Jones, Richard explained why he felt so strongly on this point.

> The entrance to the kingdom of heaven is by a strait gate. The irreverent crowd cannot enter. If our teachers and preachers were to say this instead of Ye cheats and scamps adulterers and perjurers and all the general loungers and pests of society— Come! Come! [Y]ou have food and raiment (sooner or later) and the company of the best in foreign lands. In fact they court you. They have enriched many of you and clothed many of you with decency and honoured many of your like with confidence in spite of villainy and rottenness. I have heard such sermons preached until I am sick of them. I do not wonder that the devout turn away with disgust. These people oil their lips but if you try to move the good and noble instincts of the heart they are like old rusted locks [that] will break before they yield as they ought to. Go ye to the city and ask who is worthy is our Lord's command for God wishes to send them a message of love. It is the glory of Christianity that the greatest of sinners *can* be saved but to preach as some do is to prostitute the most sacred on earth. It is against this I object. Unworthy men often pick holes (real too) in their fellow inquirers or Christians if they are likely to be preferred by their religious teachers. There is much jealously unexpressed and almost unknown to themselves. These worthy ones are the chosen of God declared in our Sacred Books and by honouring them we shall honour God—and save many a sleepless night and many a pang in the heart and a life from being spent in vain. What an alarming thought. After a life time of toil to have none but thorns and briers about us. May God deliver us from getting entangled in such fuel.[57]

---

56. Irving and Carlyle, *Collected Writings*, 1:457.
57. Richard to Jones, 16 January 1878, pp. 30–32, BMSA CH/4.

Much of what Richard says in this passage is negative: he devotes the majority of his energy to railing against the unworthy, a group he describes as "loungers and pests"—opportunistic troublemakers who are seeking after material gain rather than spiritual truth. At the same time, these "adulterers and perjurers" are possessed of hearts that are rusted and will not yield to the gospel. It is Richard's contention that too much of the mission project is tied up with attracting and then benefiting just these unworthy ones who are unlikely to experience a true change of heart. While not denying that Christ could save even the worst of sinners, Richard was eager to avoid spending his life in vain, chasing after what in the end would be only fuel for the fires of hell. Thus, it was better to expend precious missionary time and resources on those who were worthy—upon the devout ones already seeking after truth. This was the idea of seeking the worthy that Richard claimed he learned from Irving.

It is significant that in all of Irving's writings—from the entire text of *Missionaries after the Apostolical School*—this is the one idea that Richard latched on to. Certainly, Richard showed little patience for Irving's abiding distaste for anything prudent. While Irving called for "disembodied . . . spiritualised men," Richard demonstrated from his earliest years in China a willingness to employ any practical techniques or methods that might promote the gospel. The same man who was so eager to see modern subjects taught in his theological school in Wales did not hesitate once on the field to employ medicine, local dress, and even local belief in Chinese geomancy (*fengshui*) to advance the Kingdom of God.[58] Perhaps more strikingly, the implications of Irving's address that went beyond seeking the worthy failed to attract Richard's interest. Richard did not leave his sending organization or refuse their financial support, even though both points are central to Irving's exposition.[59]

Likewise, Richard eschewed the historical pessimism of Irving and his fellow Romantics, and seemed unaffected theologically by his early attraction to the Guinnesses and the CIM. Although it is important to avoid overstating its influence upon James Hudson Taylor and his organization, premillennial eschatology certainly contributed to Taylor's promotion of both rapid evangelism and personal holiness.[60] Charismatic CIM trainer

---

58. For other examples of Richard's pragmatic bent while on the field, see Richard, *Forty-Five Years*, 78–81.

59. The importance of refusing financial remuneration and support from overseas and relying entirely upon the support of the local worthy is central to Irving's argument, and held little interest for Richard prior to his late 1880s conflicts. For a typical passage, see Irving and Carlyle, *Collected Writings*, 1:475–80.

60. There is still no agreement on the precise connections between Taylor, the

Henry Grattan Guinness was author of the premillennial text *The Approaching End of the Age*, and the story of Taylor and the CIM cannot be told without reference to the people and the theology of the Christian (Plymouth) Brethren.[61] Richard, despite his Haverfordwest training, showed little interest in biblical prophecy, and maintained throughout his days a confidence in human agency—aided by God—to dramatically better the world, as demonstrated by his long-standing commitment to national reform in China and around the world.[62] Despite these seeming indications of his postmillennial optimism, Richard never debated or formally identified himself with any particular view of the end times: as will be explored in chapter 6 below, it was the practical implications of God's Kingdom reign for people's lives on earth that excited him.

Interestingly, Richard and Irving both viewed Jesus's words in Matt 10 as universally applicable in all their particulars.[63] Neither man attempted to make any allowances for a unique apostolic role or function distinct from modern missionaries, or for any special circumstances contingent upon evangelistic ministry in Palestine prior to Christ's death. Without looking back, both assumed the text spoke directly to their lives in the present. Richard, however, took this exceptionalism one step further and ignored both the otherworldly emphasis of Irving's message as well as his comments on anything other than the worthy of Matt 10:11. Employing the same hermeneutic he had used to read the Bible, Richard seized on the one aspect of Irving's text that supported the new methods he had already found to be effectively contributing to mission goals, and largely ignored the rest of the text.

While scholars often note Richard's indebtedness to Irving for his idea of seeking the worthy, they at times mistakenly connect it to his later interactions with Chinese intellectual and political elites.[64] And yet in this

---

Brethren, the CIM, and dispensationalist premillennial theology. Toward the end of his days, Taylor expressed regret over the excessive emphasis on eschatology in the early days of the mission. See the nuanced discussion throughout Wigram, *Bible and Mission,* especially 76, 179; as well as Austin, "Pilgrims and Strangers," 41–47, 55.

61. For Guinness's views and their influence on the CIM see Austin, "Only Connect," 291. CIM historian A. J. Broomhall differs from Austin, arguing that Taylor associated with the earliest independent (Open) Brethren and had little to do with Darby and the so-called Plymouth Brethren. See "Appendix Two: James Hudson Taylor and the Brethren" in Broomhall, *HTCOC,* 3:447–50; and Wigram, *Bible and Mission,* 61–63.

62. See chapters 2 and 6 of this thesis.

63. Calvin warned against such readings of Matt 10 in his *Commentary on a Harmony,* 388.

64. See, for example, Xu Yanmin's conflation of the *guanshen* (officials and gentry) with the religious leaders in Richard's worthy. "'Dingwu' zhenzai," 76. Peter Ng seems more aware of Richard's intent, situating his discussion of the worthy within the

area, Richard remained uncharacteristically faithful to Irving's intentions. The extensive engagement with Chinese scholar-officials that featured so prominently in Richard's post-famine missionary work was not a reflection of his concept of seeking after the worthy. Like Irving, Richard recognized that men of power and authority—"the high and noble and princely of the nations"—were not generally counted among the spiritually worthy.[65] It was Richard's firm conviction that the worthy were first and foremost the devout; it was to people already seeking after truth that he was to take God's message.[66] Writing after his work during the famine, Richard explained to one of his colleagues:

> As foreigners in this land we must deliver our message to the rulers of the land. They are appointed by God in his Providence over the people. But being first officials and only secondly religious, if at all, we cannot be much surprised at little success amongst them, further than the removal of prejudice, and prevention of persecution.[67]

Since officials were only incidentally, if at all, interested in matters of religious truth, they were not well disposed to receive the Christian gospel. While Richard might focus his attention upon the officials for all sorts of reasons—out of obligation or respect, or in hopes that they might be induced to rule China in ways advantageous to Christian witness—his interest in Chinese mandarins was unrelated to the idea of seeking the worthy, because for the most part *the officials were not worthy*.[68]

Richard's faithful apprehension of this one singular aspect of Irving's *Missionaries after the Apostolical School* occupied an important place in his conception of the missionary endeavor. And despite the fact that the rest of the document seems to have had little direct effect on his practice and understanding of mission, he remained firmly convinced of the value of the entire address for the larger mission world. In 1887, thanks to the financial support of an unnamed "brother missionary," Richard was able to reprint Irving's address and then distribute it to "every Mission in China, India and Japan." In his "Note on Republication," Richard was quite explicit regarding his high opinion of Irving's text:

---

context of Richard's early interactions with Chinese religionists. Ng, "Timothy Richard," 116–18.

65. Irving and Carlyle, *Collected Writings*, 1:457.
66. Cohen understood this point. Cohen, "Missionary Approaches," 35–36.
67. Richard to Baynes, 2 February 1884, BMSA CH/2.
68. This will be discussed again in chapter 6 below.

It is true we have invaluable helps in several excellent works published during the last twenty years. But I know of none dealing with the MOST FUNDAMENTAL principles of Christian Missions so applicable to all times and circumstances that will for a moment compare with this of Edward Irving's on MISSIONARIES AFTER THE APOSTOLIC [sic] SCHOOL.[69]

In total, Richard claimed to have mailed two hundred copies to Japan, five hundred copies to India, and eight hundred copies within China, a concrete demonstration of his belief in the value of Irving's ideas—or at least one of his ideas—for the mission community.[70]

As early as 1872 or 1873, Richard was already practicing his method of seeking the worthy, having been convinced by his many conversations with local religious leaders that those who were already spiritually inclined "constituted the 'good ground' in which to sow the seed." On one memorable occasion, Richard set out to visit a devout man he had heard of who resided a short distance from Chefoo. The potentially worthy man, a salt manufacturer by trade, welcomed Richard and showed him into an inner room where he conducted his own daily worship. As Richard showed the man his hymn book—he had also brought along Gospel portions and some Christian tracts—he was stunned to hear the man observe that one of the hymns therein was used regularly in his sect's worship.[71] Like many missionaries before, Richard was surprised to find such deep religious experience and piety among the people he had come to save. After a long day of fellowship and conversation it occurred to Richard that while not a Christian, the salt manufacturer "was at any rate not far from the Kingdom of God."[72]

Having found in this salt manufacturer a man that was worthy, Richard encountered a new difficulty. As he wrote, "My knowledge of the Chinese language and history of religion was too imperfect at that time for me to take advantage of that most rare opportunity."[73] From this point onwards, Richard's desire to seek the worthy would be paired with an equally ardent attempt to understand China's own religious and philosophical traditions and the language with which they were expressed. Richard's acculturation process was bringing him into yet closer empathy with the Chinese other.

69. Irving, *Missionaries after the Apostolical School*, 3.
70. Richard to Baynes, 16 July 1888, BMSA CH/2.
71. The shared hymn, possibly a vestigial Catholic Psalm adopted over the centuries by a local sect, was later viewed by Richard as an indication that this man may have been "a lost Nestorian." Richard, *Forty-Five Years*, 48.
72. Richard, *Forty-Five Years*, 48–49.
73. Richard, *Forty-Five Years*, 49.

4

Indigenous Impulses in Practice
Chinese and Western Influences

WITH THE DEPARTURE FROM the mission of his colleague Dr. Brown in April 1874, Richard was once again the only expatriate representative of the BMS in China. By this time, his encounters with worthy Chinese truth-seekers were propelling him further along his empathetic trajectory of acculturation, resulting in both the intentional borrowing of techniques from Chinese religious sectarians and an increasing emphasis on indigenous participation in mission. Richard had become convinced that in order to present the gospel more effectively, he would need

> to continue my study of the Chinese classics, and to read up the current Chinese religious books and tracts of the day, so as to be able to give answers to *Chinese* difficulties and such answers as would satisfy *them* and compel genuine inquirers to become Christians.[1]

Driven by his evangelical desire to promote religious conversion, and tempered by the pragmatic needs of his mission context, Richard was making adaptations to both his audience and his method. As discussed in the previous chapter, Richard had decided to focus on an audience comprising worthy individuals, and he believed that he would find these people among China's most devoted religious practitioners. Once access to this new audience was secured, Richard could then turn his attention to developing a method of evangelism that was fully adapted to the Chinese context.

In January 1875 Richard left the foreign community in Chefoo and settled in Qingzhou, a prefectural town two hundred miles west of Chefoo.[2] As he moved inland in pursuit of people who had not heard the gospel, Richard

---

1. Richard, *Fifteen Years*, 8.
2. Richard, *Forty-Five Years*, 66. Richard claims to have begun work there in 1874. Richard, "English Baptist Mission," 2:42. Tsingchowfu, Ch'ing-chow fu, Ts'ing Chou Fu, and others are different romanizations for the inland Shandong city of Qingzhou near Weifang.

demonstrated once again the mission priorities he shared with James Hudson Taylor. By the mid-1870s the coastal port of Chefoo already had a strong and well-established mission presence. Richard's previous itinerations in the company of local evangelists had made him well aware that there remained vast stretches of interior Shandong without Christian witness: remote Qingzhou was one such region. Perhaps more importantly for Richard's purposes, these same travels had also revealed that "[t]he country all around Tsingchowfu is a perfect hotbed of religious sects, which are neither Confucian, Buddhist, nor Taoist—the three national religions of China. The leaders of these sects are generally accepted as worthy men, who try to do good."[3] Richard accordingly chose Qingzhou for his new work, convinced that among the followers of sectarian religions in the area he would find many "genuine inquirers" who were ready to accept the gospel message. He had his audience of worthies; now it was time to work on his method.

In the relative isolation of Qingzhou, Richard was not bound by existing church or mission structures. Demonstrating once again the kind of pragmatic borrowing that epitomized his appropriation of Edward Irving's ideas, Richard—ever the intellectual magpie—synthesized ideas and practices he had acquired from a number of different sources in China, both Western and Chinese, and produced in Qingzhou a way of doing mission that was distinctively empathetic to Chinese needs and priorities. This approach was impulsively indigenous, both in its willingness to learn from local religious practices and in its eagerness to see authority and responsibility in the hands of local believers.

4.1 Learning about the Three Teachings

The "three national religions of China" mentioned by Richard above, referred to the widely recognized Three Teachings (*sanjiao*) of Buddhism, Confucianism, and Daoism. In the interest of control and social harmony, the imperial state had over the centuries encouraged these three diverse sets of religious and philosophical teachings to pursue political and moral harmony.[4] Although no institutional unity ever existed, whatever toleration Qing

---

3. Richard, *Fifteen Years*, 10; on mid-century Shandong sectarianism in general, see Esherick, *Origins of the Boxer Uprising*, 38–68.

4. Gentz, "Religious Diversity," 134. In a May 2014 conversation, Gentz noted that missionary use of the Three Teachings discourse was curious given its decline among Chinese elites throughout the Qing Dynasty. While recognizing the scholarly debates over the comingling of philosophical and religious components within Confucianism in particular, this thesis will refer to these disparate forms as "religions," reflecting the language of Richard and the majority of the missionary community at the time.

Confucian elites extended to the mainstream Buddhist and Daoist groups of their days led many of the missionaries to borrow the conceptual category of the Three Teachings in their writings on China's religions.

Timothy Richard's initial interest in the religions of China was encouraged and shaped by a number of factors on the field. The "excellent training in comparative religion" that Richard claimed to have received from Williamson, Mateer, and other missionaries during his early years in Chefoo certainly encouraged him to take the Chinese religious world very seriously.[5] Richard had also made an early study of James Legge's translation of the Confucian classics. Legge—a key figure in the burgeoning new field of comparative religious studies—would eventually become known for his accommodationist approach to Confucianism; however, these ideas were not yet clearly developed in the first editions of his texts which Richard would have encountered.[6] Richard's interest in comparative religion, as was the case with Legge and most other similarly inclined missionaries in nineteenth-century China, was driven by his desire to communicate the truths of the gospel effectively: Richard was seeking points of contact between the existing religious beliefs of Chinese people and the Christian faith.[7]

At the 1877 Shanghai GCPMC, two papers were presented on China's religions: "Confucianism, in its relation to Christianity" by James Legge and "The Popular Aspects of Tauism and Buddhism" by Joseph Edkins. While Legge's essay was omitted from the proceedings for contravening conference restrictions on discussing the Term Question, Edkins's essay captured the understanding of Chinese religion most prevalent among the mission community at the time:[8]

---

5. Richard, "Autobiography of the Author" in *Conversion by the Million*, 1:81. Comparative religion was not part of Richard's Haverfordwest studies; it did not come into its own as an organized academic discipline until after 1869. Sharpe, *Comparative Religion*, xi–xii, 28.

6. On accommodationism or "Leggism," see Pfister, "Legacy of James Legge," 79. On the early development of Legge's understanding of the relationship between Confucianism and Christianity see Pfister, *Striving*, 2:221–23, especially.

7. Scott, "Timothy Richard," 61–62. Scott notes that Richard himself did not use the term "comparative religion." While true for the early part of Richard's ministry in China, he did employ the term retrospectively in both of his post-1900 autobiographies to describe his interests during those early years. Richard, "Autobiography of the Author" in *Conversion by the Million*, 1:81; Richard, *Forty-Five Years*, 159. Comparative religion is discussed further in chapter 6 below.

8. Girardot claims that the prevalence of Term Question discussions in the other included papers suggests that Legge's essay was omitted for theological reasons related to his budding accommodationism. Yates, *Records of the GCPMC: Shanghai, 1877*, 20; Girardot, *Victorian Translation*, 218–27. Legge's essay represented one of his earliest statements of his accommodationist attitude toward Confucianism. "I feel increasingly

> Our great contest as Christian missionaries is with Confucianism. There is found the intellect, the thought, the literature, the heart of the nation. But we have also a preliminary struggle with Buddhism and Taoism. These constitute three mighty fortresses erected by satanic art to impede the progress of Christianity.... Let the Christian host of soldiers press on and detail its battalions first to overthrow these strong holds [Buddhism and Daoism] of sin and Satan, and when they are destroyed let another earnest effort be made to destroy the last and strongest of the towers of the enemy [Confucianism].[9]

Although there were no representatives of the BMS at the 1877 conference, this antagonistic attitude toward Chinese religions would have been familiar to Richard.[10] The Presbyterians Mateer and Williamson—both men who influenced Richard during his early days in Chefoo—were present, and their comments echoed Edkins's perspective. Largely agreeing with Edkins's assessment, Mateer added a plea for the "the general diffusion of scientific truth" as a means of combatting the "lies" of Chinese religion.[11] Williamson, also in agreement, reflected on the incongruities between formal Buddhist belief and actual practice, suggesting that "[t]he best way therefore for missionaries to meet such ideas as were under discussion, was to make themselves masters of the history of the false religions around them."[12] One of the few conference delegates to admit anything positive regarding Chinese religions was Griffith John. While condemning the Three Teachings in no uncertain terms, he at least acknowledged that they had preserved—albeit imperfectly—a few contact points for Christian evangelists, such as a belief in the supernatural and the concept of redemption from sin.[13] While Richard absorbed much from Mateer and Williamson—particularly their insistence that missionaries make greater use of science and study China's religions—he preferred John's more optimistic view that there existed within Chinese religions some key aids for Christian evangelism.

---

that we, as missionaries, ought to congratulate ourselves that there is so much in Confucianism about God, of which we can avail ourselves in setting forth our fuller truth." Legge, *Confucianism*, 3; Pfister, *Striving*, 239.

9. Yates, *Records of the GCPMC: Shanghai, 1877*, 71.

10. The only foreign missionaries of the BMS in China at the time, Richard and Jones remained in Shandong battling famine.

11. Yates, *Records of the GCPMC: Shanghai, 1877*, 73.

12. Yates, *Records of the GCPMC: Shanghai, 1877*, 75.

13. In a passing comment, John mentioned the Christian adoption of the Chinese Buddhist term "shuh tsuei" (*shuzui*, or atonement) as evidence of Buddhism's concern with these issues. Yates, *Records of the GCPMC: Shanghai, 1877*, 74.

Like many other missionaries, Richard's interest in China's religions strengthened as he explored his ministry context. According to his autobiographies, Richard's years in Shandong involved frequent interaction with a wide-ranging variety of Chinese religionists. From his early attempt in Jinan to ascertain if the Koran had been translated into Chinese, to interactions with a Daoist hermit and a group of female Daoist petitioners in a temple in the mountains near Qingzhou, Richard presents himself as always being eager to increase his understanding of the religious world of the Chinese people around him, and often humbled by their piety—however misdirected he thought it to be.[14] Certainly, Richard did share his missionary colleagues' negative assessment of the Three Teachings, especially with regards to the leaders and the priests associated with the Three Teachings. In 1874 he recounted having a fruitful discussion with two Buddhist priests in Laiyang, eighty miles south of Chefoo—a remarkable event, for "There I met two intelligent priests (*a rare thing hitherto in my experience*), open to discuss freely the respective merits of Christianity and Buddhism."[15] These kinds of inter-religious interactions were apparently such a significant component of Richard's experience as a missionary that in 1876, for his first contribution to the influential *Chinese Recorder*, he chose to share with his missionary colleagues an account of his debates and discussions at the Islamic theological college outside of Qingzhou.[16]

Richard expected to find many sincere seekers of truth within China's religions. From his reading of Irving, Richard believed that these worthy individuals were especially inclined to accept the Christian gospel. His own experiences, however, suggested that these genuine inquirers were more likely to be found outside the Three Teachings, in the Chinese religious milieu known as sectarianism. It was the leaders of these "Secret Sects" that Richard believed to be "the religious cream of the land."[17]

4.2 Learning from Chinese Sectarians

Though the usage is challenged by scholars today for enshrining elite prejudices,[18] Richard, along with many nineteenth-century missionaries in China, used the English terms "sect" or "society," often paired with the

14. For these incidents see Richard, *Forty-Five Years*, 57, 92–94.
15. Richard, "Missionary Labour in China," 158 (emphasis added).
16. Richard, "Mohammedan and Christian Evidences," 129–31.
17. Richard, "Autobiography of the Author" in *Conversion by the Million*, 1:81.
18. Compare the views of Tiedemann and Ter Haar in Tiedemann, "Christianity and Chinese," 342–43.

adjectives "heterodox" or "secret," to indicate the various Chinese religious associations outside of the Three Teachings.[19] Like the more acceptable Three Teachings, these groups were often referred to in Chinese official records as teachings (*jiao*), though typically delineated as heterodox ones (*xiejiao*).[20]

When distinguishing between these heterodox sects and the relatively more respected Three Teachings, the state focused on unacceptable rites and practices rather than theological or philosophical differences.[21] In the wake of the devastating mid-century quasi-Christian Taiping Rebellion, extended networks of hereditary leaders and increased millenarian emphases within Qing dynasty sectarian groups often served as lightning rods, attracting the negative attention of the state.[22] By noting their departures from the more generally accepted "orthodox" (*zheng*) Three Teachings, the state could then declare particular sects to be morally (and politically) heretical teachings susceptible to legal proscription. Thus, unlike most groups positioned within the Three Teachings, the secret sects were located—regardless of their actual intentions—at the crossroads of political and religious rebellion, and repeatedly exposed to official persecution.[23] In late imperial China "heretic" was a political as well as religious term.[24]

19. In the 1870s these groups were rarely discussed by missionaries, with the term "society" at times used interchangeably with "sect." See, for example, Joseph Edkins's brief comment in Yates, *Records of the GCPMC: Shanghai, 1877*, 365. As awareness of the phenomenon grew, "sect," while at times also used to refer to smaller divisions within Buddhism, Islam, and especially Christianity, gained in popularity for describing what the missionary community called the offshoots of the Three Teachings. See the use of *mimi jiao* terminology in Henry D. Porter, "Secret Sects of Shantung," in *CR* 17, no. 1 (1886) 2–3; as well as comments during the 1890 GCPMC in Barber, Hykes, and Lewis, *Records of the GCPMC: Shanghai, 1890*, 125, 249, 327, 522, 560–61, 569.

20. See, for example, the usage of the term *xiejiao* in the official Chinese regulation "Jinzhi shiwu xieshu: Against Heresies of Religious Leaders or Instructors, and of Priests," as recorded in De Groot, *Sectarianism and Religious Persecution*, 137–48. Although the title of the regulation under review mentioned only heretical leaders and practices, De Groot titled his chapter "The Law Against Heresy and Sects," adding "sect" as a term for voluntary associations of those whom the Chinese regulation labeled as "heretics." De Groot's translation of the regulation's title was generous, softening the pejorative bias inherent in the Confucian state's attitude toward these groups by obscuring the negative attributions of sorcery and witchcraft originally intended.

21. Note the emphasis on ritual in the prohibitions aimed at constraining unorthodox religious activity in the "Jinzhi shiwu xieshu" in De Groot, *Sectarianism and Religious Persecution*, 137–40.

22. Seiwert, "Transformation of Popular Religious Movements," 41–42.

23. The literature on sectarian rebellion and suppression in late imperial China is extensive. See, for example, the foundational Naquin, *Millenarian Rebellion*; and Overmyer, *Folk Buddhist Religion*.

24. Note the official fear of sects collecting money from the population and

The modern category of "Chinese popular religion," denoting the diverse religious concepts and beliefs practiced during imperial times by the majority of Chinese lay people in order to secure personal and communal welfare, was not recognized or employed by Richard or his fellow missionaries.[25] Many of the practices and beliefs later scholars associated with Chinese popular religion were dismissed by the missionary observers in the field at the time as superstition—and similarly viewed by most Chinese at the time as "customs" (*fengsu*) rather than "teachings."[26] Richard, however, rarely used the language of superstition—hardly ever in his personal correspondence, and only ten times in his lengthy 1916 autobiography. Chinese geomancy, for example, was one set of beliefs singled out by Richard as superstitious; but even though he eagerly hoped the teaching of science would replace the practice, on the one occasion when he was asked to assist a Qingzhou official in the selection of a new burial place, Richard gave his opinion without discrediting the practice. In this case, his pragmatic need for official support in securing a residence appears to have overcome his distaste for the superstition.[27] Perhaps more significantly, Richard's recording of demon possession in Shandong was completely free from the language of superstition, noting with admiration the "thousand instances" of effective Christian exorcism known to missionaries in China. Richard placed his entire account of spirit possession within the context of the experiences of the early church in the Book of Acts, while observing that each of the Three Teachings had practitioners engaged in exorcisms.[28] For Richard, both possession and exorcism were accepted as real phenomena and situated within a religious rather than mythical or superstitious world. Richard's interest in each of these aspects of popular religion, however, was of a very limited nature in comparison to his primary concern with the institutional manifestations of these beliefs—with the sectarian associations of China.

Hubert Seiwert has emphasized the eclectic and fundamentally popular nature of Chinese sectarian religion.[29] At the local level, popular religious life in China involved a bricolage of practices from within and outside the Three Teachings, as demonstrated by David Johnson in his study of the officially sanctioned yet religiously varied late imperial opera festivals

---

establishing "connections" within the state bureaucracy as seen in De Groot, *Sectarianism and Religious Persecution*, 139.

25. The definition is from Gentz, *Understanding Chinese Religions*, 112.
26. Gentz, *Understanding Chinese Religions*, 113.
27. Richard, *Forty-Five Years*, 81–82, 123–24.
28. See Richard's report as recorded in Nevius, *Demon Possession*, 63–72.
29. Seiwert and Ma, *Popular Religious Movements*.

of Shanxi.[30] Practically, this resulted in sets of practices that while varying with respect to specific details nevertheless found expression through a common range of general modalities.[31] As Robert Weller observed long ago, sectarian associations—the religious communities that so intrigued Richard—were, in addition to collections of individuals who embraced certain popular religious beliefs and practices, "established institutions that must be officially joined."[32] At the time of Richard's arrival in China, these sectarian groups—borrowing eclectically in their practices—also tended to be textually promiscuous, making use of various collections of popularly circulating morality scrolls (*baojuan*).[33] As Richard sought to further expand the Christian community around him, he naturally turned toward these popular institutions with their own bodies of literature as local examples of successful, thriving religious association.

A number of scholars have explored the suggestive similarities between late Qing religious sectarianism and the earliest forms of indigenous Chinese Christianity. Daniel Bays's 1982 article "Christianity and the Chinese Sectarian Tradition" was one of the first pieces of academic writing to advance the thesis

> that in nineteenth-century China, Christianity should not be seen only as a "foreign religion." In terms of the way in which it functioned in Chinese society, it can and should be seen as a variety of the wide range of heterodox religion or sectarianism which was already well established and flourishing in many parts of China. In religious ideas and in the structure and role of local religious groups, significant parallels appear when we consider Christianity and indigenous Chinese sectarianism.[34]

More recently, R. G. Tiedemann has advanced Bays's position, establishing that these connections went back to the eighteenth century, and were recognized and exploited by both sectarians and Christians.[35] Furthermore, Tiedemann argues, acceptance of and conversion to Christianity in North

---

30. Johnson, "'Confucian' Elements," 126–61. De Groot early on noted sectarian indebtedness to the Three Teachings. De Groot, *Sectarianism and Religious Persecution*, 155–57.

31. For a recent promising attempt to index these shared modes of religious expression, see Chau, "Religious Diversity," 141–54.

32. Weller, "Sectarian Religion," 465.

33. Overmyer, *Precious Volumes*.

34. Bays, "Christianity and the Chinese Sectarian Tradition," 33.

35. Tiedemann, "Christianity and Chinese," 339–82.

China was most common in areas with strong sectarian traditions and histories of sectarian violence.³⁶

Alan Richard Sweeten's detailed analysis of the religious cases (*jiao'an*) involving purported Christian persecution in nineteenth-century Jiangxi supports these claims, demonstrating how local conflicts with Christians were similar in number, scope, and nature to conflicts between villagers and religious sectarians.³⁷ Contrary to the conventional image of local communities rising up in protest against the unjust access to external power made available to local Christian adherents, Sweeten uncovers the tremendous degree of day-to-day interaction between Christians and non-Christians. Similar to what Ryan Dunch discovered in his study of Fuzhou Protestants, the very normality of the conflicts themselves—largely economic and social in nature—further supports the argument that there was no need for local people to develop new categories to explain or process the Christians in their midst.³⁸ This suggests that Richard's sympathy for Chinese sectarians was a practical strategic option that reflected his growing understanding of local conditions: many Chinese at the time recognized Christianity at the local level as a new form of sectarian religion.

Catholics were aware of the conversion potential often found in Chinese sectarian groups, having witnessed mass conversions from Shandong sectarians in the eighteenth century, as well as more recent waves of conversions during the second half of the nineteenth century.³⁹ However, during Richard's first decade in China, the larger Protestant mission community showed little interest in Chinese sectarianism. At the 1877 Shanghai GCPMC the Chinese sectarian world received only one passing mention: Edkins referred to the Zaili sect (*zaili jiao*), but only as a possible native ally of the missionaries' anti-opium activities.⁴⁰ By 1890, however, sectarians had attracted enough interest to warrant their own essay at the second meeting of the GCPMC—in part due to the success of the work in Shandong. The essay, written by Richard's eventual colleague and friend in Shanxi Francis H. James, was entitled "The Secret Sects of Shantung" and contained an appendix listing ten of the more prominent sectarian groups that were active in Shandong, as well as a

---

36. Tiedemann, "Conversion Patterns," 107–34.

37. Sweeten, *Christianity in Rural China*.

38. Dunch also noted that these conflicts were regular occurrences in "resource poor" communities. Significantly, in the Fuzhou context Western missionaries were almost completely peripheral to the *jiao'an* conflicts. Dunch, *Fuzhou Protestants*, 25.

39. Tiedemann, "Christianity and Chinese," 339–82.

40. Yates, *Records of the GCPMC: Shanghai, 1877*, 365; Shek, "Revolt of the Zaili," 194 n. 1; Soothill and Hodous, *Dictionary of Chinese Buddhist Terms*, 206. This thesis accepts Soothill's characters for the Zaili sect, despite Shek's claim of uncertainty.

Chinese index of fifty texts utilized by the various groups.[41] In his discussion of the nature and beliefs of the "over one hundred" sects active in Shandong, James echoed Richard's convictions, pointing out that while "as yet, but little has been done for them . . . [t]here is more inquiry, receptiveness and earnestness among them than among any other class in this land."[42] In addition to indicating the extent and prevalence of sectarianism in Shandong during this period, James's essay also claimed that "large numbers of Christians in this province have been gathered from these sects. . . . Some of the best and most consistent Christians I know were once the devoted followers of these societies."[43] James's testimony suggests that, as will be discussed below, Richard's attention to sectarianism did indeed produce fruit; but in the early years few missionaries shared Richard's interest.

Missionaries located in the sectarian hotbed of Shandong were most likely to echo Richard's conviction. Like Richard, ABCFM missionary Henry D. Porter was impressed by the openness to the gospel he encountered among the sectarians of Shandong. He recounted finding one group of sectarians who had been waiting for missionaries to visit them with the gospel, claiming that they been prepared to believe it by a previous "prophet" within their own sect.[44] Porter believed these sectarians were drawn to Christianity for its monotheism and injunctions against idolatry, though he did not begin writing about these connections until well after Richard's realization.[45]

One other Shandong missionary, John Nevius, was also attentive to the Christian-sectarian connections, possibly even earlier than Richard. On a visit to the village of "Chi-mi" during an extended evangelistic tour in the summer of 1873, Nevius observed that the high level of local interest in the gospel was "of an unusual and peculiar kind. Nearly every one of the inquirers has belonged to a secret and proscribed religious sect which I am very desirous to know more about."[46] Nevius was surprised by the familiar nature of many of the doctrines professed by the members of this sect:

41. The sects profiled included the Sun Society (*taiyang jiao*), the Light Worship Society (*chao guang jiao*), the White Lily Sect (*bailian jiao*), the Sz Ch'wan Province Sect (*Sichuan jiao*) which James claims is an alternative name for the Golden Elixir sect (*jindan jiao*), the Non-action Society (*wuwei jiao*), the White Cloud Society (*baiyun jiao*), Sect of the Sages and Worthies (*shengxian jiao*), the Eight Diagrams Society (*ba gua jiao*), the Mother and Son Society (*zi mu jiao*), and the Sect of the God Fah-lu (*falü jiao*). These are the English names given in James, "Secret Sects of Shantung," 196–202. On James's complex relationship with Richard and the BMS, see chapters 7 and 8 below.

42. James, "Secret Sects of Shantung," 200.

43. James, "Secret Sects of Shantung," 198.

44. Henry D. Porter, "Modern Shantung Prophet," *CR* 18, no. 1 (1887) 12–21.

45. Henry D. Porter, "Secret Sects in Shantung," *CR* 17, no. 2 (1886) 65–66.

46. This and the following quotation are from Nevius, *Life of John Livingston Nevius*,

> They believe in one supreme Deity, whom they call the Heavenly Ruler or the Heavenly Father. They speak of the world as having gone astray from the truth, and look forward to a period of reform and restoration at the end of the world, when the Lord or Head shall appear to teach and save men.

Since, at the time, Richard and Nevius were both based in Chefoo, it is quite possible that Richard's initial introduction to sectarianism came from Nevius; the men were friends, and at times shared their work quite closely. Even so, Nevius's interest cannot have been much earlier than Richard's: as late as his 1868 *China and the Chinese*, Nevius gave each of the Three Teachings its own chapter, while still maintaining that "[o]ther minor sects of religionists, which have not exercised a decided and permanent influence on the Chinese race as a whole, need not be particularly mentioned."[47]

Beyond his underlying conviction that the "worthy men" of these sects were uniquely open to Christian evangelism, Richard was impressed by their simple piety. His mother's reputation for pious faith, as well as his own revival experience and baptism into a nonconformist chapel may have predisposed Richard to sympathize with people exhibiting sincere devotion. This seems to have been the case with what may have been Richard's first encounter with Chinese sectarianism. Though admittedly writing some decades after the fact, what most impressed Richard in his encounter with the salt manufacturer discussed at the end of chapter 3 above was "that his religious experience was not only much earlier than mine, but possessed a *depth* which astonished me." Richard was struck not just by the man's sincerity or surprising familiarity with a Christian hymn, but also his "spotlessly clean" inner room where he worshipped on a daily basis.[48] So different from what he had encountered from the leaders of the Three Teachings, this kind of regular and sincere pious worship echoed the daily devotions Richard would have witnessed and practiced as a youth in Wales.

Likewise, the similarity in status between the officially proscribed "heretical" sects in China and the nonconformist Baptist congregations in Wales did not go unnoticed by Richard. When introducing the sectarians to the BMS in England during his 1885 furlough, he referred to them as "what we might call the nonconformists in China" for their staunchly local autonomous organization. He then made the emotional connection with

---

300–301. "Chi-mi" was a common nineteenth-century romanization for the eastern Shandong city of Jimo.

47. Nevius, *China and the Chinese*, 81.

48. This and the previous quotation are from Richard, *Forty-Five Years*, 49 (emphasis added).

his audience complete by pointing out that "[b]esides being our brethren in nonconformity, some of them unquestionably have a still nearer relationship. They are being perpetually persecuted."[49] And while these comments were made while speaking in England, the association would have seemed stronger for Richard himself: his own experience as a Baptist teacher and student in Wales around the time of the 1870 Education Act would have made him quick to sympathize with the oft-oppressed Chinese sectarians.[50]

While he had little interest in the strictly political or experimental societies, Richard's interest in sectarianism was general—seeking the worthies—and did not focus on particular sectarian groups.[51] In his discussion of Pastor Xi, Alvyn Austin suggested that Richard may have had significant exposure to the Golden Elixir sects (*jindan jiao*) while in Shanxi, although this is conjectural.[52] Perhaps more convincing, a large excerpt from James's 1890 "Secret Sects of Shantung" opened Richard's brief essay on Chinese sectarianism in the 1896 *China Mission Handbook*, while his own three-page gloss on the Zaili and Golden Elixir sects served as its conclusion.[53] Given their pursuit of immortality, abstention from opium and alcohol, and aversion to idol worship in any form—and that both groups were active in Shandong and Shanxi—it is possible that adherents from these societies comprised the majority of Richard's sectarian interlocutors.[54]

While he clearly sympathized with and even admired many aspects of Chinese sectarianism, Richard went a step further. In a remarkable demonstration of his willingness to recognize the good in China's religions, many of the practical adaptations that Richard had made to his mission methods were derived directly from the practices of the sectarians. As he explained,

> I had noticed that the Chinese had a method of their own in carrying on education and the propagation of their religious doctrines.

49. Richard, *Wanted: Good Samaritans for China*, 13.

50. Richard was fully aware of the persecution faced by sectarians, including the early Nestorians. Richard, "Christian Persecutions in China," 244; Richard, "Secret Sects of China," 1:41–45.

51. Richard, *Wanted: Good Samaritans for China*, 13.

52. Austin, *China's Millions*, 163–66. Some scholars have suggested that the Golden Elixir Sect is, contrary to James, a later development of the Zaili Sect. Overmyer, *Precious Volumes*, 48, 86–88. See n. 40 above.

53. Richard, "Secret Sects of China," 1:41–45.

54. For a brief description of Zaili Sect beliefs, see Soothill and Hodous, *Dictionary of Chinese Buddhist Terms*, 206. James claimed that the Golden Elixir sect was the largest of its kind in Shandong. James, "Secret Sects of Shantung," 200. Joseph Esherick describes post-famine Shandong sectarianism as "popular" and tending toward the "apolitical," but mentions no sects near Qingzhou. Esherick, *Origins of the Boxer Uprising*, 210–11.

> Their [sectarian] societies were self-supporting and self-managing. It occurred to me that the best way to make Christianity indigenous was to adopt Chinese methods of propagation.[55]

Richard's application of indigenous principles thus involved a conscious borrowing of practices from Chinese religious sects—quite a remarkable thing for a nineteenth-century Baptist missionary from Wales! But before looking at the precise nature of these sympathetic adaptations in his mission methods, it is necessary to look briefly at the many Western sources shaping Richard's interest in developing indigenous Christian churches.

4.3 Learning from Western Missionaries

While Richard learned much from his observation of Chinese religionists, he was also influenced by the larger expatriate Christian community in his pursuit of more sympathetic approaches to mission. In particular, "indigenous principles"—a catch-all phrase for mission methods that emphasized the creation of local churches that would be managed by local leadership, supported by local income, and actively engaged in carrying the gospel into their own communities—recommended themselves to Richard from a number of different directions.

Most immediately, circumstances at the time of Richard's arrival in China had forced him to accept a certain degree of local participation. The field he inherited from Laughton, where Pastor Zheng featured so prominently; the fruit he saw as he traveled out from Chefoo in the company of effective local evangelists; and especially his earlier successful attempt to encourage local fellowships to send out and support their own evangelists—these experiences encouraged him to believe that the application of similar ideas in a more intentional way was likely to be practicable and effective.

Secondly, many of these concepts had existed within the Protestant mission world for quite some time. Gathering threads and ideas that had been around since William Carey's days, Rufus Anderson of the ABCFM and Henry Venn of the Church Missionary Society had arrived at similar conclusions regarding the importance of indigenous principles in mission.[56] While Anderson tended to emphasize developing indigenous leadership and Venn focused on encouraging the self-support of local churches, both

---

55. Richard, *Forty-Five Years*, 107.

56. While they both arrived at the ideas independently and nearly simultaneously, Shenk is correct to point out that the concepts were not original to Anderson or Venn. Shenk, "Origins and Evolution," 28. Anderson was aware of this fact and seemed willing to share the credit for the ideas he helped popularize. Anderson, *Foreign Missions*, 111.

men were instrumental in promoting what became known as the "three-self principles": self-governing, self-supporting, and self-extending/propagating churches as the model for missions.[57] These three concepts quickly became popular foci for debate among missionaries of all affiliations. The China missions community during Richard's days actively engaged the topic, devoting large portions of the 1877 Shanghai GCPMC to discussing one or more of the three-self principles in their Chinese context.[58] While the discussion often touched on practical issues, and the consensus was in favor of putting the principles into practice, the absence of Chinese delegates at the 1877 Conference suggests that—at least in China at the time—the three-self principles were more theory than practice.

Thirdly, Timothy Richard was a Baptist. Nonconformity in Britain was composed of local believers who dissented from the interference of outsiders—especially the state—in their religious life. They knew that financial self-support was essential to the survival of their congregations, for there was no aid from any external source. In Wales especially, the nationalist (and indeed cultural) nature of this conflict with the established Church of England was explicit, and gave shape to Welsh notions of independence as well as Welsh religious order and practice. In his home while growing up, Richard witnessed his father's role in the care and ordering of local Baptist chapels, providing an example from his earliest days of the priority of the local and the indigenous in the community of faith—the bases of nonconformist life in Britain.

Finally, and for similar reasons, at the time of Richard's departure for China these concepts regarding local management and responsibility in church affairs were promoted within his own BMS in the persons of both Trestrail and Underhill, as mentioned in chapter 3 above. Whatever advice Trestrail gave Richard prior to his departure, Richard's experiences in China had already confirmed the value of seeking the worthy. At the same time, Underhill had also been speaking out in support of local participation in mission. Published after Richard's departure for China, Underhill's *The Principles and Methods of Missionary Labour* (1896), a compilation of shorter works written years previously, contains his most robust statement on indigenous principles.[59] While there is no indication that Richard had seen

---

57. For one of the earlier occurrences of the formulation, see Venn, *Retrospect and Prospect*, 5. Although Venn and Anderson both favored local churches choosing their own polity, Venn wanted those churches to be radically separated from all European influences. Wood, "John Livingstone Nevius," 30.

58. Yates, *Records of the GCPMC: Shanghai, 1877*, 283–334.

59. Key portions were originally composed in the 1850s, including the first two selections "On the Pastorate of the Mission Churches" and "On the Missionary and His

these compositions by the time he had moved to Qingzhou, it is reasonable to take their content as indicative of the kinds of advice Underhill might have passed on to Richard either directly prior to Richard's departure or more generally through his influence as Secretary of the BMS during Richard's first six years on the field.[60]

In his 14 January 1852 presentation to the BMS Committee in London, as recorded in his *Principles and Methods*, Underhill's concerns went beyond Trestrail's call for local pastors and addressed the cultural and intellectual differences that hindered the missionary's effectiveness at his or her task. Along the way, he defended the importance of locally appropriate manifestations of church life and devotion:

> May there not also be an unfavourable influence exercised by the presence of the European pastor, on the legitimate development of the Christian life? Piety, like learning, will have its characteristics in accord with the genius of the people. Its growth and expression will be marked by the leading peculiarities of the race among whom it finds a home. It may confidently be affirmed, that the piety of an Oriental will differ in some important particulars from that of a European.[61]

This sentiment is very similar to Richard's emphasis on the need for finding answers to specifically Chinese difficulties. Indeed, the portion of Underhill's address that deals with common objections to increased native agency relies heavily on the conviction that local Christians would be gifted for ministry, if only the Europeans would allow them opportunity to serve.[62] Retiring from his position as Secretary in 1876, Underhill would have found Richard's confidence in the wisdom and ability of the local Chinese believers as evidenced in his mission practices in Qingzhou to be most refreshing.

Richard's confidence can be seen, for example, in the ways he handled the thorny issue of payment for local church workers. In Qingzhou, Richard avoided establishing resident Chinese pastors salaried by the mission. On the contrary, he wrote, "The aggressive work among the heathen; the instruction of inquirers and church members in the stations, and

---

Work." Underhill, *Principles and Methods*, 25–53.

60. Unfortunately, whatever correspondence Richard may have exchanged with Underhill does not seem to have survived.

61. Underhill, "On the Pastorate of the Mission Churches: Presented at the Quarterly Meeting of the Committee of the Baptist Missionary Society, 14 January 1852" in *Principles and Methods*, 29. Underhill lists this presentation as having been made "by the Secretaries," which suggests that Trestrail at least agreed with the material it contained and may have had a hand in its authorship.

62. Underhill, *Principles and Methods*, 33–38.

the conducting of worship on Sunday, are for the most part attended to voluntarily by the Christians in the different stations."[63] At times, a small number of local Christians might be employed by the mission to assist with itinerant work visiting the various out-stations of the mission. As a rule, these would only be employed outside of their own counties, so as to avoid jealousy and dependence.[64]

This is not to say that Richard's reliance on Chinese colleagues was free from difficulty. Disputes over finances, questions over appropriate standards of living for itinerant Chinese evangelists, disciplinary issues involving moral failures—there was plenty to occupy Richard's attention. The goal for Richard was not merely to involve local people but rather to enable Chinese Christians to worship God in spirit and in truth. In the midst of a series of points addressing various aspects related to Chinese church workers in Shandong, Richard showed this concern:

> Rather than put the holy and tremendously responsible work of leading the church members in worship to the hands of young or frivolous men I would rather that they should have none to lead them lest that which is *holy be* cast to the dogs. Devout men alone can lead in the worship of God.[65]

Such sentiments would have been familiar to his Baptist constituents back home. What many of them might have found more surprising was his growing conviction that this purpose was best achieved by increasing the role of Chinese ministers and Chinese ideas in the mission.

4.4 Richard's Qingzhou Adaptations

Whether drawn from his observations of Chinese religious life, or reflecting the influence of any number of Western pastors and mission workers, the practices Richard employed in his Qingzhou mission marked a departure from what he and many others had done before. His move into the isolated interior gave Richard a blank canvas upon which he was free to sketch his own image of effective Christian mission. Having identified the audience for his evangelistic work most likely to produce fruit, it was

---

63. Nevius, "Mission Work in Central Shantung," CR 11, no. 5 (1880) 360–61. This article examines Richard's BMS work Qingzhou, supplying details not available elsewhere.

64. Nevius, "Mission Work in Central Shantung," CR 11, no. 5 (1880) 361.

65. Richard to Jones, 16 January 1878, pp. 2–3, BMSA CH/4. The list of difficulties related to Chinese church workers above was selected from the numerous examples found throughout this letter.

now time for him to develop his methods—to find locally acceptable answers to the things that prevented Chinese people from coming to faith in Christ. Methodologically, this would mean giving Chinese believers a larger stake in the work of evangelization.

Relocating to remote Qingzhou both enabled and forced Richard to engage more closely with Chinese cultural patterns, resulting in a telling transformation in his life and ministry. When Richard first arrived in Qingzhou in 1875, he was in the habit of wearing Western dress as he had done in the treaty port of Chefoo. Here, however, there were no other foreigners, and the curiosity engendered by his daily strolls through town produced more gawking than meaningful interactions. It soon occurred to Richard that he might "have more visitors of the better class if I wore Chinese dress. So one day I put on the native dress, shaved my head, and wore an artificial queue." The results were immediate, and he was gratified to overhear the onlookers during his afternoon stroll remark, "Ah! He looks like a man now." That very day he received his first invitation to tea in a Chinese home.[66] The comparative isolation of Qingzhou also meant that Richard's diet was now intensely local, though his relative wealth enabled him to eat most of his evening meals in an inn.[67] This afforded him the chance to keep up with local news as he conversed with townspeople over the table, as well as opportunities to engage in religious discussion—especially on the occasions when he dined at Muslim establishments. These discussions were greatly valued by Richard, and much of his traveling in the Qingzhou region was intended to create strategic encounters with various local religious—especially sectarian—leaders. Empowered by his newfound adaptability to Shandong life and culture, Richard was actively scouring the ranks of the Qingzhou religious in search of those who were worthy.[68]

This was a significant step in Richard's sympathetic acculturation to the Chinese local context. His transformations in attire, diet, and daily rhythms contained a tacit acknowledgment of the authority of the local people—the other—to determine what was normal and acceptable within their own context. By conforming to their patterns, Richard submitted to their standards.

Once established in Qingzhou, Richard commenced a study of the "popular religious books used by the devout sects. The most important of

66. Richard, *Forty-Five Years*, 78, 80. This idea was not original to Richard, but the transformation was nonetheless significant for him.

67. Richard's one concession was that he spread "foreign butter" on his breakfast millet cakes. Richard, *Forty-Five Years*, 82–83.

68. His autobiography recounts a number of these encounters (with Daoists, Muslims, Buddhists, sectarians), as well as the distances he traveled in order to secure audiences. See, for example, the journey outlined in Richard, *Forty-Five Years*, 86–94.

these was the 'King Shin Lu [*Jingxin lu*]' ('Record of Devout Faith'), a collection of the most popular Confucian and Taoist tracts in the language."[69] From these studies of Chinese religious texts as well as his own encounters with local religious leaders, Richard hit upon the idea of focusing his evangelistic work on appeals to Chinese consciences. In his many conversations, Richard had noticed that arguments dependent on the accepted authority of the Bible carried little weight with Chinese people for whom the Bible was not a known sacred book. On one occasion, while debating religion with the faculty and students of a nearby Islamic college, Richard struggled to make headway until some of his listeners cheered after his discussion of biblical ethics and Christian moral exemplars.[70] Richard thereafter adjusted his evangelistic arguments to address Chinese rather than Western concerns, employing a new form of apologetic wherein "I avoided the ordinary evidences of miracles and prophecy which I was taught to rely on in my theological training at home . . . [and] so I proceeded to dwell on the moral evidences."[71]

Surprisingly, Richard makes no mention at this point of his earlier studies of Joseph Butler, whose apologetic arguments also proceeded from the belief that moral evidences were evangelistically efficacious. In Part One of his *Analogy of Religion* Butler commenced his apologetic by establishing God's self-evident moral governance of the world before arguing that humankind's divinely-given moral faculty enabled all people to recognize this "moral system" of rewards and punishments, and to see them reflected perfectly in the Christian scriptures. In Part Two Butler then appealed to miracles and fulfilled prophecy to confirm the uniqueness of God's revelation in the Bible and thus the truthfulness of Christianity.[72] Using the same practical hermeneutic that shaped his reading of the Bible and his appropriation of Irving, Richard incorporated the first step of Butler's evangelistic argument—God's moral system—into his new apologetic, reflecting his success attracting Chinese attention through presentations of the superior Christian ethic. Butler's arguments in Part Two regarding miracles and prophecy, however, received far less attention from Richard. For many Victorians, scientific progress and the rise of biblical criticism had weakened their confidence in these lines of argument. Perhaps more significantly for Richard, Chinese religionists were unmoved by appeals to the uniqueness of Christian revelation.

69. Richard, *Forty-Five Years*, 86.
70. Richard, "Autobiography of the Author" in *Conversion by the Million*, 1:83–85.
71. Richard, "Autobiography of the Author" in *Conversion by the Million*, 1:85.
72. On Butler, see chapter 2 above. Butler, *Analogy of Religion* (1852) 319–20.

In response to his actual interactions with Chinese religious leaders, Richard was finding ways to present Christian truth that spoke directly to the needs and desires of Chinese people. As he explained:

> When I learnt that the Confucianists asserted that their Book of Changes was also the word of God, it was necessary to find something more convincing than the mere assertion that the Bible was the word of God. Then it was clearer than ever to me that our Lord Jesus Christ's method was not on these lines, but lay in appeals to conscience and reason . . . as evidenced in the Sermon on the Mount and the final judgment described in Matthew 25. . . . If we could excel the Chinese in charity to the sick, the poor, the suffering, and in giving education, then we should possess evidences which the Chinaman's conscience would approve and follow.[73]

The ever-pragmatic Richard was endeavoring to confront Chinese truth seekers with the simple idea that Christianity worked—that it excelled, or exceeded their own religions, in ways that were of practical merit. Contrasted with the greed and indifference he had found from many within China's religions, particularly within the Three Teachings, Richard was eager to demonstrate the superior worth of Christian love.

Without eschewing persuasive words, Richard was aware that actions could also be used to appeal to Chinese consciences. Medicine had been a part of Protestant missions in China since the very beginning: Robert Morrison had trained in medicine at St. Bartholomew's Hospital, and ABCFM missionary Peter Parker opened his Ophthalmic Hospital—the second Western medical institution in the land, and the first associated with a mission—in 1835.[74] Medical work soon became accepted as a valuable means by which to earn good will and increase opportunities for proper evangelistic work: influenced by W. H. Medhurst, James Hudson Taylor prepared for missions in China from the age of sixteen by training as a physician.[75] Early in 1874 Richard toured the Shandong promontory with BMS colleague Dr. Brown. As Dr. Brown healed the sick in the towns and villages they visited, Richard would "preach in the waiting room." Their journey took them through the village of Songcun where Richard had stayed prior

---

73. Richard, "Autobiography of the Author" in *Conversion by the Million*, 1:85.

74. British East India Company surgeon Thomas Richardson Colledge's 1827 Macao Ophthalmic Hospital was the first western medical institution. Anderson, "Peter Parker," 203–6.

75. Taylor engaged in medical work during his early years in China. Taylor and Taylor, *Story of the CIM*, 1:60, 138.

to the Temple Festival at Huilong Shan. The local innkeeper remembered Richard from before, and refused to accept any payment from his guests, explaining, "You have come here, giving medicine gratis to our people; it would be wrong to charge you for the night's lodging." Perhaps more significant to Richard, the man remembered their previous discussions about religion and said as they parted that he himself wanted to "have a share in doing good to people."[76] In this instance medical work had provided a clear demonstration of the validity of the moral claims of Christianity. Richard's convictions regarding the efficacy of combining words and actions to appeal to Chinese consciences would strengthen over time, especially after being tested during the North China Famine.

Brown's April 1874 exit from the BMS owing to "his refusal to engage in evangelistic work alongside medical work" was a disappointment to the mission community in Shandong.[77] At the time, the question of the relationship between the oral preaching of the word of God and so-called subsidiary means of evangelism was far from settled. For missionaries more influenced by Romantic spirituality, the suitability of relying on earthly means and provisions in the course of a life of ministry could become a matter of debate and anxiety: witness James Hudson Taylor's angst when offered a floatation device on his first voyage to China, or the conviction among some of the Cambridge Seven that Mandarin proficiency ought to be attainable without rigorous study.[78] This, however, was quite different from the matter of how much time, energy and resource should be spent on activities other than the telling of the gospel with words. Rufus Anderson, Secretary of the ABCFM, gave voice to the conservative position in a sermon preached in 1845.

> The object and work of the missionary are preeminently spiritual. . . . And the means he employs in this ministry of reconciliation, are as single and spiritual as the end he has in view. He preaches the cross of Christ. . . . [His] grand agent is oral instruction. . . . And now, perhaps not less than in the days of the apostles, the Holy Spirit appears to restrict his converting influences among the heathen chiefly to this species of agency.[79]

---

76. Richard, *Forty-Five Years*, 64–66.

77. Brown is also noteworthy as being "the first professional medical missionary to be sent by the BMS to any field." Stanley, *History of the BMS*, 181. Stanley, referencing later correspondence, says that Brown was recalled, while Williamson claimed that Brown resigned. Williamson, *British Baptists in China*, 33.

78. Taylor and Taylor, *Story of the CIM*, 102; Broomhall, *HTCOC*, 6:375–76.

79. Anderson, *Theory of Missions*, 8, 11. On Anderson and subsidiary means in the early ABCFM mission to China, see Kaiser, "S. Wells Williams," 70–76.

Dr. Brown's single-minded devotion to the practice of medicine challenged this viewpoint by suggesting that medical care in itself was sufficient to justify the support of a missionary. Despite Brown's absence and his own lack of training, Richard engaged in medical work in Qingzhou for typically pragmatic reasons: whether dispensing quinine for malarial complaints or administering chlorodyne against cholera, medical work saved lives and demonstrated the good will of the missionary.[80] The streams of people that came to Richard seeking help or as a result of help already received were evidence that this medical form of "doing good to people" was appealing to their consciences.

With these insights in mind, Richard began to adapt the literary aspects of his mission work as well.[81] In addition to translating Jeremy Taylor's *Holy Living* and James Walker's *Philosophy of the Plan of Salvation*, Richard prepared a catechism and a hymnbook.[82] For the catechism, Richard drew from various English and Welsh catechisms he was familiar with, all the while making "use of Chinese religious terms, instead of foreign ones, so as to make the gospel commend itself better to the Chinaman's conscience."[83] Here again the empathetic trajectory of Richard's acculturation was evident, as he laid aside transliterated Western terms in favor of words that resonated with Chinese readers. Though none of this literature has survived to enable a full analysis, in his autobiography Richard mentioned that he "translated" the foreign sounding name Jesus "and called him Saviour." His translation of *Philosophy of the Plan of Salvation* also suggests that he likely followed Legge, Medhurst, Muirhead and most of the British missionaries by using the "thoroughly Chinese" *shangdi* when rendering God's name in Chinese, taking advantage of its ties to ancient Chinese religious rites.[84] As he sought to make fuller use of Chinese religious terms within his own Christian texts Richard's study of Chinese religious texts and practices was proving invaluable. Although his catechism was composed primarily of

80. Richard, *Forty-Five Years*, 78–79.

81. For nineteenth-century Chinese scholarly reactions to Chinese Christian literature, see Starr, "Reading Christian Scriptures," 32–48.

82. On the two translated works, see the discussion in chapter 3 above. As with his catechism, no copies of Richard's hymnbook have survived.

83. This and the following quotations are taken from Richard, "Autobiography of the Author" in *Conversion by the Million*, 1:82. Richard does not mention precisely which catechisms he relied upon. Richard, *Forty-Five Years*, 94.

84. Legge, *Confucianism*, 3–4; Muirhead, *China and the Gospel*, 291–92. For a documentary history of the early Protestant "Term Question" debates surrounding the translation of the biblical words for God into Chinese, see Williams, "Controversy Among the Protestant Missionaries," 732–78. The best modern analysis is Eber, "Interminable Term Question," 134–61.

scripture quotations, Richard selected texts that he believed appealed to Chinese consciences, rather than those typically chosen as "proofs from a God-sent book." The thirty hymns that made up his hymnbook likewise were selected "because they appealed to the conscience of the non-Christian as soon as he heard them. . . . [T]hose which needed explanation" were excluded from the collection.

Richard also prepared some tracts for his use in and around Qingzhou. These were markedly brief, between six and eighteen characters each, with necessarily abbreviated content. Richard explained:

> In these tracts I endeavoured to follow the principle of our Lord in his marvelous parables, not to explain his sacred truths to the masses at large, but only to dwell on their importance and value. The interpretation was only given to those who had open minds.[85]

These tracts were also printed up as big character posters which Richard carried as he rode on horseback through each of the eleven cities within the prefecture of Qingzhou. Upon entering a new city, Richard would put up the posters on the city walls before retiring to an inn for a meal. Before long, he would be thronged by "parties of devout men coming to the inn kneeling before me and begging me to tell them what this wonderful Gospel was." By focusing on one idea, and then stressing its importance rather than trying to explain all in detail, Richard hoped to draw out the genuine truth seekers. As with the adjustments he made to his language, here too Richard was borrowing from local religious practices—in this case, by consciously imitating the sectarian habit of presenting truth as single, simple ideas.[86] As he explained, "It seems to me that single ideas propagate faster than many and with far greater intensity . . . the native sects turn on on [sic] one or two points discovery of the mystery of all, longevity, etc."[87]

Finally, Richard required all those who came to learn from him to memorize his books. Beginning with the catechism and hymnbook, inquirers were expected to memorize portions before being tested by himself, an evangelist, or a local Christian leader at a subsequent date. Learning by rote would have been familiar to Richard from his intimate experience with the Welsh education system, particularly during the

---

85. This and the following quotation are from Richard, "Autobiography of the Author" in *Conversion by the Million*, 1:83.

86. Nineteenth-century sectarian literature also adapted to incorporate Christian missionaries and their world into its narratives. Henry D. Porter, "Modern Shantung Prophet," *CR 18*, no. 1 (1887) 12–21; Jansen, "Sectarian Religions."

87. Richard to Jones, 16 January 1878, pp. 28–29, BMSA CH/4.

primary years. It is more likely, however, that his interest in employing memorization in the Chinese context was influenced by the great emphasis placed upon memorization through all levels of Chinese education, something he would have experienced personally through his own efforts to learn Chinese. Tellingly, this emphasis on learning texts by rote was also present in Chinese sectarianism. Richard quickly found that this greatly increased the speed at which people learned the basic truths of the gospel, even noting the effects of memorizing different scripture portions on the believers: "Those who had committed Ephesians to memory all became strong Calvinists. . . . Others who had committed the Gospel according to John to memory became lovable mystics."[88] This program of text memorization also had the added advantage of teaching people to value the literature of the Christians, all the while increasing literacy throughout the church. Knowing they would be tested on the materials in the books—and be forced to surrender materials they had not learned—inquirers and Christians alike were quick to form groups to aid in study during the times when the evangelists or missionaries were traveling elsewhere. Thus in one stroke, Richard raised the social status of the Qinzhou Christians—they were becoming literate—and created a church that organically developed its own native teachers and Sunday Schools.[89]

Taken together, Richard's early adaptations produced a method of mission that engaged in very little street preaching, but rather focused on influencing those individuals whom he identified as the worthy, employing "great pains . . . to convince the people that we are really interested in them, and desire their good."[90] While some Shandong missionaries such as Nevius and Mateer employed a pattern of regular, lengthy itinerations, typically lasting several months and covering hundreds of miles, Richard adopted a comparatively settled ministry which placed a priority on being available to meet with people. Perhaps as a reflection of his desire to enable Chinese people to witness Christian character in action for themselves, Richard's openness to receiving inquirers in his home was utilized to such a degree that it limited his ability to travel away from his home.[91] He did, of course, make regular trips into the surrounding countryside in search of worthy inquirers or to encourage new believers or church leaders, but these excursions were generally brief and limited to locations in and around Qingzhou.

88. Richard, *Forty-Five Years*, 106.
89. Richard to Jones, 16 January 1878, p. 6, BMSA CH/4; Richard, *Fifteen Years*, 12; Richard, "Autobiography of the Author" in *Conversion by the Million*, 1:81.
90. Nevius, "Mission Work in Central Shantung," *CR* 11, no. 5 (1880) 361.
91. Richard, "An Appeal from China," 234.

In the villages around Qingzhou, Christians were encouraged by Richard to set up their places of worship in the homes of individual believers; as such, these chapels tended to be simple and thus were able to proliferate quickly. In keeping with Richard's Baptist roots and his growing emphasis on empowering local leaders, Sunday services were generally conducted by the local Christians themselves, although visiting Chinese evangelists or preachers would be utilized from time to time.[92] With local Christian leaders entrusted with managing much of their own affairs—including evangelism in their communities—Richard focused his attention on equipping these new leaders. In order to make the most efficient use of his own time, Richard arranged for Christian leaders to visit him in Qingzhou at regular intervals to recite their memorized texts and receive further instruction. One of the larger of these trainings involved sixty Christian men from throughout the area, as well as a separate group of women leaders. In addition to instruction, Richard provided empty rooms for lodging during their few days stay in Qingzhou while the believers themselves supplied their own bedding, food, and travel expenses—some having come from as far as forty miles away.[93]

This emphasis on empowering locals suffused all the work of the mission:

> The duty is inculcated in those out-stations of all church members being learners and teachers at the same time. The foreign missionary or native pastor teaches the leaders or heads of the stations, and they teach the rest, and in general each one communicates what he or she knows to others less instructed. In the Baptist churches these leaders are collected together every month for receiving a day's instruction, and have lessons assigned to them for study, to be examined in at the next meeting. . . . Inquirers have put in their hand a catechism, some portion of the Scriptures, a hymn book, and forms of prayer, which they are to study, and upon which they are examined preparatory to baptism. Church members are expected to continue the study of the Scriptures, or manuals prepared for them, and are examined as to their progress in study whenever the missionary or native helper visits them.[94]

Expanding upon his early reliance on local evangelists in Chefoo, Richard's method in Qingzhou now empowered lay leaders to become trainers as well.

---

92. Nevius, "Mission Work in Central Shantung," *CR* 11, no. 5 (1880) 361–62.
93. Richard, *Forty-Five Years*, 106.
94. Nevius, "Mission Work in Central Shantung," *CR* 11, no. 5 (1880) 362.

Though rarely acknowledged by scholars, this highly independent mode of missionary work as pioneered by Richard in Qingzhou was the inspiration and model behind Nevius's influential 1886 *Methods of Mission Work*.[95] Nevius often stayed with Richard during his journeys into the Shandong interior, and was deeply impressed with the indigenous nature of the BMS work in Shandong, collecting and recording "hints and suggestions" for his own work during the visits.[96]

As Richard enlarged the role of local believers in the development and operation of the local church, he also worked to see moral evidences—his appeals to conscience—demonstrated in the actual life of the church. Just as medical work was supposed to demonstrate Christian goodwill, benevolent contributions from local Christians were encouraged as an indication not only of sacrificial devotion to God but also of a willingness to bless fellow human beings. For probationers, Richard required a year of "doing good" and making "contributions in aid of the orphan or destitute" as well as the more typical year of "devout attendance at the religious gatherings."[97] This same liberality was also to be extended toward the maintenance of the believers' fellowships. "In the Baptist churches, besides supplying and furnishing their own chapel, the Christians, after they are received into the church, buy their books, and some of them contribute money for printing books for distribution to others."[98] Richard had no hesitation making these financial demands on the new Christians, for he had already observed that within Chinese sectarianism, "They all propagate themselves more or less—they *all* subscribe in aid of their religion and the support of their teachers."[99] Not only were the sects self-supporting, but the followers understood the payment of regular dues to be a perfectly normal part of religious life—so much so that some of the leaders amassed fortunes from their sects.[100] Having witnessed self-support at work among Shandong sectarians, Richard was confident enough to write that "If any [Christian church communicants] asked for pecuniary help, we felt they had not got the love of God into their heart!"[101]

Never simply a means for economizing in the mission, this emphasis on financial contributions was part of Richard's larger drive to empower

---

95. Richard, *Forty-Five Years*, 107; Nevius, *Methods of Mission Work*.
96. Nevius, *Life of John Livingston Nevius*, 352–53.
97. Richard to Jones, 16 January 1878, p. 6, BMSA CH/4.
98. Nevius, "Mission Work in Central Shantung," *CR* 11, no. 5 (1880) 363.
99. Richard to Jones, 16 January 1878, p. 29, BMSA CH/4.
100. Richard to Jones, 16 January 1878, p. 4, BMSA CH/4.
101. Richard, *Fifteen Years*, 12.

local believers: in his mind increased Chinese financial participation necessitated greater local authority. When discussing the best means for maintaining and operating a Christian orphanage immediately following the North China Famine in Shandong, he explained,

> As we should expect the Chinese to support it they should have a share in the consultation about the best means of saving these helpless children from beggary, etc. No taxation without representation principle. This I believe would give greater satisfaction all around.[102]

In addition, Richard also saw Chinese financial participation as an example of the kind of Christian devotedness that would testify within Chinese society to the transforming power of the Christian gospel. The generosity of local believers was to function as yet another moral evidence of the superiority of Christianity—another means by which to appeal to Chinese consciences. Moreover, when this new attitude toward money was combined with empowered and committed participation in the work of the church, the results could be remarkable. Looking back on the church in Qingzhou just ten years later, Richard wrote,

> The instances of zeal and devotion and consecration of many of these Christians, not only in enduring persecution with patience, but in devoting their time and property, leaving their farms and their shops, and sometimes selling their very land in order to have means to go about to preach the Gospel, are simply astounding.[103]

Richard took this as a powerful affirmation of his adaptations, and convincing proof that the church could thrive and expand in the hands of Chinese believers.

Adjusting his methods in ways that prioritized the Chinese context as well as Chinese participants had resulted in precisely the kinds of evangelistic success Richard had originally sought. His combination of seeking the worthy, developing indigenous ministers, adjusting his language, dress and literary work to better match the local context, and appealing to Chinese consciences through moral evidences—all this was beginning to bear fruit. In just over a year, the Qingzhou mission had already baptized more than ten converts while caring for a total of over twenty communicants, all despite the absence of a central preaching chapel.[104]

102. Richard to Jones, 16 January 1878, pp. 24–25, BMSA CH/4.
103. Richard, *Fifteen Years*, 20–21.
104. Nevius, "Mission Work in Central Shantung," *CR* 11, no. 5 (1880) 357; Richard,

Richard's hopes for building upon this encouraging growth, however, were soon to be interrupted. Less than two years after his arrival in Qingzhou, Richard found himself on the front lines of a war against one of rural China's greatest foes: famine.

Forty-Five Years, 95–96. The recollections of Richard and Nevius differ, but the total number of new baptisms was no less than ten and no more than eighteen in the span of less than two years.

Part Two

Richard Encountering Famine

Application and Justification of His Missionary Thought

5

Practice Shaping Theory

Moral Evidences in the North China Famine

TIMOTHY RICHARD'S IMPRESSIVE RESPONSE to the suffering of the North China Famine cannot be understood apart from his evangelicalism and the trajectory of his empathetic acculturation to China. It was these two factors that compelled him in the midst of the disaster to provide practical relief while continuing to evangelize and build the local church. The success of both those endeavors, particularly the evangelistic effectiveness of his use of moral evidences, gave Richard great confidence in his adaptations, setting the stage for his brief period of theological reflection and justification that followed after the famine. For Richard, the disaster marked the watershed between practical mission experiments and confirmed theories of mission.

During the 1870s, regions of the globe as diverse as Australia, Brazil, and India came under the influence of an El Niño weather pattern that wrought devastating drought and famine across the world.[1] This extreme weather phenomenon was manifested in north central China with drought conditions across the five provinces of Shandong, Zhili (modern-day Hebei province), Henan, Shanxi, and Shaanxi. Owing primarily to the recent series of frontier wars and rebellions that had consumed imperial resources in the decades leading up to the drought, Qing treasury and grain reserves were at the time seriously depleted. The increasing expense of maintaining the imperial household as well as a political shift in the court in favor of external security over internal prosperity further contributed to a situation where the state was unable to respond to disaster as quickly and effectively as it had in the past.[2]

---

1. The global nature of this extreme weather event was observed (unintentionally) by former United States President U. S. Grant during his post-retirement world tour. Echoing Richard's subsequent advice to Chinese officialdom, Grant lectured Li Hongzhang on the importance of developing rail and telegraph systems, explaining that based upon the experience of the United States these could have helped prevent the famine disaster in China. See Davis, *Late Victorian Holocausts*, 1–6.

2. Bohr, *Famine in China*, 27–82; Edgerton-Tarpley, *Tears From Iron*, 28–39; 90–113.

The subsequent North China Famine lasted from 1876 to 1879, and became known in China as the *Dingwu qihuang* or "Incredible Famine of 1877–1878."[3] The devastation across the region during these years was shocking, resulting in the deaths of somewhere between nine and thirteen million people out of the combined population for the five affected provinces of 108 million people.[4] Writing in April 1878, the *London Times* correspondent in Shanghai reported that the North China Famine, "In its horrible details as given by all witnesses, foreign and native, official and missionary, . . . is the direst calamity that this or any country has been visited with."[5] When confessing the difficulty of recording the exact number of deaths that occurred during the North China Famine, the "Famine Administration" section of the *Shanxi Provincial Gazetteer* for the Guangxu reign period observed "*cheng zilai wei you zhi qi can ye* (there had never before occurred such extreme distress)."[6] Qing Dynasty officials referred to it as "*wei jian zhi can qi, wei wen zhi beitong* (distress unseen, and tragedy unheard of)" for over two hundred thirty years.[7]

In the late spring of 1875 drought symptoms began to appear in the imperial capital, soon spreading throughout Zhili and into Shandong province as well.[8] By the following spring, conditions in Shandong were especially dire. When the rains that were vital to the planting of the summer crops failed to materialize in already drought-stricken central Shandong, famine conditions

---

3. *Dingwu* is a conglomerate of the Heavenly Stem and Earthly Branch dates for 1877–1878, the most severe years of the famine. The English translation—often shortened to "Incredible Famine"—is from Edgerton-Tarpley, *Tears from Iron*, 1. Bohr's otherwise sensible adoption of the phrase "The Great Famine" to refer to the 1870s famine in North China (echoing the terminology of the various 1870s famine relief committees) is no longer practicable, since this same English term is now used for the 1958–1961 famine, known in Chinese as the *san nian da jihuang* (the great three-year famine). Note also that in many parts of southern Shanxi (where famine suffering was most acute) the event is still commonly referred to as *Guangxu san nian* referring to the third year of the Emperor Guangxu's reign (1877) when things were locally most difficult. For other Chinese nomenclature prevalent at the time, such as *Guangxu daqin* (Guangxu great assault), see Hao, "Shanxi 'Dingwu qihuang,'" 86. This thesis will follow Edgerton-Tarpley's practice, using "North China Famine" to refer to the 1870s disaster.

4. Watkins and Menken, "Famines in Historical Perspective," 650. This still broadly accepted estimated range for the total number of famine-related deaths comes from the official reports of the various famine relief committees at the time. China Famine Relief Fund Shanghai Committee, *Great Famine: Report*, 7.

5. As recorded in "Famine in China," *CM* (September 1878) 114.

6. From "huang zheng ji" in *Guangxu Shanxi tongzhi* [*Shanxi Provincial Gazetteer*], no. 82 as recorded in Gao and Chi, "Li Timotai zai 'Dingwu qihuang,'" 135 (translation mine).

7. Li, *Zhongguo jindai shi da zaihuang*, 81 (translation mine).

8. Li, *Zhongguo jindai shi da zaihuang*, 81–82 (translation mine).

began to appear.⁹ Public processions entreating rain became increasingly prominent and elaborate, with officials wearing chains in symbolic humiliation and joining with villagers in the penitential abstention from meat. The rains still did not come; food became scarce and acts of violence became more common. The number of beggars grew daily and robberies increased to such a level that any kind of travel became dangerous.¹⁰ The provincial gazette for that year summarized the situation with the four simple characters *da han min ji*: "massive drought, starving people."¹¹

As Shandong governor Ding Baozhen acknowledged in his report to the Emperor on the situation in his famine-stricken province, the suffering in the area around Qingzhou was so severe it was unbearable to describe.¹² In the winter months pits were dug in the eastern suburbs of Qingzhou where people would huddle together in groups of up to fifty persons for warmth. Within six weeks two hundred forty of these desperate souls had perished, their places rapidly taken by others.¹³ In Linzi County toward the west of Qingzhou it was claimed that one hundred thousand women and children had been sold in order to provide money to feed their remaining family members.¹⁴ According to Richard's own estimates, of the roughly two or three million people starving in Qingzhou Prefecture, by March 1877 over half a million had perished.¹⁵

5.1 Missionary Identification and the Famine

These and other symptoms of famine distress were quickly recognized by Richard, and presented him with a real dilemma. As incidents of violence escalated through the spring and into the summer of 1876, Richard's Chinese coworker suggested that they flee to the relative security of coastal Chefoo as soon as possible. But for the young man who grew up in the farming country of rural Wales, the existential issue outweighed concerns

---

9. Hao et al., "1876–1878 nian Huabei da han," 2322–24.

10. These details are from a 19 August 1876 letter written by Timothy Richard while in Chefoo, and published in December as "China," 246. See also *NCH* 17, no. 480 (22 July 1876) 70–71.

11. As quoted in Li, *Zhongguo jindai shi da zaihuang*, 83 (translation mine).

12. Li, *Zhongguo jindai shi da zaihuang*, 84.

13. J. H. Ferguson, "Famine in Shantung," *NCH* 18, no. 515 (22 March 1877) 303.

14. Morse, *International Relations*, 2:309 n. 8.

15. From *WGGB* (17 March 1877), as recorded in Li, *Zhongguo jindai shi da zaihuang*, 84.

for personal safety—no matter how real the danger. Ten years later, Richard recalled his reaction and response to his colleague's proposal.

> Here was the crisis. Should I go away to save my life, or should I remain to do what I could at all risks? Had many of these poor people any more sin than I, that they should perish and I should live? I vowed that night that I would share the last I had before leaving them, and then would only go away to seek for further help. God seemed to accept the vow.[16]

The next morning, Richard set himself to aid those in his community who were suffering the most, marking the beginning of his influential involvement with relief efforts during the North China Famine.

For the two years leading up to the famine Richard had been living in the geographically isolated interior of Shandong. Substantial portions of his missionary career up to this point had been spent working as the sole representative of his society, while during his years in Qingzhou he was the only expatriate missionary of any agency resident in the region. As a young single man traveling, living, and working closely with Chinese Christians throughout rural Shandong, his experience of Chinese people and their way of life was intimate and highly participatory. Perhaps also drawing on his own experiences growing up on a farm in Wales, it was not difficult for Richard to imagine himself in the place of the Qingzhou famine sufferers.

Timothy Man-kong Wong notes that Richard's activities during the famine reflected his "passionate identification with his contemporary China at the material dimension as well as the political-economic dimension."[17] Richard had by this time adopted local dress, and was eating local food—often at local inns; his facility with the language, his familiarity with local religious life, and his close cooperation with Chinese Christian workers further contributed to the overall impression of a foreign missionary whose sense of identification with the Chinese people in his community was unusually high for his time.[18] Compelled to take action by this strong sense of identification with the people suffering around him, Richard's own intimate experience of the famine through both his presence and his labors on the victims' behalf only deepened his empathy.

---

16. Richard, *Fifteen Years*, 13.

17. Wong, "Timothy Richard," 54; for Wong's discussion of missionary identification, see pp. 51–52.

18. In this respect, the contrast between the manner of Richard's life and work in Shandong at this time and that of the LMS central China field is striking. See the analysis of Griffith John and his LMS colleagues throughout Bonk, *Theory and Practice*.

The traumatic scenes of suffering observed by Richard as he went about relief work—work that he claimed "cost me so much peril of life"—are difficult for modern readers to conceive.[19] Through the publication of portions of his famine diaries in the *North China Herald*, Richard revealed harrowing scenes of cannibalism, human trafficking, death, and violence to a wide audience that could not help but share his sympathies.[20] The traumatic effect of these sights on Richard's psyche can be seen in his own reflections written at the time.

> [A]s it was, such scenes as I have not half described, and such tales as I cannot venture to do more than hint at, repeated daily, and several times in the day, too, made me afraid almost to mention the subject. It was like re-opening a painful wound to me.[21]

The intense, macabre nature of scenes such as Richard and his companion waving their arms and crying out to frighten wild dogs away from feeding on the famine corpses strewn by the side of the road, evoked images of the battlefield as much as natural disaster. When trying to describe the suffering of the North China Famine to a British audience a few years later, Richard resorted to a martial analogy: "Think of all the horrors of the destruction of Jerusalem, and those of the most desperate sieges recorded in history. And extend that over hundreds and thousands of towns and villages, and then you will have some conception of it."[22] The volume of death witnessed, not to mention the undoubted recognition of many of the dead from his years in Qingzhou, created in Richard's mind a deep-seated

---

19. When forced to leave Shanxi in the late 1880s, this was how Richard recalled the famine-related founding of the Shanxi mission. Richard to Glover, 2 August 1887, BMSA CH/2. The copy of this letter that exists in the BMS Archives is most likely incorrect in its claim that Richard Glover's more famous son Terriot Reaveley (T. R.) Glover was the intended recipient, rather than the father. Although T. R. Glover did remember Richard's visits to their family home with fondness, the serious tone of the letter combined with the fact that T. R. Glover was at the time only seventeen years of age make it unlikely that Timothy Richard was writing to the younger Glover. For T. R. Glover's recollections, see Soothill, *Timothy Richard of China*, 151.

20. The text of Richard's winter 1878 tour of southern Shanxi as recorded in his 1916 autobiography differs from that originally printed in the *North China Herald* newspaper. The later autobiographical account emphasizes the narrative and its dramatic elements, while the newspaper account has the feel of a statistical catalog of events intended to persuade. It is possible that both the autobiographical and newspaper accounts were purpose-suited reworkings of an original diary no longer extant. Richard, "Shansi Famine," 296–98; Richard, *Forty-Five Years*, 129–34.

21. Both this quotation and the following encounter with the wild dogs are from Richard, "Shansi Famine," 296–98.

22. Richard, *Fifteen Years*, 15.

compassion—no doubt mingled with the nightmarish visions that were not soon (if ever) forgotten—that found expression in his commitment to prevent such a thing ever happening again.

Richard's famine experiences pushed his acculturation still further along its Chinese trajectory. In the aftermath of his famine work, Richard published an essay in the main periodical of the China mission community wherein he challenged his colleagues to recognize the essentially Chinese nature of the task before them. In his passionate conclusion, he called on his fellow workers to rise to the call, proclaiming "we will guard against the insidious but wicked habit of running down the Chinese, we will give them fair play, we will make ourselves acquainted with all they value highest."[23] For Richard, effective mission required a deep respect for the Chinese context wherein he and his colleagues were serving—a serious commitment to a form and method of mission that was sensitive to Chinese realities. While visible in his early emphasis on the practice of indigenous principles in mission, Richard's commitment to the Chinese context was strengthened powerfully during the North China Famine. For when the world around him was overwhelmed by famine, Richard's sense of identification meant that Chinese concerns became his concerns, and therefore a quite natural part of his mission for China; and so Richard took action to help.

5.2 Famine Relief Work

Isolated in Shandong's interior and thus removed from the larger foreign community, Richard adopted letter writing as a convenient means for soliciting the funds he so desperately needed to save the people around him from starvation.[24] His life-long penchant for education revealed itself again, as he sought to inform his readership, which quickly and intentionally expanded to include foreign and Chinese readers of various newspapers in the West and in China. Western readers in the Chinese treaty ports and across the oceans were moved by the famine-related reports from Richard and others in the *North China Herald*, *Celestial Empire*, the *Times*, or the various mission periodicals such as the Baptist *Missionary Herald* and the CIM's new *China's Millions*, resulting in donations being sent around the world to support the foreign-run relief efforts. Public subscriptions in the treaty

---

23. Richard, "Thoughts on Chinese Missions," 440.

24. For an example of one such letter—a first-hand account of the famine-related suffering of the communities around Qingzhou—see Richard, "Famine in Shantung," 129–32.

ports and in Hong Kong raised thirty-six thousand taels (ounces of silver) or roughly £10,000 for the Shandong famine relief effort.[25]

In the coastal cities of China, reports by Richard in various Chinese-language periodicals, including the *WGGB* and the more broadly read Shanghai-based *Shenbao*, produced some Chinese donations for the foreign famine projects as well. While the funds generated for foreign relief efforts through the Chinese-language press were small, the written articles themselves had a significant impact on non-governmental Chinese relief work.[26] Details of the methods and motivations of Western relief efforts during the North China Famine provided a suggestive introduction to the practical application of Western values such as transparency and efficiency.[27] In this sense, the famine, its domestic causes, and in particular Richard's activities during and after the famine played a much more significant role in the formation of the late Qing Chinese reformers than is typically acknowledged by Chinese historians.[28] With his reports reaching so many concerned readers—both foreign and Chinese—Richard then made use of the good will and donations generated by these propaganda efforts to support his personal participation in the famine relief efforts. For Richard, this work fell into three broad categories.[29]

Initially, Richard's relief efforts in the famine districts were as simple as distributing from his own personal funds to those around him who were in need. In a drought-induced famine, not only is food scarce, but also the further planting of crops fails to produce new resources. In agrarian societies, this means the destruction of people's livelihoods, leaving them without means to generate the income by which they might hope to buy what little food may have been imported from elsewhere. Even a modest rise in food prices could be devastating to a farmer who due to drought conditions had lost his primary means of earning money. In Shanxi, grain prices peaked in the spring of 1878, reaching levels that according to local gazetteers "*heng*

---

25. From the *Parliamentary Papers*, China, no. 2 (1878) as reported in Foster, *Christian Progress in China*, 220.

26. Janku, "Sowing Happiness," 100–105.

27. On the *Shenbao*'s coverage of the North China Famine, see Edgerton-Tarpley, *Tears from Iron*, 142–55. Edgerton-Tarpley is correct to observe that the *Shenbao*'s reportage on the famine, including their publication of Richard's reports, seems to have been advancing the interests of China's self-strengthening clique—a suggestive connection, given Richard's later role in the reform movement.

28. Janku, "Drought in Northwest China."

29. For a detailed review of Richard's specific relief activities, see: Bohr, *Famine in China*, 81–94, 102–28.

gu wei you (had never occurred before)."[30] This is one of the reasons why the famine in southern Shanxi was particularly severe. Accordingly, as the famine developed—and as the foreign response expanded—the distribution of funds to famine victims remained the primary means of relief provided by Richard and his fellow missionaries.

Distribution, however, was never as simple as it sounded. Worsening conditions meant an increase in violence toward aid workers, but also between different groups of famine victims: Richard's proximity to the execution ground in Qingzhou provided regular reminders of the range of human cost associated with famine. His own life was often at risk as he traveled and distributed aid, and on two separate occasions he was implored by large groups of people to lead a rebellion against the local officials.[31] The same desire for effective results that drove his pursuit of better evangelistic methods led Richard—more so than his fellow missionaries—to experiment with creative ways to distribute aid while ensuring public safety and fair distribution, including advance home inspections, chit distributions, and various hand-marking systems. Unfortunately, as his efforts to alleviate suffering became well known, distribution became increasingly problematic as the sheer numbers of victims invariably overran his meager means. When Richard's personal funds were exhausted, he risked bandits and mobs of starving farmers and traveled to the provincial capital to intercede with the governor of Shandong on behalf of those suffering in Qingzhou. He then headed for Chefoo to publicize further the needs of the famine victims among the wealthy expatriates. A relief committee was quickly formed within the foreign community, and Richard returned to Qingzhou to distribute the monies raised by himself as well as those entrusted to him by others.

In addition to financial distributions, Richard also established orphanages—a common expression of Victorian evangelical activism—for the many children dislocated or orphaned by the famine. Richard began accepting abandoned and disadvantaged children into his care at least as early as winter 1876–1877.[32] To care for these children, Richard used a portion of the money collected from the foreign community in Chefoo to establish five different orphanages of about one hundred children each spread across the hard-hit Yidu and Linqu counties of the Qingzhou region.[33] More than just

---

30. As recorded in Hao and Zhou, "'Dingwu qihuang' shiqi de Shanxi liangjia," 85–86 (translation mine).

31. Richard declined both requests. Richard, *Forty-Five Years*, 100, 103.

32. He described his acquisition of three such boys in Richard, "Famine in Shantung," 131–32.

33. The locations are given in "Xi jiaoshi quan juan shu bing shanzuo zaimin qingxing [Western Missionary Appeals for Donations and the Shandong Famine Victims'

food and a bed, Richard's orphanages also provided the boys between the ages of twelve and eighteen with training in traditional local employments such as "smith-work, carpentering, silk-weaving, [and] cord-making" in the hopes that this might secure their future livelihoods.[34] Once the immediate famine danger had passed, the orphanages were closed and the children returned to what remained of their extended families who were no longer so desperate that they could not feed an extra mouth. Revealing once again his indigenous priorities, Richard discussed in a letter to a colleague at the time that this decision was based on the simple fact that he saw little value in maintaining an orphanage if it was neither supported by local Christians, nor managed by them.[35] While suspicion of the reasons behind his interest in the famine orphans at times created difficulties in the local communities, Richard considered this work important enough that he continued it again following his subsequent move to Shanxi.[36]

Finally, Richard demonstrated a willingness from the very beginning of the famine to cooperate with Chinese officials. Certainly, he obeyed government instructions regarding relief distribution whenever given: at one point the number of starving in Qingzhou grew so large, and their condition so desperate, that the magistrate issued a proclamation forbidding private distribution of funds for fear of riots. Richard complied.[37] Similarly, Richard sought approval and guidance from the Shanxi governor Zeng Guoquan before distributing relief funds in that province.[38] In both cases, his obedience subsequently earned him further opportunities to provide assistance. As an organic outgrowth of his empathetic identification with those suffering from the famine and the encouragement he received from his experiences respecting and cooperating with Chinese officials in his earliest relief activities, Richard soon began to advocate various reform measures that he believed would ensure that future droughts would fail to reproduce the acute famine conditions of the 1870s. In the summer of 1876 Richard met with the prefect of Qingzhou to encourage him to memorialize the Emperor requesting the opening of free grain trade with Japan and Korea, as eliminating

---

Situation*]," *WGGB* (14 April 1877), as cited in Zhang, "Xifang xinjiao chuanjiaoshi," 22.

34. Richard, *Forty-Five Years*, 109–10.

35. Richard to Jones, 16 January 1878, pp. 20–24, BMSA CH/4.

36. For one example of such difficulties, see Richard, "Rev. Timothy Richard," 7–8. Fears surrounding child kidnapping and orphanages were a longstanding anti-Christian trope in imperial China. Ter Haar, *Telling Stories*, 152.

37. Richard, *Forty-Five Years*, 101–2.

38. Richard's letter dated 11 December 1877 as reprinted in his "China Famine," 99–100.

tariffs would result in lower prices.[39] Once conditions began to improve in Qingzhou in the spring of 1877, and then again from nearly the beginning of his time in Shanxi, Richard actively encouraged government officials to consider practical reforms including building railroads for grain transportation and promoting drought-immune industries such as mining—all in order to prevent future droughts from becoming famines.[40] As will be discussed in chapter 6 below, this aspect of his work would become increasingly important in the years following the famine in Shanxi.

Recent scholars have been quick to point out that despite the attention it garnered at the time, the actual foreign contribution to the overall relief effort was quite small. While private Chinese philanthropy was not insignificant, for the victims of the North China Famine, survival was ultimately a matter of securing access to the massive government relief effort.[41] One Chinese scholar has argued that the warm response to the missionary message that often followed in the wake of the foreign relief effort owed less to the small amounts of financial aid distributed than to the access to divine assistance that the missionaries supposedly represented. With the local community's faith in the state and their local deities exhausted by the extreme conditions of the famine, the sudden appearance of the missionaries offered a lifeline for which many were grateful.[42] In practical terms, the scale of the official relief program as well as the ability of the state so effectively to advance or restrict his own relief efforts further impressed upon Richard the importance of seeking official support or at least approval for any scheme that sought to transform the nation. But these same facts also demonstrate that Richard's respectful interactions with officials of various levels—whether seeking increased fund distribution during the famine or the adoption of reform measures to prevent future suffering after the famine—represented a clever, effective, and locally appropriate strategy calculated to improve material conditions for the people of North China.

In light of all Richard did during the North China Famine, both in Shandong and later in Shanxi, Richard earned a reputation as "the Founder

39. Richard, *Forty-Five Years*, 99.

40. Richard, *Forty-Five Years*, 121–22, 136–37. See, for example, Richard's brief pamphlet *Fu jin xin gui*.

41. On the central importance of the government effort, with special attention to Shanxi, see Hao, "Guangxu chu nian Shanxi zaihuang"; and Gao and Chi, "Li Timotai zai 'Dingwu qihuang,'" 135.

42. Yuan, "'Dingwu qihuang' zhong chuanjiaoshi," 102. Especially in the isolated communities of rural southern Shanxi, the foreign missionary may indeed have appeared as a *deus ex machina* sent for the people's almost magical deliverance.

of 'Famine Relief' in China."[43] While not unwarranted, this statement requires clarification. As the famine spread across North China, many others joined in the relief work on the front lines as well as in the treaty ports. Richard's friend John Nevius quickly assumed responsibility for distribution in the nearby region of Gaoya to the south of Qingzhou.[44] Corbett and Mateer eventually joined Richard and Nevius in working to alleviate famine suffering across Shandong, while various Chinese and foreign committees soon rose up to solicit funds to support the relief efforts of Richard and the others.[45] By the time Richard commenced relief work in Shanxi, many missionaries from a variety of agencies were engaged in front-line relief work across the five affected provinces.[46] David Hill (Wesleyan Methodist Missionary Society or WMMS), Joshua Turner (CIM) and Albert Whiting (APM) in particular provided early assistance to Richard in remote Shanxi. Over and above these foreign efforts, Chinese philanthropists were also engaged at varying levels. And yet all these works were subsidiary to the massive state-sponsored programs aimed at alleviating suffering, using techniques and procedures that had been honed over centuries of famine-fighting experience. In this light, Richard's role—though perhaps larger than the other foreigners—was indeed small.

If Richard deserves any exemplary credit for his work during the North China Famine, it must be confined to three areas where his contributions, though small, were significant. First, Richard was one of the earliest foreigners to engage in direct relief in both Shandong and Shanxi. In this sense, he truly was a foreign "pioneer" of famine relief work in China, and

43. Evans, *Timothy Richard*, 60. Bohr appears to sympathize with this view of Richard, although preferring the language of "pioneer" in more recent writings. Bohr, *Famine in China*, 126–28; Bohr, "Legacy of Timothy Richard," 78.

44. Nevius, *Life of John Livingston Nevius*, 318–33. The rest of the foreign community did not necessarily share Richard's attitude toward the famine. For an indication of the variety of opinion within the foreign community, see Edgerton-Tarpley, *Tears from Iron*, 114–30.

45. Prior to the establishment of the overarching Shanghai Committee of the China Famine Relief Fund, a Shandong-specific committee had existed in Shanghai (largely created in response to Richard's accounts of suffering in Qingzhou) as well as a smaller Chefoo-based foreign committee and a Chinese-run Kiangsu Relief Fund based in Qingzhou itself. Bohr, *Famine in China*, 89–91, 92–93.

46. Although it only refers to the latter period of the famine (hence, the work of Richard, Nevius, and others from 1876–1877 is not included), there is a list of the names of Protestant missionaries engaged in relief work on behalf of the Shanghai Committee arranged according to province in China Famine Relief Fund Shanghai Committee, *Great Famine: Report*, 157. This same page contains a note stating that "upwards of 40" Roman Catholic missionaries were also engaged in relief work during the North China Famine.

was thus viewed by many of his peers as the leader of their efforts. Second, Richard did much to publicize the dire nature of the disaster, especially during its earliest phase—both across the English-speaking world and within the limited scope afforded by the growing Chinese press. He was personally responsible for increasing both awareness of the devastation and financial support for its alleviation, and the letters which helped achieve this admirable result were one reason why so many at the time associated his name with famine relief in China. Finally, Richard's experiments in the techniques of famine relief were his own, and were more extensive than those of the other missionaries; to the degree that they were successful and employed by others, he deserves credit for their development. For these reasons, as well as what R. J. Forrest called "his great tact and power of organization," it was not wholly inappropriate for Richard to be singled out for praise in one of the famine relief committee's reports.

> It would be invidious to make any distinction in recording the services of this devoted band [of relief workers], but Mr. Richard, whose Chinese name, Li Ti-mo-t'ai, is known far and wide among all classes of natives, stands out so prominent that he must be regarded as chief of the distributors.[47]

5.3 Evangelism During the Famine

Richard did not begin his career as a missionary in China with the expectation that he would be engaged in caring for people's physical needs. As Gao Pengcheng and Chi Zihua observe, "disaster relief was not the reason Timothy Richard came to China, evangelism (*chuanjiao*) was his initial motivation."[48] And yet, the actual practice of engaging in famine relief did not represent a radical theological departure for Richard. Neither the result of an all-or-nothing choice to engage in relief work rather than evangelism, nor the expression of a preference for material provision over spiritual conversion, Richard's personal participation in alleviating the physical suffering

---

47. This is taken from Forrest's report to the Tianjin relief committee following a tour of Shanxi at the very end of the famine. Forrest's comment regarding Richard's popularity with local people is particularly impressive, though just how "far and wide" Forrest's journeys in Shanxi would have taken him is questionable. R. J. Forrest, "Report of R. J. Forrest," *CM* (November 1879) 138. Note also that this accolade to Richard was printed in Taylor's CIM publication *China's Millions*, suggesting that at this point Taylor had no animosity toward Richard.

48. Gao and Chi, "Li Timotai zai 'Dingwu qihuang,'" 132. Gao and Chi describe the relationship between Richard's evangelistic and relief efforts as "interlaced, interwoven and organically integrated." Gao and Chi, "Li Timotai zai 'Dingwu qihuang,'" 133.

that accompanied famine was an "organic" development of his empathetic identification with the people around him as well as of his convictions as an evangelical missionary: this was compassionate, evangelical activism in practice. The North China Famine merely provided a new context for the application of the understanding of mission Richard had been developing since his first arrival in China.

Rather than resenting relief work as a distraction from the more typical work of the mission, Richard came to see the famine as yet another chance to work with the kinds of moral evidences he had found to be so important during his early years in Qingzhou. Christian participation in famine relief work not only provided a model of precisely the sort of ethical action that he expected from members of the local church;[49] participating in famine relief work also presented an excellent opportunity to "excel the Chinese in charity to the sick, the poor, the suffering," thus producing more of the moral evidences which Richard had come to believe were essential to evangelizing the Chinese worthy.[50]

Shortly after he began personally to distribute his own funds, Richard decided to give some of his limited resources to the most needy of the scholars in the surrounding area. By presenting these moral evidences to a particularly resistant sector of society, Richard hoped to begin to break down literati opposition to Christianity.[51] Alleviating their very real poverty (lower-level scholars typically struggled to earn money to feed their families) while also demonstrating that the Christian God cared even for those who were committed to other philosophical systems also showed sensitivity to local concerns by mirroring cultural ideals that favored support for impoverished scholars. Guided by his identification with and participation in the community, Richard was able to meet locally perceived needs in ways that honored local social structures. By acting out of his awareness of his situatedness in rural Shandong—rather than from the standpoint of his identity as a foreigner—Richard revealed "his ingenuity, determination, and concern for the Chinese as they were rather than as evangelicalism demanded they become."[52] Revealing once again his empathetic prioritizing of the Chinese context, Richard was now developing through his relief work moral evidences that were designed to appeal to specifically Chinese consciences.

49. Recall Richard's requirement, discussed in chapter 4 above, that probationers engage in "doing good" and making "contributions in aid of the orphan or destitute" before being accepted into full membership. Richard to Jones, 16 January 1878, p. 6, BMSA CH/4.

50. Richard, "Autobiography of the Author" in *Conversion by the Million*, 1:85.

51. Richard, *Forty-Five Years*, 110–11.

52. Treadgold, *West in Russia and China*, 59.

On the surface, Richard's emphasis on the moral aspects of the gospel appears to follow larger changes taking place within British Protestantism at the same time. Anglican missionary J. W. Colenso's gospel of liberation, John Seeley's presentation of Jesus as a good-intentioned moralist in his anonymously published *Ecce Homo*, and Oxford professor Max Müller's 1873 call for missionaries that would seek to influence through moral behavior rather than creedal formulas were all indicative of the emphasis on the ethical that was a hallmark of the broad church movement in the 1870s and 1880s.[53] However, the generally traditional nature of the Haverfordwest curriculum during Richard's years in attendance, his attraction to the staunchly evangelical CIM during the late 1860s, his relative isolation in China from 1869 through to his 1885 furlough, and the total lack of references to higher criticism in his writings throughout these years, all suggest that this was not a primary influence on Richard. Rather, beginning with the exigencies of his circumstances, Richard found a method that simply worked. The fact that during the famine he was reading Joseph Butler, as well as the equally morally concerned *Essays* of Francis Bacon, suggests that there may indeed have been influences shaping this innovation other than the demands of the missionary context.[54] However, unlike with Irving and the worthy, Richard did not give Butler (much less Bacon) credit for inspiring his new method.

Without downplaying the theological relationship between effective evangelism and the moral evidences which Richard found so compelling, Richard's persistent interest in evangelism throughout the Shandong famine must also be recognized as a natural outgrowth of the fact that Richard and his Chinese coworkers were still responsible for maintaining the work of the church during the period of suffering. Richard did not cease to be a missionary while engaged in famine relief; and the mission—and in particular the growing number of local believers and teachers associated with the mission—continued to develop in the midst of the famine. The daily schedule Richard set for himself in 1876 gives an indication of his commitments, precisely when the famine was most severe in Shandong.[55]

---

53. Brown, *Providence and Empire*, 238–44.

54. On Richard's reading habits during the famine, see the following paragraph. In the 1870s Bacon and his inductive method—with which Richard was clearly sympathetic—were already being presented to Chinese scholars by LMS missionary William Muirhead and others through the burgeoning Chinese-language press. Kurtz, *Discovery of Chinese Logic*, 97–101.

55. Richard, *Forty-Five Years*, 110. While this schedule no doubt reflects an ideal to which Richard strived, his reputation for industry and discipline suggests that his actual practice may not have fallen too short of his expressed goal.

7:30–8 a.m.	Breakfast.
8–8:30	Worship.
8:3–10	Translation of English into Chinese.
10–12:30	Teaching of inquirers or preaching.
12:30–2 p.m.	Overseeing of orphans, teaching Sol-fa music, etc.
2–5	Translation into Chinese.
5–7	Miscellaneous work, walk, and dinner.
7–8	Church history in English.
8–8:20	Chinese worship.
8:20–9	"Bacon's Essays" and Butler.
9–10	Conversation with teachers.

Despite the famine and Richard's personal involvement in alleviating its deprivations, the schedule he set for himself is tied to the rhythms of church and mission. While "overseeing orphans" and "miscellaneous work" no doubt brought him into direct contact with the realities of famine relief, he continued to devote large parts of each day to working on Chinese translation and the production of written materials for the use of local believers. Significantly, worship alone or with Chinese colleagues as well as the teaching and training of local teachers and inquirers punctuated his day, clear evidence that while Richard may not have been standing on the street corners preaching—though his placards were evident in many village squares—he continued to urge the people around him to accept the gospel and to live it out more faithfully, even as he sought to deliver them from physical suffering.

This overarching ministry context also helps explain Richard's persistent willingness to interpret the famine spiritually. Given Richard's evangelical upbringing, his conversion during the mid-century Welsh revivals, and his strong roots in nonconformist ministry, it should come as no surprise that one of Richard's first acts when confronted with the threat of famine was to exhort people to pray. In response to imperial commands, officials in the drought-affected regions across North China wrapped themselves in penitential chains, ordered everyone to abstain from meat, and led processions to local temples to call on their gods for rain.[56] Richard

---

56. Beijing officials were doing so as early as December of 1875. "Abstract of Peking

responded by writing a brief eighteen-word tract copying the form of the yellow placards used in local intercessory processions. The content of his message was simple: "that repentance for sin and kind deeds to each other were more acceptable to God than all fasting from meats; that prayer to the true God, and firm resolve to learn all His ways, were better than all their prayers to the other gods combined."[57] In these efforts to encourage people to "pray to God instead of idols," Richard was heartened by the earnestness with which the petitioners inquired of him "How shall we pray?"[58] More encouraging still, many were willing publicly to heed his warnings, with on at least one occasion "a thousand men, including women and children" kneeling with Richard in prayer for rain.[59]

Soothill's 1924 attempt to excuse Richard's faith in divine intervention as an outdated folly—"In those days we all still believed in praying for rain"— reflects Soothill's own biases rather than any theological proclivities on Richard's part.[60] Reflecting on this period in his 1916 autobiography, Richard recalled that on at least two occasions local Christians in and around Qingzhou independently led groups of villagers to pray to the Christian God for rain, prompting Richard with "joy to record the fact that, despite the sneers of the sceptics, rain did fall in both instances."[61] The fact that Richard published these thoughts only eight years prior to Soothill's biography suggests that doubts about the efficacy of prayer were Soothill's and not Richard's. On the contrary, Richard believed that even his material efforts during the famine were of spiritual significance. As he explained to his mother, ministry in one sphere could produce fruit in the other:

Gazettes, Dec. 17," *NCH* 33, no. 453 (13 January 1876) 30.

57. Richard, *Fifteen Years*, 12. Notice Richard's use of moral evidences, as seen in his first clause's juxtaposition of repentance and "kind deeds" with local notions of piety (vegetarianism).

58. Richard, "China," (1876) 246; Richard, *Forty-Five Years*, 97–98. Without Richard's early diaries for comparison, it is impossible to know if the account of this event in his later autobiography represents an idealized dramatization of the event as recorded in this letter reprinted in the *Missionary Herald*, or a more faithful transcription of a (now missing) full diary entry that was edited and condensed into the letter reprinted in the *Missionary Herald*. The later version claims that Richard exhorted the people to "turn from dead idols to the living God and pray unto him and obey His laws and conditions of life."

59. This instance occurred just before Richard distributed the last of his personal funds and made his first trip to Chefoo in search of assistance. Richard, "China," (1876) 246.

60. Soothill, *Timothy Richard of China*, 86–87.

61. Richard, *Forty-Five Years*, 123. This kind of independent action on the part of local believers also provides further evidence of the relatively advanced sense of empowerment present in the churches associated with Richard's Shandong mission.

Three years have passed since I started the [famine relief] work and I shall be very glad when everything will be finished and the people again enjoying plenty of their daily bread and showing their thankfulness by asking for the bread of heaven by fearing God and turning away from all wickedness.[62]

On one occasion in 1880 Richard informed his mother that a number of orphans had "made up their mind to go with God and to abandon every idol. This is the greatest pleasure we had this year."[63] Without in any way detracting from his real efforts in pursuit of the material betterment of the famine orphans (including the provision of vocational training), Richard's "greatest pleasure" was over their spiritual transformation. This evangelistic integration of the material and the spiritual perfectly reflected Richard's evangelical activism.

Nor was Richard's belief in a spiritual component to the famine and its physical suffering uniquely Western. For Chinese farmers dependent upon the seasonal fall of rain for their livelihood, there were primarily two means by which to understand—and thus have the sense of some control over—the natural world. For many people in late imperial China, particularly those with more education, Confucian teaching suggested that diligence in the practice of the cardinal virtues was the primary factor determining the natural order, including disease and weather.[64] For others, the natural world was more capricious, its blessings and curses understood to flow from the whims of particular spiritual forces or deities, such as local river spirits and earth gods, or an imbalance in the mutually opposing forces of *yin* and *yang*. In both cases, human behavior was linked to natural phenomena in what Mark Elvin terms "moral meteorology."[65] Accordingly, the promulgations against meat eating that appeared early in the drought, the penitential posturing of local officials carrying chains about their necks, as well as the popular temple processions appealing for rain[66]—all these acts situated the cause for the drought at the intersection

---

62. Richard to his mother, 31 March 1879, trans. by Thomas Evans, 31 December 1964, BMSA CH/4A.

63. Richard to his mother, 17 Jan 1880, translated by Thomas Evans, 25 January 1965, BMSA CH/4.

64. For an example of a Shanxi Confucian scholar's understanding of the close link between personal morality and physical health around the time of the famine, see Harrison, *Man Awakened from Dreams*, 52.

65. Elvin, "Who Was Responsible for the Weather?," 213–37.

66. For an eyewitness account of Shanxi rain processions during the North China Famine, see Harrison, *Man Awakened from Dreams*, 29.

of the spiritual and the moral, precisely the spheres in which Richard conceptualized his own famine relief actions.

As the famine spread and Western relief efforts expanded, reportage on Western and missionary relief work in the *Shenbao* and other Chinese-language periodicals presented coastal Chinese elites with an ethical challenge. The Western appeal for funds relied on moral suasion, and the scale and degree of the foreign philanthropic response raised the question for Chinese readers: was the West morally superior to China? Chinese gentry and religious leaders responded by expanding their own relief work, often phrasing their requests for donations in terms that made it clear that Chinese morality was not to be outdone by foreign charity. Donations to the relief effort were frequently encouraged by the promise of accumulated merit, a spiritual reward that would accrue to the generous donor. In one instance, a letter was published telling of a man whose father was ill and dying, and whose prayers seemingly were of no avail; he recalled that contributing to famine relief was promised to prolong life, and so vowed to donate if his father was healed. This prayer was answered, demonstrating the spiritual power available through participation in unofficial Chinese relief efforts.[67] By validating the moral and spiritual vitality of specifically Chinese interpretations of the value of explicitly Chinese famine relief, Chinese publishers were defending their society against the spiritual pollution of foreign ideas.

Western and Chinese notions of the spiritual import of the physical famine come together in one incident from Richard's time in Shandong. In 1877 reports of Richard's orphanages appeared in the *Shenbao*, inspiring Suzhou philanthropist Xie Jiafu to call on other local Jiangnan gentry to give subscriptions to establish a Chinese orphanage for the children suffering in Shandong.[68] Xie and many of his fellow philanthropists were no doubt motivated by concern for the condition of the famine orphans. However, drawing on a long tradition of rumors and fears regarding child kidnapping in general and—more recently—the abduction of Chinese children by foreign missionaries for nefarious purposes, they were also explicitly seeking to compete with Richard for the souls of their young compatriots.[69] Richard, meanwhile, was also keeping score, noting in his autobiography that the Jiangsu orphanage was from the beginning "dogged with misfortune." When an epidemic of smallpox killed a large number of the famine orphans under the care of the Jiangsu-run institution, "not a

67. Janku, "Sowing Happiness," 98–99.
68. Edgerton-Tarpley, *Tears from Iron*, 139.
69. Ter Haar, *Telling Stories*, 106–34, 154–76; Cohen, *History in Three Keys*, 162–72.

single child in our Orphanage suffered any illness, and more were sent to us than we were able to take in."[70] In Richard's mind, he—and by extension his God—were winning the moral contest.

Richard's work in Shandong—his activism, without distinguishing between his relief work and his evangelistic work—produced results that for the mission were significant. The church associated with the BMS in interior Shandong grew during the period of the famine. On an 1877 trip into the countryside during harvest time (for the drought was finally abating) Richard visited the five or six hundred men and women associated with the mission who were meeting regularly for worship at six different centers spread throughout the region; half of them were people who did not receive any aid from the mission, and "three-fourths or two thirds, at any rate, have committed Christian books more or less to memory."[71] By March 1878, when the desperation of the famine had already passed, the mission included eight to ten separate fellowships of roughly fifty persons each, including thirty baptized believers and an additional two to three hundred applicants for baptism.[72] While it is tempting to view these new members with cynicism, it should be recalled that, as discussed in the previous chapter, the BMS in Qingzhou required a lengthy period of faithful witness and attendance as well as demonstrated mastery of Richard's catechism and other literature prior to baptism.[73] Moreover, being fully aware of the dangers of "prostitute Christians" who approached the church purely as a means of securing material aid, Richard had decided "in the interests of true Christianity" to put a hold on all baptisms until the "relief temptation" had passed.[74] The result of all this was the emergence in the wake of the famine of a strong, growing, Chinese church in and around Qingzhou that was for its time relatively self-supporting, self-governing, and self-propagating, with what Richard

---

70. The Shandong prefect governing Qingzhou during the famine happened to be from Jiangsu. According to Richard, the magistrate divided up the region's relief work between Richard and his Christian colleagues, and the gentry from Jiangsu who most likely included Xie's workers. Richard, *Forty-Five Years*, 119.

71. Richard, "China," (1878) 15.

72. From a 10 March 1878 entry in Nevius's journal as recorded in Nevius, *Life of John Livingston Nevius*, 352.

73. Richard to Jones, 16 January 1878, p. 6, BMSA CH/4; Nevius, "Mission Work in Central Shantung," *CR* 11, no. 5 (1880) 362.

74. The term "prostitute Christians" is Richard's own, used to refer to those who seek the church for their own material advantage. Richard to Jones, "Post Script," 24 January 1878, pp. 8–9, BMSA CH/4. On the suspension of baptisms during the famine, see Richard, *Fifteen Years*, 14.

claimed to be "over two thousand inquirers meeting regularly for worship at some scores of centres."[75]

Given Richard's persistent interest in effective means, he viewed the increase in inquirers to the faith, as well as the good favor earned with local officials, as clear vindications of his evolving mission methods. The larger mission world also took notice: from the time of the North China Famine, Western missionary consciousness would ever after include emergency relief within its mandate.[76]

Richard did not, as some have suggested, decide to undertake famine work *because* it was a means to win converts.[77] Rather, as discussed above, he identified with the suffering of his neighbors, and relief work then emerged as the natural expression of his evangelical activism within that context of empathetic identification. As the famine progressed and his own experience of ministering in the midst of the subsequent devastation evolved, Richard discovered that the compassion demonstrated through famine relief functioned as yet another form of moral evidence; his primary concern to alleviate suffering had incidentally yielded evangelistic opportunities similar to those fostered by medical work. Richard saw the growing number of devout persons who came to Qingzhou seeking him in response to the literature he had spread throughout the area during the famine as confirmation that "the knowledge that I was distributing relief to the famine sufferers was a convincing proof to the multitude that my religion was good."[78] Richard's observation that through the famine "God was giving us an opportunity of exercising influence over many millions of people" was made after he had been engaged in famine relief work in Shandong for over a year and had witnessed its practical results on the local Christian community. It was the thought of seeing these proven results repeated and perhaps expanded in heretofore-unreached Shanxi that so excited him.[79]

---

75. Richard, *Forty-Five Years*, 106.

76. Walls, "Multiple Conversions," 249.

77. See, for example, Yuan, "'Dingwu qihuang' zhong chuanjiaoshi," 101. While it may accurately describe the attitude of some missionary relief workers, Yuan's observation that "disaster relief was the path; evangelism was the goal" does not reflect Richard's earliest motivation for distributing aid.

78. Richard, *Forty-Five Years*, 105.

79. Richard, *Forty-Five Years*, 124–26. Many scholars miss this point, viewing Richard's entry into famine relief work as an expression of crusading evangelistic expediency. See, for instance, the construal of Richard's motivations in Janku, "Sowing Happiness," 91–92, 105–8.

5.4 Famine Relief Work and Early Ministry in Shanxi

In November 1876 Alfred Jones arrived in Chefoo to join Richard as the newest full representative of the BMS in China.[80] Richard made a special trip away from the Qingzhou famine relief work in order to welcome Jones, immediately providing Jones with a Chinese teacher so that, having arrived on a Saturday, Jones was able to begin his language studies on Monday. Richard also wasted no time in introducing Jones to "Edward Irving's famous missionary sermon," arguing his case with passion and conviction. Jones had experience running his own successful business back in Ireland, and so it was agreed before Richard's return to Qingzhou that Jones would join him there in March 1877 to assist Richard with the bookkeeping for the famine relief monies. As the Society's long-awaited answer to Richard's many requests for reinforcements, Jones was to become Richard's first long-serving colleague in the BMS and the friendship that quickly developed between the two men proved strong, weathering the storms that were to rage around Richard during his second decade in China.

By autumn 1877 news of an even greater famine threat in interior Shanxi had reached coastal China, motivating William Muirhead to write to Richard on behalf of the Shanghai Famine Relief Committee requesting him to apply his hard-won famine fighting experience in the new area. From the beginning Richard was drawn to Shanxi not just for "the unparalleled opportunity this gives us of introducing the Gospel," but also for the "friendly relations" the relief work would help establish. Moreover, Richard also recognized "the moral effect this [work] will have on the young Christians here [in Qingzhou], showing how Christianity works as well as preaches."[81] Finally, with conditions in Shandong improving, and with a new BMS coworker to manage the work in Qingzhou, the move to Shanxi seemed to make sense. Following a period of prayer, Richard, Jones, and—significantly—Pastor Zheng all agreed to release Richard for the new work in Shanxi.[82]

Chinese assistants and coworkers had been active in Shandong throughout this period, both in the famine relief work and the ongoing operations of the mission and its growing church. While details regarding the exact nature and scope of Pastor Zheng's contribution to the Shandong church or the BMS famine relief work are limited, Richard offered his highest praise for

80. Richard knew of the possibility of a new colleague sometime before August 1876. Richard, "China," (1876) 247; and "Missionary Notes," 171.

81. From Richard's 30 October 1877 letter to C. M. Bailhache (Secretary of the BMS) as reprinted in *MH* 74, no. 3 (1878) 60.

82. Richard, *Forty-Five Years*, 125–26.

Zheng during his reflections on precisely this period of his career.[83] It was Zheng's steady competence that gave Richard the confidence to leave Jones in Shandong and head for distant Shanxi: "Pastor Ch'ing [or Zheng] was one of the finest Christians ever found in China, and as a colleague was equal to any two or three average foreign missionaries. . . . His faith in Christianity never failed, and during his life he baptized over two thousand converts."[84] While Zheng stayed behind to care for the growing Shandong church, a number of other Chinese Christians offered to join Richard on his Shanxi adventure, a great testimony to the degree to which Richard had encouraged the missionary spirit in the young Qingzhou church.[85]

Catholic missionaries had been working in Shanxi since the early seventeenth century, and by the time of the North China Famine the Catholic community in Shanxi was well established.[86] In 1866 Alexander Williamson had passed through Shanxi on an exploratory tour, providing the earliest Protestant description of the province and noting especially the relative beauty of the capital city Taiyuan and the mineral, agricultural, and entrepreneurial wealth of the cities to the south on the plains around Taiyuan and Pingyang.[87] By the time of Richard's arrival in November 1877, these same areas had been devastated by the famine, resulting in a striking loss of prosperity from which the province has even today yet to recover fully.[88] Richard was not, however, the first Protestant Westerner to have visited since Williamson. Joshua Turner and Francis H. James, both at the time associates of the CIM, had also passed through Shanxi, first on an evangelistic tour in the autumn of 1876 and then later in the spring of 1877 with the intent of establishing a permanent Protestant mission presence in Taiyuan.[89] As the famine intensified around them, both

---

83. Pastor Zheng's importance was recognized by the BMS early on: Zheng had been ordained by Richard in 1873 and granted status as an associate missionary of the BMS, complete with a salary supported by the Grosvenor Baptist Church, Manchester. Cliff, "History of the Protestant Movement," 110.

84. Richard, *Forty-Five Years*, 125.

85. The Shandong Baptists were open to migration, as exemplified a few years after the famine by the exodus of eighty-seven church members including four trained leaders as part of a group of roughly forty thousand emigrants to inland Shaanxi province. Henderson and Myers, *Centenary Volume of the BMS*, 14–46.

86. Harrison, *Missionary's Curse*, 17–18, 66–74.

87. Williamson, *Journeys in North China*, 1:151–69, 309–17.

88. Edgerton-Tarpley, *Tears from Iron*, 15–24, 28–39; Harrison, *Man Awakened from Dreams*, 22–23.

89. Francis James, "First Journey to Shan-si," *CM* (May 1877) 56–57; J. J. Turner, "Province of Shan-si," *CM* (December 1877) 154–56; J. J. Turner, "Report of Work in the Province of Shan-si (or Western Hills)," *CM* (June 1878) 80, 82. Interestingly, the

men were eventually forced by illness to retire to Hankou after less than a year's residence.[90] Arnold Foster of the LMS in Hankou also passed briefly through Shanxi sometime late in 1877, before returning to the coast and eventually England in order to solicit funds for the relief of the disaster.[91] Unlike these other missionaries, Richard was able to secure and maintain a residence in Taiyuan making him the first long-term Protestant missionary in Shanxi, prior to being joined in March 1878 by Turner, James, and Hill bearing some thirty thousand taels from the Shanghai relief committee for distribution among the Shanxi famine victims.[92]

The nature of the suffering in Shanxi was similar to what Richard had seen in Shandong: dead bodies by the roadside, cannibalism, family members sold into slavery, but now on an even larger scale.[93] Drawing on his experience, Richard once again focused on the same three relief activities: he distributed monies to the starving using the same techniques he had pioneered in Shandong; he opened orphanages, taking in children left abandoned by the famine; and he sought the approval and cooperation of the local officials, both as a practical means for advancing the work of the mission and as a vehicle for promoting the kinds of reforms which might alleviate the present suffering and prevent any future disaster of similar magnitude.[94] Throughout, he continued his practice of displaying simple gospel posters and tracts in order to inform the people of the larger context for his assistance.

All told, Richard and his fellow Protestant relief administrators distributed 127,110 taels to 100,641 individuals in Taiyuan, Pingyang, and Zezhou Prefectures, while the Catholic missionaries already resident in

---

CIM publicly dated its mission in Shanxi from the beginning of Turner and James's first visit to the province in November 1876. See the chart in *CM* (September 1877) 116.

90. James and Turner, "Scenes in the Famine Districts," *CM* (May 1878) 69–71.

91. Barber, *David Hill: Missionary and Saint*, 189. Foster, a close friend of David Hill's, played a significant (and heretofore unrecognized) role in mobilizing missionary relief during the later stages of the North China Famine. See, for example, his lengthy letter discussing relief coordination: Foster to Taylor, 6 October 1877, CIM Papers CIM/JHT/235, SOAS.

92. Turner and James arrived earlier, and did engage in preaching and literature distribution; the BMS North China workers claimed precedence in the field citing Richard's "settled residence from 1877" as prior to the CIM's 1878 "settled residence." See "Statement of Facts," 5.

93. See Richard's observations from his winter 1877–78 tour of Southern Shanxi in Richard, *Forty-Five Years*, 129–34. James and Turner reported similar scenes: "Scenes in the Famine Districts," 69–71. For local Chinese accounts of the suffering, see Edgerton-Tarpley, *Tears from Iron*, 42–66.

94. The best summary of Richard's Shanxi relief work remains Bohr, *Famine in China*, 102–13.

Shanxi (mostly Italian Franciscans) distributed thirty-five thousand taels among the large Catholic population in Taiyuan.[95] Despite the much larger relief provided by the state, Richard and Hill were spoken of reverentially throughout the distribution areas, and along with Turner they were eventually commemorated with monuments and emblems of imperial recognition, including promotion to the rank of Mandarin, an honor they declined.[96] One grateful village sent a delegation to the Richard home to confirm the characters for his Chinese name so that they could inscribe it on the wall of their local temple. Richard declined the honor.[97]

With the end of the famine in sight, some of those who had joined in the Shanxi famine relief work returned to their previous fields.[98] Others, recognizing the opening for evangelistic work created by the missionary relief efforts, determined to establish a firm Protestant presence in Shanxi. Turner and James now followed through on their earlier commitment to Shanxi, establishing a mission base in Pingyang where they had been dispensing aid during the famine. On 23 October 1878 their numbers were augmented by the arrival of Misses Horne and Crickmay, along with James Hudson Taylor's second wife Jane "Jennie" Taylor (formerly Faulding), all of the CIM. Accompanied from the coast by veteran CIM missionary and gifted linguist Frederick Baller, the women had been sent to take over the care and education of the female orphans in Taiyuan that remained after the famine.[99] Perhaps owing to the value attributed to male offspring in Shanxi at the time of the famine, there seemed to be relatively few young girls in the

95. Bohr, *Famine in China*, 192–93. Bohr's numbers for the Protestant effort in Shanxi, derived from the official famine relief committee reports, are still broadly accepted. Thompson, "Twilight of the Gods," 56. Bohr's numbers for Catholic relief (14,416 taels distributed among 2,800 local families), however, do not include monies raised by Catholics through channels other than the Shanghai Committee. Harrison, *Missionary's Curse*, 96.

96. 1879 report from Walter Hillier of the British Consulate in Shanghai in China Famine Relief Fund Shanghai Committee, *Great Famine: Report*, 152. See also "Record of the Famine Relief Work in Lin Fen Hien," David Hill, trans., *CR* 11, no. 4 (1880) 260–69, 464; Barber, *David Hill*, 217; Richard, *Forty-Five Years*, 143–44. Curiously, local observers in Shanxi made no mention of the foreign presence or relief work during the famine. Edgerton-Tarpley, *Tears from Iron*, 131.

97. 19 January 1879 letter from Mary Richard reprinted in "China," *The Missionary Record of the United Presbyterian Church* 7 (May 1879), 485–86.

98. Capel and Scott, for instance, returned to Chefoo in May of 1879 after a stay of some six months. J. J. Turner, "Shansi Province," *CM* (December 1879) 148.

99. This work they inherited from the Richards, although Mary Richard continued to be involved with the orphanage for some time. "A Day in the Country with Some of the Famine Orphans," *CM* (June 1880) 77. Horne and Crickmay were pioneers, the first foreign single women to reside so far inland.

area, thus making this educational initiative slow to develop.[100] David Hill also remained for an extended period to help with literature distribution and evangelistic outreach to local scholars. He left in May 1880, planning to return again, only to be forced by circumstances back to England and then on to other fields in China.[101]

At about this same time Richard also received an additional coworker of his own, in the form of his new wife, Mary. Mary Martin, a member of the United Presbyterian Church, was born in 1843 into a "pious and exemplary family" in Edinburgh, where she taught at the Merchant Company's College School. She left Britain on 29 July 1876, having been appointed by the United Presbyterian Mission to take charge of a Chinese girls school in Chefoo under Alexander Williamson.[102] The recommendations accepted in support of Mary Martin's application to the mission give ample testimony to her many gifts: her Christian character, service in the church, gift for teaching, and her beautiful singing voice were all widely noted.[103]

Following a brief correspondence, Timothy and Mary were married in Chefoo in October 1878, and then spent their honeymoon passing through famine-ravished North China on their way to their new home in Taiyuan.[104] As time did not permit while still in Chefoo, they held their wedding banquet in Taiyuan, providing a meal for forty of the poorest members of the local community. As Timothy explained to his mother in Wales, "[the banquet] did not cost much but it brought pleasure to many

---

100. David Hill, address at the Fifteenth Anniversary meeting of the CIM, reprinted in *CM* (July–August 1881) 90. More recent scholarship, however, questions the prevailing narrative of greater female suffering during the famine. See Edgerton-Tarpley, *Tears from Iron*, 178–87.

101. Barber, *David Hill*, 220–21.

102. United Presbyterian Church of Scotland, *Minutes of Foreign Mission Committee*, 30 May 1876, minute no. 511; and 25 July 1876, minute no. 555: CSWCA; see also Reeve, *Timothy Richard*, 62.

103. United Presbyterian Church of Scotland, *Minutes of Foreign Mission Committee*, 30 May 1876, minute no. 511, CSWCA. Mary's "Scottish" qualities—"educational attainment, theological rigour [often defined as membership in the kirk], and practicality"—were sought after by many missionary societies of the time. Semple, *Missionary Women*, 10.

104. Richard to his mother, 30 April 1879, translated by Thomas Evans, 1 January 1965, BMSA Box CH/4A; Reeve, *Timothy Richard*, 62. Initially believed to be an American, Timothy Richard was required upon marriage to compensate the Scottish Presbyterians for Mary's passage and outfit. "Extract from the minutes," 4 November 1878, United Presbyterian Church of Scotland Letter-books, MS 7657, nos. 193–94, NLS.

widows and let's hope that the feast was acceptable in the sight of God who is in heaven."[105]

Mary and Timothy were well-suited companions.[106] In a letter to his mother Richard explained the many ways in which he had "been blessed with a very valuable wife."

> She is always at some work or other. She is an exceptionally good singer.... [H]er greatest pleasure is to teach people to fear God and to keep away from all evil. She is religious, good and of tender heart, learned, hard working, in one word an unequalled help to me.[107]

In his wife Mary, Timothy Richard had found a companion uniquely suited to share the labors of his life's work as well as his devotion to that work, a fact ably demonstrated by her impassioned defense of her husband's missionary efforts written when Richard was being challenged by colleagues during the 1880s.[108] Perhaps most importantly, Timothy Richard esteemed his wife's opinion so highly that her voice would reach him when the warnings of others could not.[109]

One of the first evangelistic plans entered upon by the pioneer Protestants in Shanxi involved the distribution of simple gospel tracts to each of Shanxi's counties. As the two missionaries in Shanxi with sufficient language skills to undertake the task, Richard and Hill set about producing something that would inform the common people all across the province

---

105. Richard to his mother, 12 February 1879, translated by Thomas Evans, 29 March 1965, BMSA Box CH/4A.

106. On companionate missionary marriages, see Manktelow, *Missionary Families*, 70–73.

107. Richard to his mother, 3 July 1879, translated by Thomas Evans, 29 March 1965, BMSA Box CH/4A.

108. Mary Martin Richard, "Sketch of Mr. Richard's work since coming to Shansi," MS dated 11 May 1887, BMSA CH/4A. In addition to her technical contributions to the Richards' popular 1885 book of Chinese hymns *Xiao shipu*, Mary Richard also produced a number of learned papers on Chinese music history and theory for the foreign community in China, as well as a ten-volume series of Chinese-language Christian biographies. Mary Martin Richard, "Chinese Music," *CR* 21, no. 7–8 (1890) 305–14, 339–47; Mary Martin Richard, *Paper on Chinese Music*; Mary Martin Richard, *Jiaoshi liezhuan*; Liu, "Li Timotai furen yu *Xiao shipu*," 22–27. For her publications, see MacGillivray, *Descriptive and Classified*, 9, 14, 55, and 82–83. Johnson incorrectly credits Timothy Richard with authorship of the biographies, and lists the publication date for the entire series as 1896. It is likely that individual volumes were available earlier as they were completed. Johnson, "Educational Reform in China," 229.

109. Soothill suggested that some of Richard's final flights of idealism would have been restrained had Mary Richard lived longer. Soothill, *Timothy Richard of China*, 280.

(not just in the famine districts) "that we had come also for a spiritual famine that was though not so apparent, yet infinitely more serious in all its varied consequences, temporal and eternal."[110] The project was distinctly ecumenical, with missionaries from the various agencies choosing the districts for which they would be responsible.[111] Richard and Hill's tracts were thus distributed in all of the major market towns within a year, with the BMS handling the distribution in "over seventy-one counties of the province."[112] In March 1881 this effort gained institutional support through the formation of the Shanxi branch of the Chinese Religious Tract Society, with some thirty thousand pieces of literature distributed in that year alone in the various county seats of the province.[113]

According to Mary Richard, this entire work was undertaken "at Mr. R.'s suggestion, he taking through natives the biggest share."[114] Richard likely made use of evangelists from Shandong in this work; soon afterwards the BMS was employing eight native evangelists (six from Qingzhou) on regular tours of the major population centers around Taiyuan, with each month spent enjoying a week of instruction and three weeks of itineration.[115] It is also possible that Gao Daling, who assisted Mary Richard with her *Christian Biographies*, may have been involved in this work as well.[116] Gao, a scholar official from the Taiyuan area, served as Timothy Richard's Chinese language teacher and soon became an exemplary member of the nascent Baptist community in Taiyuan. Despite having taken two wives prior to his conversion, Gao eventually pastored a local independent church, which during the Republican period became the local branch of the True Jesus Church.[117] Given the Richards' linguistic reliance on Gao Daling during

110. Richard, *Fifteen Years*, 18.

111. David Hill, address at the Fifteenth Anniversary meeting of the CIM, reprinted in *CM* (July-August 1881) 89 and 91.

112. "Statement of Facts," 7; see also Barber, *David Hill*, 213.

113. "Missionary News," *CR* 10, no. 2 (1882) 156–57. In 1882 Richard served as President, with Dr. Schofield of the CIM as secretary.

114. Mary Martin Richard, "Sketch of Mr. Richard's Work," 3.

115. "Statement of Facts," 9–10. These evangelists also distributed literature among leading officials in Henan when traveling to and from Shandong.

116. Soothill, *Timothy Richard of China*, 119. Utilizing equipment supplied by Timothy Richard, Gao became an accomplished photographer. Richard, *Forty-Five Years*, 154, 160.

117. I am indebted to Henrietta Harrison for these fascinating insights into Gao Daling. See "Ben hui Shanxi shilue" and "Gao Daling jiandu xing shu" in Wei, *Zhen Yesu jiaohui*," C18 and M10, respectively. Gao is still recognized today for his contributions to the development of independent—specifically True Jesus—churches across Shanxi. See, for example, Hu, *Hondong jidujiao shi*, 24–26, 30–32.

their time in Shanxi, it would be surprising if Gao was not at least in some way involved in this shared missionary endeavor to produce and then distribute Christian literature across Shanxi.

Hill and Richard became close friends during the famine, with Richard recalling in later years that their "friendship was the closest, happiest, and sweetest, and lasted till his death."[118] Known for his passion for prayer, Hill, like Richard, came to Shanxi wearing Chinese dress and contributed his own personal funds to aid in the famine relief.[119] Though Hill had struggled with the tones of spoken Chinese, his ability to write Chinese by hand humbled Richard, who despite an attempt to carry on a Chinese-language correspondence with Hill during their time together in Shanxi, was forced to dictate his publications to Chinese amanuenses.[120] When the men first began working together, Hill's humble personality inclined him against Richard's policy of seeking cooperation from local officials, though he peaceably acquiesced and soon recognized the plan's effectiveness for relief work.[121] Throughout their time in Shanxi, the two men retained the distinct tendencies that would mark their lives and ministry: "David Hill became especially the friend of the poor, with an open heart for officials and gentry; Timothy Richard, with an open heart for the poor, became especially an associate of officials and gentry."[122]

Writing from Taiyuan in December 1878, James Hudson Taylor's second wife, Jennie, described Timothy Richard at this time as "a thorough Chinaman in dress, food, manners, and love, and sympathy for the people."[123] This pattern seems to have continued as the Richards began their new life together in Shanxi.[124] In 1881, Dr. Harold Schofield of the CIM in Taiyuan noted in his diary a typical meal shared at the Richard's home: "December 9th. —Chinese meal at Mr. Richard's, cooked by Mohammedans.

---

118. Richard, *Forty-Five Years*, 149.

119. Pritchard, *Methodists and their Missionary Societies*, 126.

120. Pritchard, *Methodists and their Missionary Societies*, 126; Soothill, *Timothy Richard of China*, 113.

121. See Foster's comments and Hill's own April 1878 letter on the subject in Barber, *David Hill*, 193–95.

122. This apt description is from an unattributed quotation in Evans, *Timothy Richard*, 78–79.

123. Jennie Taylor to Mrs. C. T. Fishe, 3 December 1878, as recorded in "Tidings from Shan-si," *CM* (November 1879) 50.

124. On the Richards' daily life in Shanxi, see the hand-edited copy in BMSA CH/8 of Jones, *Hints about Climate*. The appendix to this booklet includes a lengthy description of domestic life from "one of the Ladies of the Mission." Jones's edits to adjust for Shandong, as well as references in the text to the female missionary's "girls" and a persistent preference for accepting Chinese customs suggest that Mary Richard may be the appendix's author.

Many dishes really excellent . . . we ate it with chopsticks."[125] In the Richard home, as was typical in residences throughout Shanxi, the coal-heated raised brick sleeping platform, or *kang*, was central to their lives, providing a place to entertain guests or continue with their work studying and writing literature in Chinese.[126]

The Richards soon established a pattern of daily ministry. As Richard described in a letter to his mother from this time, "Mary visits the wives in the town in order to inform them of the good news which have [sic] come to our land."[127] As she sat with the women on their heated *kang*, sewing and knitting, Mary was granted access into the daily lives of local women through the gossip and conversations that accompanied these sewing sessions. Richard, meanwhile, devoted himself to "visiting the men and writing books to reach their hearts and to bring them to the savior of their souls."[128]

Throughout these years of physically demanding labor, Richard found his newly emerging understanding of the missionary task—in particular, his emphases on empathizing with local habits and priorities, and the efficacy of moral evidences—affirmed, but in a new and previously unexplored context. Andrew Walls's observation that "Richard's view of the missionary task was diversified in an unexpected way" by the famine is correct, but only if diversification is understood as the extension and application of existing notions into new areas of life and ministry.[129] Richard's actual participation in famine alleviation, including his fund-raising, distribution of relief monies, opening of orphanages and interactions with officials, did not at this point indicate a "radical alteration in the direction of his ministry in China"; any alteration, if at all, was to come later.[130] Rather, the famine years were for Richard a period of "widening vision," an extension of notions he had previously developed into new territory, and not a departure from his previous ways of doing mission.[131]

125. Schofield, *Memorials of R. Harold A. Schofield*, 173.

126. Richard to his mother, 17 Jan 1880, translated by Thomas Evans, 25 January 1965, BMSA CH/4A; see also Soothill, *Timothy Richard of China*, 115.

127. Richard to his mother, 17 Jan 1880, translated by Thomas Evans, 25 January 1965, BMSA CH/4A.

128. Richard to his mother, 17 Jan 1880, translated by Thomas Evans, 25 January 1965, BMSA CH/4A.

129. Walls, "Multiple Conversions," 247.

130. Bohr places this observation in his discussion of Richard's work following the famine, leaving open the possibility (as argued in this thesis) that the famine work itself was not a departure. Bohr, *Famine in China*, 171. This point is often missed. The supposed alteration in the direction of Richard's ministry will be discussed further in the next chapter.

131. Latourette (*History of Christian Missions*, 378) was correct to describe Richard as a missionary who served in China "always with a widening vision of the task of the Christian mission," a view more recently echoed by Bohr ("Legacy," 77).

6

Richard after the Famine

Accommodationism, the Kingdom of God, and the Broadening of Christian Mission

WITH THE FAMINE RECEDING, Shanxi was now the focus of Richard's missionary efforts. Richard soon found his previous methods challenged in new ways, as he struggled to compensate for the lack of a pre-existing Protestant Chinese church while adjusting to the demands of working in cooperation with other expatriate missionaries.[1] With the confidence gained from the growth of the church in Shandong and the effectiveness of his work during the famine, Richard exhorted his fellow Shanxi missionaries to adopt his missionary methods, turning to scripture to justify the techniques he had already found so effective.

In this post-famine context Richard began to explore two "new" theological formulations that, though strikingly similar to ideas developing within British Protestantism at the time, appear not to have been borrowed by Richard from other individuals or books. First of all, the empathetic trajectory of Richard's earlier adaptations was now extended into a more fully developed accommodationist approach to mission, grounded in the gospel promise that Jesus came to fulfill rather than destroy. Second, the apologetic use of moral evidences Richard had found so effective also acquired a more robust theological justification, in this case via Richard's realization of the relevance of the Kingdom of God to all aspects of life on this earth. Far from marking a radical turning in his practice and understanding of mission, Richard's embrace of these two theological formulations represented a sophistication—a maturing—of ideas already present, now given scriptural warrant and grafted into his previous theology of mission.

---

1. Richard, "Rev. Timothy Richard on the Recent Famine," 6–9.

6.1 Fulfillment Theology and Accommodating Mission

In 1880 Richard published in the *Chinese Recorder* a passionate appeal to the larger China mission community to reform the ways in which it practiced mission in China. His most public and polemical essay to date, "Thoughts on Chinese Missions; Difficulties and Tactics" first presented what Richard perceived to be the barriers to evangelizing China before challenging his fellow China workers to take their context more seriously and to engage China in ways that appealed to the Chinese. While mostly a summary of Richard's mission practices since his move to Qingzhou, the essay's most striking contribution was its closing exposition of Richard's newfound theological justification for his empathetic adaptations to his context.

> Now let us look at the principles which our Lord himself laid down and see if they agree with what we draw from experience. In the Sermon on the mount after the glad music of the first verses.... He tells them he came to show them a more excellent way. The key to all the music on the mount is in *surpassing* the past. He in substance says, don't be alarmed, I am not come to destroy what you hold most sacred, but to fulfil. The righteousness of the kingdom of Heaven must *exceed* that of the scribes and Pharisees; ... it is not something less but ever something more that He expects of His followers.[2]

As with his earlier creative application of Jesus's feeding of the multitudes, Richard brought his experience of mission in China—namely, his Shandong successes with Chinese adaptations—to his reading of the Sermon on the Mount. Through this novel mingling of Jesus's words regarding the Old Testament Law in Matt 5:17 with Jesus's criticism of the Pharisees and scribes in Matt 5:20, Richard was defining how the aspects of Chinese religious and cultural life which he believed were compatible with the truths of Christianity were related to those aspects which were not. Now with the imprimatur of Jesus's own words, the mission task for Richard was to fill up or complete the portions of the gospel message that were lacking from China's own traditions by building upon—and surpassing—whatever truths they already contained.

Arising from the challenges of the mission context, fulfillment theology was an explicitly Christian expression of the ideas of the academic field of comparative religion, a newly-minted discipline that by the 1870s was rapidly growing in popularity throughout the West. Both influencing and benefiting from the work of Christian missionaries, scholars such as

2. Richard, "Thoughts on Chinese Missions," 439–40.

F. Max Müller and Oxford Professor of Sanskrit Monier Monier-Williams placed rapidly expanding Western understandings of the variety of religions around the world within an evolutionary hierarchy with Christianity at the top.[3] There is, however, little evidence that Richard was aware of these developments prior to his 1885 furlough.[4] The only possible hint is the observation, supplied in Richard's 1916 autobiography, that between 1881 and 1884 he ordered "books on the Comparative Study of Religion, Church History, and biographies; [and] a complete set of Max Müller's 'Sacred Books of the East.'"[5] Curiously, given the personal nature of his relationship with the author, Richard did not mention Rowland Williams's 1856 *Christianity and Hinduism*.[6] Though he may have viewed Williams with some suspicion following the *Essays and Reviews* controversy, Richard ought to have known of this scholarly reflection on Indian mission, wherein Williams described Hinduism as a sort of training or preparation for Christianity.[7] The lack of strong connections between Richard and the discipline of comparative religion is ultimately, however, unimportant. For Richard, as for most missionaries, it was not the broad comparativist schema but rather the more specific idea of Christianity as fulfillment—with its rich implications for expanding Christian conversion—which he found compelling.

As with comparative religion, there appears to be no direct chain of influence between the early proponents of fulfillment theology such as T. E. Slater and Richard's theological insights.[8] And yet, by 1885, this idea of Christ as fulfillment, already visible in Richard's earlier "Thoughts on Chinese Missions," had become fully incorporated into his mission methods. In his address to the BMS Committee of that year, Richard concluded his

---

3. Hedges, "Post-colonialism," 55–75.

4 While concerned primarily with Richard's later interest in Mahayana Buddhism, the best attempt to situate Richard's thinking within developments in comparative religion during his lifetime is Scott, "Timothy Richard," 53–75.

5. Richard, *Forty-Five Years*, 159. On the comparativist nature of Müller's *Sacred Books* project, see Girardot, "Max Müller's 'Sacred Books,'" 213–50.

6. Williams, *Parameswara-jnyana-goshthi*.

7. Hedges, *Preparation and Fulfilment*, 63–87.

8. While fulfillment theology was popularized by Farquhar's *Crown of Hinduism*, it was founded upon Slater's practical sympathy for Hindu followers and Scottish Free Church missionary to India William Miller's more systematic development of "Christ the Fulfiller." Kalapati, "Edinburgh to Tambaram," 11; Sharpe, *Not to Destroy*, throughout, especially 87, 101–3, 337, and 345–47; Farquhar, *Crown of Hinduism*. Slater's empathetic attitude toward Indian religious practitioners—a significant departure from the negative view of Alexander Duff—was very similar to Richard's approach to the Chinese worthy. Slater, *God Revealed*, 8; Sharpe, *Not to Destroy*, 63–64, 98.

description of his interactions with Chinese sectarian worthies by pointing out the centrality of fulfillment ideas to his method.

> In all my interviews I never forgot that Christ came to fulfil and not to destroy. He comes to save, to regenerate, and to sanctify, and to make divine. To fulfill their noblest aims better than any other Teacher the world has ever yet seen. And He will not destroy one iota of good in *their* systems more than in Judaism of old.[9]

Significantly, for Richard it was not Christian civilization or Christian institutions, but rather Jesus Christ who fulfilled the "noblest aims" of these devout Chinese truth-seekers.[10]

The development of comparative religion as an academic discipline at just this time and the explorations of fulfillment theology by some of the missionaries to India both contributed positively to the spread of accommodationist notions among many Protestant missionaries, particularly in China. Grounded in a robust natural theology, the method of accommodating missionary endeavors to accord with the more positive aspects of other religions had a long pedigree in China missions, dating back to Matteo Ricci's "intellectually flavored Christianity" and the Jesuit mission to late Ming China.[11] More cynically summarized as "what you cannot suppress, reinterpret," accommodationism was further developed and refined as an evangelistic technique by seventeenth-century Chinese Christians such as Xu Wending (Guangqi) and Shang Huqing.[12] Over two hundred years later, accommodationism continued to influence mission in China through the writings of James Legge and his characteristic support for both the Christian supplementation of Confucianism and the rejection of Buddhism.[13]

---

9. Richard, *Fifteen Years*, 11.

10. In this sense, Richard's thinking is remarkably similar to Farquhar's as expressed in *Crown of Hinduism*. Sharpe, *Not to Destroy*, 339–45.

11. Mungello, *Curious Land*, 13–20, 43–73. Zupanov cites the following definition of accommodation: "Originally a device of humanistic rhetoric, the ability to adapt oneself and one's speech in order to be in touch with the feelings and needs of the audience, this became a device of all Jesuit ministries which spanned many cultures and contexts." Zupanov, "'One Civility,'" 286.

12. Zupanov, "'One Civility,'" 322. Accommodationism was also visible in the work of Chinese Christians, and Dominican and Franciscan priests, as well as Jesuit missionaries. See Mungello, *Spirit and Flesh in Shandong*, 38–41; and Tiedemann, "Christianity and Chinese," 373.

13. On the roots of Legge's supplementary principles in the much earlier Chinese Christian concept of *bu ru yi fo*, or "supplement the Literati, displace the Buddhists," see Mungello, "Confucian Voice," 590; Mungello, *Spirit and Flesh in Shandong*, 38–41.

Richard's personal course of study on China's religions undertaken just prior to his move to Qingzhou made regular use of James Legge's translation of the Confucian Classics.[14] At the time, Legge was one of the most prominent missionary scholars of China's religions, eventually (1876) serving as Oxford's first professor of Chinese. Ideologically as well as geographically positioned between Müller and the more evangelical Monier-Williams, Legge was immersed in comparativism, leading to the inclusion of his translations of Chinese religious and philosophical texts in Müller's *Sacred Books* series.[15] Legge's extensive study of Chinese religious texts had made him one of the most prominent advocates of an accommodationist attitude toward China's religions within the China mission community. Norman J. Girardot explains Legge's position:

> From the relativizing perspective of a translator and comparativist, as was Legge, the ancient Chinese already possessed a partial or natural revelation from God, which needed supplementation and fulfillment in the way that the Christian New Testament completed the Old Testament of the Hebrews.[16]

Legge, much like Richard, Slater, and the early Jesuits in China, was compelled by his missionary concern for non-Christians to develop and promote the practical applications of accommodationism;[17] the abstract construction of a comparative theory of world religion was less important than bringing China into God's Kingdom.

Along with Richard and Legge, W. A. P. Martin (APM), Gilbert Reid (APM), and Alexander Williamson were some of the missionaries in the closing decades of the nineteenth century who believed that a more sympathetic or accommodating reading of China's religions would speed the conversion of her peoples.[18] Recognizing the partial truths of other religions, and acknowledging the good they had contributed to society, these

---

14. Richard, *Forty-Five Years*, 86.

15. On Legge and Monier-Williams see Girardot, *Victorian Translation*, 350–51, 465–66.

16. Girardot, *Victorian Translation*, 249.

17. Precisely because of his overriding mission concerns, Legge's accommodations toward China's religions are still considered by some to be a "destructive act of cultural imperialism." See, for example, Wang, *Translating Chinese Classics*, 76–77.

18. This is contrary to Xiaoqun Xu, who follows Smythe and Rawlinson and views the prevalence of more accommodating attitudes toward China's religions and culture as a post-1915 phenomenon. Xu, "Dilemma of Accommodation," 24–25. While these ideas were more widely accepted within the Republican China missionary community, they were present in the writings and practices of an outspoken and highly visible group of nineteenth-century China missionaries.

missionaries argued that since Christianity fulfilled these religions—since it was the necessary supplement that filled up what they were lacking of divine revelation—then effective evangelism required accommodating mission practice to take advantage of the common areas of truth and goodness that these religions shared with Christianity.

Lee Chi-Ho sees Richard's 1880 *Chinese Recorder* article "Thoughts on Chinese Missions; Difficulties and Tactics" as proof that in his accommodation Richard was removing Jesus from the center of his message.[19] Richard, however, made it clear that he was doing something altogether different, as seen in his opening description of the progression of his own thinking during his first ten years in China.

> That mission work consists of nothing more than declaring that "God so loved the world that he gave his only begotten Son that whosoever believeth in him should not perish but have everlasting life," is only the thought of the most romantic of missionary tyros. That it involves extensive travelling for the distribution of books, daily preaching of the 'cross,' and a constant testimony against the sin of idolatry, is evident from the lives of most missionaries. But that it should involve much study of native books, much giving up of personal feelings for the sake of intercourse with the heathen, and much humble learning from many of their most devout minds, is not thought so necessary. Still in war nothing can be more disastrous than to underestimate the enemy's forces and power. It is no less so in religious conquest. Yet this often happens, partly out of our partial systems of education at home, and partly from our having little leisure for study after commencing work in China. Knowing the true strength of the enemy, success will be on the side where numbers, ability, virtue, spirituality and art are on the whole the stronger.[20]

Lee cites only the first sentence of the above quotation, before cementing his view of Richard's 1880s theology with a quotation on the Kingdom of God taken anachronistically from the opening of Richard's 1906 *Conversion by the Million*.[21] More fundamental than this problematic use of texts, Lee's line of argument does not give adequate weight to Richard's intentions in

---

19. Lee, "Qing mo ming chu jiduxinjiao lai Hua chuanjiaoshi," 24.

20. Richard, "Thoughts on Chinese Missions," 430. Note that the article was not titled "Thoughts on Christian Missions," perhaps reflecting Richard's abiding interest in the explicitly Chinese nature of the mission task.

21. Lee, "Qing mo ming chu jiduxinjiao lai Hua chuanjiaoshi," 24, especially n. 73. The citation is from Richard, *Conversion by the Million*, 1:4.

writing his 1880 essay: Richard was not questioning the message itself, but rather the notion that its simple declaration alone was sufficient to produce results. Motivated by his abiding evangelical desire for conversions, Richard was exhorting his colleagues to adopt more effective methods by following his trajectory of empathetic acculturation and accommodating their mission methods to meet China's needs.

Gregory Adam Scott is right to view Richard's interest in recognizing truth within other religious traditions as being driven by his desire to seek the worthy.[22] In his interactions with devout Chinese seekers after truth, Richard had personally witnessed the openness to the gospel that was created by showing respect for China's own religious forms and texts. This was, after all, why he had found the devout members of China's sects to be so worthy. In the aftermath of the famine, Richard's reading of the Sermon on the Mount now supplied a theological justification for what he had already found to be practically effective. Combined with the confidence born of famine relief success, this theological conviction encouraged Richard to begin a more active promotion of his mission methods among his colleagues.

Richard's emphasis on the importance of adjusting methods to take the Chinese context more seriously persisted through the next decade of his ministry, retaining always the interest in effectiveness and results that shaped both "Thoughts on Chinese Mission" and his early years in Shandong. Richard's presentation to the 1890 GCPMC on official persecution of Christians within China, despite its ostensible focus on the legal and political aspects of the foreign missionary presence in China, still placed heavy emphasis on the need for Western missionaries to reflect on the suitability of their methods, warning them to avoid confusing "the traditions and practices of Northern Europe and Northern America for that pure Gospel, which is suitable for all climes and times and nations."[23] Lest anyone mistook this questioning of the normative nature of Western Christian "traditions and practices" for an attack on the content of the gospel itself, Richard elaborated his meaning on the next page as the first of his three practical suggestions for his colleagues.

> [W]hile sacrificing no truth of Christianity, our attitude must be less foreign and more sympathetic. Our brethren in the home lands adapt Christian teaching and methods to Western needs; our task is to adapt Christian teaching and methods to Chinese needs.[24]

22. Scott, "Timothy Richard," 75.
23. Richard, "Relation of Christian Missions," 413.
24. Richard, "Relation of Christian Missions." The other suggestions included the

When considering the persecution of Christians at the hands of Chinese citizens and officials, Richard believed that it was the methods of mission activity more than the content of the message that brought about so much of the misunderstanding and conflict. Nor was this an abstract theory for Richard. The churches in Shandong so dear to his heart had struggled with persecution from the beginning. The fact that under the leadership of Pastor Zheng the Christian community grew in faith and numbers during some of the early periods of suffering only strengthened Richard's convictions that it was these adapted, Chinese expressions of Christianity that held promise for the future of the church in China.[25] Accommodation—adjusting mission methods to take advantage of the ways in which Christianity fulfilled or completed what was lacking in existing Chinese religious traditions—thus remained a key component of Richard's efforts to increase mission effectiveness.

Richard's activities surrounding the 1879 triennial provincial-level (*juren*) examinations in Taiyuan provide an example of his accommodationism at work. At least initially, Richard, David Hill, and the CIM workers appeared to have been of one mind regarding the most effective methods by which to establish the gospel in Shanxi. As Hill explained in 1879,

> The Missionaries resident in Tai Yuen Fu, held united consultation and prayer, as to the plans to be adopted, and agreed, that, as this was the first Examination during which Protestant Missionaries had resided in this city, the time had not yet come for street preaching, nor yet for the opening of a Public Preaching Hall, but that the Residences of the Missionaries should be advertized on the gates of the city, and, supposing that this would bring quite a crowd of visitors, that another house should be rented, in addition to the two already occupied.[26]

Next, over ten thousand pieces of literature, complete with instructions on how to contact the missionaries, were distributed during the exams, both to the students as they exited the examination hall and to the officials throughout the city. In addition to "a little book, written by a native Christian in the south . . . called 'The Mirror of Conscience'" and a few other tracts, a sheet specially written by Hill for the examinations entitled "Thanksgiving

---

production of textbooks introducing the truthfulness and value of Christianity to all levels of Chinese society, and the formation of a commission to formally present the needs of the foreign mission community to the imperial throne.

25. Jones noted that in his absence Pastor Zheng added 130 members to the Shandong church during the 1879–80 persecutions. "China," *MH* 76, no. 5 (1880) 152–53.

26. David Hill, "The Triennial Examinations for the Ku Jen Degree," *CR* 10, no. 6 (1879) 463–64.

for the Cessation of the Famine" was handed out. Perhaps drawing upon the example of the Jesuits, a map of the world was printed on the outside of one of the books, in order "that the people might be interested and enlightened in geography." All this effort resulted in "a good number of students" seeking out the missionaries, the visits being most cordial.[27]

Moving beyond linguistic adaptation in literature, Hill and Richard then demonstrated their confidence in Christianity's ability to fulfill or exceed China's own traditions by holding an essay contest alongside the examinations. The contest promised cash prizes for winning contributions on six themes related to "Revelation, Holiness of heart, Atonement for sin, Prayer, Idolatry, and Opium smoking," each question phrased in such a way "as to give scope for the introduction of Buddhist, Taoist, Mahommedan and Christian teaching,—lines of thought, excluded from the Government examinations."[28] The answers they received were generally Confucian in outlook, though some included Buddhist or other religious concepts as well. Confirming Richard's expectations, some did touch on matters perceived by the missionaries as truth, providing evidence of the existence of at least some common ground between Christianity and China's religions.

Out of the 110 responses they received, three contributions from the county-level (*xiucai*) degree holder Xi Zizhi of Pingyang were eventually awarded prizes for their marked approximation to Christian truth. Xi had not attended the exams, and thus had not seen the literature the missionaries distributed; moreover, he was deeply suspicious of the foreigners, initially attempting to have his wife's brother collect the prize money in his stead. Xi was eventually hired by Hill to serve as his language tutor. Not long afterwards—in Hill's home and with his medical assistance—Xi broke his opium habit and became a Christian.[29] Xi quickly became a leader among

---

27. "Letter from Mr. Francis James," *CM* (April 1880) 50. Details of *The Mirror of Conscience* (*Tianliang mingjing*) are given in MacGillivray, *Descriptive and Classified*, 97, 121. Richard and Hill both wanted to use *The Mirror of Conscience*, a circumstance Hill recorded as an answer to prayer. David Hill, "A Register of Matters on wh. I have been much pressed in spirit." 15–16 July 1879, David Hill Papers MMS/17/02/09/02, Reel 27, no. 1159, SOAS.

28. David Hill, "The Ku Jen Examination," *CR* 11, no. 2 (1880) 143. In addition to posting placards, the missionaries advertised the contest in the 19 September 1880 *WGGB* under the title "niti qiwen gaobai [Announcement of Proposed Themes for Solicited Essays*]." For a translation of the notice, as well as a listing of the essay questions, see Guinness, *One of China's Scholars*, 155–56.

29. On the exams and Xi's conversion see Guinness, *One of China's Scholars*, 153–72. In his letter to Taylor on the occasion of Xi's baptism, Turner does not mention Hill's role. Turner to Taylor, 29 November 1880, CIM Papers CIM/JHT Box 10, SOAS. Xi, however, remembered Hill in his testimony recorded in Beauchamp, *Days of Blessing*, 122–27.

the local believers in Pingyang, assuming the name Xi Shengmo, Xi "the overcomer of demons."

Thanks to the efforts of the CIM, few nineteenth-century Chinese Protestants are as well known as "Pastor Hsi."[30] A renowned healer within Golden Elixir sectarianism, Xi represented precisely the kind of devout worthy individual Richard had been seeking.[31] At the same time, Xi's conversion cannot be separated from Richard's expansion of missionary work to target the literati class through literature. Soliciting essays on Christian topics from those who were not only largely ignorant of Christianity but who often owed allegiance to other religious or philosophical systems reflected Richard's accommodationism. Richard and Hill were willing to entertain discussions of Christian truths in Chinese cultural terms, and this willingness created the conditions for Xi's eventual conversion.[32] Moreover, Xi's actual moment of conversion appears to be closely linked with his deliverance from opium with Hill's assistance, suggesting that the practical demonstration of moral evidences that played so large a role in Richard's method of mission also had a place in the winning of this Chinese saint.[33] These initial factors that were so important in the formation of Xi the Christian minister owed much to the particular missionary vision of Timothy Richard.

A few months after the conclusion of the essay contest, Hill described what he saw as the primary benefits of this scheme:

> [B]oth Mr. Richard and myself have been impressed, as never before, with the importance of this method of missionary work. It has brought us into living sympathy with the minds of men we should otherwise have never met, it has thrown light upon the views they hold on the most vital questions, it has supplied us with a series of valuable essays on these subjects written in a

---

30. The more common "Hsi" spelling reflects an earlier romanization of the *pinyin* "Xi." Xi's significance for the CIM's self-constructed identity can be seen in the persistent publication of the Guinness Xi biographies. In Mainland China today, most biographies of Xi are abridged translations of Taylor's earlier work. See, for example, Dai, *Xi Shengmo zhuan*.

31. On Xi's involvement in Chinese sectarianism, a connection that likely continued after his conversion, see Austin, *China's Millions,* 163–66, 171–77, 260–67, among others.

32. Toward the end of the famine Hill was convinced of the need for missionaries to adapt their methods to "the capacity of the hearer." See his argument for distributing preparatory literature in Hill to Brother [John or Edward Hill], 3 August 1879, David Hill Papers MMS/17/02/09/02, Reel 26, no. 1104, SOAS.

33. Much like Xi's encounter with the powerful medicine of the Christian missionaries, demonstrations of efficacy (*ling*) were of great importance for southern Chinese believers around the close of the nineteenth century. Dunch, *Fuzhou Protestants*, 6–9.

style thoroughly Chinese, and in some instances by really able men, and it has in many minds, I doubt not, led to wider views of truth, to a more earnest discussion and more testing scrutiny of the tenets held, and by a previous study of the books distributed, it has led to a more intelligent appreciation of the teaching of Christ than ever before.

All this ferment of thought is so much to the good, for there is no surer way of winning the Kingdom for Christ than by placing Confucius, Buddha, Lao Tsz and Mahomet side by side with Jesus Christ, and showing that as humble seekers after truth, we enter the arena without a shadow of doubt as to the result.[34]

By accommodating their presentation of the gospel to the context of China's religions, Richard and Hill were demonstrating their confidence in the superiority of Christianity. Not surprisingly, when the examinations were held again in 1882, Richard and his wife were already hard at work translating and composing books suitable for distribution to the scholars. This scheme was also influenced by Richard's abiding interest in local self-support, with the result that the materials produced for the literati were being purchased willingly by local leaders, generating some thirty-two pounds of income in 1881 alone.[35]

6.2 The Social Implications of the Kingdom of God

In his 1906 autobiographical essay, Richard placed what he called his "Rediscovery of the importance of the Kingdom of God" within the context of his early work in Qingzhou prior to the North China Famine. According to this account the idea emerged directly from his own unencumbered reading of the Bible: "By carefully analyzing the Scriptures I found that the usual Gospel preached by ordinary evangelists is only a fraction of the glad tidings of great joy which are to regenerate the whole earth." Noting the centrality of the Kingdom in the words of Moses, the prophets, John the Baptist, and Jesus, Richard realized that "It was that the Kingdom of God should come and His will be done on earth as it is in Heaven, that he commanded us to pray."[36] After this epiphany, Richard then went on

---

34. David Hill, "The Ku Jen Examination," *CR* 11, no. 2 (1880) 145. On page 146, Hill concluded by noting "this department of Christian work, carried on in connexion with Tract distribution and colportage may be made a means of influencing rightly the thinking men of China, one-third of the literati of the world, to a mighty and marvellous extent."

35. "Ninetieth Report: China," *MH* 78, no. 5 (1882) 150.

36. BMS Shanxi missionary Arthur Sowerby recounted a conversation wherein

to discuss how the Jubilee year promised in the Kingdom was the only antidote for the injustice, starvation, and poverty prevalent in the world—injustices which he illustrated at the time via a lengthy diatribe against the "accursed land-laws" of Britain.[37]

Later, in 1916, Richard presented his understanding of the Kingdom of God and its implications for mission as arising in a rather different context. Omitting the idea from his discussions of his work in Qingzhou, he instead placed the emergence of the idea in the context of his subsequent relief work in Shanxi, this time including David Hill in the narrative as well. In Richard's words,

> One evening, when Hill, Turner, and I were sitting at a Chinese meal, David Hill told us that after preaching for a number of years without the great success he expected to see he had restudied the New Testament, and discovered that instead of emphasizing the Kingdom of God on earth, as our Lord did, he had been preaching another doctrine, and from that time he began to be more scriptural and less theological. He had discovered a gospel in the New Testament which made Chinese as well as Europeans glad—the gospel of the Kingdom of God wherein dwelleth righteousness, peace on earth, goodwill to men. We had come to China not to condemn, but to save; not to destroy, but to fulfil; not to sadden, but to gladden.
>
> On hearing this I rose from the table, walked into my bedroom, and brought out a notebook in which I had written out my experiences. I read out my conclusions, which were precisely the same as Hill's. At which we had a hearty laugh.[38]

This latter presentation of the idea appears more palatable to evangelical sensibilities. Though lacking the biblical and theological reflection of the earlier presentation, this account is significantly free from the political haranguing that accompanied his 1906 discussion of the idea. And yet both of these accounts were written decades after the idea presented itself.

David Hill's letters from the time—while neither controverting nor confirming Richard's 1916 story—do give testimony to the presence of new ideas in Richard's missionary thinking toward the end of the famine work. At first, writing to his family in May of 1878, Hill testified that Richard

---

Richard claimed to have discovered his "enlarged conception of the Kingdom of Heaven" as something "vastly more" than a mere spiritual Kingdom, through his study of the Old Testament prophets. Sowerby to BMS Committee, 1 August 1888, p. 13, BMSA CH/64.

37. Richard, "Autobiography of the Author" in *Conversion by the Million*, 1:85–87.
38. Richard, *Forty-Five Years*, 145–46.

was continuing with the methods developed during his years in Qingzhou, noting that

> [Timothy Richard] thinks works of charity should form a great part of our plan. In this latter point I agree with him. He thinks, too, that what I may call the eclectic plan should be the one we ought to act on more; probably, in the first instance, this is the better —finding out, making selection of the worthy men of a place and working out from them.[39]

Barely a year later, however, Hill was already expanding on his conviction that the "active duties of benevolence" could not be separated from the preaching of the gospel.[40] Writing again from Taiyuan, Hill called for a larger recognition within the "science of missionary evangelism" of the truth he had come to believe—namely, that the most inveterate skeptic can "not with impunity resist peaceable men whose only idea is to do good." While on the surface merely an endorsement of Richard's abiding belief in the value of moral evidences, this statement from Hill on the importance of engaging in acts of material benefit was expressed in the context of Hill's impassioned plea for his fellow evangelists to employ "more adaptation in presenting the fuller blessings which the Son of God brought to all men."[41] These "fuller blessings" that were part of doing good were similar to the kinds of ideas Richard ascribed to himself and Hill in his 1916 autobiography.

Richard's earlier writings are of little help in determining which if either of his accounts is true. They do, however, provide ample indications of how he understood the Kingdom of God to relate to Christian mission. The same article that revealed Richard's convictions regarding Christianity's ability to fulfill China's religions also provided the earliest published evidence of Richard's growing appreciation for the relevance of the Kingdom of God for this life. In his 1880 *Chinese Recorder* article, "Thoughts on Chinese Missions," Richard's interest in moral evidences was clearly present as he

---

39. Hill to E. Hill, 29 May 1878, as recorded in Barber, *David Hill*, 207. David Hill shared Richard's interest in seeking the worthy, as seen in his prayer diaries from the time of the famine. David Hill, "Summary and Review," 26 June 1879, David Hill Papers MMS/17/02/09/02, Reel 27, no. 1159, SOAS. Even prior to his acquaintance with Richard, Hill was convinced that seeking after the worthy—what the more exegetically-gifted Hill glossed as the "sons of peace" from Luke 10:6—would greatly increase mission effectiveness and strengthen the local church. David Hill, "Cursory Notes on the New Testament," Matt 10:11, David Hill Papers MMS/17/02/09/02, Reel 26, no. 1104, SOAS. While there are few dates in this twenty-four volume manuscript, some of Hill's comments on Matt 10:11 appear to be dated 12 March 1876.

40. Hill to [Foster?], 5 April 1879, David Hill Papers MMS/17/02/09/02, Reel 26, no. 1116, SOAS.

41. Hill to R. J. Hill, 20 June 1879, as recorded in Barber, *David Hill*, 208–9.

demonstrated both the positive aspects of China's own beliefs and practices, as well as the importance of superior ethical and intellectual achievements in the historical expansion of Christianity.[42] Toward the very end of the essay, immediately after the passage wherein he presented his understanding of Christ as fulfillment (see section 6.1 above), Richard called on his fellow China missionaries to

> take the Sermon on the Mount as our text, and for motto, that we have not come to destroy but to fulfill; not to expect to be considered worthy of the kingdom of Heaven except we *exceed* the best in China, endeavouring to be perfect as our Father in Heaven is perfect . . . prepared to "*exceed*" in every branch.[43]

This call to demonstrate the superiority of Christianity—to engage in an even broader application of moral evidences—occurred directly following his discussion of "the righteousness of the kingdom of Heaven." Within this exhortation to exceed "in every branch" lay a new conviction for Richard—namely, that the Kingdom of God was not only concerned with the state of the human soul after death, but that it was also concerned with every aspect of life on this earth.

By 1885 this broadening of the implications of the Kingdom of God was explicit. Showing once again his empathetic identification with the people of China, Richard explained in his recruiting pamphlet *Wanted: Good Samaritans for China* what it was that propelled his work as a missionary in China:

> Whilst I am not blind to the wonderful resources of China in its land, its people, and its institutions, which call forth much praise, it would be unfaithfulness on my part, as the minister of God, if I did not call your attention to these many open sores of China. Nor do I believe it to be the duty of missionary societies to go and do the work of statesmen, of manufacturers, of tradesmen, of educationalists, or even of priests of China. But if all who have charge of these are more or less ignorant of the causes which bring untold misery on millions of their people, and if we know them, and will not do something towards calling their attention to this, how can we be considered to be acting the Good Samaritan towards China?

---

42. Richard showed this same confidence in moral evidences in his 1880 published recommendation that probationary missionaries be required to engage in charitable work alongside Chinese non-Christians. Richard, "Some Thoughts about Christian Missions," 295.

43. Richard, "Thoughts on Chinese Missions," 439–40.

> I understand the Kingdom of God to take cognizance of all in this world as well as the next, in a word, of MAN—*body* and *soul*. Our Lord healed diseases and preached the Gospel.[44]

Pairing his love and respect for China with his deep awareness of her "many open sores," Richard explained that his burden was still for the *missionary* task—no other—which after the example of Jesus he now understood to involve acts of mercy ("healing diseases") as well as the proclamation of the Christian message. His 1885 autobiographical address to the BMS Committee resonated with this same sense of purpose. When describing his missionary activities following the North China Famine, Richard grounded them in his assertion that "Christianity has the promise of the life that now is, as well as of that which is to come."[45] With his "discovery" of the social, this-worldly implications of the Kingdom of God, Richard was developing a theological justification that supported the extension of his previous evangelistic use of moral evidences into a widening range of missionary activities.

Scholars have tended to view developments in Richard's post-famine understanding of the Kingdom of God as signifying a departure from or a break with his previous work as a missionary. In his early work on Richard, Bohr claimed that, stirred by the famine suffering, Richard "radically altered the direction of his Christian ministry in China." This change was reflected in what Bohr called his "radical theology of social action" rooted in a "social interpretation of the Kingdom of God," an idea which Bohr claimed Richard developed "as a response to the wretchedness of the Chinese countryside."[46] One of the earliest studies of theological development within the Protestant mission community in China viewed Richard's supposedly newfound interest in social action as still more momentous, marking it as the birth of the social movement within Christian missions in China.[47] Richard's biographer Soothill also saw this shift as significant, referring to Hill and Richard's "revelation" of the social implications of the Kingdom of God as a personal "metanoia."[48] While Richard was one of the earlier China missionaries to practice social concern as an organic

---

44. Richard, *Wanted: Good Samaritans for China*, 15.
45. Richard, *Fifteen Years*, 18.
46. Bohr, *Famine in China*, 171–72.
47. Smythe, "Changes in the Christian Message," 50–51.
48. Soothill, *Timothy Richard of China*, 113–14. In this passage Soothill says more about himself than Richard, especially in his criticism of "old-style missionaries . . . who still live in Old Testament times, . . . still hold the same views," and have yet to accept Hill and Richard's insight.

component of mission evangelism (the moral evidences of chapters 4 and 5 above), the idea was neither original to him nor a radical departure from his previous understanding and practice of mission.

Since Robert Morrison's employment as translator with the British East India Company, Protestant missionaries to China had often been involved in so-called secular pursuits.[49] In the first half of the century, Karl Gützlaff (inspiration for the Chinese Society for Furthering the Promulgation of the Gospel in China, and Adjacent Countries, by Means of Native Evangelists, later simplified to the Chinese Evangelization Society or CES) and Samuel Wells Williams (ABCFM) had engaged in labors outside of the traditional confines of mission work.[50] Later on, medical work became an increasingly accepted sphere of missionary endeavor—though not without disagreement, as evident in the departures from their mission agencies of Dr. Peter Parker (ABCFM) and Richard's BMS colleague Dr. William Brown.[51] By Richard's day, W. A. P. Martin's employment in the Chinese government School of Combined Learning (*tongwen guan*), and Young J. Allen's transformation of his Shanghai periodical *Jiaohui xinbao* (*Church News*) into the *WGGB*, a key vehicle for the communication of political and technical as well as religious knowledge to the Chinese elite, marked the frontline of expanded missionary activity.[52] Nevertheless, Richard's determination to include a widening sphere of social concerns within the scope of legitimate missionary employment was pushing the boundaries of contemporary missionary practice still further.

Similar ideas had been simmering within British evangelicalism for some time, coming to a boil just as Richard concluded his famine relief work. The 1851 census in Britain and increased reporting on the injustices and immorality in Victorian society had heightened evangelical sensitivities to sin in its various private and public guises.[53] More so than in the earlier parts of the century, it was also becoming acceptable to read the Christian Scriptures as historical documents placing the story of Israel and

49. Though Morrison was not always happy with this arrangement. Daily, *Robert Morrison*, 126–29.

50. See chapter 4, "Anxious To Cultivate Friendship," in Fischer, "'Opium Pushing and Bible Smuggling,'" 245–72; and Lutz, *Opening China*. As an unordained printer, Williams was not always supported in his more integrated understanding of mission work. Kaiser, "S. Wells Williams," 70–76.

51. On Peter Parker, see Anderson, "Peter Parker," 203–38. For Brown's departure, see Stanley, *History of the BMS*, 181.

52. Covell, "Legacy of W. A. P. Martin," 28–31; Bennett, *Missionary Journalist in China*, especially the chapter "The Chinese Globe Magazine, 1874–1883," and p. 226.

53. On perceptions of "sin" driving Victorian social engagement, with particular reference to nonconformity, see Bebbington, *Nonconformist Conscience*, 37–60.

the ministry of Jesus within their larger social and political contexts—even within evangelical circles that remained resistant to any radical conclusions that might be drawn from higher criticism.[54] These two factors combined producing a "ripple of socialism" that swept across England in the 1880s revealing both the extent of popular concern for those less fortunate as well as the increase in public willingness to use the state to do something about that concern.[55] Within nonconformity, this "Christian Socialism" was not initially concerned with redrawing the boundaries of the Kingdom of God, but rather reflected the growing awareness that in the Old and New Testaments was present a "social Gospel" that addressed collective as well as individual moral issues.[56]

While the term "social Gospel" certainly was in use within British evangelicalism during the 1880s, it was not yet encumbered by the implied rejection of theological orthodoxy with which it became associated in twentieth-century America.[57] From the 1880s onwards, higher criticism began to find broader acceptance within nonconformity, transforming nonconformist theological education.[58] Higher critical works such as former Free Church professor William Robertson Smith's *Prophets of Israel* were noting the ways in which the Old Testament prophets targeted the social conditions and civic duties of God's people and the surrounding nations, leading some Protestants to abandon narrowly Christo-centric readings of the Hebrew Bible.[59] At the same time, the Congregationalist R. W. Dale had been defending Christian political activism since the early 1870s, while the Baptist John Clifford had been exploring social Christianity since before the 1880s.[60] During these decades, the idea that a faith that took

---

54. In the 1880s nonconformists in Britain were still confident that higher criticism of the Bible could result in the confirmation of traditional understandings of the atonement and supernaturalism. Glover, *Evangelical Nonconformists*, 18–20, 25, 69–70, 108–10.

55. Thompson, "Emergence of the Nonconformist," 257–58; Brown, *Providence and Empire*, 327–31, 338–43, 353–55.

56. Thompson, "Christian Socialist Revival," 273–95.

57. John Clifford was one of the earliest to employ the term, in his address, *The New City of God*; see Thompson, "John Clifford's Social Gospel," 199–218. On the relationship between the early Social Gospel and twentieth-century American liberalism, see Stanley, "Evangelical Social and Political Ethics," 30–36.

58. Bebbington, *Dominance of Evangelicalism*, 162–66; Glover, *Evangelical Nonconformists*, 71.

59. Smith, *Prophets of Israel*. See the discussion in Thompson, "Christian Socialist Revival," 293–94.

60. Thompson, "Emergence of the Nonconformist," 273–74; Thompson, "John Clifford's Social Gospel," 202–4, 215; Glover, *Evangelical Nonconformists*, 140.

the gospel seriously must also be concerned with injustice and suffering in the world was still closely tied to its evangelical roots, combining rather than separating the priority of individual salvation and the imperative of social concern in expanded evangelical activism.[61] What was new was the conviction that God was also interested in saving societies or nations, in a material as well as spiritual sense. Hence, for many British evangelicals—particularly nonconformists—in the second half of the nineteenth century, the Kingdom of God and by extension the gospel were now understood in social as well as individualistic terms.

There is no evidence either supporting or denying Richard's awareness of or interaction with any of these influential individuals from Britain, nor does Richard credit any other person or book for inspiring his new understanding of the Kingdom. While it is possible that the idea did in fact arise out of his own personal reading of the biblical texts, its growing prominence in Britain at just this time suggests at least the possibility of cross-pollination. Even without clear evidence of a particular connection, it is worth remembering that Richard had been raised within the Victorian evangelical world, the same world that had shaped the proponents of the new social Christianity. Many of the same historical influences that eventually led so many of his peers in Britain to become fixated on the social implications of Christian faith were also at work, though perhaps indirectly, on Richard as well. Rural poverty, financial and class disparity, technological and scientific advance, educational theory, the challenges and promises of higher criticism—despite his many years in China, Richard was acquainted with all these issues. Regardless of the causes and influences, Richard in Shanxi seems to have grasped the passion for social Christianity at roughly the same time that it swept through evangelicalism in Britain.

Richard's newly developed understanding of the full scope of God's Kingdom provided the theological justification for the broadening of his mission work following the famine, but was only expressed by Richard after he had become convinced of the evangelistic effectiveness of mission carried out along the lines of this broadening mandate. As an example, the orphan care programs that emerged in Shandong as a natural response to the needs around him were, by the time he arrived in Shanxi, viewed by Richard as an integral part of his mission strategy.[62] As had been true

61. Bebbington, *Evangelicalism in Modern Britain*, 210–11; Thompson, "Christian Socialist Revival," 295.

62. On the orphanage work in Taiyuan, see "The Orphanage Work—From Mrs. Hudson Taylor. To A Friend," *CM* (February 1879) 19; as well as the report in "Province of Shansi," *CM* (July–August 1880) 88–89. On its value for Richard, see Richard to his mother, 17 January 1880, translated by Thomas Evans, 25 January 1965, BMSA CH/4A.

previously in Richard's life, theory once again was following practice in an organically connected way.

Expanding the scope of the Kingdom of God to include its implications for all aspects of life on earth as well as life after death was an idea that for Richard emerged from earlier actions made possible by his interest in moral evidences, a method that had likewise arisen as a practical response to the ineffectiveness of still earlier apologetic techniques. Richard was not discarding old models and creating new ones. Rather, he was engaged in the classic Chinese practice of *mo-shi-guo-he*, or "feeling the stones as one crosses the river." Recalling his experience in Shandong, Richard in Shanxi continued to be driven by his desire for more effective mission—to see better results, with more people saved more quickly—and so he once again pragmatically adapted his methods, grafting any techniques or ideas that worked into his existing practice and understanding of mission. The difference was that now he believed that saving the body was a key component of saving the soul.

In early 1881 Richard produced a Chinese-language pamphlet entitled *Jinshi yaowu*, or *Present Needs*, which was shortly afterwards serialized in the *WGGB* over a twelve-week period around Christmas 1881.[63] Written under the pen name "friend of China and the West" (*zhong xi you*), the work contained one hundred suggested reforms for China—a practical expression of Richard's desire to prevent future disasters similar in magnitude to the North China Famine.[64] The many proposals regarding transportation and industry, education and agriculture were presented as the righteous fruits of running a nation in accordance with the principles of God's Kingdom—and thus as moral evidences that demonstrated the superior efficacy of Christian truth.

Although at this point Richard did not appear to have formally identified with the mid-century Chinese reformers of the *yangwu* or "self-strengthening" (*ziqiang*) movement, in *Present Needs* his emerging

---

63. For precise *WGGB* references (12 November 1881 to 28 January 1882) see Bennett, *Missionary Journalist in China*, 283 n. 291. On the original date of composition see Bohr, who provides an excellent summary of the scope and content of *Present Needs* based upon the text as serialized in the *WGGB*. Bohr, *Famine in China*, 145–62. Since Bohr's work, at least one copy of the separate pamphlet (with a penciled-in English title) has been found, an autumn 1882 reprint discovered by this author in the Angus Library at Regent's Park College, Oxford. Richard, *Jinshi yaowu*. All references in this thesis will be to this 1882 reprint, using its more common English title, *Present Needs*.

64. Timothy Wong has shown that Richard, on a much smaller scale than *Present Needs*, had previously published reform-minded essays in the Chinese press as early as 1876. Wong, "Timothy Richard," 55.

sympathies were apparent.⁶⁵ The Chinese term *ziqiang* first came into use among Chinese scholars in the early 1860s, and Richard used it twice on the first page of the preface to his 1882 reprint of *Present Needs*. Throughout this period, Richard had interacted with prominent reforming officials Li Hongzhang, Zuo Zongtang, and Zhang Zhidong, as well as Zeng Guofan's younger brother Zeng Guoquan—the first four of whom held to the self-strengthening ideal of adopting Western technology to Chinese ends with varying degrees of commitment.⁶⁶ While Richard shared many of their ideals, his proximity to the self-strengtheners is most apparent in their adoption and promotion of many of the reforms actively promoted by Richard.⁶⁷ As Andrea Janku has suggested, the North China Famine and its revelation of the limitations of the state, the nature of the foreign relief effort led by Richard, and Richard's resulting reform advocacy and subsequent publications with the SDCK, were key to the development of the second generation of self-strengtheners (the more constitutionally-minded modernizers of the *weixin pai* or reformist faction).⁶⁸ Accordingly, it is not coincidental that Richard was an early subscriber to the *weixin* clique's 1895 *qiang xue hui* or Strengthening Society, nor that the turn-of-the-century reformists Kang Youwei and Liang Qichao were so deeply influenced by Richard and his publications.⁶⁹

While Richard, like many Chinese reformers, distinguished between the accouterments of civilization and the gospel, he also insisted that both Western technology and Christian faith were necessary for the healthy development of China.⁷⁰ As Bohr has argued, Richard's obvious interest in especially "the technological blessings of western civilization" was always

---

65. The standard English-language account of the self-strengtheners and their *yangwu yundong* remains Kuo and Liu, "Self-strengthening," 491–542.

66. Li and Zeng occur frequently in Richard's autobiography; on Zhang and Zuo, see Richard, *Forty-Five Years*, 166–67 and 172–73, respectively. In the 1890s the bureaucratic ideals of proper comportment and efficient capability, or *ti-yong*, were re-appropriated by the reformers as "Chinese learning for fundamental principles and Western learning for practical application." Kwong, "T'i-Yung Dichotomy," 260–63.

67. Richard saw his influence clearly, as indicated in Richard, *Forty-Five Years*, 191–92.

68. This is one of the reasons, Janku argues, that the North China Famine deserves more attention from Chinese historians. Janku, "Drought in Northwest China." For the relationship between some of the earlier reformers and the later Kang and Liang, see Hon, "Zhang Zhidong's Proposal for Reform," 80–86.

69. See the discussion of Richard's impact on their thinking in Chen, "Liang Qichao yu Qing mo xifang chuanjiaoshi," 85–90.

70. This integrated approach had been recognized as effective by British mission agencies at least as early as the 1830s. Stanley, "Christianity and Civilization," 192–93.

undergirded by the need for the "moral regeneration" which Richard located within the Christian faith.[71] The bulk of the suggestions offered by Richard in his *Present Needs* were practical, focusing on China's economic conditions and the potential benefits of new technologies. Nevertheless, the entire work, in the words of one Chinese historian, "obviously possessed a Christian flavor and an intention to cause China to return to the Lord."[72] Ten or so of Richard's suggestions explicitly called for spiritual reform along expressly Christian lines, with titles such as "Fear the Lord of Heaven to Save Your Soul" and "Imitate the Savior to Receive Eternal Blessing."[73] But beyond the direct theological focus of certain sections, Richard made the relationship between the spiritual and the material explicit by closing his work with the observation that the so-called wise man who seeks reform without serving God falls into self-deception: he should instead both listen to God and study all manner of knowledge and skill.[74] These twin interests, indicative of his expanding sense of the implications of the Kingdom of God, neatly encompass Richard's work in Shanxi.

Richard's 1885 pamphlet *Wanted: Good Samaritans* illustrates how closely he connected these two imperatives. According to Jesus's parable in Luke 10:29–37, the "good Samaritan" was the foreigner who refused to ignore the suffering of a fellow human being, and took action to deliver that person from physical suffering even at some inconvenience to his or her self. Richard began his reflections in this pamphlet by exhorting his readers to "re-study the principles of the Kingdom of God, and come once again among the civilized nations to defend the sufferers against their oppressors, and point them to an ideal kingdom which all men must uphold and reverence." Most of the pamphlet was then devoted to cataloguing China's historical achievements and present deficiencies in the areas of government, industry, distribution (transportation), education, and religion, with the intention of demonstrating "how sadly [China] needs godly men, with the spirit of Salvation in them, to come and be her best friends in her present time of helplessness."[75] Toward the end of the document Richard explained why he was so interested in transforming Chinese society. "Our Lord healed diseases and preached the Gospel. Some feel themselves called to follow in His footsteps by dealing with nations as He dealt with

71. Bohr, *Famine in China*, 147.

72. Guo, "Li Timotai lai Hua," 97 (translation mine).

73. These are the titles of sections 96 and 97 from *Present Needs*, 34 (translation mine).

74. This is a summary of the final paragraph of the last section in *Present Needs*, 36.

75. This and the preceding quotation are from Richard, *Wanted: Good Samaritans for China*, 2.

individuals."[76] If God's people were to seek his Kingdom, and that Kingdom was concerned with life on earth as well as in heaven, then Richard was justified—obligated—to work as he was able *both* to preach the gospel and to heal diseases. And this applied not just to individuals, but to nations as well. Though there is once again no evidence of direct influence, these ideas—ideas which suggestively appeared in Richard's writings during his 1885 furlough—were already being expressed in Britain by influential nonconformists such as J. B. Paton and R. W. Dale.[77]

By 1890 Richard had achieved a high degree of synthesis in his practice and understanding of mission. Following presentations on missionary qualifications by Taylor and Hill at the 1890 GCPMC in Shanghai, Richard commented that while Chinese Christians were the most efficient and economical pastors and evangelists, it was the missionary's responsibility "to present the claims of God and the blessings of Christianity in such a way that the *prepared* in China shall accept," while also ensuring that "all things necessary for the building up of the church are properly established." All this work, however, could be summarized under one task: "to *establish* the *kingdom* of God in China." This Kingdom certainly entailed the salvation of souls, but much more as well:

> If the kingdoms of this world take into consideration the physical, mental, social, national and international interests of their subjects, how much more does our Father in Heaven pity all the sufferings arising from these. We are therefore, as members of the Body of Christ, to embody this in the world; in other words to mould the many in a mass, as well as to save individual souls.[78]

The priority and effectiveness of indigenous pastors and evangelists, the missionary focus on the worthy in terms that resonated with them, the relevance of God's Kingdom for conditions on earth, the sympathetic drive to alleviate human suffering, and the interest to save nations as well as individuals—all these ideas were now grafted into one another, collectively shaping Richard's expanding, activist view of the missionary task at the close of the 1880s.

---

76. Richard, *Wanted: Good Samaritans for China*, 15.

77. Thompson, "Emergence of the Nonconformist," 265, 269.

78. This and the preceding are from Barber, Hykes, and Lewis, *Records of the GCPMC: Shanghai, 1890*, 163–64.

6.3 Seeking Officials for Strategic Rather than "Worthy" Reasons

At the time of the North China Famine, it was common in China to view natural disasters as the unavoidable *yin* in a cyclical pattern of want and plenty that would be balanced by the inevitable *yang* of abundance at some future date.[79] The governor of Shanxi during the famine, Zeng Guoquan, shared this attitude toward droughts, although he also believed that the famine conditions were the result of human error—namely the effects of excessive planting of opium crops on the limited supply of arable land and on the ability of the labor force to work that land.[80] Richard, along with many foreign observers, agreed with Governor Zeng's diagnosis that the roots of the famine lay in human decisions. The same sense of compassionate identification that led Richard to participate in the relief effort in the first place, having been heightened by the tremendous suffering he witnessed during the famine itself, subsequently compelled him to take measures to ensure that those human factors would be mitigated in the event of any future droughts. As he explained in his 1885 autobiographical address,

> When the relief was over we naturally inquired into the cause or causes of the famine, so as to prevent the recurrence of that terrible calamity. In this way God seemed to drive us to the officials and the educated gentry of the land, for *they* are chiefly responsible for the good and ill of the people. The remedy must be applied there.[81]

Richard's "rediscovery of the Kingdom of God" made it possible to view striving for the betterment of conditions in this world as not just moral evidence but also as advancing God's Kingdom in its own right. In this sense, Richard believed it was God who was leading him to engage with the literati. If changing the minds of Chinese officials and scholars could result in material advance for the people living in China, then as a Christian he was obliged to do so.

One of Richard's earliest post-famine activities was to provide scientific lectures in response to requests from Chinese scholar-officials after the famine.[82] Unfortunately, no materials from these lectures have survived,

---

79. Edgerton-Tarpley, *Tears from Iron*, 78–79.
80. Edgerton-Tarpley, *Tears from Iron*, 107–8.
81. Richard, *Fifteen Years*, 17.

82. On the idea that these lectures were given in response to local invitations, see "Statement of Facts," 10. Significantly, Dixon, Farthing, Morgan, Sowerby, and Turner all affixed their signatures to this report.

leaving little indication of their content other than Richard's much later recollections. In *Forty-Five Years in China* Richard supplied dramatic accounts of a handful of his scientific demonstrations on topics such as "the miracles of steam" and other innovations that were "bringing incalculable blessings to every country that adopted them," along with a list of some of the equipment he purchased for use in the lectures.[83] While "Geissler tubes" and "pocket aneroids" seem removed from typical mission activity, Richard's procurement of such a variety of technological tools was understandable (and reminiscent of Ricci) since, as he explained, "the questions put to me by the officials here are about machinery, engineering [and] commercial principles more than anything else."[84] Lasting from 1879 to 1884, these "frequent lectures to the rulers and scholars" were recognized a few years later by the BMS Shanxi field as having resulted in Richard having "almost daily intercourse" with Chinese elites.[85]

In Richard's writings there are a few tantalizing hints of books and authors that may have influenced his plans for giving educational lectures to local scholar-officials. As discussed previously, Butler's *Analogy* had featured prominently in Richard's early theological education, and he continued to use it while in China. Butler's emphasis on the evangelistic value of things naturally observable, such as the human moral faculty, may have led Richard to believe that encouraging officials to understand better the natural world would increase their curiosity regarding the one who established that world.[86] Sometime between 1879 and 1884 Richard translated "the better part" of Horace Bushnell's *Sermons for the New Life*.[87] Bushnell's resistance to systematic theology and emphasis on the elevated status of humankind would likely have resonated with Richard, and Bushnell did believe in a this-worldly expression of the Kingdom of God; however, given the broad range of topics included in Bushnell's *Sermons* it is difficult to say just what Richard felt was of particular interest or worth translating, and thus what he might have valued in Bushnell's writings.[88] Finally, Richard was also reading the *Essays* of Francis Bacon, the founder of empirical scientific method,

---

83. Richard, *Forty-Five Years*, 160–63.
84. Richard to Baynes, 2 February 1884, BMSA CH/2.
85. "Statement of Facts," 10.
86. "[T]en thousand thousand instances of design cannot but prove a designer." Butler, *Analogy of Religion* (1852), 320.
87. "Statement of Facts," 8. There is no known copy of Richard's translation of Bushnell.
88. On Bushnell's understanding of the Kingdom of God, see Cracknell, *Justice, Courtesy and Love*, 302 n. 152.

during the famine.[89] While less directly interested in scientific matters than some of his writings, the concern of Bacon's *Essays* for proper governance and the true greatness of kingdoms may have suggested to Richard that there was much that Chinese officials could learn from the West.

Although Richard's interest in Chinese scholar-officials has often been equated with his pursuit of the devout worthy, Richard's motives for interacting with the local elite at this time were not primarily evangelistic.[90] Richard did feel an obligation to communicate the Christian gospel to Chinese officials, but (as discussed in chapter 3 above and contrary to the view of most interpreters) he did *not* count them among the worthy—the religiously inclined devout seekers after truth—whom he believed were most likely to convert to Christianity.[91] Writing to BMS Secretary Alfred Baynes in 1884, Richard said:

> As foreigners in this land we must deliver our message to the rulers of the land. They are appointed by God in his Providence over the people. But being first officials and only secondly religious, if at all, we cannot be much surprized at little success amongst them, further than the removal of prejudice, and prevention of persecution.[92]

Though conversion was unlikely, he did hold out hope that his efforts might help some of the officials move closer to the Kingdom. As he explained to the BMS Committee in 1880, "If through these [lectures and demonstrations] the authorities will have reverence for and gratitude to God for His marvelous works, then they may listen without prejudice to other manifestations of His goodness."[93]

More so than evangelism, two other factors were compelling Richard to go after the hearts and minds of the officials. Firstly, Richard had long since recognized the influence that scholar-officials had over the living conditions of the people of China. Accordingly, mitigating the human factors that contributed to disasters such as he had just experienced would

89. Richard, *Forty-Five Years*, 110.

90. Instrumental motivations, such as securing residency in the Chinese interior, also influenced initial Jesuit interactions with high-ranking Chinese officials. Standaert, "Matteo Ricci."

91. For a recent example tying Richard's work with officials to his pursuit of the worthy, see page 1 of Scott, "Famine and Political Reform"; and, to a lesser extent, Pfister, "Rethinking Mission in China," 209 n. 66; Stanley, *History of the BMS*, 182; Walls, "Multiple Conversions," 252.

92. Richard to Baynes, 2 February 1884, BMSA CH/2.

93. "BMS Annual Report," 1880, p. 101, as cited in Bohr, *Famine in China*, 262 n. 159.

be difficult without the support and participation of the Chinese elite. Secondly, Richard also believed that removing official prejudices could result in more freedom for foreign and Chinese Christians to practice and spread Christianity. Already evident in his 1878 reminder to Baynes and the BMS to take special care of Chinese ambassadors in Britain, Richard's desire to soften Chinese elite attitudes toward Christianity and the Western nations from whence the missionaries had come had grown over time to become the driving force behind at least some of the literature he was producing in 1884.[94]

The first time Richard formally addressed the GCPMC, his topic was the "Relation of Christian Missions to the Chinese Government."[95] Richard's 1890 address analyzed in detail the depth of official enmity toward Christianity before proposing specific steps aimed at reducing instances of persecution. Following an initial plea for a more empathetic attitude toward China and her people, Richard's recommendations for alleviating official harassment involved the preparation of literature to introduce Chinese scholar-officials to both Christian truths and the modern techniques and technologies of the West, accompanied by a program of increased and intentional interaction with Chinese officialdom.[96] Richard saw a direct connection between changing negative official opinions of Christianity and the progress of the gospel in China.

While Richard's newfound grasp of the scope of the Kingdom of God provided justification for the expansion of his missionary activities to include giving scientific demonstrations and publishing articles on reform, this did not mean he no longer supported or participated in other more traditional forms of missionary activity. While much of his time and energy were devoted to interviews with scholar-officials and delivering his scientific lectures, these projects were not independent from his work with other missionaries to put suitable Christian literature into the hands of the thousands of scholars who attended the triennial examinations in Taiyuan. Likewise, the broader task of distributing scripture tracts in all of the major market towns of Shanxi was advanced even as Richard prepared literature that was intended to bring material progress to the people of China. Richard's willingness to set aside his Shanxi work to superintend the church work of the BMS Shandong field during Jones's 1882–1883 furlough, his pride over the health of the Chinese church in Shandong, and his evident care

94. Richard to Baynes, 2 December 1878, as recorded in "Our Missionaries in China," *MH* 75, no. 3 (1879) 59. See, for example, Richard's two brief pamphlets *Zhongxi heyi lun* and *Min jiao zhi'an zhi ce*.

95. Richard, "Relation of Christian Missions," 401–15.

96. Richard, "Relation of Christian Missions," 414–15.

for the linguistic struggles and missionary zeal of his new BMS Shandong colleague Dr. J. Tate Kitts, all show his attentiveness to and involvement in missionary endeavor beyond the scope of his work with officials.[97] Rather, without repudiating church-focused work, Richard had made a calculated decision to put less of his energies into visiting the various rural fellowships and evangelizing the masses. After explaining the unique position Timothy Richard was in of being actively sought after by Chinese mandarins, Mary Richard rhetorically asked the BMS Committee,

> Would Mr. R. have been justified in turning his back on such an opening and *confining* himself to work among the lower class, especially when there were so many natives and foreigners to do that part of the work quite as well as he could, and they not yet fitted to do his new work?[98]

Richard was not rejecting the kinds of evangelistic work he had done in Qingzhou prior to the famine in order to bring science and civilization to the upper classes of China. Rather, God had presented him with an urgent task; and while there were comparatively many others who could do the kinds of work he had done before in Qingzhou, he felt uniquely suited to pursue this new area of mission work. With the legitimate scope of missionary activity now broadened by his understanding of the Kingdom of God, Richard the missionary chose to focus on Chinese officials and scholars. For him, they represented an effective means both to prevent the future sufferings of the people of China, and to remove what he perceived to be some of the key barriers to the conversion of large sections of China's population.

Richard's attitude toward the officials was shared by at least some of his BMS colleagues. In their 1886 report on the BMS work in Shandong, James and Jones demonstrated their agreement with Richard's interest in Chinese officials. In his description of the state of mission work in Jinan, James—who had first-hand knowledge of Richard's efforts in Shanxi—stated the case plainly:

> We feel ourselves bound as much to *work* for those in authority as to *pray* for them (1 Tim. I, i-iv.) Abundant evidence has convinced us that the cause of much opposition to Christianity, persecution of native converts, and hatred of foreigners, is to be found in the neglect or failure of Protestant missionaries

---

97. Richard to Baynes, 1 February 1883, BMSA CH/2; Richard, *Forty-Five Years*, 178–84.

98. Mary Martin Richard, "Sketch of Mr. Richard's Work," 3.

to convey to the rulers and teachers of China, a correct understanding of Christ's religion and of the motives and aims of its advocates.[99]

Jones, who had known Richard for so long, associated himself more directly with Richard's methods in his contribution.

> I can well fancy someone thinking thus: "Oh, this is the old thing over again, Mr. Richard and Mr. Jones always wanting to reach the upper classes, to get hold of the influential, the same worldly tendency to forsake the good near you for some visionary thing far away."
>
> I rejoin "Precisely so, the same old thing, but the 'old thing' is the furtherance of the gospel of Christ not among the rich but among the *poor*. We seek the few for the sake of the many—the city, for the sake of the country. What we have got to do with are the *hindrances* of the gospel." Living force differs essentially from a dead lubricant—yet, how necessary the proper application of the lubricant at the exact point of friction and strain.[100]

Jones thus saw not only the value of such work, but also the necessity of the kind of division of labor which Mary Richard saw in her husband's engagement with Chinese officialdom. Richard was willing to focus on applying the "lubricant" of educational and literary endeavors to influence the scholar-officials of the land, in order that the living force of the gospel could work more effectively among the larger population.

6.4 The Coming "National Conversion"

Over the course of his first fifteen years as a missionary in China, Richard had laid the foundations for what he expected to be the extraordinary progress of Christianity in China. Two conditions, both of which were the focus and result of Richard's own mission activities, served as evidence that the moment was at hand. First, he had seen "the Chinese government and the devout people on the one hand getting gradually convinced of the goodness of Christianity."[101] This was the fruit of Richard's interactions with Chinese religious leaders (seeking the worthy) and his work

---

99. Francis James, "On the Occupation of Tsi-nan-fu" in Jones, et al., *Baptist Missionary Work in North-China*, 6.

100. Alfred Jones, "On the Indispensability of one Missionary especially to work the City of Ts'ing Chou Fu," in Jones et al., *Baptist Missionary Work*, 21.

101. This and the following two quotations are from Richard, *Fifteen Years*, 22–23.

promoting education and reform among the officials (presenting evidence of the moral superiority of Christianity). Second, he had seen "the formation of Churches, on the other hand, getting more and more general, kindling up the love of God in the hearts of men throughout the [Chinese] Empire." Richard believed that the rapid spread of Chinese churches he had witnessed in his Shandong ministry was intimately connected with his emphasis on the empowerment and agency of Chinese believers in all aspects of church life (indigenous principles).

With these preparations in hand, China was on the cusp of a spiritual breakthrough that would rapidly and decisively involve the entire nation.

> If we add can to these two growing blessings an adequate literature, and continue to live adequate lives, *can* we then doubt our being near the time when a nation shall be born in a day? This is what I call extraordinary statistics.
>
> *We* had planned individual conversions. God had also planned national ones. We ought to thank God and take great courage. It is to this *national* conversion that God calls us now.[102]

Read in light of the rest of his comments in *Fifteen Years*, Richard's vision of "national conversion" included both the spiritual blessings that would accrue to millions of individuals as they turned to faith in Jesus, as well as the material benefits that would flow naturally throughout Chinese society as the nation recognized and embraced God's laws.[103] This was Richard's understanding of what the Kingdom of God promised.

Compelled by his evangelical desire for conversions and in line with the empathetic trajectory of his response to the Chinese other, Richard's pre-famine missionary adaptations emerged from the disaster strengthened by newly conceived theological underpinnings. The emphasis on seeking the worthy that had grown from his idiosyncratic appropriation of Irving and his encounters with Chinese religious leaders, found its theological justification in Richard's eminently practical reading of Jesus's claim to fulfill

---

102. This passage is significant as the background for understanding his 1901 address to the Shanghai Semi-General Conference of Missionaries, "How to Make a Million Converts," in Richard, *Conversion by the Million*, 1:211–31. The "Laws" of mission work that Richard outlined in that essay were for the most part already present in his thinking in the early 1880s, as demonstrated in this thesis. On the other hand, Richard's 1889 paper for the North China Religious Tract Society on "How One Man can Preach to a Million," was—not surprisingly, given his audience—devoted almost exclusively to the importance of the prompt and wide distribution of suitable literature for the evangelization of China. See the abridged version in Richard, *Conversion by the Million*, 1:197–210.

103. See, in particular, Richard, *Fifteen Years*, 9–13, 17–23.

rather than destroy the religion of Israel. This gave Richard confidence to develop his missionary methods along accommodationist lines in order to better appeal to people within a Chinese religious context. Likewise, the emphasis on moral evidences in evangelism—on appeals to conscience— that emerged from his early work in Shandong had by the end of his intimate participation in the North China Famine found its theological roots in Richard's conviction that the Kingdom of God was concerned with this world as well as the next. This resulted in a broadening of the legitimate scope for mission endeavor to include a host of activities that for Richard were focused on bringing material benefit to the people of China who had so recently suffered so greatly, as well as breaking down official prejudices against Christianity. Through both of these progressions, Richard's preference for indigenous solutions and indigenous results remained visible, as seen in his pride over the growth and strength of the Shandong church, and his expectation of still more rapid results in Shanxi.

However, not everyone welcomed Richard's innovations. Following his famine success, Richard faced criticism throughout the 1880s from outside and within his own mission. The nature of these criticisms, and Richard's responses to them, revealed his commitment to his missionary adaptations as well as the degree to which his peers accepted or rejected those innovations. The next two chapters will examine these attacks; first, from the CIM he earlier had so admired, and second, from his own Shanxi coworkers in the BMS.

Part Three

Richard Encountering Conflict

Confirmation and Conviction of His Missionary Thought

7
Richard and the China Inland Mission

BY THE TENTH ANNIVERSARY of his arrival in China, Timothy Richard was an established and successful missionary, filled with confidence in the new understanding and practice of mission that had developed from the confluence of his evangelical impulses and his empathetic acculturation. With the famine in the past, Richard was now the senior missionary on the Shanxi frontier, surrounded by a growing group of colleagues from a range of missions. This last section of the thesis will analyze the conflicts and confusion that emerged as Richard began to work more closely than ever before with a host of other missionaries—first with the members of the CIM Shanxi mission, and then with colleagues of his own in the BMS North China Mission.

Historians record that at some point during the first half of the 1880s the spirit of cooperation that existed between the missionaries in post-famine Shanxi began to crumble, resulting in a severing of ties between Richard and the CIM. While it may seem inevitable to modern readers that James Hudson Taylor and Timothy Richard would disagree over missionary work, such distinctions were not obvious at the time. During and after the famine, Richard had shown a generous spirit to other missions, especially Taylor's CIM, with all the early Shanxi workers enjoying the resulting cooperation and fellowship. But as issues within the CIM itself led the Shanxi workers to transfer to Richard's BMS one after another, Taylor's frustration grew, and soon he took action to stem the flow. Taylor became convinced that the cause for these desertions was Richard, as expressed in his two primary criticisms: first, Taylor believed that Richard was "not orthodox" but had "Romish" tendencies; and second, he thought he was too influential within the CIM Shanxi field. While the paucity of evidence makes it difficult to speak conclusively about the theological issues that caused Taylor to break with Richard, there is ample documentary proof to demonstrate that while Richard was respected by his CIM neighbors, the exodus of Shanxi workers from the CIM had little to do with Richard or his paradigm of mission. This suggests the need for revision to the scholarly consensus regarding these events and what some recent writers have termed the "Shanxi spirit."

7.1 Mutual Cooperation

One of the first things Richard did after arriving in Taiyuan was send word to the coast seeking the whereabouts of "Mister Xiu and Mister Teh."[1] Somehow Richard had discovered that he was not the first foreigner to visit Shanxi during the famine, and with only their Chinese names at hand Richard was able to contact Francis James and Joshua Turner at the CIM headquarters in Shanghai where they were recovering from illness. Richard's purpose in writing was to invite these Shanxi veterans to join him in famine relief work in the province—a task they heartily agreed to undertake as some of the first contributors to what would become the multi-mission effort to help alleviate famine conditions in Shanxi.

This minor incident reveals an aspect of Richard that remained fairly constant throughout his years of service in China. Whether by temperament or perhaps as a reflection of his revivalist conversion experience, Richard maintained an open and welcoming attitude toward other Christian organizations and associations.[2] In his pursuit of effective mission in China, Richard, like many other missionaries around the world, was led by issues of efficacy and practicality rather than organizational or even denominational fealty.[3] This pattern of open ministry had been set during Richard's earliest years in Shandong, as he learned from his fellow Chefoo missionaries and enjoyed close cooperation with Nevius in Qingzhou. It then found confirmation in the multi-agency Shanxi relief effort within which Richard functioned as de facto leader and coordinator.

When the BMS was slow to send out coworkers for the new Shanxi field, Richard contacted the ABCFM and CIM who responded quickly, sending out laborers.[4] Martin and Emily Stimson of the ABCFM—bound for Shanxi as the first of the "Oberlin Band"—were hosted by the Richards when they initially arrived in China.[5] Richard was mentioned often during

---

1. "Shansi Province," *CM* (December 1879) 147–48.

2. Although, like most nonconformists, Richard "could not tolerate" the "anythingism of modern Broad Churchism." Schofield, *Memorials of R. Harold A. Schofield*, 233.

3. See Stanley, "Reshaping of Christian Tradition," 399–426.

4. The Religious Tract Society was also contacted, and responded by sending money and loaning Dr. Murdoch from India to assist with organizing Society work in China. Richard to Baynes, "For the Committee," 1 March 1887, BMSA CH/2.

5. Brandt, *Massacre in Shansi*, 29.

the first few years of the ABCFM Shansi Mission's minutes, as he worked successfully with Stimson and Charles Tenney to establish a comity agreement to avoid reduplication of efforts.[6] Relationships were cordial enough for Richard to be invited to lead "devotional services" on one evening of the Shansi Mission's first annual meeting in May 1882, an evening also attended by Dr. Schofield of the CIM.[7]

Richard also hosted the first group of CIM reinforcements for Taiyuan, inviting them to reside at his home until they could arrange suitable housing for themselves.[8] There was real admiration in these early relationships, as recorded by Jennie Taylor, who found the Richards to be "both very nice people. Mrs. Richard is very humble and earnest, and he is a splendid missionary."[9] In the pages of the CIM *China's Millions* periodical Richard's central role in the famine relief work was warmly acknowledged, while he and his wife were praised as "noble, unselfish missionaries." Readers were enjoined to remember them as well as David Hill alongside their prayers for James, Turner and the other CIM workers in Shanxi.[10]

The work itself also reflected the respect shared between the various missionaries: the tract distribution project, the work surrounding the examinations, and the various schools and orphanages around Taiyuan all involved members of more than one mission. In many instances, particular initiatives or promising converts were transferred between the missionaries and their respective agencies. Pastor Xi is the best known example of these exchanges, but Richard transferred other new converts to the CIM as well, and was quite proud of the success enjoyed by the CIM in Pingyang following his own post-famine removal to Taiyuan.[11]

During its early years, the CIM was quite comfortable receiving assistance from other missions, even going so far as to view its work as dependent on that of the other more established agencies. Writing in 1877, James

---

6. "Records of Special Meetings: 1882–1883," vol. 1:15, 17, Shansi Mission (ABC 16.3.15), ABCFMA; "Records of the First Annual Meeting: 27–31 May 1882," vol. 1:23–26, 29, Shansi Mission (ABC 16.3.15), ABCFMA.

7. "Records of the First Annual Meeting: 27–31 May 1882," vol. 1:25, Shansi Mission (ABC 16.3.15), ABCFMA.

8. Richard, *Forty-Five Years*, 141.

9. Jennie Taylor to Mrs. C. T. Fishe, 3 December 1878 as recorded in "Tidings from Shan-si," *CM* (April 1879) 50.

10. R. J. Forrest, "Report of R. J. Forrest," *CM* (November 1879) 138; "Tidings from Shan-si," *CM* (March 1879) 40; "Tidings from Shan-si," *CM* (April 1879) 51.

11. Mary Martin Richard, "Sketch of Mr. Richard's Work," 5; Richard, *Fifteen Years*, 19. On Pastor Xi, see chapter 6 above.

Hudson Taylor explained his understanding of the relationship between the CIM and other mission agencies at work in China:

> We aim at being an auxiliary agency; and but for the work of our honoured predecessors, and of our esteemed fellow labourers, from Europe and America, the work we are doing would have been an impossibility. We learn the language from the books they have prepared, circulate the Scriptures they have translated, and sell the tracts they have written and printed. We should not advise them, nor do we wish them to leave undone the work they are doing so well.[12]

Taylor went on in his editorial to describe his agency's plan to mimic the wide itineration habits of the colporteurs, but to devote its energies more to preaching than to literature distribution. This self-perception as "auxiliary" may not have survived the organization's growth and increasing institutionalization, but it may help explain the hesitancy of the CIM to enter into a comity agreement with Richard and the BMS: building upon the work of others naturally required geographical overlap.[13]

For this "happy circle of friends," the early phase of the Protestant mission work in Shanxi indeed possessed "a charm of unity and simplicity all its own."[14] More than a reflection of a healthy community, the cooperation that Richard had appreciated and fostered throughout his first ten years in China had become for him by 1880 an essential component of effective mission. In his "Thoughts on Chinese Missions" essay, Richard highlighted the "want of system" in missionary work as a key hindrance to Christian advance in China.

> The Government distributes its power into provinces, circuits, prefectures, and hiens [xian], and who is there that does not admire the system as far as it goes? And what is *our* system? It is nothing but an absolute chaos, scarcely showing a trace of being the work of men with a common aim, except in the few reforms that have of late been made in the southern ports. For instance: I was once foolish enough to take a three days' journey after one convert who lived in the same village with converts of the Presbyterian church, as though I could not trust

12. James Hudson Taylor, "Work of the China Inland Mission," *CM* (April 1877) 43.

13. One ABCFM missionary present at the time, however, ascribed the lack of comity between the BMS and CIM in Shanxi to the reluctance of the many Christian Brethren in the CIM to be led by unspiritual concerns. Stimson to Smith, 13 February 1885, Shansi Mission (ABC 16.3.15), vol. 2, part 2 (Reel 318: 0632), ABCFMA.

14. Barber, *David Hill*, 205.

my brethren to give him all, essential advice. I have known others go an eight days' journey to look after converts who lived within a couple of hours' walk of another missionary. The same with colleges, schools, mission stations, medical missions and book-making; instances might be multiplied to any extent to show waste of power.

In the face of this, what sensible Chinaman can be expected to help us with funds to travel hundreds of li on such conceited errands? Nay, what sensible foreigner would do so either unless blinded by habit and conceit of his own denomination's surpassing excellence? It was refreshing to see the [1877 GCPMC] Conference calling attention to the necessity of greater unity of action, and it is to be hoped that the suggestion will be carried out by all throughout China.[15]

Richard had been reading from Francis Bacon's *Essays* since at least 1876.[16] In his third essay, "Of Unity in Religion," Bacon had stressed the dire consequences of any breach of unity within the body of Christ.[17] In particular, Bacon's warning against schism over matters either too small or—though large—too subtle and ingenious, seems to accord well with Richard's own sensibilities. He would have ample opportunities to reflect on just these questions during his remaining years in Shanxi. For despite the happy fellowship that pervaded during these early days, the Shanxi field was to witness tremendous upheaval over its first few decades, with many workers resigning from or transferring between missions.

7.2 Separating from Richard: The Question of Orthodoxy

Richard enjoyed very close, cordial relations with the CIM, as seen in the repeated favorable mentions he received in the pages of *China's Millions* throughout the early days of the Shanxi mission. At first, Taylor viewed Richard almost as if he were one of his own, including the Richard family in a list of China workers for use at an 1879 prayer meeting in England—alongside David Hill of the WMMS, the only other non-CIM person mentioned.[18] Taylor's second wife Jennie acknowledged (gratefully) having

---

15. Richard, "Thoughts on Chinese Missions," 436.

16. Bacon is mentioned in sections 5.3 and 6.3 above; and Richard, *Forty-Five Years*, 110.

17. Bacon and Whately, *Bacon's Essays*, 24–27. While Richard does not indicate which edition he read, Whately's was popular in the mid century and Richard may have encountered it during his school days.

18. Taylor to Benjamin Broomhall, 20 February 1879, CIM Papers CIM/JHT/242,

learnt famine relief techniques from Richard, while CIM missionary Celia Horne—noting the absence of James from Taiyuan, and the lack of language skills of her newest colleagues—made special mention of Richard's "kind help" and service to her.[19]

Initially, the small foreign community located in Taiyuan worshipped together as one at the Richards' home.[20] This unity began to crumble when, according to the retrospective account in Richard's 1916 autobiography, "Mr. Hudson Taylor, of the Inland Mission, broke our harmony by ordering his members, in 1881, to have a separate place of worship, on the ground that I was not orthodox."[21] In an effort to preserve the earlier accord on the field, Richard then made a special trip to Tianjin to meet with Taylor in person—perhaps the occasion when Richard claimed to have heard the phrase "not orthodox." This was the earliest recorded meeting between the two men. Richard's trip, however, was in vain: Taylor was apparently unwilling to remove his injunction or to agree to any sort of comity or division of the field.

According to Richard's 1916 recollections, CIM Taiyuan workers Robert Landale and Dr. Harold Schofield were initially distressed and surprised at Taylor's decision.[22] Schofield continued to worship at least intermittently with Richard, recalling "an admirable and most powerful address" delivered by Richard on Sunday, 1 January 1882 "on God's majesty and the fulness of Christ's redemption."[23] When Schofield died in 1883, the CIM Taiyuan workers spoke repeatedly of Richard's indispensable kindness and care during and after the crisis.[24] Schofield's account of Richard's pastoral ministry during the earlier passing of Mary Landale in January 1882 as reported in *China's Millions* strengthens this impression, showing not only the esteem in which Richard was held by each of the CIM Taiyuan workers, but also their affirmation of his theological orthodoxy.[25]

Box 10 (513-10), SOAS.

19. Jennie Taylor to Mrs. C. T. Fishe, 3 December 1878 as recorded in "Tidings from Shan-si," *CM* (April 1879) 50; "Brief Notes: Miss Horne," *CM* (October 1881) 128.

20. Richard, *Forty-Five Years*, 152; Barber, *David Hill*, 205.

21. Richard, *Forty-Five Years*, 152–53. This also, according to Richard, resulted in the opening of a separate CIM school in Taiyuan.

22. Richard, *Forty-Five Years*, 152–53.

23. Schofield, *Memorials of R. Harold A. Schofield*, 190.

24. "Tidings from T'ai-yuen Fu, Shan-si Province," *CM* (November 1883) 155–57. Broomhall mistakenly lists Schofield's date of death as 1 August 1881. Broomhall, *HTCOC*, 6:501.

25. "In Memoriam," *CM* (June 1882) 70–73. According to Schofield, Richard was invited to give the address at the funeral, reading from 1 Cor 15 and reflecting on the

For his part, Richard had continued in his practical ecumenism on the field after the breach in fellowship, entrusting various new believers and enquirers to the care of CIM workers. On one occasion in 1882, Richard introduced to the CIM a local temple-keeper initially evangelized by one of Richard's Shandong evangelists. The man was soon baptized and employed in the CIM Taiyuan mission as one of their native helpers.[26] Arriving in Shanxi just after the supposed division, the new workers from the ABCFM shared in the communal spirit by deciding in November 1882 to invite their "friends of other missions" in Taiyuan—Baptist and CIM—to join them in worship "on alternate Sabbaths."[27] Clearly, whatever Taylor's intent, his workers on the field ignored his injunction and continued to cooperate and share fellowship across organizational lines.[28]

Given what little difference it seems to have made, what precisely was the nature of the complaint against Richard that led to this division? Richard's claim, written forty years after the fact, that Taylor believed he was "not orthodox," indicates that the dispute was theological, an assessment further strengthened by Taylor's intention to hold separate worship services. Beyond this entry from the last years of his life, however, Richard makes no other references to this event: his personal correspondence from the time as well as his two earlier autobiographical accounts make no mention of any separation of worship or theological dispute with Taylor.

The correspondence of the other missionaries in Shanxi at the time is also silent on the division. The break in fellowship is absent as well from the biographies of the missionaries who served in Shanxi during those years, save a fleeting acknowledgment by David Hill's biographer that at the time of the famine "the worship in Taiyuen had not yet crystallised into the separate services supported by separate societies."[29] Apart from Richard's 1916 account, and this brief comment in an 1899 biography of Hill, there is no indication that the community ever divided.

Most surprising of all, none of the existing CIM materials from the time mention a breaking of fellowship in Taiyuan. As mentioned above, the

---

theme, "To me to live is Christ, to die is gain."

26. "Tung" was among the first six people baptized by the CIM in Taiyuan. 6 July 1882 letter, as printed in "Province of Shan-si: From Mr. Pigott," *CM* (July 1883) 84–85.

27. "Records of Special Meetings: 1882–1883," vol. 1:15, 17, Shansi Mission (ABC 16.3.15), ABCFMA.

28. McKay has suggested that Taylor intentionally divided his workers on the field according to their denominational backgrounds. McKay, "Faith and Facts," 143. While beyond the scope of this study, it would be fascinating to see how or if this holds true for the Shanxi field.

29. Barber, *David Hill*, 205.

CIM members in Taiyuan gave no indication of dissatisfaction with Richard. Taylor's own communications did not mention separate worship services. In fact, in all of Taylor's extant correspondence prior to 1890 Richard's name only appeared twice. These two brief references—which again, are silent regarding the division in Taiyuan—are the only direct evidence available for reconstructing the content of Taylor's accusation of "not orthodox."

Taylor's first mention of Richard occurred in a letter to Benjamin Broomhall written in response to the news of a May 1880 letter from James requesting transferal to the BMS. Taylor informed Broomhall that

> Richard is driving a good theory to death. He refuses to preach to the masses, is for circulating moral and theistic tracts not containing the name or work of Christ, to prepare the way as he thinks for the gospel, and in some respects is dangerously near Rome.[30]

In this letter Taylor expressed clear dissatisfaction with the way in which Richard was going about mission, criticizing the methods—the preaching and tract circulating—that had emerged from Richard's somehow excessive application of his "good theory." For his part, Richard certainly spent less time preaching on Chinese street corners, preferring to train Chinese evangelists instead. And while still in Shandong Richard had become convinced of the efficacy of simple Christian messages in attracting the worthy and preparing people to accept the gospel. Richard—along with Hill—was also convinced that colportage that allowed only for scripture distribution, while perhaps good in other places, was premature in Shanxi.[31] Both Richard and Hill believed that "adapting" missionary methods in pursuit of more effective evangelism meant beginning with basic, simple truths to lay the groundwork for accepting the necessary full teaching of salvation through Jesus.[32] The bills posted by Richard during the famine in Shandong and Shanxi reflected this technique—one he had found to be effective.[33]

Taylor, on the other hand, was much more interested in unadulterated scripture colportage. Discounting the tract distribution that Richard,

---

30. Taylor to Benjamin Broomhall, 24 May 1880, CIM Papers CIM/JHT/256, Box 10, SOAS.

31. While on furlough, Jones, likely channeling what he had learned from Richard, aggressively defended the need for the preaching of basic gospel ideas to precede the distribution of whole scriptures, ironically citing Taylor's own words at the 1877 GCPMC. Jones, *North China BMS*, note on p. 7.

32. See, for instance, Hill to his brother [John or Edward Hill], 3 August 1879, David Hill Papers MMS/17/02/09/02, Reel 26, no. 1104, SOAS.

33. See the discussion of evangelism during the famine in chapter 5 above.

Hill and the Shanxi workers of the CIM had carried out across the entire province, Taylor explained to one donor in the spring of 1880 that he had "been unable to get colportage or evangelistic work carried on there up to the present time."[34] For Taylor, true "colportage or evangelistic work" meant passing out scripture rather than the "moral and theistic tracts" which the other Shanxi missionaries (including the CIM workers) were already distributing throughout the entire province. While this difference may have shaped Taylor's criticism in this letter, it provides only scant grounds for claiming that Richard was so far from orthodoxy that he ought not to be joined in worship.

Taylor's focus may have been on specific "moral and theistic tracts" used by Richard which did not contain "the name or work of Christ." Unfortunately, no information is available regarding which of Richard's Chinese-language materials may have been known to Taylor. Richard's catechism and his translations of *Holy Living* or *The Philosophy of the Plan of Salvation* contained the name of Christ and it seems implausible that these could be called "moral or theistic tracts."[35] Though no copies survive for analysis, the tracts distributed throughout Shanxi after the famine, as well as those prepared for the provincial examination candidates were used by the CIM missionaries in Shanxi and prepared with the assistance of Hill, who was respected by the CIM in China and in England.[36] If specific literature was being targeted, then Taylor was most likely criticizing the materials passed out by Richard during the famine (none of which has survived), and thus was attacking a specific example of his general complaint discussed in the paragraph above regarding Richard's use of literature in evangelism.

Taylor's mention of "the name or work of Christ" appears to come closer to challenging the orthodox nature of Richard's Christianity. Though he did not say so directly in this document—a personal letter written only for his friend Broomhall's eyes—Taylor may have feared that Richard did not recognize the centrality of Jesus and His cross in evangelism. If connected

---

34. All quotations in this paragraph are from Taylor to Benjamin Broomhall, 6 March 1880, CIM Papers CIM/JHT/256, Box 10, SOAS.

35. The fact that no one ever complained of his catechism suggests it did not fail to mention Jesus or his cross. While no copy of Richard's translation of *Holy Living* exists, Jesus's name appears throughout the translated *Philosophy of the Plan of Salvation*. See, for example, the title given by Richard and Zheng to chapter 16: "*Jiushi dangran zhi li*: di shiliu zhang lun xin Yesu ganhua ren [*Philosophy of the Plan of Salvation*: chapter sixteen, concerning faith in Jesus and its improving effects on man*]," *WGGB* (14 June 1875) 608a.

36. As demonstrated by his prominent role in the 1881 CIM Fifteenth Anniversary meetings, recorded in *CM* (July–August 1881) 89–92. On Hill's role in producing tracts during and after the famine, see chapters 5 and 6 above.

with the final phrase that Richard was "dangerously close to Rome," it is even possible that Taylor was suggesting that by eschewing mention of the name or work of Christ Richard held a (deficient) Catholic understanding of salvation. Only a few years later when speaking to a gathering of Shanxi missionaries Taylor criticized the Jesuit mission in China for obscuring the cross in their presentation of Christianity.[37] The tone of Taylor's complaint (Richard apparently possessed a "good theory") and the—admittedly self-reported—coolness of Richard's response, however, do not seem proportionate to so serious an attack.[38]

Only slightly less inflammatory, Taylor's reference to preparing the way and his characteristic emphasis on preaching Jesus to as many people as possible may indicate a difference of opinion over eschatology. While recent studies have injected welcome balance into scholarly understandings of Taylor's enthusiasm for premillennialism, this belief nevertheless formed an important aspect of his understanding of and motivation for mission.[39] Like many evangelical missionaries, Taylor's sense of evangelistic urgency was derived from the premillennial conviction that Jesus would return to reign in glory once the gospel was preached to the ends of the earth.[40] Richard, however, did not discuss the end times in any of his writings during the years covered by this thesis. As discussed in chapter 3 above, while Richard's actions may suggest an affinity with postmillennialism he gives no indication in his writings of either embracing or rejecting his earlier Haverfordwest training in prophecy and premillennialism. Regardless, Taylor's acknowledgment of some merit in Richard's theory, his interest in the nature of the tracts being circulated, and the concluding allusion to Rome all suggest that, while eschatological differences may have existed, they were not the focus of Taylor's complaint in this quotation.

Taylor's final criticism that Richard was "dangerously close to Rome" is especially ambiguous.[41] Catholicism was a strong presence in nineteenth-century Shanxi, and would have been difficult to avoid completely in the

---

37. Beauchamp, *Days of Blessing*, 30.

38. Taylor was not completely dismissive of the early Jesuit missionaries, at times praising them for their faithfulness to God's call. Taylor, *China's Spiritual Need*, 13–14; Taylor and Taylor, *Story of the CIM*, 1:17–20.

39. Wigram, *Bible and Mission*, 55–56, 58–63, 162–66.

40. This hope was based upon texts such as Matt 24:14. See also Pfister, "Rethinking Mission in China," 199, 205 n. 55; and Pocock, "Influence of Premillennial Eschatology," 129–34, 136.

41. Catholicism, with respect to Richard and Shanxi, will be discussed further in the following chapter. For more on the Catholic Church in Shanxi during Richard's lifetime, see Harrison, *Missionary's Curse*, 62–108.

course of one's missionary duties.⁴² In Shandong and especially Shanxi Richard had associated with and on rare occasions assisted and even cooperated with Catholic missionaries.⁴³ Even though at least some of Richard's interactions involved intentional confrontations over the nature of the true church, for British evangelicals shaped by several waves of public anti-Catholicism since the 1850s, such physical proximity to Catholic leaders may have seemed "dangerous."⁴⁴

During the famine Richard made a special trip to Shanghai to acquire a complete set of "Roman Catholic Chinese books," which almost certainly included the works of Ricci.⁴⁵ And yet he also ordered a copy of the popular anti-Jesuit tract *Secret Instructions of the Jesuits*, which he hoped would help him to understand the "immoral teachings" of the Jesuits so that he might better "direct at once those under our care to avoid falling upon the quicksands where they (Roman Caths) shipwreck themselves."⁴⁶ Nowhere in his writings from the time did Richard mention the Jesuits' so-called "top-down" approach to evangelism.⁴⁷ When he did mention the Jesuits, as in his marginal notes for Irving's *Missionaries After the Apostolical School*, Richard was critical of the Jesuit focus on the elites, approving Irving's observation that the first disciples "were not like the Jesuits to lay their artful toils around the high and noble and princely of the Nation."⁴⁸ Given all this, it seems difficult to imagine the CIM missionaries in Shanxi mistakenly reporting Richard as being in danger of embracing Catholicism. Indeed, Taylor most likely had no knowledge of Richard's interactions with Catholic missionaries or their literature.

Taylor's second mention of Richard provides a further possible clue to his concerns regarding Richard's "Romish" views. In response to

---

42. Harrison, "Village Politics," 2. Latourette claimed there were over twenty thousand Catholics in Shanxi in the 1830s, while at the end of the century the local scholar Liu Dapeng wrote (with some exaggeration) that Catholics made up from 30 to 40 percent of the population on the central Shanxi plain. Latourette, *History of Christian Missions*, 183; Liu, "Qianyuan suoji," 34.

43. Richard, *Forty-Five Years*, 129, 173–76.

44. Richard, *Forty-Five Years*, 174, 202–3; Wheeler, *Old Enemies*; Wallis, "Anti-Catholicism," 1–17.

45. Richard, *Forty-Five Years*, 144–45.

46. Richard to Baynes, 17 December 1877, BMSA CH/2.

47. Recent studies of the late Ming Jesuit mission to China have highlighted the scope and effectiveness of their equally contextualized evangelistic efforts among the less educated population. Laven, *Mission to China*, 212–21.

48. See MacGillivray's transcription of Richard's handwritten notes in the margin of page 457 of Irving's *Collected Writings*, as recorded in Soothill, *Timothy Richard of China*, 78.

Broomhall's recommendation of a letter printed in the *Baptist Magazine*, Taylor explained what he felt was Richard's role in the feared departure of CIM workers from the mission:

> [Richard's] presence in Shan-si caused me great anxiety for some of his views are so Romish, and his personal influence so strong that the CIM has no existence scarcely, or place or work or claims in the minds of Turner and James. This is not necessarily Mr. R.'s fault, it is rather the inevitable result of a strong and attractive character over weaker minds.[49]

It is not clear which *Baptist Magazine* article was being shared by the two men, but it may have been a January 1880 publication of a letter from Richard wherein he discussed the changing opinions of Shanxi officials, the reasons for the relatively slow growth of the church in Shanxi, and made brief mention of his practice during the famine of writing "bills urging the people to pray to the true God" which were then posted on walls and in temples, and carried throughout the countryside on a white flag hoisted by Richard himself.[50] If Taylor's comment was a response to this letter, then he may have been objecting to Richard's use of flags and parades as reminiscent of Catholic processions and the panoply of saints they invoked.[51] Such a criticism would help explain Taylor's insistence on separate worship services and Richard's claim that he was accused of being "not orthodox." These specific famine-related evangelistic activities, however, played so small a part in Richard's letter—a few lines in a lengthy report much more concerned with relating to Chinese officials and exploring techniques likely to produce evangelistic progress—that it seems more likely that Taylor was reacting to Richard's excessive comfort with these methods that seemed so similar to those of the early Catholic mission in China.

Before turning to consider Taylor's comments regarding Richard's influence over the CIM missionaries in Shanxi—for these concerns occupy three of the four lines of his second quotation—it is important to remember that all of the previous analyses of the possible theological complaints leveled by Taylor against Richard are based on two four-sentence quotations from letters that were only incidentally about Richard. Nowhere in his references to Richard does Taylor say he is "not orthodox," mention separate places of worship, or refer to Richard as if he no longer believes him to be a converted Christian. At the same time, the historicity of the

---

49. Taylor to Benjamin Broomhall, 6 March 1880, CIM Papers CIM/JHT/256, Box 10, SOAS.

50. Richard, "Rev. Timothy Richard on the Recent Famine in China," 6–9.

51. Reinders, *Borrowed Gods*, 100–131.

division of worship in the Taiyuan Christian community is based upon one eyewitness account—admittedly unchallenged—written nearly forty years after the fact, and that eyewitness is not Taylor, the man who supposedly ordered the division. If the two men did in fact meet in Tianjin to discuss their differences, no detailed account of their conversation exists. With so little evidence available, it is dangerous to suppose that the full nature of their dispute can be ascertained from the source material that has survived. It is possible that the emotional tension surrounding the encounter of these two strong characters led Richard nearly forty years after the fact to recall a word that Taylor never spoke. It is also equally plausible that some piece of information that has since been lost convinced Taylor for reasons completely outside those discussed in his two letters above to consider Richard outside the bounds of orthodox Christianity. While a comparison of their entire lives' output provides ample evidence for positing real theological differences between them, the contours of this particular event are much less clear.[52] There are simply too many unknowns. Accordingly, while there is no reason to question the existence of some kind of disagreement at the time that involved these two missionaries, readers should be warned against constructing an argument regarding the theological or missiological differences between Timothy Richard and James Hudson Taylor using the dangerously rickety scaffolding of this poorly documented event.

7.3 Richard and Attrition within the CIM

While it is impossible to specify the ways in which Taylor did or did not consider Richard at this time to be "not orthodox," Taylor's second quotation suggests an alternative understanding of the division for which more evidence is available. It is possible that overwhelmed with threatened departures from the CIM, Taylor found in Richard a convenient scapegoat, enabling him to claim that the departures were not the fault of Taylor or his policies, but rather were "the inevitable result of [Mr. R's] strong and attractive character over weaker minds."[53] A closer look at the evidence, however, demonstrates that CIM losses at the time had little to do with Richard, his theology, or his approach to mission.

Whether in relief distribution, orphan care, and official cooperation during the famine, or later works such as the initial tract distribution scheme and outreach initiatives targeting the triennial provincial examinations,

---

52. For one recent comparison, see Winter, "How To Best Help China?," 12–14.

53. Taylor to Benjamin Broomhall, 6 March 1880, CIM Papers CIM/JHT/256, Box 10, SOAS.

Richard was guiding and directing much of the multi-agency mission effort in Shanxi. The CIM, however, was explicit in its intentional emphasis on Taylor's sole authority in all matters related to the operations of the mission—a policy decision driven by practical convictions rather than personal megalomania.[54] Experienced and dynamic, Richard represented an alternative authority. Moreover, Taylor was far removed from the Shanxi field, forced to rely on slow, unreliable post to assert his authority while Richard was on the ground and ready to help.[55] Accordingly, it is no surprise that Taylor felt he had little influence on his workers there. Likewise, it seems only natural that any disaffected Shanxi workers—regardless of their reasons for feeling dissatisfied with their own organizational affiliations—would be drawn to Richard and the alternative he (and by extension his mission) represented.

If Taylor's intent in separation was to prevent the flow of workers out of the CIM by curtailing the influence of Richard and his ideas, it was in vain. By the end of 1884 nearly all of the earliest CIM Shanxi pioneers had one way or another left the mission, while the BMS Shanxi team that the Richards left behind at the start of their first furlough was composed entirely of former CIM workers.[56] Taylor claimed that Richard and his incorrect or "Romish" ways of doing mission were drawing people away from the CIM. A closer look at the transfers themselves, however, reveals very different reasons for the departures.

The first Shanxi CIM worker to transfer to the BMS, Shanxi pioneer Francis Huberty James, did not come to Richard for theological or missiological reasons; even Taylor admitted that finances were "probably" the "larger" reason for James's resignation.[57] James was dissatisfied with the CIM "plan of support" and, after having been involved for some time in an ongoing financial dispute with Taylor and the London Committee, chose to

---

54. McKay, "Faith and Facts," 147–48. Reacting to his personal experience with Gützlaff and the CES, Taylor believed centralized authority was key to efficient mission management. Austin, *China's Millions*, 103–4.

55. James, in his explanation letter to Taylor, specifically mentioned his frustrations waiting for guidance by post. James to Taylor, 20 June 1881, CIM Papers CIM/JHT/261, Box 10 (5228), SOAS.

56. Austin, *China's Millions*, 268. Austin mistakenly lists Celia Horne among the CIM deserters. Interestingly, not all who resigned from the CIM were welcomed into the BMS. On Richard's recommendation, the application of *Lammermuir* party member Josiah Jackson of Zhejiang was declined by the BMS Committee in 1885. BMS China-Japan Sub-Committee Minutes, 23 April 1885, vol. 2:33–34, BMSA; Broomhall, *HTCOC*, 6:297.

57. Taylor to Benjamin Broomhall, 24 May 1880, CIM Papers CIM/JHT/256, Box 10, SOAS.

move to a "Society giving a stated salary."[58] Following his resignation, James sent a letter to Taylor explaining why he had chosen to leave the mission. Apart from suggesting that an assistant be found to allow Taylor more time for correspondence, James explained his departure solely in terms of his desire for a more comfortable and perhaps more certain level of financial support. While acknowledging that there were other "minor matters" influencing his decision, James stated that these were "personal and private," even noting that he might wish to seek Taylor's advice on them at a later date. There was no mention of disagreements over the method of conducting mission or its message and goals, and no mention of Richard.[59] In fact, as James wrote upon his departure:

> In all your labours for China, you [James Hudson Taylor] and all the members of the mission, will have my continued sympathy and prayers. Our points of agreement are more in number and greater in importance than those concerning which our opinions differ; so that we may hope to enjoy fellowship and seek to render spiritual assistance in the future, whenever opportunity offers.[60]

James was not so much joining Richard and his mission as he was leaving the CIM and its policies, and the information available suggests James left the CIM in search of more satisfactory financial arrangements. Following a period of rest in England, James returned to China in 1882 as an associate of the BMS.[61]

It seems unlikely that Richard's influence on the field involved the spread of financial dissatisfaction among the CIM Shanxi workers. As discussed in chapter 3 above, Richard showed little anxiety for his personal financial situation, refusing secular employment and returning any excess income back into the work of the mission.[62] On the one occasion when he

---

58. James to Taylor, 20 June 1881, CIM Papers CIM/JHT/261, Box 10 (5228), SOAS. See Taylor's alarmingly detailed record of the financial history and its effects in Taylor, "Remarks on Mr. James' [sic] Memo," [prior to 24 March 1880?], CIM Papers CIM/JHT/261, Box 10 (5228), SOAS.

59. Although not surprising, Taylor's recommendation of James to the BMS is likewise free from any mention of different ideas of mission or methods, commending James's "useful work" to "my own" denomination's missionary society. Taylor to Baynes, 24 May 1880, CIM Papers CIM/JHT/257, Box 10 (5224), SOAS.

60. This and the previous are from James to Taylor, 20 June 1881, CIM Papers CIM/JHT/261, Box 10 (5228), SOAS.

61. BMS China-Japan Sub-Committee Minutes, 20 November 1882, vol. 1:129–30, BMSA.

62. In 1897 Richard told his daughters that he and Mary had given all their earnings to missions. Johnson, "Timothy Richard's Theory," 218.

received a substantial personal bequest, he spent it on scientific equipment for use in his work with officials.[63] The only times Richard corresponded with his society over finances were when requesting more funding for new ministry initiatives or the expansion of the mission.[64] While it is possible that Richard's relative contentment may have been attractive to the less financially secure CIM workers, there is nothing suggesting he was actively feeding their pecuniary dissatisfaction.

In October 1881 Joshua Turner, James's co-pioneer of the Shanxi field, was in Chefoo prostrate in bed with illness and, according to Taylor, "utterly down in body, and mind," while his wife remained behind in Taiyuan. Although this was not the first time during his few years in Shanxi that Turner had been forced to flee owing to ill health, Taylor was deeply concerned, for it seemed that Turner "wants to go home and to leave the mission."[65] Not long after, Turner, having recovered from his fever and dysentery, returned to Taiyuan in the company of Timothy Richard. Taylor remained uneasy, observing that Turner "has made up his mind to leave us I feel sure, and does not believe in looking directly to God."[66]

This phrase, "looking directly to God," was typically used within the CIM to describe attitudes toward financial matters rather than salvation. The *Principles and Practices of the China Inland Mission*, a three-page compilation of the main policies of the organization that each new associate was required to read and sign before departure, stressed that all CIM missionaries were "to look for their supplies to God." Even when receiving extensive support from the mission, workers were reminded, "their faith must be in God, their expectation from Him."[67] Turner apparently also had expectations regarding his missionary finances: while making no mention of his opinions regarding mission methods, discussion in the April 1883 CIM London Council Minutes showed that Turner had asked for an increase in support beyond what Taylor had offered—an offer the Council

63. Richard's uncle, Welsh Baptist preacher and scholar Joshua Lewis, left him a legacy following his death in 1879 that covered some portion of Richard's £1000 outlay on scientific books and instruments. "Lewis, Joshua (1816–1879)," *Welsh Biography Online*; Richard, *Forty-Five Years*, 159.

64. See for example, BMS China-Japan Sub-Committee Minutes, 18 July 1882, vol. 1:93, BMSA; and BMS China-Japan Sub-Committee Minutes, 16 January 1883, vol. 1:140, BMSA.

65. Taylor to Jennie Taylor, 29 October 1881, CIM Papers CIM/JHT (5231z), SOAS.

66. Taylor to Jennie Taylor, 10 November 1881, CIM Papers CIM/JHT (5231a), SOAS.

67. *Principles and Practices of the China Inland Mission*, SOAS.

flatly rejected.⁶⁸ Like James before, Turner found himself at odds with CIM financial policy, as did other CIM missionaries who were criticized for their supposed unwillingness to "live by faith," an indicator within the CIM that they were breaking with the spiritual lifestyle of dependence that formed a key unifying force within the organization.⁶⁹

Given the scarcity of documentation from Turner's own pen, it could be claimed that his transfer to Richard's BMS may have been at least partly related to disagreements over evangelistic method. However, at the end of the famine Turner turned his attention to itinerant evangelistic work, accompanying new CIM colleagues W. L. Elliston (who later became first headmaster of the CIM Chefoo school) and A. G. Parrott (who later served as Taylor's corresponding secretary) across post-famine southern Shanxi in order "to become acquainted with the people, and by conversation and by tracts to lead them to Christ."⁷⁰ While not far from Richard's methods as practiced in Shandong, surely this kind of work shows Turner at that time to be in at least broad sympathy with Taylor's emphasis on preaching and—since he was also cooperating with Parrott who initially received financial support from the British and Foreign Bible Society (BFBS) and therefore was committed to Bible colportage—the distribution of scripture. It should also be recalled that the early CIM Shanxi baptisms, including Xi Shengmo, were largely at Turner's hands.⁷¹ All this makes it unlikely that Turner was in rebellion against Taylor's drive for itinerant evangelism.

Certainly, Turner's ideas regarding mission methods may have changed during the year between his itinerations in Shanxi and when Taylor encountered him in Chefoo in October 1881. But the record of his denied request in 1881 for an increase in the expenses allowed for his family remains in suggestive proximity to the acceptance of the Turners into the BMS

---

68. London Council Minutes, April 1883, vol. 5:3, CIM Papers CIM/01/01/2/05, SOAS.

69. The "revivalistic spirituality" personified in Taylor's way of living by faith—concepts derivative of holiness ideas that emerged and rose to prominence within British evangelicalism in the 1870s and 1880s—was more significant for CIM identity than any particular doctrinal formulation. Bebbington, *Evangelicalism in Modern Britain*, 151–52; McKay, "Faith and Facts," 145. For a critical analysis of "living by faith" in Taylor's mission, and its relation to material supply, see Rowdon, "Concept of 'Living By Faith,'" 339–56.

70. "Shan-si Province," *CM* (January 1881) 10. It is not clear which tracts Turner and Elliston were distributing. For more on these tours, see W. L. Elliston, "Distribution of the Famine Relief Fund in Tseh-Chau Fu," *CM* (April 1880) 49–50; A. G. Parrot, "Itinerant Work in North China: Second Journey," *CM* (December 1881) 150–52.

71. See the four biographies of early baptisms recorded in Turner to Taylor, 29 November 1880, CIM Papers CIM/JHT, Box 10, SOAS.

in June 1883.⁷² Their return to Taiyuan under their new affiliation in February 1884 was a double loss for the CIM,⁷³ since Turner had married Anna Crickmay, an early reinforcement of the CIM staff in Shanxi, in February of 1881, necessarily taking her with him to join the Baptists.⁷⁴

Like Anna Crickmay Turner, many single women left the CIM through marriage.⁷⁵ But some CIM associates across China resigned less amicably over the question of marriage—specifically, because of their unwillingness to abide by the mission's policy forbidding marriage to associates prior to the completion of their two- to three-year probationary (language study) period.⁷⁶ At the same time that Arthur Sowerby came out to join the BMS work in Shanxi in 1881, his brother Herbert resigned from the CIM over the marriage restrictions as well as frustrations with what he perceived to be the lack of organizational support during his early attempts to secure a residence in Shandong.⁷⁷ Sowerby's sister Florence married Samuel Drake of the CIM Shanxi field in 1882, expressly against the regulations of the CIM regarding the marriage of probationers.⁷⁸ In 1886 the Drakes resigned from the CIM and joined the BMS work in Shandong.⁷⁹ As letters from

72. BMS China-Japan Sub-Committee Minutes, 20 January 1891, vol. 2:174, BMSA. The Turners' exact dates for leaving the CIM and joining the BMS do not seem to have been entered into the existing minutes of either organization.

73. BMS China-Japan Sub-Committee Minutes, 18 February 1884, vol. 1:247, BMSA.

74. "Province of Shan-tung," *CM* (June 1881) 67. In 1880 Taylor wrote that Crickmay and single colleague Celia Horne were "true to the mission [and] have had a very trying time of it." Taylor to Benjamin Broomhall, 6 March 1880, CIM Papers CIM/JHT/256, Box 10, SOAS.

75. On marriage in general within the CIM, see Austin, *China's Millions*, 232–33, 238–39, 390–91.

76. By 1884 the exact period of time forbidding marriage had been removed from the *Principles and Practices*, stating instead the inviolability of "the period [of singleness] specified in their respective agreements." *Principles and Practices*, 3 point 15.

77. Taylor to Sowerby, 26 October 1880, CIM Papers CIM/JHT Box I, SOAS; Taylor to Jennie Taylor, 29 October 1881, CIM Papers CIM/JHT (5231z), SOAS; "Reinforcements for India, China and Africa," *MH* 77, no. 2 (1881) 46. Citing Broomhall who is unclear, Austin may have conflated the two Sowerby brothers into one. Austin, *China's Millions*, 269. Prior to resigning, Herbert Sowerby served CIM stations in Nanjing and Anqing. See references in the June, July–August, and October *CM* (1880) 78, 85, and 132, respectively; and H. Sowerby, "Gan-k'ing," *CM* (June 1881) 74.

78. Austin, *China's Millions*, 269; Williamson, *British Baptists in China*, 364. Florence Sowerby may have been working in Pingyang as early as 1881, prior to their marriage. "Pingyang Fu Station," *CM* (July 1883) 86; and "Tidings From Miss Lancaster, Of Tai-Yuen Fu," *CM* (May 1883) 57.

79. BMS China-Japan Sub-Committee Minutes, 13 July 1886, vol. 2:96–7, BMSA. Their reasons for resigning are not clear.

the 1880s show, Taylor and his second wife Jennie exerted much effort to maintain the policy against early marriages in the face of frequent disobedience, at times involving subterfuge and desperate actions in pursuit of illicit betrothals.[80] Richard, meanwhile, shared at least some of Taylor's ideas regarding the disadvantages of being engaged to be married in pioneering mission work, recommending—though not demanding—single men for the itinerant work in his 1885 *Scheme for Mission Work in China*.[81] The responsibility for these transfers and resignations, however, lies not with Richard but rather with the engaged couples themselves and with those in the CIM who enforced their marriage policies.

Ultimately, it was disillusionment with the management of their own organization that led the CIM workers on the Shanxi field to transfer to the BMS. They were escaping from a regime of policies that they had found too burdensome, and the already comfortable cooperation they had experienced with Richard—as well as his seeming contentment with the arrangements of his own organization—provided a convenient local alternative to the CIM. Significantly, it was an alternative that allowed them for the most part to continue their present employment in Shanxi, continuing in many instances in projects that Richard had helped establish. Certainly, Richard's openness to cooperating in mission with workers from any broadly evangelical society helped pave the way for their easy transfers; but, to whatever degree the CIM workers on the Shanxi field were aware of the missiological differences between James Hudson Taylor and Timothy Richard, theology does not seem to have significantly influenced their decisions to transfer to the BMS.

Taylor's attacks—in the form of the breaking of fellowship and whatever words the two exchanged in Tianjin—no doubt caused pain to Richard, the man who had so earnestly desired to work with and in the manner of Taylor's CIM when he first pursued China service. But within the Shanxi mission community, Taylor's criticisms seem to have had little effect: Richard continued to enjoy the respect of those around him, they continued to work alongside him in projects and initiatives that in many cases he himself had begun, and in time those ordered to distance themselves from him left the CIM to join his own organization. Despite distant criticisms, Richard's

---

80. Taylor personally witnessed one woman's successful attempt to escape her guard and sneak into her suitor's quarters in order to secure her unapproved marriage. Taylor offered the gentleman the option to either send the woman away (as a "ruined" woman for having entered the man's compartment inappropriately attired) or marry her immediately and leave the mission. Taylor to Jennie Taylor, 12 March 1881, CIM Papers CIM/JHT/262, Box 10 (5231e), SOAS.

81. Richard, *Scheme for Mission Work*, 5 point VIII.

personal experience with the mission community on the ground was one of great affirmation and cooperation.

As Lauren Pfister has recently highlighted, Richard and Taylor were similar in many ways.[82] Nonconformist in churchmanship, with strong Baptist sympathies, wearing Chinese clothes, willing to carry out medical and other humanitarian work, and committed to pioneering inland mission work and the development of indigenous churches, these two evangelical missionaries shared much, with their wives also working together to care for orphans in post-famine Shanxi.[83] Whatever conflict occurred between them following the North China Famine must be viewed with this in mind. And while theological differences did exist, the existing evidence makes it very difficult to specify what was behind Taylor's challenge to Richard's orthodoxy—if in fact such a challenge was made. What is certain from the available evidence is that the early 1880s were difficult for Taylor's mission, particularly on the Shanxi field. And while Taylor's missionaries complained about him and his policies, they respected Richard and in many cases joined his mission.

7.4 Revisiting the "Shanxi Spirit"

In his massive seven-volume *Hudson Taylor and China's Open Century* (*HT-COC*), CIM historian A. J. Broomhall, introduced a term one hundred years later to try and capture the difficulties the CIM was facing in the 1880s. He wrote:

> A phrase "the Shansi spirit," found in a few letters, described a whirlpool of complaints, misunderstandings, derelict spiritual morale and finally resignations from the CIM and BMS. At the vortex was the remarkable personality of Timothy Richard, still young and developing but intellectual, original and inevitably influential.[84]

---

82. Pfister, "Rethinking Mission in China," 183–212. See also Walls, "Multiple Conversions," 245.

83. Denominational affiliations were never particularly important for Taylor. Raised Wesleyan and heavily influenced by the Brethren, Taylor also spent at least some time worshipping at Westbourne Grove Baptist Church, Paddington, considered the Baptist denomination "his own," was (according to Austin) an ordained Baptist minister, and on at least one occasion self-identified as theologically Baptistic. Taylor to Baynes, 24 May 1880, CIM/JHT/257, Box 10 (5224); Austin, "Only Connect," 286; Broomhall, *HTCOC*, 2:207; Wigram, *Bible and Mission*, 62–63, 161.

84. Broomhall, *HTCOC*, 6:288.

Certainly, this was a difficult time for Taylor's young organization. Likewise, as shall be seen in the next chapter, the second half of the decade would see the BMS Shanxi field disrupted by conflict. Broomhall's statement, however, must be read with two cautions in mind.

Firstly, there is little evidence to suggest that "the Shansi Spirit" was a phrase used at the time within the CIM. Checking the limited references given in Broomhall's work yields only one instance that even approximates to the phrase. Writing to her husband from Chefoo in August 1879, Jennie Taylor explained, "I have not seen much of [George] Clarke yet, having been [myself] so much with Mrs. M[oore] but enough to find him to be a faithful reflection of the present *Shan-si state of mind*."[85] The letter itself gives no indication of what this last phrase means. George Clarke was only in Shanxi for about three months, assisting in famine relief work after escorting Parrott to his first station.[86] During the journey to Shanxi, Clarke repeatedly engaged in the kind of evangelistic open-air preaching Taylor advocated.[87] The only indication of dissension in Clarke's distinguished missionary career was his marriage to Fanny Rossier, a Swiss associate of the CIM stationed in Yangzhou (not Shanxi), in September 1879, less than one year after her arrival in China.[88] Not long after, the Clarkes were en route to Yunnan, determined to persevere in scripture colportage regardless of criticism or hardship. A strong advocate of wide itineration and straightforward scripture distribution, Clarke passionately cautioned a friend to "put your fingers in your ears to arguments against the distribution of God's Word."[89] Whatever Clarke's state of mind, it owed little to Shanxi or Timothy Richard, and was concerned more with rebelling against a forbidden marriage than bucking recommended evangelistic methods.

---

85. Jennie Taylor to Taylor, 20 August 1879 (emphasis added), CIM Papers CIM/JHT/250, Box 10 (5212), SOAS.

86. G. W. Clarke, "Diary of Mr. Geo. Clarke while in the Famine Districts," *CM* (June 1880) 71–73; A. G. Parrott, "For the Young: A Letter from Shan-si," *CM* (November 1879) 145–46; Broomhall, *HTCOC*, 6:183. Parrott and Clarke were quickly driven out of Zezhou (modern-day Jincheng), joining Elliston and Turner in Pingyang. Though punctuated with grief (Clarke was widowed twice in China) Clarke's service in the CIM was long and faithful, pioneering new territories in northern Shanxi and western China.

87. A. G. Parrott, "Itinerant Work in North China: First Journey," *CM* (November 1881) 136–39.

88. "Recent Intelligence," *CM* (March 1879) 40; "Recent Tidings," *CM* (December 1879) 158; Broomhall, *HTCOC*, 6:501.

89. G. W. Clarke, "Letter from Yun-nan Fu, en route for Ta-li Fu," *CM* (December 1881) 145–46.

Reading more broadly within the extant CIM materials, the phrase or its near equivalents are absent from correspondence at the time. CIM publications prior to Broomhall, whether biographies or histories, also do not use the phrase. Moreover, Broomhall himself may not have placed much stock in the term: his surviving notes for *HTCOC* make no mention of the phrase in the historical reconstructions of the early 1880s, while showing only two occurrences of "Shansi spirit" in his detailed source notes, both of which refer to the "state of mind" quotation regarding George Clarke.[90] It also does not appear in the BMS materials or any of Richard's writings. The term, in short, appears to have been developed by Broomhall for his own purposes.

Secondly, it seems inaccurate to place Timothy Richard at the vortex of the difficulties the CIM was facing in Shanxi and beyond. While James Hudson Taylor may not have approved of Timothy Richard's theology or the methods by which he conducted missions in Shanxi, the documentary evidence suggests that this had little to do with the departures rocking the CIM in Shanxi or elsewhere during the 1880s. The Shanxi workers of the CIM may have been drawn to the BMS by Richard's care and charisma, but they were leaving Taylor's organization for reasons intrinsic to the CIM, its policies, and its leader. The CIM was struggling, but it was hardly Timothy Richard's fault. Taylor and his organization's policies must bear responsibility for this phenomenon.

There were individuals on the Shanxi field who changed their allegiances for explicitly theological reasons, although none did so in order to work with Timothy Richard. Charles Tenney left the ABCFM Shanxi mission in 1885 owing to his departure from the faith of his colleagues.[91] James, having initially left the CIM for financial reasons, left the BMS, Richard, and the rest of the mission world entirely in 1891 because he no longer held "the orthodox teaching on the Trinity and Atonement."[92] Contrasted with Taylor's long-standing tolerance of Cambridge Seven Shanxi missionary Stanley Smith's unorthodox ideas, these departures only highlight the rela-

---

90. "A. J. Broomhall's MS Notes," CIM Papers CIM/04/05/12, Box 15 (11 a, b; 12 a, b), SOAS. See also Broomhall's handwritten loose-leaf source notes in the CIM Papers for August 1879 and May 1881.

91. Tenney to Judson Smith, 7 June 1885, Shansi Mission (ABC 16.3.15), vol. 2, part 2 (0174–0177), ABCFMA. While rejecting the orthodoxy of his colleagues, Tenney stressed his strong agreement with missionary methods similar to those advocated by Richard.

92. James to Baynes, 21 December 1891, as reprinted in BMS China-Japan Sub-Committee Minutes, 15 February 1892, vol. 2:209–11, BMSA. Asserting that he was still passionate about mission work and the Kingdom of God in China, James soon returned to China, teaching in both the Shanghai Arsenal and the Imperial University before his execution during the Boxer Uprising.

tive absence of resignations over theological issues within the CIM Shanxi expatriate community.[93]

The difficulties weighing down Taylor and his organization extended well beyond Shanxi. On half a page of one letter written in 1880, Taylor listed five different situations where he foresaw sending workers home—none were related to Shanxi, the BMS, Richard, or evangelistic methods.[94] Eventually, in 1886, the CIM formally requested that the BMS cease from accepting further applications from CIM workers, for fear of "setting up estranged relations" between the two missions and their directors.[95] The BMS immediately agreed, perhaps reflecting hesitancy among BMS field workers regarding the difficulties of cooperating with members of the CIM who came from a Brethren background.[96] Despite this complaint from the CIM, the evidence is clear that early workers left the CIM Shanxi field not in order to ally themselves with Timothy Richard or his missionary methods; they left out of frustration with the CIM's own policies. Timothy Richard was not the vortex of the CIM's problems.

Since Broomhall's work, the phrase "Shanxi spirit" has been employed by various scholars examining China missions at this time.[97] Alvyn Austin, in particular, has dramatically enlarged the scope and content of the phrase in his colorful exploration of the CIM and its work in Shanxi.[98] Though

93. On Stanley P. Smith, see Austin, *China's Millions*, 337, 385–87. While little documentation exists, the Pigotts (wealthy and financially independent of the mission) severed ties with the CIM in 1890 "owing to a difference of opinion with Mr. Hudson Taylor on the new rules then introduced into the principles and practice of the Mission," possibly related to their employment of an English governess on the field. Their formation of the independent Shouyang Mission in May 1892, as well as CIM Taiyuan doctor Eben Edwards's transfer to that mission in 1896, appear to have been for similarly practical reasons. Pigott, *Steadfast Unto Death*, 142, 171–72.

94. Taylor to Benjamin Broomhall, 6 March 1880, CIM Papers CIM/JHT/256, Box 10, SOAS. The passage begins with the last line of the ninth page.

95. The request came to the BMS via Sir Morton Peto. BMS China-Japan Sub-Committee Minutes, 13 July 1886, vol. 2:98–99, BMSA.

96. See Jones's comments on CIM personnel, that while their bodies resided in China, "their minds are back either in Palestine and Asia Minor or at the time of Cromwell.... The Director is practically a Diocesan Bishop." Jones to Short, 9 February 1884, BMSA CH/8. The ABCFM Shanxi workers were similarly frustrated with many of their CIM neighbors. Stimson to Smith, 13 February 1885, Shansi Mission (ABC 16.3.15), vol. 2, part 2 (Reel 318: 0632), ABCFMA.

97. See, for example, Pfister, "Rethinking Mission in China," 208; Wigram, *Bible and Mission*, 133–35, 170. Wigram, despite his familiarity with the Taylor materials in the CIM archives, makes no reference to personal correspondence involving Taylor or Richard in his discussion of the so-called controversy.

98. Austin cites Broomhall for the provenance of the phrase. Austin, *China's Millions*, 268–69, especially n. 46.

such a catchphrase may have its uses, it is important to remember the limitations of its origin: there is no extant evidence of the phrase being used at the time, nor is the phenomenon it was supposed to have described especially related to Timothy Richard.

This last point, of course, only holds true with respect to the CIM. Richard's interactions with the missionaries of the CIM field for the most part served to confirm his confidence in the new understanding and practice of mission that he had developed during his first ten years in China. However, as Richard would soon discover, not all of his colleagues in the BMS agreed with his methods. More to the point, their complaints against him would prove to be both personal and expressly theological. For the conflict that tore through the BMS China mission in the late 1880s, Richard was indeed the focus, if not the vortex.

8

Substituting Another Gospel?
Timothy Richard and His Critics in the Baptist Missionary Society

WHILE THE MANY TRANSFERS to the BMS China mission in the first half of the 1880s owed little to Richard's particular understanding and practice of mission, the conflict that developed between him and his Shanxi colleagues following his first furlough focused on precisely these issues. When his BMS coworkers challenged nearly all of his missionary adaptations, Richard rigorously defended his methods and his message revealing once again his persistent evangelicalism and the empathetic trajectory of his acculturation. Ultimately, the BMS Committee in London sided with Richard against his detractors in all areas save one: they asked Richard to devote less of his time to the indirect aspects of missionary work. Richard's commitment to all his adaptations, and the strength of his convictions regarding them nevertheless remained firm. When he took up his position with the SDCK in 1891, he viewed this new role not only as a strategic platform for speeding the conversion of the nation of China but also as a fitting venue for the further application of his key missionary adaptations.

8.1 The First Furlough: Disappointment with the BMS

Throughout his years of service in China, Richard had resisted calls from family to return to Britain for rest and relaxation. As he explained to his mother just after the North China Famine,

> You are asking when I shall be coming home. I would be very glad to see you all. Yet the work here is so much and the workers so few that it is not easy to return when there are thousands without a knowledge of the way to flee from the wrath to come. Some have advised me to go to England to bring more labourers out here. I do not consider that so far the call is from God. When

I shall believe that God wants me to go then the way will be clear and my return a pleasure to me and to you.[1]

By spring 1884 the moment had apparently arrived, as the BMS Committee unanimously recommended that since "the health of the Rev. T. and Mrs. Richard has become much impaired by their long and arduous labours, especially during the disastrous years of famine," the Richard family should be urged "to take without delay a period of rest and change in England."[2] While in Shandong during Alfred Jones's earlier furlough in England, Richard had fallen ill twice, once so seriously that he penned a farewell note to his wife in Taiyuan and gave instructions to be buried in Qingzhou.[3] Recognizing the wisdom in the committee's suggestion, the Richards agreed and made plans to set off on their first furlough, Richard having served continuously in China for nearly fifteen years.

Richard toured eastern China on his way to Tianjin and then Britain. He visited Qingzhou, for a strategic conference with the recently returned Jones, and Nanjing, where Richard and David Hill petitioned Zeng Guoquan to promote religious protection for Christians in China.[4] While in Nanjing, Richard also visited the Buddhist scripture press of Yang Wenhui.[5] Having lived overseas as part of the Chinese Embassy in London, Yang had converted from Confucianism to become, according to Richard, "the most intelligent Buddhist I had ever met." When asked to explain his transformation, Yang told Richard that the Buddhist text *Dasheng qi xin lun* or *The Awakening of Faith* had convinced him with its clear teaching on "the most important questions." Richard immediately purchased a copy and read it that evening, exclaiming to Hill on its surprisingly Christian character.[6] A few months later, Richard purchased Samuel Beal's newly published *Buddhism in China* in an Edinburgh bookstore, having discovered that the author supported Richard's suspicions with his assertion that *The Awakening of Faith* was "based on doctrines foreign to Buddhism and allied to a perverted form of Christian dogma."[7] Sensing confirmation of his previous experiences with sectarian religious groups, Richard began from this time to explore the early historical relationship

1. Richard to his mother, 13 October 1880, translated by Thomas Evans, 25 January 1965, BMSA CH/4A.
2. BMS China-Japan Sub-Committee Minutes, 26 May 1884, vol. 2:2, BMSA.
3. Richard, *Forty-Five Years*, 177, 180.
4. Richard, *Forty-Five Years*, 194–95.
5. Welch, *Buddhist Revival in China*, 2–9.
6. Richard, *New Testament of Higher Buddhism*, 43–47.
7. Beal, *Buddhism in China*, 138.

between China's religions and Christianity.⁸ For Richard, the Mahayana Buddhism contained in *The Awakening of Faith* was a lost, "higher" form of Buddhism that had been profoundly shaped by its exchanges with first-century Christianity—one whose existence strengthened his belief in the potential rapid conversion of the Chinese nation.⁹ This interest would grow during the second half of Richard's ministry, beginning with his idiosyncratic 1894 translation, with Yang Wenhui's assistance, of *The Awakening of Faith*, a work he did not publish until 1910.¹⁰

Informed by his discussions with Jones, Richard returned to Britain prepared to present the BMS Committee with his vision for the China mission. Since Jones in his 1883 report to the BMS Committee had so ably introduced the general principles he and Richard had been employing in their work in China, Richard felt free to focus on securing support for specific projects.¹¹ In addition to his autobiographical essay *Fifteen Years*, Richard prepared a separate report titled *A Scheme for Mission Work in China* to present what he believed was a timely and vital new endeavor in China mission.¹²

Richard cast his new project as a plan for bringing about the conversion—spiritual as well as material—of the entire nation.¹³ This involved influencing the mandarins and scholars of China as well as evangelizing the religious sectarians, both natural expressions of his foundational convictions regarding the value of changing negative official attitudes toward

---

8. See, for instance, his comments while on furlough: Richard, *Fifteen Years*, 3; Richard, *Wanted: Good Samaritans for China*, 12–15, citing Beal.

9. Richard used the adjective "higher" not so much in an evolutionary sense but rather to indicate that Chinese Mahayana had more in common with Christianity than the earlier Hinayana school. Richard, *New Testament of Higher Buddhism*, 1–9.

10. Though Richard's interest in Buddhism was born during his first twenty years in China, the subject achieved true significance for him only after 1890. See Richard, "Influence of Buddhism in China," 49–64. For current scholarship on Richard and Buddhism see Lai, "Timothy Richard's Response," 30–39; Lee, "Qing mo ming chu jiduxinjiao lai Hua chuanjiaoshi," 19–92; and Scott, "Timothy Richard," 53–75.

11. See Jones, *North China BMS*.

12. Richard, *Scheme for Mission Work*. The version included in Richard's later publication differs with the addition of a few rhetorical and emphatic statements, but is the same in particulars. See Richard, "A Scheme for Mission Work in China: A University College in each Provincial Capital" in *Conversion by the Million*, 2:60–73. Richard claimed that his interest in "national conversion" as discussed in his *Fifteen Years* was mistaken by his nonconformist brethren to be a call for a national church in China. He then published *Scheme for Mission Work* to clarify his ideas. Richard, *Fifteen Years*, 23; Stanley, *History of the BMS*, 189.

13. Johnson emphasizes the educational as opposed to missional aspects of Richard's scheme. Johnson, "Educational Reform in China," 49–50.

Christianity and the unique preparedness of the devout classes of China for Christian conversion. In its details, the actual scheme advanced by Richard was broad and strikingly ambitious. Although the bulk of the proposal centered on the establishment of institutions of higher learning throughout China, the project also assumed an enormous enlargement of the number of BMS China workers to supply seventeen missionaries for each of China's provinces.[14] As an indication of the scope of Richard's vision, in each province the expanded BMS staff was expected to

> divide its efforts into various branches of work, such as—
>
> Preaching and Evangelising.
>
> Preparation of Christian Literature in Chinese.
>
> Teaching at an Institution.
>
> Intercourse with Native Leaders.
>
> Examination of non-resident Students in Christian Subjects.
>
> Philanthropic Work, such as Dispensaries, Opium Refuges, &c., &c.
>
> And *all* combine in their work the *spiritual*, the *educational*, and the *practical*.[15]

Reflecting Richard's broadened conception of the Kingdom of God, relief work, education, medicine, and literature production were clearly presented in the scheme as components of a larger mission project, one that continued the more traditional missionary endeavors of preaching, evangelism and the discipleship of Chinese Christians. While much of *A Scheme* discussed the nature of the academic institutions that he hoped to establish, Richard stated at the beginning that those schools were being set up for the purposes of "Raising a large Staff of Native Missionaries," with school sessions limited to only six months of the year, "the remaining six months [to] be spent in evangelistic and pioneering work to get Christian teaching and preaching extended to all parts of the country." Similar institutions were to be set up for women as well.[16] Recalling his successes in

---

14. Arthur Sowerby suggested that Richard's interest in educational institutions was inspired by Maclear's hypothesis regarding the central role of universities in the evangelization of Europe. Sowerby to BMS Committee, 1 August 1888, p. 10, BMSA CH/64; Maclear, *Apostles of Mediaeval Europe*.

15. Richard, *Scheme for Mission Work*, 4.

16. All the above is taken from Richard, *Scheme for Mission Work*, 5.

Shandong, Richard continued to push for enlarging the role of local Christians in the advancement of the gospel.

While he only asked "that the Baptist Missionary Society undertake to establish some of these Institutions," the scope of Richard's vision was nevertheless enormous. Beyond the massive increase in mission personnel, each institution, in addition to an initial £5000 outlay for laboratory and library outfit, would require by Richard's estimate some £6600 annually to maintain its missionaries and students. Despite Richard's expectation that local Chinese officials would contribute to the project, and that back home "wealthy men would be glad" to cover some of the expenses, he was still asking the Society to commit to the provision of a prohibitive quantity of resources. Not only were there to be *nineteen* such institutions—one for each provincial capital—but Richard wanted this project for China to receive the Society's exclusive priority, enjoining that "*no further advance be made for any country, much less new fields occupied, until China's many years' wrong be righted.* Till three years ago we, at *most*, had only two Missionaries in full work here."[17]

It is a sign of Richard's commitment and passion that he failed to anticipate the BMS Committee's response to so bold a request. Jones had no doubt informed Richard that while the committee had been "strongly convinced" of the value and importance of the work and philosophy of mission outlined in Jones's 1883 report, "the income of the Society is altogether inadequate to meet the demands of any *increased* expenditures, the year just closed having left a heavy debt."[18] It should have come as no surprise that, despite professing strong support for Richard, Jones, and their vision for expanded work in China that included targeted work among the secular and religious leaders, the BMS Committee had little choice but to reject Richard's scheme as—again—beyond their financial capacity.[19] Having secured no more than a lengthy, rousing endorsement for himself in the minutes of the BMS China-Japan Sub-Committee, Richard returned to China disappointed.[20]

When Richard left China for his first furlough, the BMS China contingent was small. In 1881 Richard and Jones had been joined by John S. Whitewright and Arthur Sowerby, both of whom married in 1883.[21] Dr. J. Tate Kitts had come out earlier in 1879, but struggled with the language and eventually

17. This paragraph is from Richard, *Scheme for Mission Work*, 6.

18. BMS China-Japan Sub-Committee Minutes, 21 May 1883, vol. 1:168–70, BMSA.

19. The 1901 establishment of Shanxi University was in many ways the realization of Richard's original *Scheme*. Johnson, "Educational Reform in China," 71 n. 10; 70 n. 5.

20. BMS China-Japan Sub-Committee Minutes, 13 July 1886, vol. 2:97–98, BMSA.

21. BMS China-Japan Sub-Committee Minutes, 19 July 1881, vol. 1:44, BMSA; Williamson, *British Baptists in China*, 363.

left China.[22] The transfers of the Turners and Jameses thus made for a total force of seven BMS missionary families, four of whom had been added in the few years prior to the Richards' furlough. During the Richards' absence in Britain the BMS Committee, moved by Jones's appeal during his 1882–1883 furlough, finally began to provide some of the additional reinforcements long requested by the China field.[23] Samuel Couling, R. C. Forsyth, C. Spurgeon Medhurst, Evan Morgan, and Dr. J. R. Watson joined the work in 1884, along with Herbert Dixon who, owing to ill health, had been allowed to transfer from tropical Congo to the drier, more temperate climate of Shanxi.[24] The Richards themselves, arriving in Shanghai on 18 October 1886, were accompanied on their return by further reinforcements in the shape of E. C. Nickalls and G. B. Farthing, as well as Jessie Corpe, Annie Maitland, and Marion Weedon, the brides of Medhurst, Forsyth, and Morgan, respectively.[25] For the first time in its history, the BMS China team was growing rapidly, adding new workers who had not shared in the formative famine experiences of the pioneers James, Jones, Turner, and Richard.[26]

8.2 The Contours of the Conflict

While Timothy Richard was still on furlough, a letter from one of these new workers was published in the August 1886 *Missionary Herald* that seemed at first glance harmless, but which upset Richard. Despite having only just arrived in China, Dixon wrote publicly that

22. Though he did not formally leave the mission until 1889, Kitts was encouraged as early as 1884 to return to England. BMS China-Japan Sub-Committee Minutes, 17 March 1884, vol. 2:25, BMSA; Williamson, *British Baptists in China*, 363.

23. The Sub-Committee had agreed to Jones's suggestion that a ratio of two Shandong workers for every one in Shanxi be maintained, a decision that became a point of contention in the late 1880s. BMS China-Japan Sub-Committee Minutes, 14 June 1883, vol. 1:173, BMSA.

24. These and the previous names are taken from Williamson, *British Baptists in China*, 363–64. Sowerby had written to invite the invalided Dixon to join him. See Bell and Clements, *Lives From a Black Tin Box*, 94–95.

25. "Missionary Journal," *CR* 17, no. 11 (1886) 444; BMS China-Japan Sub-Committee Minutes, 7 June 1886, vol. 2:92, BMSA. Jessie Louisa Corpe (1856–96) was married to Charles Spurgeon Medhurst in Shanghai on 20 October 1896, almost immediately after her arrival.

26. This paragraph is not exhaustive: J. Percy Bruce, Moir Duncan, F. Harmon (from the BFBS), A. G. Shorrock, E. C. Smyth, W. A. Wills (from the CIM), and Miss Lila Dawburn, a self-supporting missionary about whom little is known, also joined the BMS China field in 1886–87, but for various reasons (resignations, transfers, or assignment to Shaanxi) did not spend significant time working in Shanxi or Shandong. See Burt, *Fifty Years in China*, 123.

> Mr. Richard has been working here for some six years, chiefly, as far as I know, amongst the upper classes and at translation. Mr. Sowerby and myself think the most promising mode of work to be ... dispensing medicine ... opening villages ... and following it up by regular systematic services, visitings, and teaching. City work in China seems far less paying than country work.[27]

These seemingly innocuous words were the opening salvo in what became a battle over the correct methods and message of the BMS China mission that lasted throughout the rest of the 1880s. Richard's colleagues in Shanxi—Dixon, Farthing, Sowerby, and Turner—were the primary challengers, questioning almost everything Richard was doing at the time. Morgan distanced himself from the attackers and supported Richard, as did Jones and the rest of the Shandong workers—including the recently transferred James, whose letters tended to provide a more balanced perspective to the common partisan invective.[28] Eventually, the BMS missionaries in Shandong lobbied aggressively for Richard to be released from Shanxi to join their work. The debates were all-encompassing, covering a wide range of issues, both personal and theological, all discussed through voluminous correspondence.[29] Significantly, none of the primary attackers had been with the BMS in China for very long, and as such had only limited first-hand knowledge of Richard, his Chinese context or his work.

Richard was very much aware of the grave nature of the accusations made against him. Although there was clearly animosity on all sides, Richard tried to remain hopeful in the midst of their trials: "God in His Providence has put us into a hot furnace for the present. If it will purify us though the process be painful then it will still be a blessing."[30] In his responses to his critics, Richard provided a convenient summary of the various adaptations he had made to his practice and understanding of Christian mission during his first term of service in China, expressing confidence in his methods and reaffirming his convictions regarding what mission entailed.

Currently, the fullest account of the debates is contained in Brian Stanley's *History of the Baptist Missionary Society*.[31] Rather than fleshing out Stanley's narrative, the following analysis will focus on the nature of the criticisms

---

27. Herbert Dixon to Baynes, 23 November 1885, reprinted as "Tidings from Shansi," *MH* 82, no. 8 (1886) 359–62, especially 61.

28. See, for example, James to Baynes, 19 September 1888, as recorded in BMS China-Japan Sub-Committee Minutes, 19 November 1888, vol. 2, bk. 2:7–12, BMSA.

29. Many letters were written, some of them very long: Sowerby, Turner, and Richard produced letters of forty-six, twenty-six, and twenty pages in length, respectively.

30. Richard to Baynes, 12 May 1887, p. 18, BMSA CH/2.

31. Stanley, *History of the BMS*, 189–96.

and Richard's responses, in order to elucidate the ways in which this conflict both challenged and affirmed Richard's adaptations to his understanding and practice of mission. While the letters from this period are lengthy and detailed, most of the criticisms fall into one or more of the four categories that will be discussed in turn in the four sections that follow.

8.2.1 "Another Gospel"

a) The Charges

Despite the frequent references to the *ways* in which Richard pursued mission work in Shanxi, the main detractors were insistent that their complaint was not a fit of pique over different tastes in evangelistic method.[32] Rather, as Turner explained, "Mr. Richard was working toward ends not within the proper object of the B.M.S. and substituting *something else* for the Gospel of Christ."[33] Sowerby added detail to Turner's charge, claiming that "to certain classes, and in certain books Mr. Richard does not teach Christianity as a spiritual religion, based on faith in Christ Jesus, but that he substitutes for it a secular and earthly Gospel."[34] In their letters home, Richard's detractors presented his reform proposals in *Present Needs* as proof that what he was offering the people of Shanxi and of China was something other than salvation from sin and death through faith in Jesus Christ.[35]

In the opinion of his critics, Richard had erroneously redefined the Kingdom of God. Dixon believed that Richard was preaching a "conglomerate teaching wherein Science, Heathenism, Roman Catholicism and Christianity are bundled up into a new 'Gospel for Nations.'"[36] This combination, according to Sowerby, reflected Richard's departure from the orthodox view of God's Kingdom.

> Mr. Richard's conception of the Kingdom of Heaven is that it is materio-spiritual, it does not seem to him to mean that "new order into which men are born from above" by faith in Christ Jesus, their new life being sustained and controlled by the Spirit of God, so that they live in obedience to the Divine

---

32. For example, see Sowerby to BMS Committee, 1 August 1888, p. 3, BMSA CH/64.

33. Turner to BMS Committee, May 1888, pp. 7, 13, BMSA CH/65. It is unclear whether the emphasis was in the original or was added later.

34. Sowerby to BMS Committee, 1 August 1888, p. 36, BMSA CH/64.

35. Turner to BMS Committee, May 1888, pp. 14–22, BMSA CH/65.

36. Dixon to Baynes, 25 April 1887, BMSA CH/1.

laws of the Kingdom, as laid down by our Lord in the Sermon on the Mount. This idea of the Kingdom will be sufficient to preach to some, but for others it must be represented as having "real and tangible 'blessings'" such as will commend it to unregenerate heathen men, and hence Mr. Richard finds it necessary to include all the comforts of western civilization, all the triumphs of modern science and engineering, all knowledge, and everything that is profitable, as an essential part of the Kingdom, it being our duty to teach the Chinese that these are the "blessings of Christianity" and so will they have "right conceptions of true Christianity."[37]

As Turner explained, "a kingdom can become the kingdom of Christ *only* so far as its individual members are brought to love, and serve Him. Individual conversion then is our aim." This proper missionary task of "preaching the Gospel to the people," it was argued, contrasted starkly with Richard's interest in meeting China's "*special* needs."[38]

Aware of the accusation that he and the others were attacking Richard out of personal rancor, Dixon later softened his critique of Richard's message. Richard, he wrote, "preaches science (?) to the exclusion of the Gospel. Mark that word it is *exclusion* not substitution." This in no way cleared Richard of the charges, for regardless of his understanding of the gospel, Richard "has done and would still do things that are not in harmony with his position as a missionary of the B.M.S. and which the B.M.S. could not conscientiously (supposing them to have a conscience) allow him to do in their time with their money."[39] For Richard's critics, the time and resources spent by Richard on "science"—on the various reform programs and educational initiatives he was pursuing—were not advancing the spiritual Kingdom, and thus were not within the purview of any BMS missionary. According to Richard's Shanxi coworkers, Richard had lost sight of the gospel: he was preaching something different as a result of his mistaken inclusion of the material in his understanding of the Kingdom of God. This had led him to misunderstand the proper scope of Christian mission.

---

37. Sowerby to BMS Committee, 1 October 1888, pp. 7–8, BMSA CH/64.

38. This and the preceding quotation are from Turner to BMS Committee, February 1887, BMSA CH/65.

39. Dixon to Baynes, 13 November 1888, BMSA CH/1. The question mark (Dixon's own) reflects Dixon and Turner's contention that Richard's scientific ideas were not legitimate science.

b) Richard's Defense

In October 1888, in what survives as one of Richard's clearest written statements of his own theological convictions, Richard responded forthrightly to those who questioned his commitment to the orthodox Christian gospel.

> An explanation of what I understand to be the aim and scope of the Gospel. I regard the Gospel of Christ as remedial—undoing the work of the fall—destroying the works of the devil—a Salvation from sin and suffering wherever found, so that where sin has abounded grace shall much more abound. It begins by the conversion of individual souls through belief in the incarnation, the life, death and resurrection of our Lord Jesus Christ, and then proceeds to lead these individuals to benefit their fellow men by the bearing of the various fruits of the Spirit, and as conversions multiply the converts will ultimately become a blessing to all the world. I also note this, that belief in Christ's death for us is not the end of our religious life, but a means. It is difficult to find a passage anywhere in scripture which tells the object of Christ's death to be other than Holiness. E. G. Our Lord "gave himself for us that he might redeem us from all our iniquity, and purify unto himself a peculiar people, zealous of good works.["] I hold also that our personal complete salvation is indissolubly connected with saving others.
>
> Turner agrees with me that Christ saves the soul and gives immortality, and so far destroys the works of the devil; but I believe that as sin brings a whole train of misery into the present world as well as into the next, often involving numberless other people, spiritually, morally, materially, socially and politically, Christ's salvation is not a half salvation, but will deliver the world in the long run, and is now delivering it, from all sin and misery of the present life, whether brought on us by ourselves or by others.[40]

As was the case with nearly all of his adaptations, Richard had not rejected one set of ideas in exchange for another, but rather had grafted new ideas into the old—in this case, taking his fully evangelical conception of the Christian message and broadening it to also reflect what he now recognized as the this-worldly implications of the Kingdom of God.[41] While the opti-

---

40. Richard to BMS Committee, 17 October 1888, p. 3, BMSA CH/4. The biblical citation is Titus 2:14.

41. Richard's desire for "the conversion of individual souls through belief in the incarnation, the life, death and resurrection of our Lord Jesus Christ" set him apart from his LMS contemporary T. E. Slater, who in his accommodations in India reduced

mism of Richard's second paragraph suggests postmillennial influences, he clearly had not rejected the basic components of the gospel, as one of his critics eventually conceded.[42]

In Richard's view, the main source of contention with his colleagues emerged not from differing construals of the gospel but rather from their disagreement regarding "the *scope* of the missionary's work."[43] While insisting that he had not departed from "the simplicity and spirituality of the Gospel of Christ," Richard proclaimed that he had broadened its content to include the implications of the Kingdom of God for life on this earth.[44] For his critics, Richard's hybrid focus produced what they believed to be an inaccurate version of Christianity in which "the line which separates the material from the spiritual is obliterated."[45] Richard, on the other hand, argued that the Kingdom of God as expressed by the Old Testament prophets and taught by Jesus himself was an organic combination of both worldly and otherworldly concerns.[46]

Richard was quite happy to offer a defense of his broadened understanding of the Kingdom and, by extension, the missionary task. Immediately following the lengthy quotation above, Richard provided numerous Old and New Testament proofs that "our Heavenly Father is not indifferent to our present physical suffering."[47] The challenges and isolation of living in interior China, argued Richard, often produced a narrowing of scriptural interpretation that could only be countered by the concerted practice of analyzing entire books of scripture, rather than selected passages. This more balanced reading at times resulted in departures from popular viewpoints, "especially when mainly surrounded by Plymouth Brethren, Salvation Ar-

---

the gospel to what he termed the "Divine facts and Divine life in Christianity" in recognition of his belief that "all are by nature Christians," thus granting Hinduism a status coequal with Christianity. Cracknell, *Justice, Courtesy and Love*, 109–10; Slater, *God Revealed*, iii, as quoted in Sharpe, *Not to Destroy but to Fulfil*, 98.

42. Sowerby wrote, somewhat disingenuously, that "we have never questioned Mr. Richard's orthodoxy" regarding the importance of individual conversion, or Christ's divinity and sacrifice for sin. Sowerby to BMS Committee, 1 August 1888, p. 15, BMSA CH/64.

43. Richard to BMS Committee, 17 October 1888, p. 4, BMSA CH/4.

44. The phrase is from Sowerby to BMS Committee, 1 August 1888, p. 45, BMSA CH/64.

45. Sowerby to BMS Committee, 1 August 1888, pp. 13–16, BMSA CH/64.

46. In his autobiography Richard claimed that Turner was also present when Richard and Hill realized this truth. Richard, *Forty-Five Years*, 145–46.

47. In this letter Richard specifically discussed Ps 72:2–4, 12–4; Isa 41:17–20; 61:1–11; Matt 25; and Jas 2. Richard to BMS Committee, 17 October 1888, pp. 3–5, BMSA CH/4.

myists, and Evangelists of only one school of religious thought as was the case with me in Shansi."[48] Richard then built upon these arguments from scripture by appealing to the practice of the vast majority of missionaries throughout history: political reform in medieval Europe, social equality within the Indian caste system, and building homes and supplying clothes for "Polynesians, Africans, and American Indians" were listed along with other examples as evidence of the acceptability of missionary action to improve worldly conditions. Finally, Richard suggested that his construal of the scope of missionary endeavor differed little from that of many admired missionaries of his generation, including William Knibb and David Livingstone, and was in agreement with the teaching of R. W. Dale, C. H. Spurgeon and the BMS Secretary Alfred Baynes.[49] Far from straying from the object of Christian mission, Richard believed he was following Scripture and historical mission practice by pursuing the full scope of the missionary task.

8.2.2 "Ineffective Methods"

a) The Charges

Beginning with Dixon's letter in the *Missionary Herald*, the newer BMS arrivals to the Shanxi field began to question most of Richard's missionary methods. As Dixon wrote above, he and the other members of the Shanxi BMS team believed that there was greater openness to the gospel in the countryside, and thus saw Richard's urban focus as a less effective allocation of resources. Likewise, Richard's interest in officials and gentry was perceived as an elitist mission that targeted "wealthy men," and this "at great expense": Richard was squandering too many resources on privileged men unlikely to accept the gospel.[50]

Nearly every aspect of Richard's mission to the mandarins was challenged by his critics. The science he presented was questioned, with his detractors devoting many pages of their letters to exposing what they saw as Richard's "foolish and chimerical ideas, which while they would excite a

---

48. Richard to BMS Committee, 17 October 1888, p. 6, BMSA CH/4. This phrase angered Dixon, somewhat justifiably, with its reference to the many CIM workers from Brethren backgrounds, and perhaps to Stanley Smith and C. T. Studd's experiments with Salvationist musical processions in Lu'an. Broomhall, *HTCOC*, 7:58.

49. Richard to BMS Committee, 17 October 1888, pp. 7–8, BMSA CH/4. Richard also mentioned Moses's freeing the Hebrew slaves and William of Orange's deliverance of Europe from the Inquisition as further examples of proper Christian concern for this world, noting, "I believe men do not cease to be citizens when they become Christians."

50. Sowerby to Baynes, 18 May 1888, BMSA CH/64.

little amusement at home, are cruelly misleading and injurious to a people so badly informed as the Chinese are."[51] Richard's suggestion that his interactions with officials were producing an environment more open to Christian witness was also dismissed. Dixon quoted Baron Richtofen's favorable impression of Shanxi's openness to outsiders in 1870 as proof that the province was friendly toward foreigners even before Richard began his work to foster good official relations.[52] The idea that Chinese officials could be moved to create conditions that would advance the gospel was also questioned. Criticizing Richard for having exceeded John Clifford's acknowledgment that "forces and ideas" shaped the environment within which the gospel contended, Sowerby was appalled at the suggestion that the mission ought to rely on "unconverted heathen officials" for the establishment of the church.[53] Most telling for his critics, Richard's attempts to conciliate the official and scholarly classes were not producing converts. The small size of the Baptist community in Shanxi was pointed out, as well as the questionable quality of those believers.[54] Dixon specifically claimed that there were only two "fruits" from Richard's dealings with the upper classes—one of whom, very likely Richard's teacher Gao Daling, he claimed "now cares nought for Christ."[55]

Nor were the alleged defects of Richard's methods limited to his official interactions: Turner and Dixon saw Richard's employment of Chinese evangelists in the countryside as ineffective and impracticable, suggesting instead that the missionaries themselves do the evangelism, preaching in public chapels and in the streets—the precise methods Richard had found so ineffective upon his first arrival in China.[56] In their minds, Richard's failure was complete: his work was wasting limited resources, had not improved official attitudes toward foreigners, had produced few converts (and those of questionable quality), and his reliance on local evangelists was less effective than having the missionaries themselves preach in the streets.

---

51. Sowerby to Baynes, 18 May 1888, BMSA CH/64.

52. Dixon to Baynes, 13 November 1888, BMSA CH/1. On page 3 of this letter Dixon quotes what he recalls from the Baron's 1870 and 1872 letters: "[Shanxi] IS AS SAFE AS PEKING.... THEY TREAT FOREIGNERS WITH RESPECTFUL CURIOSITY."

53. Sowerby to BMS Committee, 1 August 1888, pp. 18–19, BMSA CH/64. Sowerby's favorable reference to Clifford seems to be based upon Clifford, *New City of God*, 19–20.

54. Dixon to Tymms, 18 March 1887, BMSA CH/1.

55. Dixon to Baynes, 13 November 1888, BMSA CH/1.

56. Dixon to Tymms, 18 March 1887, pp. 3–4, BMSA CH/1; Turner to BMS Committee, February 1887, BMSA CH/65. See also chapter 2 of this thesis.

b) Richard's Defense

The evangelization and conversion of Chinese people, Richard argued, was being hindered by the anti-Christian prejudices of the official class. This reality had driven him to adopt the methods he was currently employing.[57] It was Richard's hope that his work toward the "enlightenment and conciliation of the mandarins and scholars" would gain for Christians in China a "greater freedom to preach the Gospel." Richard believed his efforts were changing official attitudes, as indicated by the fact that several Shanxi elites were now positively disposed toward Christianity and willing to promote its priorities. Beyond changes in the attitudes of individual mandarins, Richard saw the greatest proof of his method's effectiveness to be the fact that in isolated, inland Shanxi, the missionaries "live in perfect peace."[58]

With little experience of mission life in other parts of China, Richard's critics underestimated the significance of this achievement. Richard remembered being pelted with stones while traveling in interior Shandong, and the difficulties of finding a place to sleep.[59] Despite gratifying numerical growth—by 1891 there were 1,138 baptized believers meeting in over sixty small churches—the BMS mission in Shandong continued to experience persecution among its local members and restrictions on the lawful travel and residence of its foreigners in the countryside.[60] Throughout the 1880s Jones and his colleagues expressed their urgent desire for someone—initially someone like Richard, and then, as the Shanxi conflict developed, for Richard himself—to come and conciliate the official classes in the provincial capital of Jinan in order to remove some of these barriers.[61] Having arrived in Shanxi during (in the case of Turner) or after the famine relief effort which formed the foundation of Richard's conciliatory work, the Shanxi BMS workers were unable to appreciate the material advantages they received from this work.

Richard rejected the notion that his focus on the official classes was elitist. Richard's work did not exclude ministering to the poor or uneducated;

---

57. Richard to BMS Committee, 17 October 1888, p. 25, BMSA CH/4.

58. Richard to BMS Committee, 17 October 1888, pp. 26–27, BMSA CH/4.

59. Richard to Baynes, 8 June 1887, p. 2, BMSA CH/2.

60. See the letter from Richard printed in *NCH* 31, no. 845 (8 September 1883) 280–81, 290–92. This was incorrectly recorded in the BMS China-Japan Sub-Committee as being in the 28 September edition. BMS China-Japan Sub-Committee Minutes, 17 December 1883, vol. 1:232, BMSA. See also Richard to Baynes, 26 December 1887, p. 9, BMSA CH/4. For details of the growth of the Shandong Baptist church, see Armstrong, *Shantung (China)*, 135.

61. BMS, *Reports of China*, 4, 7; Jones et al., *Baptist Missionary Work*, 1–9, 19–24; Jones, *North China BMS*, 10–13.

rather, he explained, it was "simply because work amongst certain classes has not yet been properly attempted" that he had emphasized this sphere of missionary endeavor.[62] Moreover, his colleagues' lack of interest in taking the gospel to China's mandarins disregarded the simple fact that Christianity was "for all classes; to neglect the rulers is to disobey our Lord's plain command."[63] While Richard certainly hoped to see officials converted to Christianity, and become "god-fearing rulers" who would create better laws for the people of China, his focus on the educated classes was not primarily an evangelistic scheme; Richard did not expect scholar-officials to be particularly open to conversion. As he explained, even if they would "only *sympathize* with Christianity, . . . then in addition to the individual conversions themselves, the poor peasants, now often persecuted for conscience's sake will be relieved of their suffering."[64] Significantly, throughout the conflict neither Richard nor his colleagues questioned seeking the worthy, a strong indication that Richard continued to understand the worthy to be devout seekers of truth, rather than the social or political elite.[65] Richard did not seek after officials because he counted them among the worthy, but because he deemed their approval essential to the rapid conversion of China— hence, his emphasis on conciliating rather than converting the mandarins of China. As Richard's wife Mary suggested in her defense of her husband's work in Shanxi, Richard certainly desired the conversion of the large mass of Chinese people, but had strategically chosen to focus his own efforts on conciliating the officials out of an awareness of his unique suitability for this specific task and a conviction that doing so would foster precisely the conditions conducive to rapid Chinese conversion.[66]

Although Richard was devoting more and more of his energies to the indirect aspects of mission work, his ministry was not without fruit—and this despite, as his Shandong colleagues could attest, the fact "that city work is the most difficult in all mission in China."[67] After pointing out that his early years in Shanxi were devoted to arresting and alleviating the devastation of the famine, Richard noted that,

62. Richard to Baynes, 7 March 1887, p. 3, BMSA CH/2.
63. This and the following: Richard to BMS Committee, 17 October 1888, p. 25, BMSA CH/4.
64. Richard to Baynes, 19 November 1888, as recorded in BMS China-Japan Sub-Committee Minutes, 15 January 1889, vol. 2, bk. 2:39, BMSA.
65. On one occasion in the conflict, Richard did mention "work amongst the devout" as a method he hoped the BMS would continue to pursue. Richard to Baynes, 12 March 1888, p. 8, BMSA CH/2.
66. Mary Martin Richard, "Sketch of Mr. Richard's Work," 3.
67. Richard to Baynes, 12 May 1887, p. 9, BMSA CH/2.

> It is true that notwithstanding such general work as I mention above I had only 14 baptisms during my 3 or 4 years of *mission work* in Shansi having handed twenty or thirty enquirers to the C.I.M. Messrs. Turner and Sowerby have not been engaged in such general work, here each two years at work—4 between them, during my visit to England, and they have baptized *two*! Pray pardon this miserable comparison which is forced on me in self defence.[68]

Despite time spent in Shandong while officially posted to Shanxi, and having spent the more recent years in Shanxi devoted to the less directly evangelistic spheres of mission work, Richard maintained that he had seen more numerical success than his critics.

While Richard recognized the importance of individual conversions, he had made a conscious decision following the North China Famine to focus on the more indirect aspects of mission work. Twenty years prior to Richard's arrival in Shanxi, David Livingstone had experienced a similar shift in his methods in Southern Africa, increasing acquaintance with the local peoples and cultures having impressed upon him the importance of many at the time unnoticed works for the advancement of God's Kingdom.[69] Richard's post-famine shift toward doing the longer-term, less concentrated work necessary to change opinions among educated Chinese was driven by the same strategic motivations that compelled Livingstone. Thus Mary Richard argued for the effectiveness of her husband's methods by saying, "Mr. Richard's work here [in Shanxi] has been more *diffusive* but not less *successful* than that in Shantung."[70]

While Richard's promotion of reform among the officials and scholars was closely related to his plans to remove anti-Christian prejudice, he was also genuinely interested in producing changes that benefited those in China who were suffering. Turner's criticisms of Richard's interest in "political economy" downplayed the simple fact that for Richard "the end of all [his promotion of reform] was the *relief of the poor from starvation*."[71] Nor did he accept the charge that his science was foolish. In some detail, Richard pointed out that many of his ideas were already being developed by serious men of science throughout the Western world, and had already been adopted by various governments: transmission of sound by telegraph

---

68. Richard to Baynes, 12 May 1887, p. 10, BMSA CH/2.

69. See Blaikie, *Personal Life*, 203–6. Livingstone eventually left his mission so that he could continue involvement in these "indirect" mission labors. Ross, *David Livingstone*, 117–23.

70. Mary Martin Richard, "Sketch of Mr. Richard's Work," 1.

71. Richard to BMS Committee, 17 October 1888, p. 9, BMSA CH/4.

or telephone, the collection and storage of electricity, geothermal energy, the use of balloons to predict and influence weather, chemically modified food, and many others were not fancies but facts.[72] Scientific education also helped remove barriers to the gospel. As Jones had explained to the BMS Committee in 1883: "Do not for a moment think this is all so much mere secular fuss. It is also the direct helping of religion, for in China we have many obstacles which rest solely on ignorance of physical science."[73] Since Richard had used his own money to purchase the scientific equipment for use in his demonstrations in Taiyuan, all of this was accomplished without burdening the Society's finances.[74] As Richard moved through his defense of his reform-related and scientific activities he refuted his detractors' most damning critique with the repeated refrain: "there is no substitution of anything for the Gospel here."[75]

Finally, the employment of indigenous Christians was for Richard more than a matter of method. Developed during his early years in Qingzhou, and enshrined in his 1885 *A Scheme for Mission Work in China*, Richard's commitment to increased indigenization of the work of winning China for Christ was founded on his own first-hand knowledge that in Shandong "the greatest progress was when the *natives* were most at work."[76] Richard was anxious to avoid the

> error of engaging foreigners to do the same work which [Chinese evangelists] will do [but] less efficiently and at least eight times more expensively. Foreigners should be reserved to do what the Chinese cannot do, never to do what Chinese Pastors can do much better. What we want is the quickest and most efficient way of raising native missionaries.[77]

---

72. Richard to BMS Committee, 17 October 1888, pp. 9–16, BMSA CH/4. While Richard's responses to his BMS opponents, as well as the actual text of *Present Needs*, give an indication of the breadth of his scientific interests, the absence of contemporary records regarding the content of Richard's scientific lectures in Taiyuan makes it difficult to assess some of his critics' accusations.

73. Jones, *North China BMS*, 11.

74. James to BMS Committee, 19 September 1888, as recorded in BMS China-Japan Sub-Committee Minutes, November 1888, vol. 2, bk. 2:9, 19, BMSA.

75. Richard to BMS Committee, 17 October 1888, pp. 10–16, BMSA CH/4.

76. Richard to Baynes, 19 October 1888, p. 3, BMSA CH/2. Richard was puzzled as to why his Shandong colleagues—not just those from Shanxi—lacked his confidence in the effectiveness of Chinese evangelists. See his concerns in Richard to Baynes, 26 December 1887, p. 6, BMSA CH/4.

77. Richard to Baynes, 12 May 1887, p. 6, BMSA CH/2. See also Richard's comments in Barber, Hykes, and Lewis, *Records of the GCPMC: Shanghai, 1890*, 163–64.

While his colleagues contemplated eliminating Chinese evangelists and engaging in street preaching themselves, Richard was still convinced that the rapid conversion of China necessarily required a tremendous expansion of Chinese people in ministry. The missionary's job was to develop and support a gifted coterie of Chinese pastors and evangelists, who will then

> be able to tell their own country men far better than we can that Christianity has the promise of *the life that now is* as well as that which is to come, which some missionaries forget to teach, and that after the hundred fold here with persecutions there is the eternal life hereafter which their own sages did not teach them.[78]

8.2.3 "Leaning Romewards"

a) The Charges

Richard's critics were also deeply suspicious of what they perceived to be his Roman Catholic tendencies, particularly his supposed sympathy for Ricci and the Jesuit mission to China.[79] Two primary strains of argument—questioning the "flavouring of Romanism" in the Christianity presented by Richard, as well as the excessive accommodation in his methods (techniques learned from the Jesuit mission to China)—were present throughout their complaints.[80]

By the 1880s anti-Catholicism in England had lost much of its mid-century political force, yet attitudes in the Protestant churches and chapels of both England and Wales were still decidedly against the Catholic religion.[81] Most of the British missionary community in China shared this aversion to Catholicism, finding further confirmation in the apparent similarities between Chinese religious practices and the rites and sacraments of the Catholic Church.[82] Richard's new colleagues were no different, expressing strong disapproval of the services held by Richard in the main church in Taiyuan.

---

78. Richard to Baynes, 12 March 1888, p. 9, BMSA CH/2.

79. Sowerby to Baynes, 11 August 1888, BMSA CH/64.

80. Quotation from Sowerby to BMS Committee, 1 August 1888, p. 32, BMSA CH/64.

81. Arnstein, *Protestant Versus Catholic*; O'Leary, "When Was Anti-Catholicism?," 326–33.

82. Reinders, *Borrowed Gods*, throughout, especially 100–112.

[Richard] had the end of the chapel covered with crimson cloth, and in the centre of it a large white satin cross, and at either side two yellow streamers exactly like those used in Buddhist Temples; that with all the people kneeling toward the cross he led them in a chaunted [sic] litany.[83]

Dixon was so horrified at the use of a prayer book in one of these services, where "responses were chanted by the people," that he immediately stood up and left the service. "I could not stand it. I do not believe in it at home, it tends Romewards and I believe in it still less for Chinese who naturally are formal and whose own religion consists in this very chanting of litanies."[84] Likely because of his association with the Church of England, Sowerby was more nuanced in his criticism, explaining that he did not actually believe Richard to be in sympathy with Catholicism on any points of dogma. Rather, he believed Richard "had gathered from [the early Jesuit mission in China] many ideas, ideas which although he does not perceive it, are fatal to the establishment and purity of the true spiritual religion of our Lord Jesus Christ."[85]

Nor were these the only signs of Catholicism they found in Richard's work. In seeming confirmation of their worst fears, Richard's colleagues had also discovered in one of his Chinese-language pamphlets from the 1880s language that they believed advocated the establishment of a church—perhaps a national one—with an "episcopal hierarchy" that ended only one step short of its logical conclusion: "the establishment of the Papacy."[86] For Richard's nonconformist critics, the advocacy of an episcopal structure within the fledgling Chinese Baptist community was nothing less than "barefaced popery."[87]

83. Dixon to Baynes, 25 April 1887, BMSA CH/1. Curiously, in this same letter Dixon also mentioned the competition he faced from the Catholic presence and their "priestcraft" in and around Xinzhou, yet he did not make any connections between Richard's worship services and the practices of Shanxi Catholics.

84. Dixon to Tymms, 18 March 1887, BMSA CH/1.

85. Sowerby to BMS Committee, 1 August 1888, pp. 44–45, BMSA CH/64. For Sowerby's opinion of Richard's Chinese worship services, see Sowerby to BMS Committee, 1 August 1888, p. 32, BMSA CH/64.

86. Sowerby to BMS Committee, 1 August 1888, p. 23, BMSA CH/64. This criticism was built upon the various titles Richard suggested for different levels of church workers in *The Order of Learning the Doctrine*, titles which shifted—possibly in response to his colleagues' criticisms—between the two editions extant, both held in the BMSA. See, for example, the change of the term for the highest church officer, a superintendent of several fellowships, from *zhang jiao zhe* in the first edition to *jiao xian zhe* in the second edition. Richard, *Xue dao cixu*, first edition, 3; Richard, *Xue dao cixu*, second edition, 3. The first edition was produced in Shanxi "some years" before 1887. Richard to Baynes, 12 May 1887, p. 5, BMSA CH/2.

87. Dixon to Tymms, 18 March 1887, BMSA CH/1.

Richard's use of Catholic literature was considered yet another sign of his sympathy for Rome. Richard's willingness to utilize European Catholic works when developing materials for use in China was seen as inappropriate, particularly Timothy and Mary Richard's translations from Alban Butler's *Lives of the Saints* and Cardinal Wiseman's *Fabiola*.[88] Richard's distribution of Catholic Chinese-language tracts produced in China was perhaps more troubling still, for in addition to spreading errors, this involved Society funds being paid to the Roman Catholics.[89]

To support their claims that Richard was engaging in Jesuit-like accommodationism, Richard's colleagues in China sent several of Richard's Chinese-language publications to the BMS Committee, though few of Richard's critics or the committee members could read them. One document that especially attracted the attention of Richard's colleagues was his *Xue dao cixu*, or *The Order of Learning the Doctrine*.[90] Their main criticisms of the work were twofold: First, although the pamphlet mentioned the Kingdom of Heaven and talked about the way of eternal life, it failed to define either phrase or provide instruction as to how one actually achieved them.[91] Thus, a book that purported to outline what was expected of Christian workers failed accurately to represent the Christian faith. Second, the pamphlet seemed to intermingle all sorts of Chinese religious and philosophical ideas with instructions for Christian living, thus further clouding this presentation of Christianity by making it seem compatible with China's religions.

Perhaps reflecting their own limited linguistic skills, Richard's critics did not challenge any of the Chinese religious terms employed by Richard in his writings. In his Chinese texts from this time Richard had continued his earlier practice—increasingly popular among certain Protestant missionaries—of using *shangdi* to refer to God.[92] The term *tianzhu*, a Catholic gloss for "Lord of Heaven" with similar usages in Buddhism, was adopted when translating the "fear the Lord" in *Present Needs*.[93] Many other terms

88. BMS Shanxi local committee to BMS Committee, 20 April 1887, p. 15, BMSA CH/64; Sowerby to BMS Committee, 1 August 1888, pp. 32–33, BMSA CH/64. On the works of Alban Butler and Cardinal Wiseman, see n. 115 below.

89. Dixon to Baynes, 13 May 1887, BMSA CH/1.

90. See n. 86 above.

91. Sowerby to BMS Committee, 1 August 1888, pp. 7, 20–24, BMSA CH/64.

92. By the early 1880s *shangdi* was favored over *shen* and *tianzhu* by nearly 60 percent of the Protestant missionary community. Lai, *Negotiating Religious Gaps*, 50. Richard continued to use *shangdi* in his publications after the conflict. See, for instance, "Jiushi jiao yi [The Benefits of Christianity*]," *WGGB* (June 1891) 7b–11a.

93. See section 96 in *Present Needs*, 34. Although the 1872 Peking Committee translation of the New Testament used *tianzhu* when referring to God, Richard's otherwise exclusive reliance on *shangdi* suggests his use here is borrowed from Catholic or

from Chinese Buddhism were also pressed into service: *tiandao* (The Way of Heaven), a term that was also used within Daoism to refer to the laws of nature, was similarly employed by Richard, while *tiantang* (heavenly hall) was used in place of *tian* (heaven), the more common term in Protestant Chinese Bible translations at the time.[94] In *The Order of Learning the Doctrine* Richard went further—borrowing the unusual term *shen'gong* with its connotations of mystic power to describe acts of righteousness or "divine merit."[95]

Rather than challenging his word choices, Richard's critics charged that by enjoining Chinese pastors to "*select all that is good from these and use it in the service of God*," Richard was guilty in his writings of "attempting to graft heathen beliefs on to the Christian faith, [having] selected what is not good and embodied it in his work."[96] For Richard's detractors, this kind of accommodation, so reminiscent of the early Jesuits, was compromising the gospel. To make their case, Richard's attackers supplied their own English-language translations of Richard's documents to the BMS Committee, emphasizing in their renderings the "heathen" or Chinese religious roots of Richard's writings. What James Legge described as Turner's sometimes "ridiculous" interpretations of Richard's language in the religious sections of his *Present Needs* booklet contrasted strikingly with Richard's approachable English translations and their recognizable paraphrases of scriptural texts such as Matt 28:18–20.[97] Turner's decision to translate "*wei ting tianming*"

Buddhist sources. On the Peking Committee see Eber, "Interminable Term Question," 148–52.

94. Both terms occur throughout the final five sections of *Present Needs*, and in both editions of *The Order of Learning the Doctrine*. On the Buddhist provenance and meaning of the Chinese terms in this paragraph, see the relevant entries in Muller, "Dictionary of Digital Buddhism," http://www.buddhism-dict.net/ddb. Though of less interest to Richard, *tiandao* was also used within Confucianism. See, for example, *Analects* 5.13. Since Richard gives no indication of which Chinese versions of the Bible he used or preferred, comparisons between Richard's Chinese-language publications and the Chinese-language Bible are highly speculative. For reference purposes, a copy of the 1853 (*shangdi*) Delegates' Version printed in Shanghai was consulted as being Richard's most likely preference: "Chinese Delegates NT." On the characteristics of the Delegates' Version see Zetzsche, *Bible in China*, 77–101, 145–60.

95. This term appears in ancient Chinese literature, and can mean either meritorious acts or, as in the popular novel *Shuihu zhuan* [*Outlaws of the Marsh*], deeds of miraculous power. See the entry in *Han dian*. In both editions of *The Order of Learning the Doctrine*, Richard employed the term, often alongside *xingshan* (to do charitable works)—a term used widely in Buddhist texts in the same sense—to encourage Chinese believers in moral living and doing good deeds.

96. Sowerby to BMS Committee, 1 August 1888, p. 29, BMSA CH/64.

97. See James Legge's criticism of Turner's translation of Richard in Legge's assessment of Richard's writings for the BMS Committee. BMS China-Japan Sub-Committee Minutes, 19 November 1888, vol. 2, bk. 1:246–49, BMSA; and BMS China-Japan

rather woodenly as "listening to Heaven's command" when he could have chosen the equally plausible yet more culturally sympathetic "following God's will" was typical.[98] Not surprisingly, Turner was critical of Richard's accommodating attempts to present Christianity in language that resonated with Chinese sensibilities, dismissing the religious sections of *Present Needs* as "rotten to the core."[99]

For his detractors, there was too much of Rome in Richard's practice and presentation of Christianity. Moreover, by accommodating his literature to appeal to the Chinese cultural context, Richard was guilty of repeating the mistakes of the Jesuits who had come before him.

b) Richard's Defense

In his 1883 furlough report to the BMS Committee, Jones had given an example of Richard's accommodationism at work.

> Mr. Richard once had a wooden cross made with an inscription on it—the same ancient words by which the Chinese denote the God of "heaven, earth, all space, and the spirits of all flesh"—his idea being that any Chinese, who knew nothing of us, might, at a glance, see the ancient monotheistic belief of their nation obtaining its great confirmation and development in the Person and Work of Christ.[100]

Though Jones was clear that Richard merely used the wooden *pai* "as common ground," Richard in a letter written shortly after felt it necessary to caution Jones, explaining,

> I made no such wooden tablet. A paper picture of one to meet the Chinese about half way is all I *did*. Though to my mind there

---

Sub-Committee Minutes, 19 November 1888, vol. 2, bk. 2:1–4, BMSA. Richard's Chinese paraphrase of the Great Commission from Matthew's Gospel was worded to highlight the inclusive nature of God's plan as well as its corporate—rather than exclusively individualistic—scope: "When the Savior ascended to heaven he commanded [them] to go toward all land under heaven and to spread the Gospel to all peoples, not just to save a person or a region but a nation as well." *Present Needs*, 33 (translation mine).

98. Turner's translation is from Turner to BMS Committee, May 1888, p. 23, BMSA CH/65; the more sympathetic translation is admittedly modern, taken from Bohr, "The Legacy of Timothy Richard," 80 note 11. See Richard's translations of sections 94 and 98 of *Present Needs* in Richard to BMS Committee, 17 October 1888, pp. 17–21, BMSA CH/4.

99. Turner to BMS Committee, May 1888, p. 22, BMSA CH/65.

100. Jones, *North China BMS*, 8. See also the note at the bottom of the page for Jones's defense of the Christian appropriation of Chinese "pai" or tablets.

cannot be a grain of countenance to idolatry even if it were good. To ignorant years [sic] the wooden tablet sounds more idolatrous perhaps and we have to deal with those who have not had the same privilege we have had of knowing the whole truth about several of these things.[101]

Fear of being unjustly connected with idolatry, and by extension with Catholicism, led Richard to specify his actions and warn his colleague of the difficulty the uninformed might have accepting such strategic accommodations to Chinese religious practices.[102]

The animosity that Protestant missionaries and their converts encountered in China was part of a long history of anti-Christian prejudice that began with the late Ming Jesuit mission. Originally introduced by Chinese merchants and practiced in culturally acceptable forms, Catholicism had begun quite peaceably in seventeenth-century Shanxi. The growth of foreign power in the nineteenth century changed conditions so that Catholic communities became increasingly at odds both socially and culturally with local Shanxi life.[103] Further heightened by two centuries of religious and ethnic rebellions, as well as the increasing assertiveness of the foreign powers, the growing antagonism was extended to the recently arrived Protestants as well. Ironically, Richard's accommodations in church practice that were intended to change educated Chinese opinions of Christianity—adaptations that he embraced in order to *combat* a Chinese anti-foreignism frequently directed at Catholic missions—made him the object of anti-Catholic criticisms from his fellow Europeans.

Richard had little patience for his colleagues' anti-Catholic reaction to his adapted Chinese worship services. "Some of [my fellow missionaries] believed that everything Roman Catholic comes from the devil, that all written forms of prayer in worship even in the case of beginners will lead to formalism and hypocrisy. They forget how many of our Psalms and hymns are prayers."[104] As early as 1880 Richard had written about the importance that Chinese people attached to ritual (*li*), and suggested that missionaries would do well to adapt their worship services and musical tunes to conform to more formal Chinese rather than Western tastes, for "if we do not admit what the conscience of the whole world, except a section of Protestants,

---

101. Richard to Jones, 3 March 1884, p. 3, BMSA CH/2.
102. Reinders, *Borrowed Gods*, 100–120.
103. This is a central theme in Harrison, *Missionary's Curse*.
104. Richard to Baynes, 12 May 1887, p. 14, BMSA CH/2.

demands as so necessary, then it would be preposterous in us to expect success while sinning against so many."[105]

In the wake of the Tractarian push for liturgical renewal in the Church of England, Victorian nonconformity became less hostile to formalism in worship than it had been in the past. An increasingly urban, middle-class and socially accepted population of nonconformists demanded a more gentlemanly form of worship.[106] The free or "long" pastoral prayers that preceded nonconformist sermons gradually gave way to shorter, more formalized prayers; unadorned geometric chapels were replaced with soaring Gothic buildings complete with organs and stained glass windows, all in testimony to the newfound dignity in worship and social power of many nonconformist congregations.[107] By the end of the century, formal liturgical acts such as set congregational responses and infant "dedications" (not quite baptisms) were increasingly encountered in Baptist chapels.[108] At the same time, other sectors of Protestantism became obsessed with anti-Catholic fears that found their expression in the largely ineffective 1874 Public Worship Regulation Act.[109] The vehemence of Richard's critics' attack on his liturgical accommodations reflected the reactionary response of many conservative Baptists to what they perceived to be the impending Catholicization of Protestantism in Britain.[110]

Ten years later, near the end of the BMS Shanxi conflict, Richard's convictions on this matter had only strengthened:

> our modes of conducting services are often too much Western and too little Asiatic. The early Christian services in Palestine were very different from those now held in the West. If Europeans and Americans can adjust Christian services to the taste of Western nations, without harm to their devotion, may not a Chinaman do the same for his own people? . . .
>
> No nation has ever received Christianity willingly without adaptation to its own existing civilization. This imperfect adaptation, substituting adherence to traditional opinions and practices, which had arisen to meet a different civilization, for

---

105. Richard, "Thoughts on Chinese Missions," 436.

106. Munson, *Nonconformists*, 133–37.

107. Binfield, *So Down to Prayers*, 145–61; Davies, *Worship and Theology*, vol. 4:65–89, 212–22.

108. Davies, *Worship and Theology*, vol. 4:237–43.

109. Bentley, *Ritualism and Politics*, 40–75; Brown, *Providence and Empire*, 276–78.

110. Briggs, *English Baptists*, 28.

unadulterated Christianity, was the main cause of the fall of Romanism in China.[111]

Rather than moving the Chinese church toward Rome, Richard's increased use of ritual in local worship services was a strategic attempt to avoid the mistake of the Catholic mission in China—to ensure that Chinese Christian worship followed Chinese rather than European forms, whether Protestant or Catholic. Ironically, while Richard ascribed what he viewed as the "fall of Romanism in China" to its being insufficiently Chinese, his critics attacked his "Chinese-style" innovations as typically "Catholic."

Richard's suggestion that believers observe certain feast days—particularly those associated with the birth, death and resurrection of Jesus—was, he explained, not a sign of his Catholic inclinations, but rather an attempt to encourage "those Christians living too far away for ordinary Sunday services" to "come in with advantage as these days would impress upon their mind the essential doctrines of the Divinity and power of our Lord and his great atonement on the Cross."[112] Richard's proposal for the networking of rural churches under organized local supervision was driven by similarly pragmatic concerns. Far from establishing some sort of papal hierarchy, Richard's relativizing of the voluntary principle was a strategic response to this same problem of geographical diversity. "I know of no better plan for getting speedily over the ground without the unnecessary crowding of several churches in one place."[113] In light of his rich understanding of Chinese culture and its religious milieu, Richard was demonstrating the same flexibility regarding church polity that many other nonconformist missionaries in India and Africa explored toward the end of the nineteenth century.[114]

Richard also denied that there was anything unique or untoward in his use of Catholic literature.

> The London Mission has published Thomas a Kempis[.] The American Presbyterians have published a Roman Catholic tract. Jones and I ordered some and printed them for use. I added another Christian Biography and got *Fabiola* translated, but in all cases the Romish teaching was cut out.... If we could find books on the subjects wanted, from Protestant sources, we should prefer them of course.[115]

---

111. Richard, "The Relation of Christian Missions to the Chinese Government," 413.

112. Richard to Baynes, 12 May 1887, p. 7, BMSA CH/2.

113. Richard to Baynes, 12 May 1887, p. 6, BMSA CH/2.

114. Stanley, "Reshaping of Christian Tradition," 399–426.

115. Richard to Baynes, 12 May 1887, p. 8, BMSA CH/2. The portrayal in Wiseman's

Richard and his wife had translated portions of Alban Butler's *Lives* for similarly practical reasons. Given his belief in the evangelistic efficacy of moral evidences in the Confucian-influenced Chinese context, it was natural that, as Richard explained, "In training the native evangelists I often felt the need of a church hist. given in the concrete with examples of Holy Lives as well as dry fact. We have no such thing in Chinese as yet." As always, the appropriation of the Catholic text was selective and edited, with Mary Richard "leaving out what she thought Romish."[116] Furthermore, Richard explained, these so-called Catholic materials were only for use in apologetic settings. An entirely separate set of works—completely Protestant—were used for communicating Christian "Dogmatics."

> It is by *these* that I try to produce in men a sense of sin, to awaken in them a cry "what shall I do to be saved?" and tell them of the glad tidings of reconciliation to God through Jesus Christ, as the means of their individual salvation, and as the foundation of the kingdom of God which is ultimately to bless all men in this world as well as in the next. The books that I use are those of Dr. Milne,[117] Dr. Martin,[118] Dr. Williamson,[119] Dr. Allen,[120] William

---

Fabiola of a persecuted Christian minority and their struggle to persevere and transform the highest levels of national society must have struck Richard as prescient for China's small Protestant community. In Britain, however, the book—both because of its content and its association with Cardinals Wiseman and Newman—was linked to the perceived threat of resurgent Catholicism. Arnstein, *Protestant Versus Catholic*, 42–49; Howard, "Saint Fabiola," 89. Richard's "Christian Biography" was almost certainly the *Christian Biographies* his wife translated from Butler's popular Catholic devotional work, still in print long after its initial 1756 publication. Butler, *Lives of the Fathers*.

116. This and the previous quotation are from Richard to BMS Committee, 17 October 1888, p. 23, BMSA CH/4.

117. In the following the literary contributions from each of the authors mentioned that were most likely to have attracted Richard's attention are provided. See the corresponding entries in MacGillivray, *Descriptive and Classified*; and Wylie, *Memorials of Protestant Missionaries*. William Milne's 1819 *Zhang Yuan liangyou xianglun* [*The Two Friends*], noted for its Chinese context and non-confrontational tone, was voted by the 1907 China missionary conference as the "most useful in leading heathen to a knowledge of the truth." *China Centenary Missionary Conference*, 196–97; Lai, *Negotiating Religious Gaps*, 124–27.

118. Voted second "most useful" in 1907, W. A. P. Martin's extremely popular 1854 tract *Tiandao suyuan* [*Evidences of Christianity*] used the arguments of William Paley to present the Christian faith to Chinese literati. See Pfister, "Attitudes Towards Chinese Culture(s)," 406.

119. As head of the SDCK, Alexander Williamson was involved in many different publications on history, world religions, and Christianity, including his popular 1879 three-volume *Jidu shilu* [*Life of Christ*].

120. Besides his well-known periodical *WGGB*, Young J. Allen published numerous

Burns,[121] Mr. John,[122] Mr. Faber,[123] and all the leading books published by the Religious Tract Societies in China, as they appear from time to time.[124] I also use my own catechism, hymn book, portions of Jeremy Taylor's *Holy Living*, and of course the Scriptures. Does Turner use much more? I think not.[125]

The works of these authors were popular throughout the Protestant missionary community at the time and, as Richard pointed out, these were more or less the same materials that were used by Turner and the other BMS Shanxi workers.

This is also the proper context for understanding Richard's interest in the Jesuit mission to China. Richard was not interested theologically in Catholicism, but rather pragmatically in the highly contextualized ways in which the earlier Jesuit mission to China communicated the truths of the gospel. A few years after the famine, Richard was discussing with Jones the selection of illustrations for a new evangelistic book for use in Shanxi. Richard explained that, "while I bring up Roman methods so very often in order to learn from them where I think we need improvement still I am far from approving *very many things* because I believe we are far superior to them."[126] Shortly after, in the opening paragraph of his 1885 autobiographical address, Richard did praise the "Romish mission" to China for their "learning and devotion," even noting their earlier missionary successes; but then

---

apologetic materials, as well as a number of Christian biographies.

121. English Presbyterian missionary to China William Charles Burns was a "linguistic genius," and his translations of Bunyan's *The Pilgrim's Progress* [*Tianlu licheng*] into *wenyan* (1853) and Mandarin (1865) were extremely popular throughout the rest of the nineteenth century. Wu, "Bin Weilin *Tianlu licheng*," 128–31.

122. From among his many popular tracts, Griffith John's commonly used 1879 *De hui rumen* [*The Gate of Virtue and Wisdom*] had been specifically prepared by John for the 1879 Wuchang *juren* exam candidates.

123. Ernst Faber's 1876 *Make jiangyi* [*Commentary and Seventy-seven Sermons on the Gospel of Mark*] was especially popular with Chinese pastors and evangelists, although his later 1884 apologetic *Zixi cudong* [*Civilization, from West to East*, or the "Fruits of Christianity"] became even more influential. Faber, Kranz, and Haden, *Works of Rev. Ernst Faber*, 56–60, 62–65.

124. On nineteenth-century Protestant literature in China in general, see Barnett and Fairbank, *Christianity in China*, in addition to Lai, *Negotiating Religious Gaps*.

125. Richard to BMS Committee, 17 October 1888, pp. 27–28, BMSA CH/4. Significantly, none of Richard's colleagues challenged his catechism or his hymnbook.

126. Even this mention of "Roman methods" occurs in the letter within the context of the BMS literature work in North China, with no further indication of what Richard was supposedly learning from the Catholic mission. Curiously, in the preceding sentence Richard stated explicitly that his interest was in Roman "*not Jesuit*" things. Richard to Jones, 8 March 1884, p. 3, BMSA CH/2.

finished by concluding that what he saw as their failure was due to their decision "to obey the Pope rather than Christ."[127] Richard had little taste for Catholic theology, but recognized the effectiveness of their empathetic, accommodationist missionary methods.

Regarding the more general criticism that this accommodationist attitude had led him to embrace "heathen" principles, Richard responded by questioning his critics' idea of Christian truth.

> Some believe that everything that is heathen is unchristian and from the devil. I don't believe the Mohammedans are unchristian in their worship of one true God instead of idols. I don't believe that the high moral teaching of any religion is devilish and unchristian. Christianity has the power of assimilating all that is good in other religions. We come here to counteract their false teaching and to fill up what is wanting just as Christ came not to destroy but to fulfill.[128]

Repeating his conviction that Christianity fulfilled what China's best religions lacked, Richard revealed once again his parallelism with comparativist views of world religions. He did not, however, feel the need to say much more on the topic, for "On these subjects even my colleagues are by no means all agreed any more than people at home." This was demonstrated when James Legge was called upon by the BMS Committee to render verdict on the religious content of Richard's works and to assess the accuracy of Turner and Richard's translations. Not surprisingly, Legge approved of Richard's writings:

> On the whole, there is nothing in this [*Present Needs*], or in the others that I have seen, which proves that Mr. Richard's religious teaching is wrong, and if there be but little such teaching in them, that may be owing to their special purpose.... Enthusiast as he is, he is yet, as I have already said, a man in earnest, and may, when "sober-minded," do good and efficient service in the cause of Christ.[129]

Enthusiastic and perhaps uniquely purposeful in his missionary endeavors, Richard had not embraced Catholic doctrine. Rather, even as he

---

127. Richard, *Fifteen Years*, 3. This appears to refer to the Jesuit decision to obey the Pope's ruling during the Ming Dynasty Rites Controversy. See Minamiki, *Chinese Rites Controversy*; as well as, for Chinese Christian perspectives, Liu, "Chinese Converts."

128. This and the following are from Richard to Baynes, 12 May 1887, p. 14, BMSA CH/2.

129. James Legge to Baynes, 27 September 1888, as recorded in BMS China-Japan Sub-Committee Minutes, 19 November 1888, vol. 2, bk. 2:2–3, BMSA.

criticized Catholic missions in China for excessive adherence to Western traditions, Richard saw in the Chinese-language devotional literature of the Catholic mission a powerful tool (once its specifically "Romish" content was removed) for demonstrating to China's Confucian elite the moral superiority of Christian living.

8.2.4 "Personal Feelings"

a) The Charges

Given the nature of the charges, and the transparency facilitated by the open exchange of letters between the various parties involved, it is not surprising that tempers grew hot. Richard's critics, however, were quick to reject the suggestion that their reasons for objecting were primarily personal, as Turner did in the following letter:

> As to the charge of personal feeling I must confess that throughout this unhappy affair there *has* been a considerable amount of personal feeling on both sides.... [W]hen men discuss such important matters as were discussed between us it seems inevitable that personal feeling should be roused, though I assure you that the discussion was not caused by personal feeling.[130]

While the personal nature of the conflict was acute for Turner, who had known Richard comparatively longer than the rest of the Shanxi workers, the newer missionaries also wrote and acted with great passion. In early 1884 the BMS Committee, with guidance from Richard and the support of Jones and Turner who were present in England at the time, had adopted regulations to postpone the full participation of new China workers "in the direction and governance of the affairs of the mission" for a further year past the two years typically set aside for the adjustment of BMS missionaries overseas.[131] By the time of the conflict a few years later Sowerby was arguing that Richard—and indeed the entire BMS system—was too constraining of new workers, unnecessarily denigrating their ability to make positive contributions to the work during their initial years on the field. Given the variance between the content of ministerial preparation in Britain and the kind of mission advocated and practiced by Richard, the probationers (Sowerby was here thinking particularly of his friend Dixon)

---

130. Turner to BMS Committee, May 1888, pp. 6–7, BMSA CH/65.
131. BMS China-Japan Sub-Committee Minutes, 18 February 1884, vol. 2:7, BMSA.

were in his view to be commended for going against the regulations and directly petitioning the BMS Committee.

> It is a terrible thing for men in their first years in a heathen country to find their senior brethren hopelessly at variance as to the main truths of the Gospel, and to find what they have been carefully trained in, for four or five years, as formative truths recklessly trampled on or thrown away.[132]

Richard's characteristic lack of systematic clarity on matters theological did not help cool inflamed tempers. Sowerby found Richard to be "inconsistent," noting that "Mr. Richard is not very clear, and I cannot be absolutely sure that I have not misunderstood him."[133] Dixon, in particular, saw something sinister behind Richard's ambiguity, accusing him of being deliberately misleading, and of demonstrating a lack of "straightforwardness" by disingenuously agreeing with everyone so as to remove all opposition.[134] Dixon's correspondence was rife with instances of Richard's personal offences: on one occasion Richard lost his temper with the BMS Shanxi local committee and stormed out of the meeting.[135] In one letter Richard had left the title "Mr" off of Turner's name; in another, as already noted, he slandered his critics, calling them Plymouth Brethren and Salvation Armyists in order to discredit them.[136] For his part, Dixon made no effort to hide his dislike of Richard: "On his telling me he was going [to leave Shanxi] I said plainly I should be thankful to see him gone."[137]

Of course, the critics were convinced that God was on their side. Both Dixon and Sowerby referred to a series of revival meetings organized for the foreign population in Taiyuan by Stanley Smith of the CIM in the summer of 1887.[138] Smith's messages focused on the need for a "baptism of the Spirit," and produced many tears as well as great interest in the more consecrated

---

132. Sowerby to Baynes, 21 December 1887, BMSA CH/64.

133. Sowerby to Baynes, 11 August 1888, BMSA CH/64. See also Sowerby to Baynes, 1 August 1888, pp. 16, 34, BMSA CH/64; and Beauchamp, *Days of Blessing*, 100–104. Perhaps alluding to Richard, Sowerby's comments during the *Days of Blessing* meeting also mentioned the "painful feelings" he had regarding the "incompatibility of temper" that may exist among colleagues.

134. Dixon to Baynes, 18 March 1887, BMSA CH/1; Dixon to Baynes, 14 October 1887, BMSA CH/1; Dixon to Baynes, 13 November 1888, BMSA CH/1.

135. Dixon to Baynes, 13 May 1887, BMSA CH/1.

136. Dixon to Baynes, 13 November 1888 BMSA CH/1. See n. 48 above in this chapter.

137. Dixon to Baynes, 14 October 1887 BMSA CH/1.

138. Sowerby to Baynes, 11 October 1887, BMSA CH/64.

life among the missionary community.[139] The Richards attended, along with other members of the BMS, CIM, and ABCFM. Sowerby hoped that the prayers and humility engendered by the meetings might heal the division in the BMS, but Dixon was—again—less sanguine: "I am sorry to say [Richard] was apparently unbenefited by our meetings for prayers; he spoke several times, but it was like cold water thrown on me, but took no effect on any one."[140] In his critics' eyes Richard was inured to prayer, and unable to contribute meaningfully in a proper spiritual context.

b) Richard's Defense

Living as members of so small a foreign community in a remote foreign land while engaged in work that was physically and emotionally demanding, it was surprising when missionary coworkers did *not* come into conflict. Richard's sense of hurt and frustration with his colleagues came across clearly in his letters. Though he tried to be gracious, his bitterness was plain regardless of his protestations that self-defense drove him to this level.

> I would not have you think that I am blind to the varied and many excellent gifts of my brethren which are capable under the grace of God of rendering immense service to the mission cause. What I *do* think is that they have committed an error of judgment in devoting so much of the time that should have been spent in learning and earnest mission work to the teaching of a senior who thinks he knows all the lessons they can now teach him about mission work and perhaps a few more, without any disrespect to them.[141]

Having just returned from furlough to find himself surrounded with new colleagues, Richard was surprised to be attacked by men with little knowledge of China and still less knowledge of himself. Turner, with whom Richard had become acquainted during the North China Famine, had only joined the mission a few months before Richard's furlough and had come from a mission which advocated very different methods from his own; the others had arrived during Richard's absence and were still in their probationary period. Unfamiliar with China or the language, and with little practical mission experience, how could these men claim ability to judge Richard or

---

139. Smith later embraced the doctrine of annihilationism as well as the radical faith-healing notions of J. A. Dowie, resulting in his dismissal from the CIM in 1902. Broomhall, *HTCOC*, 7:310, 490–97.

140. Dixon to Baynes, 14 October 1887, BMSA CH/1.

141. Richard to Baynes, 12 May 1887, p. 19, BMSA CH/2.

his work in Shanxi?[142] For newer colleagues, connections to Britain were still fresh and paramount, sustaining priorities and values that came from those connections. For those who had served longer—those for whom the local context had become more real than their sending context—Britain was distant and the needs and habits of the Chinese community took precedence. In Richard's case this meant that worship services and literature crafted with empathy for Chinese cultural values were being measured by his newer colleagues against standards that were shaped more by conditions and priorities that persisted in Britain. Lacking his understanding of and concomitant appreciation for Chinese ways, Richard's critics were unable to acknowledge the vital contribution of his adaptations toward speeding the conversion of China. These disagreements over deeply ingrained cultural values were unavoidably personal.

Richard was eccentric, as his friend James admitted—"though there is two-tenths foolishness, or worse, in all men."[143] Richard was also sensitive to the slights of his teammates, noting that two or three of his BMS colleagues refused to attend any of the worship services he led—a very aggressive action in an intentionally Christian community. By comparison, only two out of twenty of the CIM workers in the area were unwilling to join his services, and one of those later changed his mind to such a degree that he donated one hundred pounds toward Richard's literature distribution work.[144]

His sense of hurt was especially apparent in his frustration with the unjust functioning of the BMS Shanxi local committee—the group whose meeting supposedly produced his tantrum. In particular, he complained of the excessive authority given to the local committee over its individual members.[145] With Turner and Sowerby voting en bloc against him, they exercised complete control over Richard, effectively preventing him from printing and distributing any literature, or from continuing to carry out mission work in accordance with his own proven methods. As Richard explained, "This exclusiveness is I believe *the crux* where all our differences meet. They persist in coercing me and now report home that I protest!"[146]

Richard countered by asking that he be allowed to serve as a missionary with the same freedom of conscience granted to any minister in Britain.

142. Richard to Baynes, 12 May 1887, pp. 1–3, BMSA CH/2.

143. James seemed to be thinking primarily of Richard's ideas. James to BMS Committee, 19 September 1888, as recorded in BMS China-Japan Sub-Committee Minutes, 19 November 1888, vol. 2, bk. 2:10, BMSA.

144. Richard to Baynes, 26 December 1887, pp. 3–4, BMSA CH/4. The identity of these two individuals is unclear.

145. Richard to Baynes, 26 December 1887, p. 7, BMSA CH/4.

146. Richard to Baynes, 12 May 1887, pp. 11–15, quotation from p. 15, BMSA CH/2.

Initially, Richard had voted along with the local committee and agreed with their ideas, in hopes that the BMS Committee would soon supersede the local committee's more restrictive decisions and reign in their power. When this was not immediately forthcoming, Richard recommended a division of labor in the Shanxi field that would allow each to carry on as they saw fit. "We must let each other alone. For Christ has many members in one body and has distributed different gifts to different members."[147] When this too was rejected by the local committee, Richard decided in the autumn of 1887 to leave Shanxi and remove at least temporarily to the coast because, as Legge observed, given the nature of the criticisms leveled against Richard there appeared to be no way for the BMS Shanxi workers to "walk and work together."[148]

Despite all the human frailty on display, Richard still looked for divine providence in the midst of the conflict. "The hand of man is very plain in all this matter. May we also be able to trace the hand of God bringing good out of evil."[149] This persistent faith was especially notable given the level of discouragement Richard faced following the rejection of his *Scheme* during his furlough, difficulties with health, and now the personal and professional rejection of his colleagues on the field. With nowhere else to turn, Richard looked to God for vindication.

> It is like a living death to see one's work which in my case cost me so much peril of life now being undone by changes made in Furnival Street and by new colleagues.... Still though Committees and Colleagues may oppose I hope God who has been my stay in my solitary work for the first fifteen years of my life in China will help me to succeed in whatever will be my lot next to do. No men can ask me to assist in pulling down my own work even if they won't accept a single suggestion from me. The moral, dear friend from this is: —Be sure you do the will of God always and then in the long run no individuals or body of men can do you more harm than they did to Jesus Christ. Death will be followed by a suitable resurrection.[150]

---

147. Richard to Baynes, 12 May 1887, p. 16, BMSA CH/2.

148. Richard to Baynes, 13 October 1887, BMSA CH/2; BMS China-Japan Sub-Committee Minutes, 19 November 1888, vol. 2, bk. 2:3, BMSA.

149. Richard to Baynes, 13 October 1887, BMSA CH/4.

150. Richard to Glover, 2 April 1887, BMSA CH/2. In this context, Richard's remarks on "changes made in Furnival Street" is most likely a reference to the new rules for making decisions on the field that he had found so frustrating.

8.3 Conclusion of the Conflict: Release for Expanded Ministry

Shortly after his October 1887 withdrawal from Shanxi Richard reflected on God's purpose behind the conflict. "I am myself a believer in Providence. The question I have put to myself frequently since the beginning of the difficulty is What does God mean to the Society and to me by this dead lock [sic]?" First, he thought perhaps it was a prompting from God to move to other parts of China where anti-foreign sentiments were hindering mission work and where he might be able to foster the kind of friendliness he had developed in Shanxi. Then again, he wondered if this might be an encouragement to him to begin working independently of the Society, relying solely on the support of "natives who sympathize with my work." Finally, he wondered if perhaps this whole experience was designed to force the Society to determine which methods, in fact, had proven most effective.[151] Richard believed God was working in the midst of strife to encourage him and the Society to continue developing and using his methods.

Throughout Richard's communications with the BMS Committee this confidence in the very methods under question was evident as he exhorted the Society to honor the legacy of pioneering missionary adaptation which he believed marked their mission in China.

> Consider what good work you have done in China and let your future be in harmony with the past. Hitherto you have been the first in so many mission methods and other societies are following you in almost every point. E. G. work in the interior—social intercourse with the Chinese—Christian literature, constructive instead of destructive—self teaching and self-support in the native church—work amongst the devout—work amongst the educated and governing classes: these are some of them.[152]

Not coincidentally, this list reflected both the development of the BMS and its work in China over the previous twenty years as well as Richard's own personal development as the Society's senior missionary. These were profoundly *his* adaptations, and despite all the criticism he faced he still believed that these methods represented the future of the BMS in China.

When Richard left Shanxi he did not leave the BMS. Richard had witnessed the many transfers and departures of the first generation of CIM workers in Shanxi, as well as Tenney's resignation from the ABCFM precisely

---

151. Richard to Baynes, 26 December 1887, pp. 10–11, BMSA CH/4.
152. Richard to Baynes, 12 March 1888, p. 8, BMSA CH/2.

because he no longer held to the orthodox view of the gospel.[153] Toward the end of 1888 Richard claimed that there were other BMS workers in China who were prepared to resign in response to the heavy-handed restraint of the local committee.[154] At the end of 1891, James resigned amicably from the BMS, surprising the BMS Committee by informing them that he no longer held "the orthodox teaching on the Trinity and Atonement."[155] In line with his previous refusals of secular employment outside the mission, Richard stayed with the BMS—despite the frequency of organizational changes Richard had seen in Shanxi, and in the face of the example of those who left their societies over theological questions. Even after he had fled to the coast to escape the disapproval of his Shanxi brethren, Richard continued to plead passionately with the Society to focus more of its resources and attention on his beloved "poor Shanxi."[156]

When the BMS Committee announced its final decision on the Shanxi conflict, it began by expressing its approval "of Mr. Richard's high Christian character, his devotion to the Saviour, and his fidelity and attachment to the central truths of the Gospel." This vindication was tempered, however, by their attitude toward his missionary methods. "With respect to the general subject of Mr. Richard's missionary aims and methods, and the proportion which efforts to promote the social and material welfare of the people should bear to direct Gospel teaching and work," Richard's work was found wanting. Showing the specific nature of their concern, the committee then went on to encourage Richard to return to "those earlier methods, which God so richly blessed, instead of those wider and more indirect methods upon which his heart appears to be set."[157]

Richard's missionary message had been deemed orthodox. His more empathetic attitude toward China's religions and cultures, his accommodationist approach to local Christian practice, even his use of Catholic literature—none of these had been criticized by the mission leadership. Their disapproval centered on what they referred to as his "more indirect methods;" namely, the relative amount of time and energy he expended on the

---

153. See chapter 7 above.

154. Richard to Baynes, 8 November 1888, BMSA CH/2. Richard claimed that one member "gave in his resignation" and another was "talking of leaving the Mission." Richard may have been referring to James and Medhurst, both of Shandong. Richard to Baynes, 23 July 1889, p. 3, BMSA CH/2.

155. James to BMS Committee, 21 December 1891, as recorded in BMS China-Japan Sub-Committee Minutes, 15 February 1892, vol. 2, bk. 2:209–10, BMSA.

156. Richard to Baynes, 12 March 1888, pp. 4–5, BMSA CH/2.

157. BMS China-Japan Sub-Committee Minutes, 10 December 1888, vol. 2, bk. 2:18–20, BMSA.

this-worldly aspects of his missionary work. This criticism was all the more striking given Richard's extensive medical and relief work prior to the conflict with his colleagues, and the positive effect of those so-called secular efforts on his ministry in Shandong as well as in Shanxi. While the committee did not express its unease in theological terms, Richard's broadened conception of the Kingdom of God and the expanded approach to mission that Richard felt this required had failed to secure their full endorsement.

Theologically, the Society had declared Richard and his faith to be within the boundaries of evangelical truth. To frame it differently, Richard clearly upheld the evangelical characteristics as articulated by Bebbington's famous quadrilateral. Officers of his own society, men respected within the Baptist community, had failed to find fault with Richard's views on the gospel (crucicentrism) or the need for personal salvation (conversionism)—a decision affirmed by Richard's reference to the crucifixion and resurrection in his post-conflict Chinese-language apologetic essay "Benefits of Christianity."[158] His confidence in the Bible as God's word (biblicism) was never really challenged, and his tangible manifestations of the gospel in deed (activism) were greatly admired. Richard, in fact, was very much in line with the growing social activism that was emerging as a hallmark of evangelicalism in the closing decades of the nineteenth century. As Bebbington says, "Very few in the Evangelical world saw the new social message as a diversion from the true Gospel until well into the twentieth century."[159]

From chapter 7 above, it is also clear that members of the ABCFM and CIM Shanxi teams—in as much as they knew him—also accepted Richard and even allowed him to teach and preach within their fellowships. Despite the acrimony of the BMS conflict, in the end just under half of the BMS representatives in China questioned the theological orthodoxy of Richard and his missionary methods. The BMS Committee and the rest of the China field workers accepted him, a trend that continued toward the end of the century as Richard's more accommodating missionary methodologies became increasingly accepted within the Protestant mission community in China.[160]

Richard was "deeply pained" by the BMS Committee's decision. Since the accusation of his unorthodox faith was rejected, why were his accusers not sanctioned for libel? Moreover, while he did engage in a broader range of activities than his colleagues, Richard nevertheless spent *"as much time*

---

158. See "Jiushi jiao yi [Benefits of Christianity*],", WGGB (December 1891) 13b. For more on "Jiushi jiao yi," see n. 166 below.

159. Bebbington, "Baptist Conscience," 13–24; Bebbington, "Evangelicalism," 247–48.

160. Ling, Changing Role, 28–29.

in gospel teaching—probably more time—than any of my accusers," and he pleaded for a deputation to visit the field so that the fact could be established once and for all. Finally, "[t]he assumption . . . that I have given up former methods of mission work is pure fiction."[161] Ultimately, Richard maintained that his aims were identical to those of the BMS. After pleading with Baynes to attend to what he was saying rather than what his opponents claimed he believed, Richard concluded by asking the BMS Committee to "grant that the Spirit of God may be guiding us after long experience in China if not to *better* methods than it is likely for those at home to know, at least to such as should not be entirely suppressed."[162] In the end, he was most jealous to defend his methods.

At the time, Jones and the rest of the BMS workers in Shandong were working hard to convince Richard to join their team and represent the mission to the officials and literati in Jinan. The Shandong field was aware of the BMS Committee's final judgment; and beyond their sympathy for Richard's accommodationist approach to China's religions and cultures (Jones advocated the republication and broad distribution of Richard's 1880 "Thoughts on Chinese Missions" among the Protestant mission community), they also hoped to benefit from those same indirect methods—from Richard's conciliating efforts among the official and scholarly classes—which the BMS Committee had now deplored.[163] Richard was willing to join them, but two issues repeatedly prevented an agreement.[164] First, both Richard and the Shandong field wished to open an educational institution in Jinan, a project that was still considered financially impracticable by the BMS. Second, Richard was holding out for a guarantee that the local committee would never again be in a position to interfere with his missionary work.[165] On this point, the BMS Committee insisted that Richard must function within the mission according to the same regulations that governed all other members of the Society.

While waiting for his concerns regarding Shandong to be resolved Richard remained in Tianjin where he prepared an English version of the apologetic essay "Jiushi jiao yi" or "Benefits of Christianity" which he had earlier produced as a response to Viceroy Li Hongzhang's questions about

---

161. This and the previous quotations are from Richard to Baynes, 23 July 1889, pp. 4–5, BMSA CH/2.

162. Baynes, 23 July 1889, p. 6, BMSA CH/2.

163. Jones, *North China BMS*, 26.

164. This is neatly summarized in Glover and Morris, "Report on China Missions of the BMS," 30–32.

165. Richard to Baynes, 26 December 1887, pp. 7–8, BMSA CH/4.

Christianity.¹⁶⁶ He also continued his efforts to improve official attitudes toward Christianity, gaining a few converts along the way.¹⁶⁷ Having been struck by "malarial paralysis" in his right arm after a bout with famine fever during the summer 1889 famine in Shandong, Richard had been prevented by doctors from heading directly to Jinan until his health recovered sufficiently to allow him to brave the "malaria and sun" of central Shandong.¹⁶⁸ In July of that year, as he convalesced in Tianjin, Richard accepted Viceroy Li's personal request to act as editor in chief for the new Chinese-language newspaper, *Shibao* [*The Times*].¹⁶⁹ This allowed Richard to have further interaction with Li, while also allowing him to support his family without burdening the Society. The more than two hundred editorial leaders which Richard produced during his brief tenure were copied widely, enabling him to extend his conciliatory work among the officials beyond the paper's circulation in Shanxi, Zhili, Beijing, and Shandong.¹⁷⁰

Richard recognized that editing this Chinese newspaper was only "one part of the work appointed me by the society to do in [Jinan]," and only a temporary employment until "the way opened for fuller work in connection with the Society."¹⁷¹ When he realized that the *Shibao* would be closing its doors for financial reasons in June 1891, Richard recommended

---

166. No editions of "Jiushi jiao yi" exist apart from the seven-chapter version published in 1891–1892 in the *WGGB*. For Richard's English translation, see "Historical Evidences of Christianity for China: Chapter I The Material Benefits," *CR* 21, no. 4 (1890) 145–50; "The Intellectual Benefits of Christianity," *CR* 21, no. 5 (1890) 228–32; "Political Benefits of Christianity," *CR* 21, no. 10 (1890) 435–48; and "The Social Benefits of Christianity," *CR* 21, no. 11 (1890) 500–509. While the source of Richard's *jiushi jiao* (save the world teachings) terminology is unclear, he may have been influenced by the *jiushi tang* tablet donated by grateful locals to the Taiyuan church in 1878. Williamson, *British Baptists in China*, 41.

167. Richard to Baynes, 18 March 1890, BMSA CH/2.

168. Glover and Morris, "Report on China Missions of the BMS," 32; Richard, *Forty-Five Years*, 213; Soothill, *Timothy Richard of China*, 164–67. The deputation attested that Richard was seriously ill. Soothill noted that Mary served as amanuensis, as seen in Richard's letters from the time. See, for example, Richard to Baynes, 26 June 1890, BMSA CH/2.

169. Richard to Baynes, 26 June 1890, BMSA CH/2; Xiong, *Xixue dong jian*, 589. *Shibao* became one of the key influences behind reformer Liang Qichao's own periodicals: the intentionally named *Shiwu bao*.

170. Xiong, *Xixue dong jian*, 589. Richard's *Shibao* contributions were later collected and reprinted as *Shishi xinlun*. This influential text for the Chinese reformers became one of the most-pirated publications of the SDCK. MacGillivray, *Descriptive and Classified*, 45; Shu, "Zhongguo jindai shi ziliao jianjie," 73–75.

171. Richard to Baynes, 26 June 1890, BMSA CH/2. Richard also promised at the time to compensate the Society for any fees associated with his daughters' schooling back in Britain.

that the BMS Committee purchase the paper and continue its operations, or else authorize Richard to train and direct a team of Chinese evangelists to commence work along the navigable rivers stemming out of Tianjin; both were rejected as society resources were already strained with supporting the existing work under its care.[172] Ironically, Mary Richard had already been engaged in similar work on behalf of the American Methodist Episcopal Mission in Tianjin, having provided training for fifty of their Chinese female evangelists. Once again the Richards' confidence in Chinese evangelists was confirmed as they watched these women bring many inquirers into the church.[173]

Despite his fear that the existing BMS local committee structure would still result in undue interference with his ministry, with nothing else available Richard was now prepared to join the BMS Shandong field as soon as his health permitted.[174] At just this time, less than a year after the death in August 1890 of its founding director Alexander Williamson, the SDCK invited Timothy Richard to serve as its new director, having been impressed by his work in the pages of the *Chinese Recorder*.[175] Recognizing the potential provided by the SDCK to expand his conciliatory work with officials through literature into all of China's provinces, Richard accepted the offer with the approval of the visiting BMS deputation, and took up his new position in Shanghai in October 1891, retaining his status as a financially supported member of the BMS.[176] Four years after their painful departure from Shanxi, the Richards saw God's will in this "the first satisfactory settlement of our affairs in all that time."[177] With Richard's arrival the SDCK acquired a new sense of vision and purpose, as he identified and then systematically targeted China's literati with a rich stream of publications aimed at changing their attitude toward Christianity, their own people, and the world.[178]

---

172. Richard to Baynes, 20 May 1891, BMSA CH/3; Glover and Morris, "Report on China Missions of the BMS," 31, BMSA.

173. Richard, *Forty-Five Years*, 215–16.

174. Glover and Morris, "Report on China Missions of the BMS," 30.

175. Richard, *Forty-Five Years*, 217–18. On Richard and the SDCK/CLS, see Whitefield, "Christian Literature Society"; Sun, "Li Timotai yu guangxue hui," 161–67. According to Reeves, it was the *CR* reprint of Richard's 1989 address to the North China Religious Tract Society that attracted the attention of the SDCK. Richard, "How One Man Can Preach to a Million," 487–98; Reeve, *Timothy Richard*, 35–36.

176. Richard to Baynes, 20 May 1891, BMSA CH/3.

177. Mary Martin Richard to her brother, 18 September 1891, as recorded in Soothill, *Timothy Richard of China*, 170–71.

178. Xiong, *Xixue dong jian*, 589.

Toward the end of the nineteenth century, Chinese-language Christian periodicals shifted away from direct evangelism and were increasingly focused on presenting Western knowledge as a means of removing official prejudices and indirectly promoting Christian conversion.[179] Richard and his SDCK were one of the primary driving forces behind this development. With the wide reach and influence of his literature now enabling the diffusion of his conciliatory work across the entire nation, Richard was more hopeful than ever that the day of China's conversion by millions through the agency of local Christians was close at hand.

---

179. This trend reversed itself in the twentieth century as many missionary periodicals returned to more directly evangelistic publishing aims. Zhao, "Cong chuanbo xijiao dao chuanbo xixue," 92–97; Zhao, "Chuanjiaoshi zhongwen baokan ban," 64–70.

9

Conclusion

9.1 Transformation and Continuity

THE PRIMARY FOCUS OF this thesis has been to analyze the missionary adaptations—what Andrew Walls termed the "multiple conversions"—of Timothy Richard during his first twenty years serving in China. The acculturation experienced by most cross-cultural missionaries affected this Victorian Baptist missionary from Wales deeply, resulting in a profound transformation of his understanding and practice of mission. Reading Richard's published and personal writings from the time within the multiple contexts that shaped his life, this thesis presents a significant revision to the common distorted portrayal of Timothy Richard as the "liberal" who "departed from the original missionary vocation."[1] Without denying the dramatic nature of the changes—practical and theological—experienced by Richard, the present study has drawn attention to three themes that remained constant throughout his development, providing the force and direction for this transformation: his identity as an evangelical missionary, his deep empathy for the Chinese people among whom he was living, and his pragmatic interest in methods that worked.

It is impossible adequately to understand Richard's missiological transformation without reference to his persistent evangelicalism. Throughout his first twenty years in China Richard, "then and always, was primarily an evangelist."[2] This was demonstrated in chapter 2, as Richard's characteristic passion for conversion, shaped by his formative revival experience in Wales, led directly to his initial dissatisfaction with evangelistic methods in 1870s Shandong. This provided the impetus for his subsequent efforts to develop a more effective way of rapidly bringing large numbers of Chinese people to salvation.

---

1. A distortion pointed out by Walls, "Multiple Conversions," 240; and Pfister, "Rethinking Mission in China," 186.
2. Rattenbury, *David Hill*, 75.

In all his efforts to increase evangelistic effectiveness, the trajectory of Richard's adaptations remained emphatically toward closer approximation to Chinese patterns of thinking. As a Welshman, Richard owed at least some of this cultural flexibility to the bilingualism and practical approaches to education that were common components of his upbringing.[3] In his earnest desire to see Chinese people converted to Christianity—and thus to attain all the blessings God promised for this life and the next—Richard was willing to adapt himself and his methods in order to promote a gospel that was tuned for Chinese rather than Western ears. As discussed in chapter 4, Richard's willingness to acknowledge that there was good within China's religions and culture contributed to his emphasis on local participation in mission. This also strengthened his conviction, discussed in chapter 3, that there were "worthies" among China's devout religionists who were predisposed to accept the message of salvation. Increased interaction with these pious religious leaders further reinforced his Chinese sympathies, drawing him into deeper engagement with the languages, literature, and religions of China. As chapter 4 also demonstrated, Richard's positive view of Chinese people and their traditions, as well as his commitment to grow a distinctly Chinese church, were especially evident in his borrowing of effective organizational and educational techniques from local religious sects.

As he interacted with Chinese evangelists as well as devout followers of other religions, Richard increasingly relied on literary forms of communication that reflected Chinese sensibilities. This shift soon developed beyond linguistic modifications to include a change in apologetic strategy. Finding the traditional evidences for the truth of Christianity he had learned while at Haverfordwest to be ineffective in his Chinese context, Richard deemphasized the role of miracle and prophetic fulfillment in his apologetic. Equipped with Joseph Butler's arguments regarding humankind's God-given moral faculty and the existence in nature of a divine system of rewards and punishment, Richard discovered that Chinese people conditioned by centuries of codified Confucian morality seemed to be especially responsive to historical and personal demonstrations of the ethical superiority of Christianity.[4] As discussed in chapter 5, these "moral evidences" proved evangelistically effective, and were thus quickly incorporated into Richard's mission and church. Like most missionaries, Richard was more practical than reflective, reacting to his experiences on the field in whatever fashion he believed would be most likely to advance the gospel, and only later developing theological justifications.

3. May, "Mountain Views," 244–47.
4. Butler, *Analogy of Religion* (1852) 109–10.

The merits of Richard's development of an approach to mission that appealed to specifically Chinese needs and priorities were most clearly evident in the remarkable growth and independence of the Baptist churches in Shandong. As the local Baptist community expanded, Richard turned to scripture in search of a theological justification for his already effective accommodationist approach to church and evangelism. As seen in chapter 6, Richard's discovery of the concept of Christianity as fulfilling rather than destroying existing religious traditions—an idea that was also being explored by other evangelical missionaries at the time, particularly in India—owed more to Richard's encounters with the diverse Chinese religious world than to the intellectual inheritance of any Western thinker. For Richard, missionary methods that resulted in more rapid conversions in his particular North China context could not be other than biblically sound, a further reflection of his practical hermeneutic as discussed in chapter 2.

Chapter 5 demonstrated how the tremendous suffering closely observed by Richard during the North China Famine cemented his Chinese sympathies, as his evangelical compassion led him to identify with these people and to place their best interests foremost in his heart. The result—not surprising given his earlier efforts to incorporate scientific subjects into the curriculum at Haverfordwest Baptist College—was a natural expansion (not substitution) of his scope of mission to include famine relief work and eventually educational, scientific, and reform advocacy aimed at preventing future suffering on such a scale. Such efforts also provided further evidence of Christianity's ethical and technological superiority. As the famine receded, Richard once again turned to scripture, finding a warrant for his widening missionary vision: Jesus and the prophets had spoken of the Kingdom as something not only pertaining to life after death, but with real implications for life on this earth. Theologically, Richard was tracing paths that were also being followed independently by other evangelicals back in Britain, and yet Richard's ideas and impulses arose out of the demands of his missionary context.

Unlike Lian Xi's missionaries whose growing empathy and respect for all things Chinese led them to abandon their commitment to Christian conversion, Richard during the first half of his life and ministry in China continued to pursue conversion, remaining firmly within the boundaries of Victorian evangelicalism.[5] At the same time, Richard was unashamedly empathetic; like the avowedly evangelical Martha Crawford in the latter phases of her career, Richard responded to the acculturation process with an ever-growing love for and sense of identification with the Chinese people

---

5. Lian, *Conversion of Missionaries*, 10–13.

around him, rather than a simple rejection of the values and habits of the Chinese "other."[6] Throughout his development as a missionary, Richard pursued greater evangelistic results with almost indiscriminate enthusiasm, incorporating any and all techniques that proved effective into his evolving understanding and practice of mission. The convergence of these three factors, his persistent evangelical identity, the increasingly empathetic trajectory of his acculturation, and his pragmatic inclinations, explains much that was distinctive about Richard's transformation in mission.

9.2 Implications

The analysis begun in this thesis has yet to be extended to the second half of Richard's life and ministry in China, and so it would be premature to propose any revisions to scholarly understandings of Richard's later years. At the very least, however, any future study of the later Richard must henceforth take this thesis as its starting point. While that further work on Richard remains to be done, the thesis in its present state already offers a number of suggestive contributions to more general conversations regarding nineteenth-century missions and Christianity in China.

Most strikingly, the picture of Richard that emerges in this study challenges narratives of the development of Protestant mission that characterize Richard as an exemplar of a top-down mission strategy, placing him in opposition to missionaries such as James Hudson Taylor who supposedly followed a bottom-up strategy. Richard's idiosyncratic appropriation of Edward Irving's interpretation of the Matt 10 injunction to "seek the worthy," as demonstrated in chapter 2, reflected his respect for the intelligence and good intentions of devout Chinese religious leaders. It was not an evangelistic strategy—"Jesuit" or otherwise—focused on converting the social or political elite. When Richard did approach Chinese officials, he did so, not because he counted them among the worthy, but rather, as explained in chapter 6, out of a sense of obligation to carry the gospel to *all*. And while Richard recognized that these scholar officials were unlikely to accept the Christian faith, he was confident that efforts to win their hearts and minds would lessen elite hostility to Christianity, thus creating a more conducive political and social environment for the rapid spread of the faith throughout China.

This, along with an awareness of his unique suitability for the task, led Richard to make a strategic choice to work "at the top" of Chinese society. Richard saw developments at both ends of the social spectrum (the

---

6. Vaughn Cross, "Missionary Returns," 243–60.

softening of official attitudes and the proliferation of distinctly Chinese churches) as heralding a coming age of "national conversion," whereby great swathes of China's population—both high *and* low—would embrace Christianity.[7] Richard raises the possibility that not all missionary interactions with Chinese mandarins represented trickle-down theories of evangelism; some missionaries may have followed his example, taking a strategic, instrumental approach to Chinese elites out of a pragmatic recognition of political realities.

Second, this thesis has demonstrated the value of paying greater attention to missionary interactions with Chinese sectarian religion. Missionaries in India had earlier found the anti-idolatrous and anti-Brahmanical sects of Hinduism to be especially open to Christian conversion; similarly, Richard had found the Chinese sectarian world to be disproportionately populated with worthy truth seekers.[8] As he conversed with devout leaders from the Zaili, Golden Elixir, and other sectarian associations prevalent in Shandong and Shanxi, Richard noticed a kindred piety—a passion for truth—that he believed predisposed these people to accept the gospel. The conversion of Xi Shengmo with his strong sectarian connections suggests the evangelistic potential of Richard's interest in sectarianism, while it remains for future studies to explore precisely how Richard's intimate knowledge of the sectarian milieu may have shaped or colored his admittedly idiosyncratic interpretations of Chinese Buddhism.[9] All of this suggests there may be more to tell regarding the influence of sectarianism among both missionaries and local believers in the early twentieth-century proliferation of indigenous Chinese Christian sects.[10]

Richard's interest in sectarianism also lends credence to emerging scholarly understandings of local perspectives on late-Qing Christian missions. Historians such as Daniel Bays and R. G. Tiedemann have long argued that during the Qing Dynasty Christianity was often viewed as a form of Chinese sectarianism.[11] Richard seems to have grasped this relationship intuitively, placing sectarianism at the center of his Matt 10 evangelistic strategy while also incorporating effective practices from the sectarians into his church and mission. Henrietta Harrison's further claim that initial high levels of compatibility between Christianity and the religions and culture of

7. Richard, *Fifteen Years*, 22–23.

8. Oddie, "Old Wine in New Bottles?," 57–78.

9. On Xi's sectarianism, see Austin, *China's Millions*, 163–66. For a beginning exploration of how Chinese religious literature influenced Richard's later writings on Chinese Buddhism, see Scott, "Timothy Richard," 64, 66–74.

10. Lian, *Redeemed by Fire*.

11. Bays, "Christianity," 33–55; Tiedemann, "Christianity and Chinese," 339–82.

China *decreased* as China's contact with the outside world increased, also finds support: Richard's more isolated work in Qingzhou, with its heavy reliance on many of the forms and structures of local sectarians, grew much more quickly than his earlier, more Western-informed evangelistic work in relatively foreign-filled Chefoo.[12]

Third, Richard's efforts to learn from and adapt local practices for his own mission, when considered alongside his devoted attention to Chinese language and literature, situate Richard as an instructive example of the complex and varied ways in which missionaries, culture, and religion interacted with one another in nineteenth-century China. While other China missionaries of his day also mined the Chinese religious world for evangelistic entry-points, Richard was exceptional in his pragmatic willingness to borrow organizational and educational techniques from local religious associations in the hopes that doing so would make the new Baptist churches more acceptable and more effective within their local communities. Contrary to the missionary-as-cultural-imperialist narrative, Richard allowed his familiarity with the people, organization, and literature of his sectarian "brothers in nonconformity" to color his sense of what a truly Chinese church could become, rather than seeking to impose his own cultural notions of church upon the local faith communities.[13] Richard's prioritizing of indigenous ministers, his respect for local religious sectarians, his accommodationist approach to evangelism, and his practical applications of his own version of the theological idea of fulfillment: these all serve as powerful reminders of the surprising degrees of cultural empathy of which many missionaries were capable.

Finally, this understanding of Richard's development as a missionary adds welcome complexity to traditional narratives of the evolution of Protestant missions, reminding scholars of the multiple trajectories operating in tension throughout these years. Timothy Larsen has pointed out that while nineteenth-century developments in science and biblical criticism created a crisis of faith for some, others found in these same circumstances a crisis of doubt that led them back to Christian faith.[14] Similarly, Janet Fishburn has argued that not all twentieth-century Social Gospellers valued social conversion more than individual conversion.[15] Richard embodied many of these same tensions, persisting as an evangelical missionary who embraced

---

12. Harrison, *Missionary's Curse*, 4–5. Esherick's account of the sectarian-influenced Spirit Boxers implies a similar trajectory. Esherick, *Origins of the Boxer Uprising*, 206–40.

13. A point not acknowledged in Ding, *Li Timotai*.

14. Larsen, *Crisis of Doubt*.

15. Fishburn, *Fatherhood of God*, chapter 1, especially.

scientific advances and the social implications of the gospel without repudiating the importance of saving souls.

Richard's increasing employment of the Kingdom of God as the central motif in his understanding of mission, his confidence in the evangelistic power of Christian ethical actions as moral evidence for the truth of Christianity, and even the specific activities he integrated into his expanding scope for mission, all bear comparison with the hallmarks of the early twentieth-century Social Gospel as found in China, the United States, or Britain.[16] Accordingly, it is entirely appropriate to see Richard as pointing toward those later developments. This does not mean, however, that Richard necessarily shared all the theological assumptions of the later Social Gospellers: the cultural empathy that led many twentieth-century China missionaries to "cast doubts on their Christian missions" produced in Richard a confident drive to seek the more rapid conversion of the Chinese people.[17] In his 1979 study of conservative Christian responses to the Darwinian revolution, James Moore demonstrated the danger of allowing the distortions of the fundamentalist controversies of the 1920s to influence interpretations of the Victorian debates over science and religion.[18] Likewise, it is important to avoid reading an early twentieth-century dichotomy between social concern and commitment to conversion back into the 1870s and 1880s. Viewed from within the context of the rise of social Christianity in Victorian Britain, Richard's expansion of the scope of mission to include social concern highlights Richard's identity as an evangelical rather than signaling his departure from the faith.

Protestant missionaries from very early on "were concerned with conversions *and* social and economic structures that seemed to interfere with the response of individuals to the gospel."[19] Many of the "good works" that would eventually become institutionalized foci for Social Gospel-informed mission in the twentieth century had existed throughout modern Protestant missions.[20] Like Alexander Duff's educational projects in India or Peter Parker's Canton ophthalmologic hospital, Richard's famine relief work was not a rejection of evangelism in favor of worldly service, but an organic component of his explicitly evangelical mission.[21] In this sense, divisive conservative responses to the fundamentalist-modernist theological

16. Lian, *Conversion of Missionaries*, 153–57.
17. Lian, *Conversion of Missionaries*, 11.
18. Moore, *Post-Darwinian Controversies*.
19. Fishburn, "Social Gospel," 227 (emphasis added).
20. Hyatt, "Protestant Missions in China," 93–126.
21. Stanley, "Christianity and Civilization," 181–82; Anderson, "Peter Parker," 203–38.

debates of the twentieth century should not be allowed to obscure the very real debt that the Social Gospel owed to these earlier evangelical missionary impulses. In his humanitarian response to famine-racked Shandong, Richard expressed the same sense of guilt and compassion regarding the surrounding deprivation that drove his brethren in Britain to take up the many social (and moral) causes that marked the nonconformist conscience at the end of the nineteenth century.[22]

Despite his identity as a Briton living in China in an age of growing Western imperialism, Richard passed through the acculturation process with the growing conviction that effective mission necessitated allowing one's practices and understandings to be informed by a wide and deep reading of the local context:

> [W]hile sacrificing no truth of Christianity, our attitude must be less foreign and more sympathetic. Our brethren in the home lands adapt Christian teaching and methods to Western needs; our task is to adapt Christian teaching and methods to Chinese needs.[23]

Contrary to distortions that suggest he may have abandoned his fundamental missionary vocation of converting Chinese people to Christianity or even compromised his evangelical faith, Richard remained throughout his first twenty years in China committed to the task of Christian evangelism. Increasingly, however, he chose to do so in ways that were explicitly Chinese, convinced that doing so was the most effective way to bring about the "conversion by the million" of the people of China.

This thesis has presented an analysis of the ways in which one man responded to his encounter with the Chinese other. As he sought to transform the people of China, Timothy Richard and his understanding and practice of mission were also transformed. These changes are best understood, as this thesis has demonstrated, in reference to his persistent identity as an evangelical missionary, his consistent empathy for China, and his results-oriented pragmatism. Seeking the worthy, learning from Chinese sectarians, using moral evidences, accommodating China's religions and cultures, broadening mission to include humanitarian work, interacting with Chinese officials, and focusing on literature and publication: all these adaptations to Richard's practice and understanding of Christian mission were the result of the influence of these three factors on his encounters with the people of Shandong and Shanxi.

---

22. Bebbington, *Nonconformist Conscience*, 37–38.
23. Richard, "Relation of Christian Missions," 414.

Appendix 1

Selected List of Chinese Terms

Anqing	安庆	fengshui	风水
		fengsu	风俗
ba gua jiao	八卦教	Fenyang	汾阳
bailian jiao	白莲教	Fenzhou	汾州
baiyun jiao	白云教		
bao juan	宝卷	Gao Daling	高大龄
"ben hui Shanxi shilue"	本会山西史略	"Gao Daling jiandu xing shu"	高大龄监督行述
Bixie jishi	辟邪纪实	Gaoya	高崖
bu ru yi fo	补儒易佛	guang xue hui	广学会
		Guangqi	光启
chao guang jiao	朝光教	Guangxu	光绪
"cheng zilai wei you zhi qi can ye"	诚自来未有之奇惨也	Guangxu daqin	光绪大侵
		Guangxu san nian	光绪三年
chuanjiao	传教	Guangxu Shanxi tongzhi	光绪山西通志
"da han, min ji"	大旱, 民饥	guanhua	官话
Dasheng qi xin lun	大乘起信论	guanshen	官绅
De hui rumen	德慧入门	Han dian	汉典
Dengzhou	登州	Hangzhou	杭州
Dengzhou, Henan	邓州, 河南	Hankou	汉口
		Hebei	河北
Ding Baozhen	丁宝桢	Heilongjiang	黑龙江
Dingwu qihuang	丁戊奇荒	Henan	河南
falü jiao	法律教	"heng gu wei you"	亘古未有

Huang zheng ji	荒政记	Linzi	临淄
Huilong Shan	回龙山	Lu'an	潞安
Jiangnan	江南	Make jiangyi	马可讲义
Jiangsu	江苏	mimi jiao	秘密教
jiao	教	mo-shi-guo-he	摸石过河
jiao xian zhe	教县者		
jiao'an	教案	Nanjing	南京
Jiaohui xinbao	教会新报	Ningbo	宁波
Jidu shilu	基督实录	"Niti qiwen gaobai"	拟题乞文告白
Jimo	即墨		
Jinan	济南		
Jincheng	晋城	pai	牌
jindan jiao	金丹教	Penglai	蓬莱
jing-di-zhi-wa	井底之蛙	Pingyang	平阳
Jingxin lu	敬信录		
Jinshi yaowu	近事要务	qiang xue hui	强学会
"Jinzhi shiwu xieshu"	禁止师巫邪术	Qingzhou	青州
Jiushi dangran zhi li	救世当然之理	sanjiao	三教
		san nian da jihuang	三年大饥荒
"Jiushi jiao yi"	救世教益		
jiushi jiao	救世教	Shaanxi	陕西
jiushi tang	救世堂	Shandong	山东
juren	举人	Shang Huqing	尚祜卿
		shangdi	上帝
kang	炕	Shanxi	山西
Kang Youwei	康有为	Shenbao	申报
		shen'gong	神功
Laiyang	莱阳	shengxian jiao	声贤教
li	礼	Shibao	时报
Li Hongzhang	李鸿章	Shishi xinlun	时事新论
li long wenhua	李龙文化	Shiwu bao	时务报
Li Timotai	李提摩太	Shuihu zhuan	水浒传
Liang Qichao	梁启超	shuzui	赎罪
ling	灵	Sichuan jiao	四川教
Linqu	临朐	Songcun Zhen	宋村镇

Suzhou	苏州	Xi Zizhi	席子直
		xian	县
Taiping	太平	Xiao shipu	小诗谱
taiyang jiao	太阳教	Xie Jiafu	谢家福
Taiyuan	太原	xiejiao	邪教
ti-yong	体用	xingshan	行善
tian	天	xiucai	秀才
tiandao	天道	Xu Wending	徐文定
Tiandao gongke	天道功课	Xue dao cixu	学道次序
Tiandao suyuan	天道溯原		
Tianjin	天津	yang	阳
Tianliang mingjing	天良明镜	Yang Wenhui	杨文会
		yangwu yundong	洋务运动
Tianlu licheng	天路历程	Yangzhou	杨州
tiantang	天堂	Yantai	烟台
tianzhu	天主	yin	阴
Tongwenguan	同文舘		
Tongwen shuhui	同文书会	zaili jiao	在理教
tu weiba laoli	秃尾巴老李	Zeng Guofan	曾国藩
		Zeng Guoquan	曾国荃
Wan'guo gongbao	万国公报	Zezhou	泽州
"wei jian zhi can qi, wei wen zhi beitong"	未见之惨凄, 未闻之悲痛	zhang jiao zhe	掌教者
		Zhang Yuan liangyou xianglun	张远两友相论
wei ting tianming	惟听天命		
Weifang	潍坊	Zhang Zhidong	张之洞
weixin pai	维新派	zheng	正
Wendeng	文登	Zheng Yuren	郑雨人
wenhua chuanbo	文化传播	Zhifu	芝罘
wenli	文理	Zhili	直隶
wenyan	文言	zhong xi you	中西友
Wenzhou	温州	zi mu jiao	子母教
wuwei jiao	无为教	ziqiang	自强
wuxing	五行	Zixi cudong	自西徂东
		zongjiao	宗教
Xi Shengmo	席胜魔	Zuo Zongtang	左宗棠

Appendix 2

Publications by Timothy Richard

Full Chronological List of Publications by Timothy Richard to 1891, plus selected publications thereafter

"Reception of the Gospel in China." *MH* 67, no. 11 (1871) 749–50.
"Progress in China." *MH* 67, no. 11 (1871) 750–51.
"Missionary Labour in China." *MH* 70, no. 8 (1874) 160.
"An Inquirer's Thoughts on the Gospel." *MH* 70, no. 10 (1874) 193–94, bound out of sequence at 191–92.
"An Appeal from China." *MH* 71, no. 12 (1875) 233.
Tiandao gongke 天道功课 [*Holy Living*, trans.]. Shanghai: ca. 1875.
With Zheng Yuren 郑雨人. *Jiushi dangran zhi li* 救世当然之理 [*Philosophy of the Plan of Salvation*, trans.]. Peking: 1876. Previously published in installments in *WGGB* (October 1874–August 1875).
"Mohammedan and Christian Evidences." *CR* 7, no. 2 (1876) 129–31.
"China." *MH* 72, no. 12 (1876) 246–47.
"China." *MH* 72, no. 12 (1876) 246.
"Chefoo." *NCH* (22 July 1876) 75–76.
"Sketch of the English Baptist Mission." *CR* 8, no. 5 (1877) 380–82.
"The Famine in Shantung." *MH* 73, no. 6 (1877) 129–32.
"China Famine." *MH* 74, no. 4 (1878) 99–100.
"China." *MH* 74, no. 1 (1878) 14–15.
"The Shansi Famine." *NCH* (21 March 1878) 296–98.
Xue dao cixu 学道次序 [*The Order of Learning the Doctrine*]. 1st ed. [Taiyuan?]: ca. 1878.
"Rev. Timothy Richard on the Recent Famine in China." *MH* 76, no. 1 (1880) 6–9.
"Some Thoughts about Christian Missions: Examinations." *CR* 11, no. 4 (1880) 293–95.
"Thoughts on Chinese Missions: Difficulties and Tactics." *CR* 11, no. 6 (1880) 430–41.
"Sacred Memories of Rev. J. S. McIlvaine." *CR* 12, no. 4 (1881) 297–99.
Jinshi yaowu 近事要务 [*Matters of Present Importance* or *Needs of the Present*]. [Taiyuan?]: 1882. Previously published in installments in *WGGB* (November 1881–January 1882).
"Dr. Mateer's Native College in Shantung." *NCH* (14 March 1883) 304–5.
"Missionary Troubles, Their Causes and Remedies." *NCH* (8 September 1883) 290–92.
"Christian Persecutions in China—Their Nature, Causes, Remedies." *CR* 15, no. 4 (1884) 237–48.

"The Bond of Union and Some Characteristics of the Church of the Future." *CR* 15, no. 4 (1884) 291–307.

Fu jin xin gui 富晋新规 [*Plan for Enriching Shansi, or How to Develop the Resources of Shan-si*]. [Taiyuan?]: 1884.

Zhongxi heyi lun 中西合一论 [*On the Union (or Harmony) Necessary Between China and Western Nations*]. [Taiyuan?]: 1884.

Min jiao zhi'an zhi ce 民教治安之策 [*How to Secure Amity between Christians and Non-Christians*]. [Taiyuan?]: 1884.

"The Political Status of Christians in China." *CR* 16 (1885) 96–107.

Fifteen Years' Missionary Work in China: An Address by Rev. Timothy Richard. London: Baptist Missionary Society, 1885.

A Scheme for Mission Work in China. London: Baptist Missionary Society, 1885.

Wanted: Good Samaritans for China. London: Baptist Missionary Society, 1885.

"Note on Republication." In *Missionaries After the Apostolical School: Three Addresses*, by Edward Irving, 3. Tientsin: Tientsin Printing Company, 1887.

Xue dao cixu 学道次序 [*The Order of Learning the Doctrine*]. 2nd ed. Taiyuan: 1887.

"Christian Missions in Japan." *CR* 19, no. 9 (1888) 407–18.

"Missionary Co-operation." *CR* 19, no. 12 (1888) 583–84.

"Antagonism Between Buddhism and Christianity." *CR* 20, no. 3 (1889) 231.

"The Famine in Shantung and Manchuria." *NCH* (3 August 1889) 149–50.

"How One Man Can Preach to a Million." *CR* 20, no. 11 (1889) 487–98.

"The Influence of Buddhism in China." *CR* 21, no. 2 (1890) 49–64.

"Historical Evidences of Christianity for China: Chapter I The Material Benefits." *CR* 21, no. 4 (1890) 145–50.

"Friendly Proclamations." *CR* 21, no. 4 (1890) 183.

"The Intellectual Benefits of Christianity." *CR* 21, no. 5 (1890) 228–32.

"The Relation of Christian Missions to the Chinese Government." In *Records of the GCPMC: Shanghai, 1890*, edited by W. T. A. Barber, J. R. Hykes, and W. J. Lewis, 401–15. Shanghai: American Presbyterian Mission Press, 1890.

"Political Benefits of Christianity." *CR* 21, no. 10 (1890) 435–48.

"The Social Benefits of Christianity." *CR* 21, no. 11 (1890) 500–509.

"Jiushi jiao yi 救世教益 [The Benefits of Christianity*]." *WGGB* (January 1891–February 1892).

Shishi xinlun 时事新论 [*Modern Discourses on Timely Affairs**]. Shanghai: Guang xue hui, 1895.

"Demoniacal Possession in China." In *Demon Possession and Allied Themes: Being an Inductive Study of Phenomena of Our Own Times*, by John Livingston Nevius, 62–72. 2nd ed. Chicago: Fleming H. Revell, 1896.

"The Secret Sects of China." In *The China Mission Hand-book*, 1:41–45. Shanghai: American Presbyterian Mission Press, 1896.

"The English Baptist Mission." In *The China Mission Hand-book*, 2:42–51. Shanghai: American Presbyterian Mission Press, 1896.

Conversion by the Million in China, Being Biographies and Articles. 2 vols. Shanghai: Christian Literature Society, 1907.

The New Testament of Higher Buddhism. Edinburgh: T. and T. Clark, 1910.

Forty-Five Years in China: Reminiscences. London: T. Fisher Unwin, 1916.

Bibliography

Archival Collections

Edinburgh

Archives, Centre for the Study of World Christianity, School of Divinity, University of Edinburgh:
> United Presbyterian Church of Scotland, Minutes of Foreign Mission Committee (1875–1880)

Manuscript Collections, National Library of Scotland:
> United Presbyterian Church of Scotland Foreign Missions
>> Letter-books of the secretaries (April 1875–Nov 1876) MS.7655
>> Letter-books of the secretaries (Aug 1878–July 1881) MS.7657

London

Archives and Special Collections, SOAS Library, School of Oriental and African Studies:
> China Inland Mission collection
>> London Council (CIM/01/01)
>> Personal and Private Papers: Broomahll, Anthony James (CIM/04/05)
>> *Principles and Practices of the China Inland Mission*, January 1884 version, signed by Dixon Hoste (CIM/JHT/295: 5423)
>> Taylor, James Hudson (CIM/JHT)
> (Wesleyan) Methodist Missionary Society collection
>> Special Series, Biographical Papers, China: Rev. David Hill (MMS/17/02/09/02)

New Haven, CT

Special Collections, Yale Divinity School Library, Yale Divinity School:
> Eunice Johnson Collection on Timothy Richard (Record Group 232)

Oxford

Angus Library and Archive, Regents Park College, Oxford University:

    Archives of the Baptist Missionary Society

        China-Japan Sub-Committee Minutes, vols. 1–2

        Glover, Richard, and T. M. Morris. "Report on China Missions of the Baptist Missionary Society." [London?]: Baptist Missionary Society, 1891.

        Missionary Journals and Correspondence, 1792–1914

            China

                Dixon, Herbert (Box CH/1)

                Jones, Alfred G. (Boxes CH/6–CH/8)

                Richard, Timothy (Boxes CH/2–CH/4)

                Richard, Timothy—Diaries (Box CH/4B)

                Richard, Timothy—Family Correspondence (Box CH/4A)

                    "Statement of Facts. Being the Report of the Subcommittee on the Province of Shansi." Richard to BMS Committee. 4 March 1887.

                Sowerby, Arthur (Box CH/64)

                Turner, Joshua (Box CH/65)

Wheaton, IL

Billy Graham Center Archives, Wheaton College:

    Papers of the American Board of Commissioners for Foreign Missions, Collection 261 (on microfilm—the originals are held by Harvard University)

        Shansi mission (ABC 16.3.15)

            Shansi, 1880–1890. v. 1. Documents and [letters] A–O. [440]. Microfilm A467: Reel 316.

            Shansi, 1880–1890. v. 2. Documents and [letters] P–Z. [441]. Microfilm A467: Reels 317 and 318.

Periodicals

The Baptist Magazine

China's Millions

The Chinese Recorder and Missionary Journal

The Missionary Herald

The Missionary Record of the United Presbyterian Church

The North China Herald

*Wanguo gongbao*万国公报 [This thesis utilizes electronic versions of the bound facsimiles of the *WGGB* republished in Taiwan in the 1960s, with dates given according to the Georgian calendar. *Wanguo gongbao*, reprint. Taipei: Hua wen shu ju fa xing, 1968. http://catalog.hathitrust.org/Record/002311859.]

Published Works Cited

Anderson, Gerald H. "Peter Parker and the Introduction of Western Medicine in China." *Mission Studies* 23 (2006) 203–38.

Anderson, Rufus. *Foreign Missions: Their Relations and Claims*. New York: Scribner, 1869.

———. *The Theory of Missions to the Heathen: A Sermon at the Ordination of Mr. Edward Webb, as a Missionary to the Heathen*. Boston, MA: Crocker and Brewster, 1845.

Armstrong, Alexander. *Shantung (China): A General Outline of the Geography and History of the Province, a Sketch of its Missions, and Notes of a Journey to the Tomb of Confucius*. Shanghai: Printed at the *Shanghai Mercury* office, 1891.

Arnstein, Walter L. *Protestant Versus Catholic in Mid-Victorian England: Mr. Newdegate and the Nuns*. Columbia, MO: University of Missouri, 1982.

Austin, Alvyn. *China's Millions: The China Inland Mission and Late Qing Society, 1832–1905*. Grand Rapids, MI: Eerdmans, 2007.

———. "Only Connect: The China Inland Mission and Transatlantic Evangelicalism." In *North American Foreign Missions, 1810–1914*, edited by Wilbert R. Shenk, 281–313. Grand Rapids, MI: Eerdmans, 2004.

———. "Pilgrims and Strangers: The China Inland Mission in Britain, Canada, the United States, and China, 1865–1900." PhD Dissertation, York University (Canada), 1996.

Bacon, Francis, and Richard Whately. *Bacon's Essays: With Annotations*. 5th ed. London: John W. Parker and Son, 1860.

Ballinger, John. *The Bible in Wales: A Study of the Welsh People, with an Introductory Address and a Bibliography*. London: Henry Sotheran, 1906.

Baptist Missionary Society. *Reports of China and Japan Sub-Committee on North China Mission to Be Presented to the General Committee on Tuesday, 19th June, 1888*. London: Baptist Mission House, n.d.

Barber, W. T. A. *David Hill: Missionary and Saint*. London: C. H. Kelly, 1899.

Barber, W. T. A., J. R. Hykes, and W. J. Lewis, eds. *Records of the General Conference of the Protestant Missionaries of China: Held at Shanghai, May 7–20, 1890*. Shanghai: American Presbyterian Mission Press, 1890.

Barnett, Suzanne Wilson, and John King Fairbank, eds. *Christianity in China: Early Protestant Missionary Writings*. Cambridge, MA: Council on East Asian Studies, Harvard University, 1985.

Bays, Daniel H. "Christianity and the Chinese Sectarian Tradition." *Ch'ing-shih wen-t'i* 4 (1982) 33–55.

Beal, Samuel. *Buddhism in China*. London; New York: Society for Promoting Christian Knowledge; E. and J. B. Young, 1884.

Beauchamp, Montagu Harry Proctor. *Days of Blessing in Inland China: Being an Account of Meetings Held in the Province of Shan-si, etc.* London: Morgan and Scott, 1887.

Bebbington, David W. "The Baptist Conscience in the Nineteenth Century." *Baptist Quarterly* 34 (1991) 13-24.

———. *The Dominance of Evangelicalism: The Age of Spurgeon and Moody*. Downers Grove, IL: InterVarsity, 2005.

———. "Evangelicalism." In *The Blackwell Companion to Nineteenth-Century Theology*, 235-50. Malden, MA: Wiley-Blackwell, 2010.

———. *Evangelicalism in Modern Britain: A History from the 1730s to the 1980s*. London: Unwin Hyman, 1989. Reprint, New York: Routledge, 2002.

———. *The Nonconformist Conscience: Chapel and Politics, 1870-1914*. London: G. Allen and Unwin, 1982.

Bell, Prudence, and Ronald Clements. *Lives From a Black Tin Box*. Milton Keynes, UK: Authentic Media, 2014.

Bennett, Adrian Arthur. *Missionary Journalist in China: Young J. Allen and His Magazines, 1860-1883*. Athens, GA: University of Georgia, 1983.

Bennett, Adrian Arthur, and Kwang-Ching Liu. "Christianity in the Chinese Idiom: Young J. Allen and the Early *Chiao-hui hsin-pao*, 1868-1870." In *The Missionary Enterprise in China and America*, edited by John King Fairbank, 159-96. Cambridge: Harvard University Press, 1974.

Bentley, James. *Ritualism and Politics in Victorian Britain: The Attempt to Legislate for Belief*. Oxford: Oxford University, 1978.

Binfield, Clyde. *So Down to Prayers: Studies in English Nonconformity, 1780-1920*. London: J. M. Dent and Sons, 1977.

Blaikie, William Garden. *The Personal Life of David Livingstone . . . Chiefly from His Unpublished Journals and Correspondence in the Possession of His Family*. New York: Fleming H. Revell, 1895.

Bohr, P. Richard. *Famine in China and the Missionary: Timothy Richard as Relief Administrator and Advocate of National Reform, 1876-1884*. Cambridge, MA: Harvard University, 1972.

———. "The Legacy of Timothy Richard." *IBMR* 24 (2000) 75-78.

Bonk, Jonathan J. *The Theory and Practice of Missionary Identification, 1860-1920*. Lewiston, NY: Edwin Mellen, 1989.

Brandt, Nat. *Massacre in Shansi*. New York: toExcel, 1999.

Briggs, J. H. Y. *The English Baptists of the Nineteenth Century*. Didcot: Baptist Historical Society, 1994.

Broomhall, A. J. *Hudson Taylor and China's Open Century*. Vol. 2, *Over the Treaty Wall*. Sevenoaks, Kent: Hodder and Stoughton with Overseas Missionary Fellowship, 1982.

———. *Hudson Taylor and China's Open Century*. Vol. 3, *If I Had a Thousand Lives*. Sevenoaks, Kent: Hodder and Stoughton with Overseas Missionary Fellowship, 1982.

———. *Hudson Taylor and China's Open Century*. Vol. 6, *Assault on the Nine*. Sevenoaks, Kent: Hodder and Stoughton with Overseas Missionary Fellowship, 1988.

———. *Hudson Taylor and China's Open Century*. Vol. 7, *It Is Not Death to Die!* Sevenoaks, Kent: Hodder and Stoughton with Overseas Missionary Fellowship, 1989.

Brown, Kenneth D. "The Baptist Ministry of Victorian England and Wales: A Social Profile." *Baptist Quarterly* 32 (1987) 105-20.

Brown, Stewart J. *Providence and Empire: Religion, Politics and Society in the United Kingdom, 1815–1914*. New York: Pearson Education, 2008.
Burt, Ernest Whitby. *Fifty Years in China: The Story of the Baptist Mission in Shantung, Shansi and Shensi, 1875–1925*. London: Carey Press, 1925.
Butler, Alban. *The Lives of the Fathers, Martyrs, and other Principal Saints*. 12 vols. Dublin, London: James Duffy, 18711872.
Butler, Joseph. *The Analogy of Religion, Natural and Revealed*. London: Printed for James, John and Paul Knapton, 1736.
———. *The Analogy of Religion, Natural and Revealed*. London: Henry G. Bohn, 1852.
———. *The Analogy of Religion, Natural and Revealed*. London: J. M. Dent; E. P. Dutton, 1906.
———. *Fifteen Sermons Preached at Rolls Chapel*. London: Printed by W. Botham, for James and John Knapton, 1726.
Calvin, Jean. *Commentary on a Harmony of the Evangelists, Matthew, Mark, and Luke*. Translated by William Pringle. Edinburgh: Calvin Translation Society, 1996. Reprint, 1845 ed.
Census of England and Wales: Summary Tables. London: H. M. Stationery Office, printed by Love and Malcomson, 1901.
Chambers, David H. *Tim China: Timothy Richard, The Man Who Helped Change a Dynastic Warrior Nation*. York: York Publishing Services, 2012.
Chau, Adam Yuet. *Miraculous Response: Doing Popular Religion in Contemporary China*. Stanford, CA: Stanford University Press, 2005.
———. "Religious Diversity from the Perspective of Religious Consumers." In *Religious Diversity in Chinese Thought*, edited by Joachim Gentz and Perry Schmidt-Leukel, 141–54. New York: Palgrave Macmillan, 2013.
Chen Qiyun 陈启云. "Liang Qichao yu Qing mo xifang chuanjiaoshi zhi hudong yanjiu—chuanjiaoshi duiyu weixin pai yingxiang de ge'an fenxi 梁启超与清末西方传教士之互动研究—传教士对于维新派影响的个案分析 [Liang Qi–Chao's 'Missionary Education': A Case Study of Missionary Influence on the Reformers]." *Shixue jikan*, no. 4 (2006) 79–96.
China Centenary Missionary Conference Records: Report of the Great Conference Held at Shanghai, April 5th [read 25th] to May 8th, 1907. New York: American Tract Society, 1907.
China Famine Relief Fund Shanghai Committee. *The Great Famine: Report of the Committee of the China Famine Relief Fund*. Shanghai: American Presbyterian Mission Press, 1879.
"Chinese Delegates NT." http://www.bibel-baptistengemeinde.ch/Bibel-Baptisten gemeinde/Auslandische_Bibeln_files/.
Clart, Philip. "The Concept of 'Popular Religion' in the Study of Chinese Religions: Retrospect and Prospects." Paper presented at the The Fourth Fu Jen University International Sinological Symposium: Research on Religions in China: Status Quo and Perspectives." Taibei Xian Xinzhuang Shi, 2007.
Cliff, Norman Howard. "A History of the Protestant Movement in Shandong Province, China, 1859–1951." PhD Thesis, University of Buckingham, 1995.
Clifford, John. *The New City of God: or, The Primitive Christian Faith as a Social Gospel*. London: Alexander and Shepheard, 1888.
Cohen, Paul A. *History in Three Keys: The Boxers as Event, Experience, and Myth*. New York: Columbia University, 1997.

———. "Missionary Approaches: Hudson Taylor and Timothy Richard." In *Papers on China: Volume 11*, 29–62. Cambridge: Harvard University Press, 1957.
Commissioners of Inquiry into the State of Education in Wales and Privy Council Committee on Education. *Reports of the Commissioners of Inquiry into the State of Education in Wales.* . . . London: W. Clowes and Sons, 1848.
Conference on Missions Held in 1860 at Liverpool. London: James Nisbet, 1860.
Corbett, Hunter. *A Record of American Presbyterian Mission Work in Shantung Province, China, 1861–1913*. [Shanghai?]: [American Presbyterian Mission Press?], 1914.
Covell, Ralph R. "The Legacy of W. A. P. Martin." *IBMR* 17 (1993) 28–31.
Cracknell, Kenneth. *Justice, Courtesy and Love: Theologians and Missionaries Encountering World Religions, 1846–1914*. London: Epworth, 1995.
Craighead, James R. E. *Hunter Corbett: Fifty-Six Years Missionary in China*. New York: Revell Press, 1921.
Criveller, Gianni. "Review of *Matteo Ricci: A Jesuit in the Ming Court* by Michela Fontana (Lanham, MD: Rowman and Littlefield, 2011); *A Jesuit in the Forbidden City: Matteo Ricci, 1552–1610* by R. Po-chia Hsia (New York: Oxford University Press, 2010); and *Mission to China: Matteo Ricci and the Jesuit Encounter with the East* by Mary Laven (London: Faber and Faber, 2011)." *The Journal of Asian Studies* 71, no. 03 (2012) 768–73.
Dai Cunyi Shimu 戴存义师母 [Mrs. Howard Taylor]. *Xi Shengmo zhuan* 席胜魔传 [Biography of Xi Shengmo*]. Shenzhen, China: Shenzhen guangming chubanshe, 2002.
Daily, Christopher. *Robert Morrison and the Protestant Plan for China*. Hong Kong: Hong Kong University Press, 2013.
Davies, Elwyn. *A Gazetteer of Welsh Place Names = Rhester o Enwau Lleoedd*. 3rd ed. Cardiff: University of Wales, 1989.
Davies, Horton. *Worship and Theology in England*. Vol. 4, *From Newman to Martineau, 1850–1900*. Princeton: Princeton University Press, 1962.
Davis, Mike. *Late Victorian Holocausts: El Niño Famines and the Making of the Third World*. London: Verso, 2001.
Ding Zeliang 丁则良. *Li Timotai: Yi ge dianxing de wei diguo zhuyi fuwu de chuanjiaoshi* 李提摩太: 一个典型的为帝国主义服务的传教士 [Timothy Richard: A Typical Missionary in the Service of Imperialism]. Beijing: Kaiming shudian, 1951.
Doar, Bruce. "The Boxers and Chinese Drama: Questions of Interaction." *Papers on Far Eastern History* 29 (1984) 91–118.
Dugdale, Thomas, et al. *The Topographical Dictionary of England and Wales*. 6 vols. London: L. Tallis, 1860.
Dunch, Ryan. *Fuzhou Protestants and the Making of a Modern China, 1857–1927*. New Haven, CT: Yale University Press, 2001.
Eber, Irene. "The Interminable Term Question." In *Bible in Modern China: The Literary and Intellectual Impact*, edited by Irene Eber, Sze-kar Wan, and Knut Walf, 134–61. Sankt Augustin: Institut Monumenta Serica, 1999.
Edgerton-Tarpley, Kathryn. *Tears from Iron: Cultural Responses to Famine in Nineteenth-Century China*. Berkeley, CA: University of California Press, 2008.
Edwards, Viv, and Lynda Pritchard Newcombe. "When School Is Not Enough: New Initiatives in Intergenerational Language Transmission in Wales." *International Journal of Bilingual Education and Bilingualism* 8 (2005) 298–312.

Elliston, E. S. *Shantung Road Cemetery, Shanghai, 1846–1868: with notes about Pootung Seamen's Cemetery [and] Soldiers' Cemetery*. Shanghai: [Millington?], 1946.

Elvin, Mark. "Who Was Responsible for the Weather? Moral Meteorology in Late Imperial China." *Osiris* 13, 2nd Series (1998) 213–37.

Esherick, Joseph. *The Origins of the Boxer Uprising*. Berkeley, CA: University of California Press, 1987.

Evans, Edward William Price. *Timothy Richard, a Narrative of Christian Enterprise and Statesmanship in China*. London: Carey Press, 1945.

Evans, Eifion. *Two Welsh Revivalists: Humphrey Jones, Dafydd Morgan, and the 1859 Revival in Wales*. Bryntirion, Bridgend, Mid Glamorgan: Evangelical Library of Wales, 1985.

———. *When He Is Come: An Account of the 1858–60 Revival in Wales*. London: Evangelical Press of Wales, 1967.

Evans, R. J. W. "Nonconformity and Nation: The Welsh Case." *The Welsh History Review* 25, no. 2 (2010) 231–8.

Faber, Ernst, Paul Kranz, and Robert A. Haden. *The Works of Rev. Ernst Faber, Dr. Theol.: A Champion of Faith, a Pioneer of Christian Literature in China*. Shanghai: American Presbyterian Mission Press, 1904.

Fang, Ren. "The Rural Market in Late Imperial China." *Asian Social Science* 6, no. 6 (2010) 42–9.

Farquhar, J. N. *The Crown of Hinduism*. Oxford: Oxford University Press, 1913.

Feuchtwang, Stephan. "A Chinese Religion Exists." In *An Old State in New Settings: Studies in the Social Anthropology of China in Memory of Maurice Freedman*, edited by Maurice Freedman, Hugh D. R. Baker, and Stephan Feuchtwang, 139–61. Oxford: JASO, 1991.

Fischer, Benjamin Louis. "'Opium Pushing and Bible Smuggling': Religion and the Cultural Politics of British Imperialist Ambition in China." PhD Dissertation, University of Notre Dame, 2008.

Fishburn, Janet F. *The Fatherhood of God and the Victorian Family: The Social Gospel in America*. Philadelphia, PA: Fortress, 1981.

———. "The Social Gospel as Missionary Ideology." In *North American Foreign Missions, 1810–1914: Theology, Theory, and Policy*, edited by Wilbert R. Shenk, 218–42. Grand Rapids, MI: Eerdmans, 2004.

Fisher, D. W. *Calvin Wilson Mateer, Forty-Five Years a Missionary in Shantung, China: A Biography*. Philadelphia, PA: Westminster Press, 1911.

Fitzgerald, Timothy. *The Ideology of Religious Studies*. Oxford: Oxford University Press, 2000.

Flegg, Columba Graham. *"Gathered Under Apostles": A Study of the Catholic Apostolic Church*. New York: Clarendon, 1992.

Forsyth, Robert Coventry. *Shantung: The Sacred Province of China in Some of its Aspects*. Shanghai: Christian Literature Society, 1912.

Foster, Arnold. *Christian Progress in China: Gleanings from the Writings and Speeches of Many Workers*. [London?]: Religious Tract Society, 1889.

Foster, L. S. *Fifty Years in China: An Eventful Memoir of Tarleton Perry Crawford, D.D.* Nashville, TN: Bayless-Pullen, 1909.

Gao Pengcheng and Chi Zihua 高鹏程及池子华. "Li Timotai zai 'Dingwu qihuang' shiqi de zhenzai huodong 李提摩太在'丁戊奇荒'时期的赈灾活动 [On the Influence of Timothy Richard's Relief in 'Ding-wu Disaster']." *Shehuikexue*, no. 11 (2006) 132–38.

Garnier, Albert J. *A Maker of Modern China*. London: Carey Press, 1945.

Geertz, Clifford. *The Interpretation of Cultures: Selected Essays*. New York: Basic Books, 1973.

Gentz, Joachim. "Rational Choice and the Chinese Discourse on the Unity of the Three Religions (sanjiao heyi)." *Religion* 41, no. 4 (2011) 535–46.

———. "Religious Diversity in Three Teachings Discourses." In *Religious Diversity in Chinese Thought*, edited by Perry Schmidt-Leukel and Joachim Gentz, 123–39. New York: Palgrave Macmillan, 2013.

———. *Understanding Chinese Religions*. Edinburgh: Dunedin, 2013.

Gilley, Sheridan. "Edward Irving: Prophet of the Millennium." In *Revival and Religion since 1700: Essays for John Walsh*, edited by Garnett, Jane and Colin Matthew, 95–110. London: Hambledon Press, 1993.

Girardot, N. J. "Max Müller's 'Sacred Books' and the Nineteenth-Century Production of the Comparative Science of Religions." *History of Religions* 41, no. 3 (2002) 213–50.

———. *The Victorian Translation of China: James Legge's Oriental Pilgrimage*. Berkeley, CA: University of California, 2002.

Glover, Archibald E., and Leslie T. Lyall. *A Thousand Miles of Miracle in China*. Expanded centenary ed. Fearn, Ross-shire; Sevenoaks: Christian Focus; OMF Publishing, 2000.

Glover, Willis Borders. *Evangelical Nonconformists and Higher Criticism in the Nineteenth Century*. London: Independent Press, 1954.

Goossaert, Vincent. "1898: The Beginning of the End for Chinese Religion?" *The Journal of Asian Studies* 65, no. 2 (2006) 307–35.

Goossaert, Vincent, and David A. Palmer. *The Religious Question in Modern China*. Chicago, IL: University of Chicago Press, 2011.

Grass, Tim. *Edward Irving: The Lord's Watchman*. Milton Keynes, UK: Paternoster, 2011.

Griffith, W. P. "'Preaching Second to No Other Under the Sun': Edward Matthews, the Nonconformist Pulpit and Welsh Identity During the Mid-Nineteenth Century." In *Religion and National Identity*, edited by Robert Pope, 61–83. Cardiff: University of Wales Press, 2001.

De Groot, J. J. M. *Sectarianism and Religious Persecution in China*. Taipei: Ch'eng Wen, 1970. Reprint, 1903 ed.

Gu Changsheng 顾长声. *Cong Malixun dao Situ Leideng: Lai Hua xinjiao chuanjiaoshi ping zhuan* 从马礼逊到司徒雷登来华新教传教士评传 [From Morrison to Leighton Stuart: A Critical Biography of Protestant Missionaries to China]. Shanghai: Shanghai renmin chubanshe: Xinhua shudian Shanghai faxingsuo faxing, 1985.

Guinness, Geraldine [Mrs. Howard Taylor]. *One of China's Scholars: The Culture and Conversion of a Confucianist*. 5th ed. London: Morgan and Scott, 1905.

Guo Hanmin 郭汉民. "Li Timotai lai Hua chu qi de shehui gaige sixiang [The Social Reform Thinking of Timothy Richard During his Initial Period in China*]." *Hunan shifan daxue shehuikexue xuebao* 23, no. 6 (1994) 93–97.

Guo Wuzhen 郭吾眞. "Li Timotai zai Shanxi de qinlue huodong 李提摩太在山西的侵略活动 [The Invasive Activities of Timothy Richard in Shanxi*]." *Lishi jiaoxue*, no. 4 (1964) 11–15.

Ter Haar, Barend J. *Telling Stories: Witchcraft and Scapegoating in Chinese History*. Leiden: Brill, 2006.

Hall, Catherine. *Civilising Subjects: Metropole and Colony in the English Imagination, 1830–1867*. Cambridge: Polity, 2002.

Hao Ping 郝平. "Guangxu chu nian Shanxi zaihuang yu jiuji yanjiu 光绪初年山西灾荒与救济研究 [Research on Emergency Relief and the Famine in Shanxi During the First Year of the Guangxu Reign Period*]." PhD Dissertation, Shanxi University, 2007.

———. "Shanxi 'Dingwu qihuang' bingfa zaihai shu lue 山西'丁戊奇荒'并发灾害述略 [A Brief Record of the Complications Related to the Dingwu Famine in Shanxi*]." *Jinyang xue kan*, no. 1 (2003) 86–89.

Hao Ping and Zhou Ya 郝平及周亚. "'Dingwu qihuang' shiqi de Shanxi liangjia '丁戊奇荒'时期的山西粮价 [The Food Price of Shanxi in the Great Famine in 1877 and 1878]." *Shi lin*, no. 5 (2008) 81–89.

Hao Zhixin, Zheng Jingyun, Wu Guofeng, Zhang Xuezhen and Ge Quansheng 郝志新、郑景云、伍国凤、张学珍及葛全胜. "1876–1878 nian Huabei da han: Shishi, yingxiang ji qihou Beijing 1876–1878 年华北大旱: 史实、影响及气候背景 [1876–1878 Severe Drought in North China: Facts, Impacts and Climatic Background]." *Kexue tongbao* 55, no. 23 (2010) 2321–28.

Harrison, Henrietta. *The Man Awakened from Dreams: One Man's Life in a North China Village, 1857–1942*. Stanford, CA: Stanford University Press, 2005.

———. *The Missionary's Curse and Other Tales from a Chinese Catholic Village*. Berkeley, CA: University of California Press, 2013.

———. "Village Politics and National Politics: The Boxer Movement in Central Shanxi." In *The Boxers, China, and the World*, edited by Robert A. Bickers and R. G. Tiedemann, 1–15. Lanham, MD: Rowman and Littlefield, 2007.

Hedges, Paul M. "Post-colonialism, Orientalism, and Understanding: Religious Studies and the Christian Missionary Imperative." *Journal of Religious History* 32, no. 1 (2008) 55–75.

———. *Preparation and Fulfilment: A History and Study of Fulfilment Theology in Modern British Thought in the Indian Context*. New York: Peter Lang, 2001.

Henderson, W. J., and John Brown Myers. *The Centenary Volume of the Baptist Missionary Society, 1792–1892*. London: Baptist Missionary Society, 1892.

Holloway, Brenda Wilmar. *Timothy Richard of China: A Pageant*. London: Carey Press, 1945.

Hon, Tze-ki. "Zhang Zhidong's Proposal for Reform: A New Reading of the *Quanxue pian*." In *Rethinking the 1898 Reform Period: Political and Cultural Change in Late Qing China*, edited by Rebecca E. Karl and Peter Gue Zarrow, 77–98. Cambridge, MA: Harvard University Asia Center, 2002.

Howard, H. Wendell. "Saint Fabiola in Fiction, in History, in Portraiture." *Logos–A Journal of Catholic Thought and Culture* 14, no. 2 (2011) 82–95.

Hsia, R. Po-chia. *A Jesuit in the Forbidden City: Matteo Ricci, 1552–1610*. Oxford: Oxford University Press, 2010.

Hu Shixiang 扈石祥. *Hondong jidujiao shi* 洪洞基督教史 [History of the Hongdong Christian Church*]. Hongdong: Hongdong xian renmin zhengfu minzu zongjiao ke, 1990.

Hyatt, Irwin T. "Protestant Missions in China, 1877–1890: The Institutionalization of Good Works." In *American Missionaries in China: Papers from Harvard Seminars*, edited by Kwang-Ching Liu, 93–126. Cambridge, MA: Harvard East Asian Research Center, 1966.

Irving, Edward. *Missionaries After the Apostolical School: Three Addresses*. Tientsin: Tientsin Printing Company, 1887.

Irving, Edward, and Gavin Carlyle. *The Collected Writings of Edward Irving*. Vol. 1. London: A. Strahan, 1866.

James, C. V. *The Older Mother Tongues of the United Kingdom*. London: Centre for Information on Language Teaching and Research, 1978.

James, Francis H. "The Secret Sects of Shantung, with Appendix." In *Records of the GCPMC: Shanghai, 1890*, edited by W. T. A. Barber, J. R. Hykes, and W. J. Lewis, 196–202. Shanghai: American Presbyterian Mission Press, 1890.

James, John Angell. *God's Voice from China to the British Churches, Both Established and Unestablished*. London: Hamilton, Adams, 1858.

Janku, Andrea. "Drought in Northwest China: A Late Victorian Tragedy?" Paper presented at the Chinese Studies Seminar Series, University of Edinburgh, 5 March 2014.

———. "Sowing Happiness: Spiritual Competition in Famine Relief Activities in Late Nineteenth-Century China." *Minsu Quyi* 143 (2004) 89–118.

Jansen, Thomas. "Sectarian Religions and Globalization in Nineteenth Century China: The *Wanbao baojuan* (1858) and Other Examples." In *Globalization and the Religious Field in China, 1800–Present*, edited by Jansen, Thomas, Thoralf Klein, and Christian Meyer. Leiden: Brill, forthcoming.

Johnson, David G. "'Confucian' Elements in the Great Temple Festivals of Southeastern Shansi in Late Imperial Times." *T'oung Pao* 83, no. 1/3 (1997) 126–61.

———. *Spectacle and Sacrifice: The Ritual Foundations of Village Life in North China*. Cambridge, MA: Harvard University Asia Center, 2009.

Johnson, Eunice V. "Educational Reform in China, 1880–1910: Timothy Richard and His Vision for Higher Education." PhD Dissertation, University of Florida, 2001.

Johnson, Rita Therese. "Timothy Richard's Theory of Christian Missions to the Non-Christian World." PhD Dissertation, St. John's University (New York), 1966.

Jones, Aled. "Culture, 'Race' and the Missionary Public in Mid-Victorian Wales." *Journal of Victorian Culture* 10, no. 2 (2005) 157–83.

Jones, Alfred G. *Hints about Climate, Living, and Outfit, &c.* London: North China English Baptist Mission, 1883.

———. *North China English Baptist Mission: Conditions, Needs and Claims*. London: Baptist Missionary Society, 1883.

Jones, Alfred G., et al. *Baptist Missionary Work in North-China (Province of Shantung): Letters Written by the Missionaries on the Field, Relative to its Consolidation and Development*. Shanghai: Kelly and Walsh, 1886.

Kaiser, Andrew T. "S. Wells Williams: Early Protestant Missions in China." MA Thesis, Gordon-Conwell Theological Seminary, 1995.

Kalapati, Joshua. "Edinburgh to Tambaram: A Paradigm Shift in Missions, or the Horizon of Missions Broadened?" *Dharma Deepika: A South Asian Journal of Missiological Research* 14, no. 1 (2010) 10–15.

Kuo, Ting-yee, and Kwang-Ching Liu. "Self-strengthening: The Pursuit of Western Technology." In *The Cambridge History of China*, Vol. 10, *Late Ch'ing 1800–1911*,

Part I, edited by John King Fairbank, 491–542. Cambridge: Cambridge University Press, 1978.

Kurtz, Joachim. *The Discovery of Chinese Logic*. Leiden: Brill, 2011.

Kwong, Luke S. K. "The T'i-Yung Dichotomy and the Search for Talent in Late-Ch'ing China." *Modern Asian Studies* 27, no. 2 (1993) 253–79.

Lai, John Tsz Pang. *Negotiating Religious Gaps: The Enterprise of Translating Christian Tracts by Protestant Missionaries in Nineteenth-Century China*. Sankt Augustin: Institut Monumenta Serica, 2012.

Lai Pan-Chiu 赖品超. "Li Timotai dui da sheng fojiao de huiying: Cong hou zhimin dui dongfang de pipan zhuoyan 李提摩太对大乘佛教的回应: 从后殖民对东方学的批判著眼 [Timothy Richard's Response to Mahayana Buddhism: From the Perspective of the Postcolonial Critique of Orientalism]." *Zhejiang daxue xuebao* (renwen shehuikexue ban) 40, no. 3 (2010) 30–39.

Landow, George P. *Victorian Types, Victorian Shadows: Biblical Typology in Victorian Literature, Art, and Thought*. Boston: Routledge and K. Paul, 1980.

Larsen, Timothy. *Crisis of Doubt: Honest Faith in Nineteenth-Century England*. Oxford: Oxford University Press, 2006.

———. *A People of One Book: The Bible and the Victorians*. Oxford: Oxford University Press, 2011.

Latourette, Kenneth Scott. *A History of Christian Missions in China*. New York: Macmillan, 1929.

Laven, Mary. *Mission to China: Matteo Ricci and the Jesuit Encounter with the East*. London: Faber and Faber, 2011.

Lee Chi-ho 李智浩. "Qing mo ming chu jiduxinjiao lai Hua chuanjiaoshi dui Zhongguo fojiao de quanshi—Li Timotai, Su Huilian, Ai Xiangde ge'an yanjiu 清末民初基督新教來华传教士对中国佛教的诠释—李提摩太、蘇慧廉和艾香德个案研究 [An Interpretation of Chinese Buddhism by the Protestant Missionaries from Late Ching Dynasty to the Republic of China—The Studies of Timothy Richard, William Edward Soothill and Karl Ludvig Reichelt]." PhD Dissertation, The Chinese University of Hong Kong, 2007.

Lee Chi-ho and So Yuen-tai 李智浩及苏远泰. "Hua-di-wei-you—Pouxi Li Timotai jinxing ye fo duihua de yuanyin 化敌为友—剖析李提摩太进行耶佛对话的原因 [The Reasons Why Timothy Richard the Missionary Participated in Buddhist-Christian Dialogue]." *Shandao qikan* 6, no. 2 (2003) 105–29.

Legge, James. *Confucianism in Relation to Christianity: A Paper*. Shanghai: Kelly and Walsh, 1877.

Leung, Philip Yuen-sang. "Mission History versus Church History—The Case of China Historiography." *Ching Feng* 40, no. 3–4 (1997) 177–213.

Lewis, H. Elvet. *Nonconformity in Wales*. London: National Council of the Evangelical Free Churches, 1904.

"Lewis, Joshua (1816–1879)." In *Welsh Biography Online*. http://wbo.llgc.org.uk/en/s-LEWI-JOS-1816.html.

Lewis, Thomas. *These Seventy Years: An Autobiography*. London: Carey Press, 1930.

Li Aisi. "Competition and Compromise between British Missionaries and Chinese Officials: The Founding of Shanxi University in 1902." DPhil Thesis, University of Oxford, 2012.

Li Haihong 李海红. "Shixi Li Timotai de jidujiao sixiang—yi qi zai Wan'guo gongbao shang de yanlun wei li 试析李提摩太的基督教思想—以其在《万国公报》上的言论为例 [The Tentative Analyse of Timothy Richard's Christian Ideology]." *Anhui Shixue*, no. 6 (2006) 48–51.

"Li long shanhui sheng kuang 李龙王山会盛况 [The Grand Occasion of the Dragon Lee Mountain Festival*]." Xinlang Shipin, http://video.sina.com.cn/v/b/32941096-1741684663.html.

"Li long wenhua shanhui zai Shandong sheng Wendeng shi Huilong Shan ju ban 李龙文化山会在山东省文登市回龙山举办 [The Dragon Lee Cultural Mountain Festival is held at Huilong Mountain in Wendeng City, Shandong Province*]." China News Service, http://www.chinanews.com/cul/2012/03-24/3770052.shtml.

Li Qingben and Guo Jinghua. "Rethinking the Relationship between China and the West: A Multi-Dimensional Model of Cross-Cultural Research Focusing on Literary Adaptations." *Cultura: International Journal of Philosophy of Culture and Axiology* 9, no. 2 (2012) 45–60.

Li Wenhai 李文海. *Zhongguo jindai shi da zaihuang* 中国近代十大灾荒 [The Ten Great Disasters of Modern China*]. Shanghai: Shanghai renmin chubanshe, 1994.

Li Xinde 李新德. "Li Timotai yu fojiao dianji ying yi 李提摩太与佛教典籍英译 [Timothy Richard's English Translations of Ancient Buddhist Texts*]." *Shijie zongjiao wenhua*, no. 1 (2006) 13–15.

Lian Xi. *The Conversion of Missionaries: Liberalism in American Protestant Missions in China, 1907–1932*. University Park, PA: Pennsylvania State University Press, 1997.

———. *Redeemed by Fire: Popular Chinese Christianity in the Twentieth Century*. New Haven, CT: Yale University Press, 2010.

Ling, Oi Ki. *The Changing Role of the British Protestant Missionaries in China, 1945–1952*. Madison, NJ; London: Fairleigh Dickinson University; Associated University Presses, 1999.

Litzinger, Charles A. "Rural Religion and Village Organization in North China: The Catholic Challenge in the Late Nineteenth Century." In *Christianity in China*, edited by Daniel H. Bays, 41–52. Stanford, CA: Stanford University Press, 1996.

Liu Dapeng 刘大鹏. "Qianyuan suoji 潜园琐记 [Brief Notes from Qian Garden*]." In *Yihetuan zai Shanxi diqu shiliao*, edited by Qiao Zhiqiang, 26–75. Taiyuan: Shanxi renmin chubanshe, 1980.

Liu Qi 刘奇. "Li Timotai furen yu Xiao shipu 李提摩太夫妇与《小诗谱》 [Mrs. Timothy Richard and *The Tune-book in Chinese Notation**]." *Yinyue yanjiu*, no. 1 (1988) 22–27.

Liu Yinghua. "Chinese Converts in the Chinese Rites Controversy: Ancestral Rites and Their Identity." PhD Dissertation, Graduate Theological Union, 2011.

Lu Yao 路遥. "Zhongguo chuantong shehui minjian xinyang zhi kaocha 中国传统社会民间信仰之考察 [Research on Folk Religion of Chinese Traditional Society]." *Wen shi zhe*, no. 4 (Serial No. 319) (2010) 82–95.

Lutz, Jessie Gregory. *China and the Christian Colleges, 1850–1950*. Ithaca, NY: Cornell University Press, 1971.

———. *Opening China: Karl F. A. Gützlaff and Sino-Western Relations, 1827–1852*. Grand Rapids, MI: Eerdmans, 2008.

Ma Xiaowei 马晓伟. "Lun Li Timotai de wenhua shenfen yu baokan biaoda—yi Wan'guo gongbao wei li 论李提摩太的文化身份与报刊表达—以《万国公报》为例 [Research on Timothy Richard's Cultural Identity and Expressions via Newspapers: Take *A Review of the Time* for Example]." MA Thesis, Soochow University, 2012.

MacGillivray, Donald. *Descriptive and Classified Missionary Centenary Catalogue of Current Christian Literature*. Shanghai: Christian Literature Society, 1907.

———. *Timothy Richard of China: A Prince in Israel. An Appreciation*. Shanghai: Christian Literature Society, 1920.

Maclear, G. F. *Apostles of Mediaeval Europe*. London: Macmillan, 1869.

Manktelow, Emily J. *Missionary Families: Race, Gender and Generation on the Spiritual Frontier*. Manchester: Manchester University, 2013.

Mann, Horace. *Census of Great Britain, 1851: Religious Worship in England and Wales*. London: Routledge, 1854.

May, Andrew J. "Mountain Views: Welsh Missionaries, Diaspora and Empire." *The Welsh History Review* 25, no. 2 (2010) 239–50.

McKay, Moira Jane. "Faith and Facts in the History of the China Inland Mission 1832–1905." MLitt Thesis, University of Aberdeen, 1981.

Merricks, William S. *Edward Irving: The Forgotten Giant*. East Peoria, IL: Scribe's Chamber Publications, 1983.

Minamiki, George. *The Chinese Rites Controversy: From Its Beginning to Modern Times*. Chicago, IL: Loyola University Press, 1985.

"Missionary Notes." *MH* 72, no. 8 (1876) 171.

Moore, James R. *The Post-Darwinian Controversies: A Study of the Protestant Struggle to Come to Terms with Darwin in Great Britain and America, 1870–1900*. Cambridge: Cambridge University Press, 1979.

Morgan, D. Densil. "Christmas Evans (1766–1838) and the Birth of Nonconformist Wales." *Baptist Quarterly* 34, no. 3 (1991) 116–24.

———. *Wales and the Word: Historical Perspectives on Religion and Welsh Identity*. Cardiff: University of Wales Press, 2008.

Morse, Hosea B. *The International Relations of the Chinese Empire*. 3 vols. London: Longmans, Green, 1910.

Muirhead, William. *China and the Gospel*. London: James Nisbet, 1870.

Mungello, David E. "A Confucian Voice Crying in the Victorian Wilderness." Review of *The Victorian Translation of China: James Legge's Oriental Pilgrimage* by Norman J. Girardot. *The Journal of Religion* 83, no. 4 (2003) 585–92.

———. *Curious Land: Jesuit Accommodation and the Origins of Sinology*. Stuttgart: F. Steiner Verlag Wiesbaden, 1985.

———. *The Spirit and the Flesh in Shandong, 1650–1785*. Lanham, MD: Rowman and Littlefield, 2001.

Munson, James. *The Nonconformists: In Search of a Lost Culture*. London: SPCK, 1991.

Naquin, Susan. *Millenarian Rebellion in China: The Eight Trigrams Uprising of 1813*. New Haven, CT: Yale University Press, 1976.

Nevius, Helen Sanford. *The Life of John Livingston Nevius, for Forty Years a Missionary in China*. New York: Fleming H. Revell, 1895.

Nevius, John Livingston. *China and the Chinese*. New York: Harper, 1868.

———. *Demon Possession and Allied Themes; Being an Inductive Study of Phenomena of Our Own Times*. 2nd ed. Chicago, IL: Fleming H. Revell, 1896.

———. *Methods of Mission Work*. Shanghai: American Presbyterian Mission Press, 1886.

Ng, Peter Tze Ming. "Timothy Richard: Christian Attitudes towards Other Religions and Cultures." In *Chinese Christianity: An Interplay Between Global and Local Perspectives*, 111–32. Leiden: Brill, 2012.

Ning, Lao Tai-tai, and Ida Pruitt. *A Daughter of Han: The Autobiography of a Chinese Woman*. New Haven, CT: Yale University Press, 1945.

Oddie, Geoffrey A. "Old Wine in New Bottles? Kartabhaja (Vaishnava) Converts to Evangelical Christianity in Bengal, 1800–1845." In *Religious Conversion Movements in South Asia: Continuities and Change, 1800–1900*, edited by Geoffrey A. Oddie, 57–78. Richmond, Surrey: Curzon Press, 1997.

O'Leary, Paul. "When Was Anti-Catholicism? The Case of Nineteenth- and Twentieth-Century Wales." *The Journal of Ecclesiastical History* 56, no. 2 (2005) 308–25.

Oliphant, Margaret. *The Life of Edward Irving: Minister of National Scotch Church, London: Illustrated by His Journals and Correspondence*. 3rd revised ed. London: Hurst and Blackett, 1864.

Orr, J. Edwin. *The Second Evangelical Awakening in Britain*. London: Marshall, Morgan and Scott, 1949.

Overmyer, Daniel L. *Folk Buddhist Religion: Dissenting Sects in Late Traditional China*. Cambridge, MA: Harvard University Press, 1976.

———. *Local Religion in North China in the Twentieth Century: The Structure and Organization of Community Rituals and Beliefs*. Leiden: Brill, 2009.

———. *Precious Volumes: An Introduction to Chinese Sectarian Scriptures from the Sixteenth and Seventeenth Centuries*. Cambridge, MA: Harvard University Asia Center, 1999.

Pfister, Lauren F. "Attitudes Towards Chinese Culture(s), 1860–1900." In *Handbook of Christianity in China*. Vol. 2, *1800–present*, edited by R. G. Tiedemann, 405–16. Leiden: Brill, 2010.

———. "The Legacy of James Legge." *IBMR* 22, no. 4 (1998) 77–82.

———. "Rethinking Mission in China: James Hudson Taylor and Timothy Richard." In *The Imperial Horizons of British Protestant Missions, 1880–1914*, edited by A. N. Porter, 183–212. Grand Rapids, MI: Eerdmans, 2003.

———. *Striving for the "Whole Duty of Man": James Legge and the Scottish Protestant Encounter with China: Assessing Confluences in Scottish Nonconformism, Chinese Missionary Scholarship, Victorian Sinology, and Chinese Protestantism*. Frankfurt am Main; New York: Peter Lang, 2004.

Pigott, C. A. *Steadfast Unto Death or Martyred for China: Memorials of Thomas Wellesley and Jessie Pigott*. London: Religious Tract Society, 1903.

Pocock, Michael. "The Influence of Premillennial Eschatology on Evangelical Missionary Theory and Praxis from the Late Nineteenth Century to the Present." *IBMR* 33, no. 3 (2009) 129–36.

Price, Eva Jane. *China Journal 1889–1900: An American Missionary Family During the Boxer Rebellion*. New York: Scribner, 1989.

Price, Fred S. *History of Caio, Carmarthenshire*. Swansea, Wales: Printed by B. Trerise, 1904.

Pritchard, John. *Methodists and Their Missionary Societies 1760–1900*. Farnham, Surrey; Burlington, VT: Ashgate, 2013.

Rattenbury, Harold B. *David Hill, Friend of China: A Modern Portrait*. London: Epworth Press, 1949.

Redfield, Robert, Ralph Linton, and Melville J. Herskovits. "Memorandum for the Study of Acculturation." *American Anthropologist* 38, no. 1 (1936) 149–52.
Rees, Thomas. *History of Protestant Nonconformity in Wales*. London: Snow, 1883.
Reeve, B. *Timothy Richard: China Missionary, Statesman and Reformer*. London: Partridge, 1912.
Reinders, Eric Robert. *Borrowed Gods and Foreign Bodies: Christian Missionaries Imagine Chinese Religion*. Berkeley, CA: University of California, 2004.
Report of the Baptist College, Haverfordwest for the Year 1867. Haverfordwest: Haverfordwest Baptist College, 1867.
Report of the Baptist College, Haverfordwest for the Year 1869. Haverfordwest: Haverfordwest Baptist College, 1869.
Richard, Mary Martin. *Jiaoshi liezhuan* 教士列传 [Christian Biographies]. 10 vols. Shanghai: SDCK, 1898.
———. *Paper on Chinese Music*. Shanghai: American Presbyterian Mission Press, 1899.
Richard, Mary Martin, with Timothy Richard. *Xiao shipu* 小诗谱 [*The Tune-book in Chinese Notation**]. 1885.
Ross, Andrew. *David Livingstone: Mission and Empire*. London: Hambledon and London, 2002.
Rowdon, Harold H. "The Concept of 'Living By Faith.'" In *Mission and Meaning: Essays Presented to Peter Cotterell*, edited by Antony Billington, Tony Lane, and Max Turner, 339–56. Carlisle: Paternoster Press, 1995.
Sam, David L. and John W. Berry, eds. *The Cambridge Handbook of Acculturation Psychology*. Cambridge: Cambridge University, 2006.
Schofield, A. T. *Memorials of R. Harold A. Schofield: First Medical Missionary to Shan-Si, China*. London: Hodder and Stoughton, 1885.
Scott, Gregory Adam. "Famine and Political Reform in China." http://www.buddhiststudies.net/Scott_Famine_and_Political_Reform.pdf.
———. "Timothy Richard, World Religion, and Reading Christianity in Buddhist Garb." *Social Sciences and Missions* 25, no. 1–2 (2012) 53–75.
Seiwert, Hubert Michael. "The Transformation of Popular Religious Movements of the Ming and Qing Dynasties: A Rational Choice Interpretation." In *The People and the Dao: New Studies in Chinese Religions in Honour of Daniel L. Overmyer*, edited by Daniel L. Overmyer, Philip Clart, and Paul Crowe, 39–62. Sankt Augustin: Institut Monumenta Serica, 2009.
Seiwert, Hubert Michael, and Ma Xisha. *Popular Religious Movements and Heterodox Sects in Chinese History*. Leiden: Brill, 2003.
Semple, Rhonda Anne. *Missionary Women: Gender, Professionalism, and the Victorian Idea of Christian Mission*. Woodbridge, Suffolk: Boydell Press, 2003.
Sharpe, Eric J. *Comparative Religion*. London: Duckworth, 1975.
———. *Not to Destroy but to Fulfil: The Contribution of J. N. Farquhar to Protestant Missionary Thought in India before 1914*. Uppsala: Gleerup, 1965.
Shek, Richard. "The Revolt of the Zaili, Jindan Sects in Rehe (Jehol), 1891." *Modern China* 6, no. 2 (1980) 161–96.
Shenk, Wilbert R. "The Origins and Evolution of the Three-Selfs in Relation to China." *IBMR* 14, no. 1 (1990) 28–35.
Shu Xincheng 舒新城. "Zhongguo jindai shi ziliao jianjie (qi) 中国近代史资料简介 (七) [A Brief Introduction to Modern Chinese Historical Resources*]." *Xueshu yuekan*, no. 7 (1957) 73–75.

Slater, Thomas E. *God Revealed: An Outline of Christian Truth*. Madras: Addison and Co., 1876.

Smith, William Robertson. *The Prophets of Israel and Their Place in History to the Close of the Eighth Century, B.C.: Eight Lectures*. Edinburgh: Adam and Charles Black, 1882.

Smythe, Lewis S. C. "Changes in the Christian Message for China by Protestant Missionaries." PhD Dissertation, University of Chicago, 1928.

Soothill, Lucy (Farrar). *A Passport to China; Being the Tale of Her Long and Friendly Sojourning Amongst a Strangely Interesting People*. London: Hodder and Stoughton, 1931.

Soothill, William Edward. *Timothy Richard of China: Seer, Statesman, Missionary and the Most Disinterested Adviser the Chinese Ever Had*. London: Seeley, Service and Company, 1924.

Soothill, William Edward, and Lewis Hodous. *A Dictionary of Chinese Buddhist Terms, with Sanskrit and English Equivalents and a Sanskrit-Pali Index*. London: K. Paul, Trench, Trubner and Company, 1937.

Standaert, Nicolas. "Matteo Ricci: Shaped by the Chinese." Jesuits in Britain, May 21, 2010. http://www.thinkingfaith.org/articles/20100521_1.htm.

Stanley, Brian. "Christian Missions and the Enlightenment: A Reevaluation." In *Christian Missions and the Enlightenment*, 1–21. Grand Rapids, MI: Eerdmans, 2001.

———. "Christianity and Civilization in English Evangelical Mission Thought, 1792–1857." In *Christian Missions and the Enlightenment*, 169–97. Grand Rapids: Eerdmans, 2001.

———. "Evangelical Social and Political Ethics: An Historical Perspective." *Evangelical Quarterly* 62, no. 1 (1990) 19–36.

———. "From 'The Poor Heathen' to 'The Glory and Honour of All Nations': Vocabularies of Race and Custom in Protestant Missions, 1844–1928." *IBMR* 34, no. 1 (2010) 3–10.

———. *The History of the Baptist Missionary Society, 1792–1992*. Edinburgh: T. and T. Clark, 1992.

———. "The Reshaping of Christian Tradition: Western Denominational Identity in a Non-Western Context." In *Unity and Diversity in the Church*, edited by R. N. Swanson, 399–426. Oxford: Blackwell, 1996.

Starr, Chlöe. "Reading Christian Scriptures: The Nineteenth-Century Context." In *Reading Christian Scriptures in China*, edited by Chlöe Starr, 32–48. Edinburgh: T. and T. Clark, 2008.

Sun Banghua 孙邦华. "Li Timotai yu guangxue hui 李提摩太与广学会 [Timothy Richard and the Christian Literature Society*]." *Jiangsu shehuikexue*, no. 4 (2000) 161–67.

Sweeten, Alan Richard. *Christianity in Rural China: Conflict and Accommodation in Jiangxi Province, 1860–1900*. Ann Arbor, MI: Center for Chinese Studies at the University of Michigan, 2001.

Taylor, Howard, and James Hudson Taylor. *The Story of the China Inland Mission*. London: Morgan and Scott, 1893.

Taylor, James Hudson. *China's Spiritual Need and Claims*. London: Morgan and Scott, 1887.

Taylor, Jeremy. *Holy Living and Dying: Together with Prayers; Containing the whole duty of a Christian, and the parts of devotion fitted to all occasions and furnished for all necessities*. London: Printed for Longman, Orme, Brown, Green, and others, 1839.
Thompson, David M. "The Christian Socialist Revival in Britain: A Reappraisal." In *Revival and Religion since 1700: Essays for John Walsh*, edited by Jane Garnett and Colin Matthew, 273–95. London: Hambledon Press, 1993.

———. "The Emergence of the Nonconformist Social Gospel in England." In *Protestant Evangelicalism*, edited by Keith Robbins, 255–80. Oxford: Basil Blackwell, 1990.

———. "Social Gospel." *Baptist Quarterly* 31, no. 5 (1986) 199–218.

Thompson, Roger R. "Twilight of the Gods in the Chinese Countryside: Christians, Confucians, and the Modernizing State, 1861–1911." In *Christianity in China: From the Eighteenth Century to the Present*, edited by Daniel H. Bays, 53–72. Stanford, CA: Stanford University Press, 1996.

Tiedemann, R. G. "Christianity and Chinese 'Heterodox Sects': Mass Conversion and Syncretism in Shandong Province in the Early Eighteenth Century." *Monumenta Serica* 44 (1996) 339–82.

———. "Conversion Patterns in North China." In *Authentic Chinese Christianity*, edited by Wei-ying Ku and Koen DeRidder, 107–34. Leuven, Belgium: Leuven University; Ferdinand Verbiest Foundation, 2001.

———. "Social Gospel and Fundamentalism: Conflicting Approaches in the Protestant Missionary Enterprise in China (1840–1911)." In *The Catholic Church and the Chinese World: Between Colonialism and Evangelization, 1840–1911*, edited by Agostino Giovagnoli and Elisa Giunipero, 83–105. Vatican City: Urbaniana University, 2005.

Treadgold, Donald Warren. *The West in Russia and China: Religious and Secular Thought in Modern Times*. Vol. 2, *China 1582–1949*. Cambridge: Cambridge University Press, 1973.

Underhill, Edward Bean. *Christian Missions in the East and West, in Connection with the Baptist Missionary Society, 1792–1872*. London: Yates and Alexander, 1873.

———. *The Principles and Methods of Missionary Labour*. London: Alexander and Shepheard, 1896.

Vaughn Cross, Carol Ann. "'Living in the Lives of Men': Martha Foster Crawford." *Social Sciences and Missions* 25 (2012) 102–28.

———. "Missionary Returns and Cultural Conversions in Alabama and Shandong: The Latter Years of Madam Gao (Martha Foster Crawford)." In *North American Foreign Missions, 1810–1914: Theology, Theory, and Policy*, edited by Wilbert R. Shenk, 243–60. Grand Rapids, MI: Eerdmans, 2004.

Vedder, Henry C. *A Short History of the Baptists*. New and illustrated ed. Philadelphia, PA: American Baptist Publication Society, 1907.

Venn, Henry. *Retrospect and Prospect of the Operations of the Church Missionary Society*. London: Church Missionary Society, 1865.

Walker, James Barr. *Philosophy of the Plan of Salvation: A Book for the Times*. Edited by Calvin E. Stowe. New and enlarged ed. Cincinnati, OH: Hitchcok and Walden, 1855.

Wallis, Frank. "Anti-Catholicism in Mid-Victorian Britain." *Journal of Religion and Society* 7 (2005) 1–17.

Walls, Andrew F. "The Multiple Conversions of Timothy Richard: A Paradigm of Missionary Experience." In *The Cross-cultural Process in Christian History: Studies in the Transmission and Appropriation of Faith*, 236–58. Maryknoll, NY: Orbis Books, 2002.

———. "The Translation Principle in Christian History." In *The Missionary Movement in Christian History: Studies in the Transmission of Faith*, 26–42. Edinburgh: T. and T. Clark, 1996.

Wang Hui. *Translating Chinese Classics in a Colonial Context: James Legge and His Two Versions of the Zhongyong*. Frankfurt am Main: Peter Lang, 2008.

Wang Yipu 王一普. "Shixi Li Timotai de chuanjiao celue ji qi tedian 试析李提摩太的传教策略及其特点 [On Timothy Richard's Evangelistic Approach]." *Lishi jiaoxue*, no. 10 (2009) 91–96.

Wang Yuechuan and Hu Miaosen 王岳川及胡淼森. *Wenhua zhan lue* 文化战略 [Cultural Strategy*]. Shanghai: Fudan daxue chubanshe, 2010.

Ward, W. R. "Evangelical Identity in the Eighteenth Century." In *Christianity Reborn: The Global Expansion of Evangelicalism in the Twentieth Century*, edited by Donald M. Lewis, 11–30. Grand Rapids, MI: Eerdmans, 2004.

Warr, Winifred. *Far Into China: The Story of Timothy Richard, Pioneer*. London: Carey Press, 1945.

Watkins, Susan Cotts, and Jane Menken. "Famines in Historical Perspective." *Population and Development Review* 4 (1985) 647–75.

Wei Yisa, ed. 魏以撒, 编. *Zhen Yesu jiaohui chuangli sanshi zhounian jinian zhuankan* 真耶稣教会创立三十周年纪念专刊 [Special Volume Commemorating the Thirtieth Anniversary of the Founding of the True Jesus Church*]. Nanjing: Zhen Yesu jiaohui, 1948.

Welch, Holmes. *The Buddhist Revival in China*. Cambridge, MA: Harvard University Press, 1968.

Weller, Robert P. "Sectarian Religion and Political Action in China." *Modern China* 8, no. 4 (1982) 463–83.

Wells, David F. *The Courage to Be Protestant: Truth-lovers, Marketers, and Emergents in the Postmodern World*. Grand Rapids, MI: Eerdmans, 2008.

Wheeler, Michael. *The Old Enemies: Catholic and Protestant in Nineteenth-century English Culture*. Cambridge: Cambridge University Press, 2006.

Whitefield, Douglas Brent. "The Christian Literature Society for China: The Role of its Publications, Personalities and Theology in Late-Qing Reform Movements." PhD Thesis, University of Cambridge, 2001.

Wigram, Christopher E. M. *The Bible and Mission in Faith Perspective: J. Hudson Taylor and the Early China Inland Mission*. Zoetermeer: Boekencentrum, 2007.

Williams, Glanmor. *Recovery, Reorientation, and Reformation: Wales, c. 1415–1642*. Oxford: Clarendon, 1987.

Williams, Rowland. *Parameswara-jnyana-goshthi: A Dialogue of the Knowledge of the Supreme Lord, in which are compared the claims of Christianity and Hinduism, and various questions of Indian religion and literature fairly discussed*. Cambridge: Deighton, Bell and Company, 1856.

Williams, S. Wells. "The Controversy Among the Protestant Missionaries on the Proper Translation of the Words of God and Spirit into Chinese." *Bibliotheca Sacra* 35, no. 140 (1878) 732–78.

Williamson, Alexander. *Journeys in North China, Manchuria, and Eastern Mongolia; With Some Account of Corea.* 2 vols. London: Smith, Elder and Company, 1870.

Williamson, H. R. *British Baptists in China, 1845–1952.* London: Carey Kingsgate, 1957.

Winter, Ralph D. "How to Best Help China? The Story of Two Very Different Missionaries to China." *Mission Frontiers* 30, no. 6 (2008) 12–14.

Wong, Timothy Man-kong. "Timothy Richard and the Chinese Reform Movement." *Fides et Historia* 31, no. 2 (1999) 47–59.

Wood, John Halsey, Jr. "John Livingstone Nevius and the New Missions History." *Journal of Presbyterian History* 83, no. 1 (2005) 23–40.

Wu Wennan 吴文南. "Bin Weilin Tian lu licheng hanyi pingjie 宾为霖《天路历程》汉译评介 [An Assessment of William Burns's Translation of *Pilgrim's Progress*]." *Chongqing jiaotong xueyuan xuebao* (shehuikexue ban) 10, no. 1 (2010) 128–31.

Wylie, Alexander. *Memorials of Protestant Missionaries to the Chinese.* Shanghai: American Presbyterian Mission Press, 1867.

Xiong Yuezhi 熊月之. *Xixue dong jian yu wan qing shehui* 西学东渐与晚清社会 [The Dissemination of Western Learning and the Late Qing Society]. Shanghai: Shanghai renmin chubanshe, 1994.

Xu Fang 徐方. "Lun 'Dingwu qihuang' zhong wan qing zhengfu yu chuanjiaoshi jian de guanxi 论'丁戊奇荒'中晚清政府与传教士间的关系 [The Relationship Between the Late Qing Dynasty Government and Western Missionaries During the Ding-Wu Severe Famine]." *Ningbo jiaoyu xueyuan xuebao* 12, no. 4 (2010) 102–5.

Xu, Xiaoqun. "The Dilemma of Accommodation: Reconciling Christianity and Chinese Culture in the 1920s." *Historian* 60, no. 1 (1997) 21–38.

Xu Yanmin 许艳民. "'Dingwu' zhenzai dui Li Timotai chuanjiao fangshi de yingxiang '丁戊'赈灾对李提摩太传教方式的影响 [Dingwu Disaster Relief's Influence upon Timothy Richard's Preaching Ways]." *Shantou daxue xuebao* (renwen shehuikexue ban) 27, no. 1 (2011) 75–80.

Yates, M. T., ed. *Records of the General Conference of the Protestant Missionaries of China, held at Shanghai, May 10–24, 1877.* Shanghai: Presbyterian Mission Press, 1878.

Yuan Yingying 袁滢滢. "'Dingwu qihuang' zhong chuanjiaoshi zai Shandong de zhenzai huodong kaocha '丁戊奇荒'中传教士在山东的赈灾活动考察 [An Investigation of Missionary Disaster Relief Activities During the 'Dingwu Famine']." *Liaocheng daxue xuebao* (Shehuikexue ban), no. 6 (2007) 98–102.

Zetzsche, Jost Oliver. *The Bible in China: The History of the Union Version or The Culmination of Protestant Missionary Bible Translation in China.* Sankt Augustin: Monumenta Serica Institute, 1999.

Zhang Deming 张德明. "Xifang xinjiao chuanjiaoshi yu wan qing Shandong zhenzai shulun 西方新教传教士与晚清山东赈灾述论 [Western Missionaries and Shandong Disaster Relief in the Late Qing Dynasty]." *Gujin nongye*, no. 4 (2009) 21–28.

Zhao Bingxiang. "'The Place Where the Sage Wouldn't Go' and 'The Place Where the Sage was Born': Mutual Definitions of Place in Shandong and Heilongjiang." In *Making Place: State Projects, Globalisation and Local Responses in China*, edited by Stephan Feuchtwang, 117–32. London: UCL, 2004.

Zhao Liuqing 赵柳青. "Li Timotai de chuanjiao huodong kua wenhua chuanbo celue 李提摩太的传教活动跨文化传播策略 [Study on Timothy Richard's Missionary Activities and Strategy of Cross-Culture Communication]." MA Thesis, Hebei jingmao daxue, 2011.

Zhao Xiaolan 赵晓兰. "Chuanjiaoshi zhongwen baokan ban kan zongzhi huanbian fenxi 传教士中文报刊办刊宗旨演变分析 [On the Evolution of the Aim of Missionaries' Chinese Press]." *Zhejiang daxue xuebao* (renwen shehuikexue ban) 41, no. 5 (2011) 64–70.

———. "Cong chuanbo xijiao dao chuanbo xixue—chuanjiaoshi zhongwen baokan ban kan zongzhi de yanbian 从传播西教到传播西学—传教士中文报刊办刊宗旨的演变 [From the Communication of Western Religion to that of Western Scholarship—The Changes of Objectives for Chinese Journals by the Missionaries]." *Xueshu yuekan* 40, no. 12 (2008) 92–97.

Zupanov, Ines. "'One Civility, but Multiple Religions': Jesuit Mission among St. Thomas Christians in India (16th–17th Centuries)." *Journal of Early Modern History* 9, no. 3–4 (2005) 284–325.

Index

1870 Education Act, 31, 79
1874 Public Worship Regulation Act, 206
1877 General Conference of the Protestant Missionaries of China (GCPMC), 40–41, 58n36, 70–71, 73n19, 76, 81, 163, 166n31
1890 General Conference of the Protestant Missionaries of China (GCPMC), 56, 73n19, 76, 132, 147, 151, 199n77

accommodation, 1–2, 4–5, 13, 19, 70, 126–36, 155, 192n41, 200, 203–6, 210, 217–19, 228, 230
Allen, Young J., 42, 52, 141, 208
American Board of Commissioners for Foreign Missions (ABCFM), 2, 57n34, 77, 80, 86, 87, 149, 160–62, 165, 180–81, 213, 216, 218
American Methodist Episcopal Mission, 221
American Presbyterian Mission (APM), 38, 39n73, 40, 107, 130
American Southern Baptist, 2, 38, 41
Anderson, Rufus, 80–81, 87
Anqing, 176n77

Bacon, Francis, 110–11, 149–50, 163
Baller, Frederick, 120
Baptist Missionary Society, English (BMS), 2–4, 6, 15, 17, 20–21, 35–38, 41, 43, 46n108, 48–49, 54, 55n22, 56, 58, 63, 68, 71, 78, 81–82, 83n65, 86–87, 92, 115, 117–18, 119n92, 123, 128, 136n36, 140, 141, 149–52, 155, 159, 160, 162, 166, 172–82, 183–222
Baynes, Alfred, 150–51, 194, 219
Beijing, 36, 111n56, 220
Bethel Chapel, 26–30
Brethren. *See* Christian Brethren
British and Foreign Bible Society (BFBS), 175, 188n26
Broomhall, Benjamin, 61n53, 166–67, 170
Brown, William, 41, 58, 68, 86–88, 141
Bruce, J. Percy, 188n26
Buck, Pearl, 3, 5
Buddhism, 5, 8–11, 45, 69–72, 73n19, 84n68, 128n4, 129, 134, 136, 184–85, 202–3, 227
Burns, William Charles, 208–9
Bushnell, Horace, 33n45, 149
Butler, Alban, 202, 208
Butler, Joseph, 32, 85, 110–11, 149, 224

Caio, 26–30, 35
Cambridge Seven, 87, 180
Carey, William, 80
Ch'ing, Pastor. *See* Zheng Yuren
Chalmers, Thomas, 58
Chefoo, 19, 36–43, 46, 50, 51, 67–72, 78, 80, 84, 91, 99, 104, 107n45, 112n59, 117, 120n98, 160, 174–75, 179, 228
China Famine Relief Fund Shanghai Committee, 107n45–46, 108, 117, 119, 120n95

INDEX

China Inland Mission (CIM), 6, 16, 21, 35, 41, 54, 55n22, 57n34, 61, 64–65, 102, 107, 108n47, 110, 118, 119n92, 120, 123n113, 124, 133, 135, 155, 159–82, 188n26, 194n48, 212–214, 216, 218
Chinese Evangelization Society (CES), 36n62, 141, 172n54
Christian Brethren, 65, 162n13, 178n83, 181, 193, 194n48, 212
Christian Literature Society (CLS), 7n16, 61, 221n175
Clarke, George, 179–80
Clifford, John, 142, 195
Colenso, J. W., 110
Coleridge, Samuel Taylor, 59–60
Confucianism, 13n41, 69–71, 73n20, 85–86, 113, 129–30, 134, 136, 184, 203n94, 208, 211, 224
Corbett, Hunter, 39–40, 107
Corpe, Jessie, 188
Couling, Samuel, 188
Crawford, Martha, 2, 3, 5, 38, 225
Crickmay, Anna. *See* Anna Turner

Dale, R. W., 142, 147, 194
Daoism, 18n59, 69–72, 84n68, 85, 134, 136, 203
Davies, John, 29
Dawburn, Lila, 188n26
Dengzhou, 38
Ding Baozhen, 99
Dixon, Herbert, 148n82, 188–91, 194–95, 201, 211–13
Dowie, John Alexander, 213n139
Drake, Samuel and Florence, 176
Drummond, Henry, 59
Duff, Alexander, 128n8, 229
Duncan, Moir, 8, 188

Edinburgh, 41, 58, 121, 184
Edkins, Joseph, 38, 70–71, 73n19, 76
Elliston, W. L., 175, 179n86

Faber, Ernst, 209
Farquhar, John N., 13, 128n8, 129n10
Farthing, George B., 148n82, 188–89

Faulding, Jennie. *See* Jane "Jennie" Taylor
Forrest, R. J., 108
Forsyth, Robert Coventry, 188
Foster, Arnold, 119, 124n121

Gao Daling, 123–24, 195
Gaoya, 107
geomancy (*fengshui*), 64, 74
Golden Elixir sects, 77n41, 79, 135, 227
Guinness, Henry Grattan, 35, 64–65
Gützlaff, Karl, 141, 172n54

Hall, Charles James, 36
Hangzhou, 38n72, 40, 41
Hankou, 119
Harmon, Frank, 188n26
Hartwell, Jesse, 38–39
Haverfordwest Baptist College, 31–35, 50–51, 53, 65, 70n5, 110, 168, 224–25
Helm, Benjamin, 41
Henan, 38n70, 46, 97, 123n115
Hill, David, 16, 107, 119–24, 133–38, 140, 147, 161, 163, 165–67, 184, 193n46
Holmes, James and Sally, 38
Horne, Celia, 120, 164, 172n56, 176n74
Hsi, Pastor. *See* Xi Shengmo
Huilong Shan, 43–46, 87
Hume, Edward, 3, 5

Imperial University of Shanxi, 8, 10n32, 34n53, 180n92, 187n19
Irving, Edward, 12, 20, 50, 58–67, 69, 72, 85, 110, 117, 154, 169, 226
Islam, 72, 73n19, 84–85, 124, 134, 136, 210

Jackson, Josiah, 172n56
James, Francis H., 76–77, 79, 118–20, 152, 160–61, 164, 166, 170, 172–75, 180, 188, 189, 214, 217
James, John Angell, 35
Jesuits, 4, 12, 14, 62, 129, 130, 134, 150n90, 168–69, 200–5, 209, 210n127, 226
Jinan, 46, 72, 152, 196, 219–20

Jinshi yaowu. See *Present Needs*
John, Griffith, 26, 38, 71, 100n18, 209
Jones, Alfred G., 2, 5, 61, 63, 71n10, 117–18, 124n124, 133n25, 151–53, 166n31, 181n96, 184–85, 187–88, 189, 196, 199, 204, 207, 209, 211, 219
Jones, Humphrey, 28

Kang Youwei, 145
Kiangsu Relief Fund, 107n45
Kingdom of God (God's Kingdom, Kingdom of Heaven, etc.), 13, 20, 54, 63–65, 67, 126–155, 180n92, 186, 190–93, 198, 202, 208, 218, 225, 229
Kitts, J. Tate, 152, 187–88
Kloekers, Hendrik Z., 36–37

Laiyang, 72
Lammermuir party, 35n55, 172n56
Landale, Robert and Mary, 164
Laughton, Richard Frederick, 37, 39, 41, 80
Legge, James, 4, 13, 70, 88, 129–30, 203, 210, 215
Lewis, John Gomer, 33–34
Lewis, Joshua, 26, 174n63
Lewis, Thomas, 31
Li Hongzhang, 97n1, 145, 219–20
Liang Qichao, 145, 220n169
Lilley, Robert, 41
Linqu, 104
Linzi, 99
Livingstone, David, 198
London Missionary Society (LMS), 4, 38, 40, 59–60, 61n49, 100n18, 110n54, 119, 192n41

MacGillivray, Donald, 7, 60–61, 169n48
Maitland, Annie, 188
Martin, Mary. See Mary Martin Richard
Martin, W. A. P., 130, 141, 208
Mateer, Calvin, 39–40, 70–71, 90, 107
Medhurst, C. Spurgeon, 188, 217n154
Medhurst, William H., 86, 88
millennialism, different perspectives on, 32, 59, 64–64, 73, 168, 193

Milne, William, 208
Monier-Williams, Monier, 128, 130
Morgan, David, 28–29
Morgan, Evan, 148n82, 188–89
Morrison, Robert, 86, 141
Muirhead, William, 40, 88, 110n54, 117
Müller, Max, 110, 128, 130

Nanjing, 36, 176n77, 184
National Bible Society of Scotland, 38, 41
Nestorians, 67n71, 79n50
Nevius, John Livingston, 16, 38–39, 77–78, 90, 92, 94n104, 107, 160
Nickalls, E. C., 188
Ningbo, 36n61, 38
North China Famine, 4, 7n18, 8, 10, 12, 16–17, 20–21, 53–54, 87, 93, 97–125, 136, 140, 144–45, 148, 155, 159–61, 170, 178–79, 183, 198, 213, 225, 229–30

orphanages, 17, 55, 92–93, 104–5, 109n49, 111, 113–15, 119–20, 125, 143, 161, 171, 178

Parker, Peter, 86, 141, 229
Parrott, A. G., 175, 179
Paton, J. B., 147
Pigott, Thomas Wellesley, 181n93
Pingyang, 118–20, 134–35, 161, 176n78, 179n86
Porter, Henry D., 77, 89n86
Present Needs (*Jinshi yaowu*), 15, 144–46, 190, 199n72, 202–4, 210
Price, Eva Jane, 2, 3, 5

Qingzhou, 4, 60–61, 68–69, 72, 74, 79n54, 82–84, 89–93, 99–101, 102n24, 104–7, 109, 115–18, 123, 127, 130, 136–38, 152, 160, 184, 228

Rawlinson, Frank, 3, 5
Reid, Gilbert, 130
Religious Tract Society, 123, 154n102, 160n4, 221n175
Ricci, Matteo, 4, 14, 129, 149, 169, 200

Richard, Eleanor, 27
Richard, Joshua, 30
Richard, Mary Martin, 120n99, 121–23, 124n124, 125, 152–53, 173n62, 184, 197–98, 202, 208, 220n168, 221
Roberts, Issachar, 36
Roman Catholicism, 1n4, 26n5, 67n71, 76, 107n46, 118–20, 168–70, 190, 200–211, 217
Rossier, Fanny, 179

Salem Baptist Chapel, 26–30, 35
Salvation Army, 193–94, 212
Schofield, Harold, 123n113, 124, 161, 164
Seeley, John, 110
Self-strengthening (*ziqiang*) movement, 103n27, 144–45
Sermon on the Mount, 33, 54, 86, 127, 132, 139, 191
Shaanxi, 97, 118n85, 188n26
Shang Huqing, 129
Shanghai Arsenal, 180n92
Shanghai Famine Relief Committee. *See* China Famine Relief Fund Shanghai Committee
Shanghai, 6, 36–40, 56, 61, 70, 76, 81, 98, 103, 107n45, 141, 147, 160, 169, 188, 203n94, 221
Shenbao, 103, 114
Shibao, 220
Shorrock, A. G., 188n26
Slater, Thomas E., 128, 130, 192n41
Smith, Stanley P., 180–81, 194n48, 212–13
Smith, William Robertson, 142
Smyth, E. C., 188n26
Social Gospel, 5, 142, 228–30
Society for the Diffusion of Christian and General Knowledge Among the Chinese (SDCK), 6–7, 21, 38, 50, 51n9, 61, 145, 183, 208n119, 220n170, 221–22
Songcun, 43–44, 86
Soothill, William Edward, 7–8, 11, 16, 112, 140

Sowerby, Arthur, 136n36, 148n82, 176, 186–203, 211–14
Sowerby, Herbert, 176
Spurgeon, Charles Haddon, 194
Stimson, Martin and Emily, 160–61

Taiping, 36, 38, 73
Taiyuan, 4, 8n19, 118–24, 133, 138, 143n62, 151, 160–61, 164–66, 171, 174, 176, 181n93, 184, 199–200, 212, 220n166
Taoism. *See* Daoism
Taylor, James Hudson, 6, 9–10, 16, 37n64, 51, 54–56, 58–62, 64–65, 69, 86–87, 108n47, 134n29, 147, 159–81, 226
Taylor, Jane "Jennie," 120, 124, 161, 163, 177
Taylor, Jeremy, 51, 88, 209
Tenney, Charles, 161, 180, 216
Three Teachings, 69–75, 78, 86
Tianjin, 108n47, 164, 171, 177, 184, 219–21
Treaty of Tianjin, 35, 38n70
Trestrail, Frederick, 48–50, 61n49, 81–82
True Jesus Church, 123
Turner, Anna, 120, 176
Turner, Joshua, 107, 118–20, 134n29, 137, 148n82, 160–61, 170, 174–76, 179n86, 188–92, 193n46, 195–96, 198, 203–4, 209–14

Underhill, Edward Bean, 48–50, 61n49, 81–82
United Presbyterian Mission of Scotland, 121

Venn, Henry, 80–81

Walker, James, 51–52, 88
Wanguo gongbao (*WGGB*), 15, 51n11, 52, 103, 134n28, 141, 144, 208n120, 220n166
Watson, J. R., 188
Weedon, Marion, 188
Weifang, 68n2

Wesleyan Methodist Missionary Society (WMMS), 107, 163
Whitewright, John S., 187
Whiting, Albert, 107
Williams, Rowland, 27, 128
Williams, Samuel Wells, 141
Williamson, Alexander, 38–39, 70–71, 118, 121, 130, 208n119, 221
Wills, W. A., 188n26
Wiseman, Cardinal Nicholas Patrick, 202, 208n115

Xi Shengmo (Xi Zizhi), 79, 134–35, 161, 227
Xie Jiafu, 114, 115n70
Xu Wending (Guangqi), 129

Yang Wenhui, 11n35, 184–85
Yantai. *See* Chefoo
Yates, M. T., 41
Yidu, 104

Zaili sect, 76, 79, 227
Zeng Guofan, 145
Zeng Guoquan, 105, 145, 148, 184
Zezhou, 119, 179n86
Zhang Zhidong, 145
Zheng Yuren, 37, 51, 80, 117–18, 133, 166n35
Zhili, 97–98, 220
Zuo Zongtang, 145

www.ingramcontent.com/pod-product-compliance
Lightning Source LLC
Chambersburg PA
CBHW070241230426

43664CB00014B/2377